THE
Naturalist

THE
Naturalist

THEODORE ROOSEVELT, A LIFETIME
OF EXPLORATION, AND THE TRIUMPH
OF AMERICAN NATURAL HISTORY

Darrin Lunde

CROWN PUBLISHERS
NEW YORK

Published in the United States by Crown Publishers, an imprint of the Crown Publishing Group, a division of Penguin Random House LLC, New York.
www.crownpublishing.com

CROWN is a registered trademark, and the Crown colophon is a trademark of Penguin Random House LLC.

Library of Congress Cataloging-in-Publication Data
Names: Lunde, Darrin P.
Title: The naturalist : Theodore Roosevelt, a lifetime of exploration, and the triumph of American natural history / Darrin Lunde.
Description: First edition. | New York : Crown, 2016.
Identifiers: LCCN 2015036683 | ISBN 9780307464309 (hardback)
Subjects: LCSH: Roosevelt, Theodore, 1858–1919. | Nature conservation—United States. | Natural history museums—United States. | Naturalists—United States—Biography. | Conservationists—United States—Biography. | Presidents—United States—Biography. | BISAC: BIOGRAPHY & AUTOBIOGRAPHY / Presidents & Heads of State. | NATURE / Animals / Wildlife.
Classification: LCC E757 .L95 2016 | DDC 973.91/1092—dc23
LC record available at http://lccn.loc.gov/2015036683

ISBN 978-0-307-46430-9
eBook ISBN 978-0-307-46432-3

Printed in the United States of America

Book design by Elina D. Nudelman
Jacket design by Christopher Brand
Jacket photograph: © Corbis
See page 321 for photography credits

10 9 8 7 6 5 4 3 2 1

First Edition

For Sakiko

Contents

Introduction 1

PART I

The Museum Naturalist

Chapter 1   **The Seal on Broadway**   *9*

Chapter 2   **Collections Make Museums**   *19*

Chapter 3   **The Mind but Not the Body**   *31*

Chapter 4   **Full-Bore Birder**   *43*

Chapter 5   **Egypt, Land of My Dreams**   *51*

Chapter 6   **Alone at Harvard**   *65*

PART II

All Hunters Should Be Nature Lovers

Chapter 7   **Roosevelt Rebels**   *83*

Chapter 8   **Hell with the Fires Out**   *97*

Chapter 9   **Change in the West**   *110*

Chapter 10   **Winchester Naturalist**   *125*

Chapter 11   **Real Men and Mousers**   *138*

Chapter 12   **A Tiffany Knife to the Heart**   *155*

Chapter 13   **Who's a Nature Faker?**   *168*

PART III

Roosevelt's New Naturalism

Chapter 14   **I Am Going to Africa**   *179*

Chapter 15   **A Railroad Through the Pleistocene**   *197*

Chapter 16   ***Bwana Tumbo*—Mr. Big Belly**   *213*

Chapter 17   **Deep in Prehistoric Thought**   *222*

Chapter 18   **Bent on Mischief**   *228*

Chapter 19   **Hunters and Naturalists**   *233*

Epilogue   **The End of the Game**   *249*

Acknowledgments   257

Sources and Notes   261

Bibliography   301

Photography Credits   321

Index   323

THE
Naturalist

Introduction

⚊⚊⚊⚊⚊ ◄ ► ⚊⚊⚊⚊⚊

$\mathcal{I}$magine what's behind a closed door in a natural-history museum. Back rooms lined with jars of snakes in alcohol, a vault full of hippo skulls, an attic of elephant bones. Rooms stacked with thousands of stuffed birds, basement vats of alcohol-preserved gorillas, or a closet of tanned zebra hides. All these things are hiding from museum patrons, beyond exhibitions and displays. This is the unseen world of a natural-history museum, awash with scientific specimens. Stuffed, skeletonized, or preserved whole in jars, nearly all these animals were collected by museum naturalists.

Millions of these specimens will never be displayed; the public will never see them. Instead, they are collected for scientific study, which is essential to understanding the world's great diversity of life. Every known animal species—every bird, mammal, fish, frog, and snake—was named based on museum specimens. Virtually everything we know about the morphology, geographic distribution, and ancestral relationships of animals is derived from the vast collections of specimens housed in museums. Natural-history museums represent our record of life on Earth.

Some of these rooms may have been partially filled by Theodore Roosevelt, who (among many other things) was an intrepid museum naturalist. From early childhood through his years in the White House, Roosevelt studied animals by shooting them, stuffing them, and preserving them in natural-history museums, and we should be thankful he did. One of the country's greatest museums—the American Museum of Natural History—was founded in his living room when he was just a boy. He lived in an age when natural-history museums commissioned scientists to explore and document uncharted terrain, collecting specimens for both study and exhibit. Whether sent to the deepest jungles of central Africa, the high Himalayas, or the deserts of the American West, these museum naturalists camped out in the remotest parts of the world for weeks and months at a time. They slung guns over their shoulders and fought their way into the last unknown regions of the world, all in the name of zoological exploration. Part scientist, part explorer, they collected animals by the thousand—and, for such a naturalist, *collect* meant *kill and preserve*, a fact easily forgotten today.

From a very early age, Theodore Roosevelt devoted a great deal of his energy to building up his own natural-history collection. He was seduced by the challenge of collecting something rare. Although hunting birds and mammals for science has a higher purpose (nature's mysteries are best revealed with a dead specimen in hand), for Roosevelt, collecting specimens also satisfied his desire for adventure.

Museum naturalists might be thought of as hunters for science, their "trophy rooms" the vast collections housed in natural-history museums. Despite the size of their stores, the collections of these institutions aren't limited to taxidermy exhibits. More valuable to scientists are museum study skins, prepared to be densely packed in rows of cabinets full of drawers. Bird specimens lie breast up, their wings tight against the body, and bill pointing forward. Mammal specimens lie prone, arms and legs extended, their cleaned skull in a box or vial set to the side. Museum study skins represent a compromise: they are stuffed so that they show all the external features of the animals, but in a way that will allow many examples of the same species to be stored neatly and compactly behind closed doors.

Museums put their specimens in taxonomic order, meaning one can walk down an aisle of cabinets to browse through similar species of a kind. There might be a long run of, say, voles in the rodent section of a collection, and opening drawer after drawer would gradually reveal the many different species of voles—pine voles, red-backed voles, prairie voles, and so on—each species distinguished by particular traits.

The real value of all these collections, and the thing that drives any zoological collector to want to gather more specimens in the field, is posterity; these collections are kept in perpetuity, providing a historical record of past expeditions while at the same time documenting biodiversity. Wandering the various storerooms of such a museum is like traveling around the world, thanks to the efforts of what probably amounts to thousands of years of cumulative human effort in assembling these collections from every corner of the globe.

Museum specimens are traditionally identified by a paper tag attached to the preserved animal's leg. Often yellowed with age and annotated in tight cursive, the tag gives the precise location of an expedition, the exact date the animal was trapped or shot, and the name of the naturalist who captured it. Thus, the collector is forever tied to his specimens. But who were these early museum naturalists? And why was Theodore Roosevelt so inspired by them?

Museum naturalists have seldom been well understood, but as a member of their ranks, I have some insight. I've spent my entire adult life working as a museum naturalist, and, like Roosevelt, I have specialized in mammals—the kinds of specimens you get by trapping and shooting. Starting out at the American Museum of Natural History in New York City before moving on to the Smithsonian's National Museum of Natural History in Washington, D.C., I have personally collected thousands of specimens while on expeditions for these institutions. I know something of the romance of being a museum naturalist and of the passions that motivated Roosevelt's desire to become one.

I started working for the American Museum of Natural History right after college graduation, and the ensuing years now seem like a string of continuous expeditions to the remotest regions of South America, Africa, and Southeast Asia. I have lived and worked in deep wilderness for weeks and months at a time, often toting a shotgun. Camped miles from civilization with no communication with the outside world, I spent most of this time setting traps by day or roaming the jungles alone at night in search of animals to shoot. I have been charged by forest elephants while working in the Congo Rainforest, and contracted serious tropical diseases while working in the jungles of South America. Dangers of a more human nature have included sidestepping wildlife traffickers while working in the mountainous border regions of Southeast Asia. I know firsthand what it means to be the kind of museum naturalist who embarks on these extreme sorts of specimen-collecting expeditions. Our brand of zoological exploration has remained virtually unchanged since the heyday of collecting expeditions more than a century ago; indeed, this timelessness makes the profession even more alluring to some.

Most museum naturalists were largely self-motivated and began collecting animals at a very early age. Driven by adventure, many struggled to gain acceptance as "real" scientists; collecting expeditions can seem like extreme forms of camping and sport hunting rather than serious scientific study. Yet the privations of museum collecting are substantial enough to ward off all but the most ardent adherents. Tropical disease, strained family relations, financial ruin, and the threat of violent death offer constant bedevilment, but those who persist ultimately end up at the largest and most prestigious natural-history museums—the American Museum of Natural History, Chicago's Field Museum of Natural History, and the Smithsonian Institution, to name just a few. These remain the ultimate centers of gravity for the very best museum naturalists.

From the time Theodore Roosevelt was a young boy until very near his death, he collected animal specimens for museums—and yet this fundamental aspect of his life has never been fully presented from the perspective of a museum naturalist. Natural-history museum collections and their collectors have always remained somewhat hidden from the public, not so much by design, but because our work tends to be overshadowed by our museums' public exhibits.

I got my start as a naturalist in much the same way Roosevelt did. We both grew up in New York City, but we both had access to the country and craved the chance to explore the natural world. We were enthralled with animals—birds and mammals especially—and obsessed with building serious boyhood natural-history museums. We were introduced to guns at an early age and developed a lifelong passion for hunting. Taxidermy was something we studied for a time, but I suspect that Roosevelt, like me, only did so because it was an essential skill for building museums. As was true for Roosevelt, simply being a scientist was never enough for me; we needed to get our hands dirty and catalogue the world through our experience, not just our study. The traditional museum collector pursues the thrill of discovery as eagerly as he does scientific results. Roosevelt and I may have both sought adventure, but our pursuit is no less real or sincere than that of the traditional scientist in a lab coat.

Today, we all tend to limit our interactions with nature. We glimpse it through binoculars and telephoto lenses and rarely examine an animal in our hands or contend with its death as something that is perfectly natural. Theodore Roosevelt and those who built the field of museum naturalism did something few would dream of today: they had *visceral* experiences with nature. They collected animals for science and hunted them for sport, in the process developing a very intimate connection to the way nature really works.

The depletion and degradation of natural habitats since Roosevelt's time and the rising number of endangered species preclude the vast majority of us from experiencing nature in this way, but understanding Roosevelt's motivation and perspective is the key to understanding his life as a naturalist. He wrote detailed and often graphic accounts of many big-game hunts because he knew that our more visceral connection to nature would only fade with time. He knew he was witnessing the end of an era and that public sentiment about such hunting would change. Much as Roosevelt strove to conserve species and their habitats, he was also intent on preserving the memory of his own time.

Roosevelt described himself as a *hunter-naturalist*, meaning he applied the skills of a hunter toward being a better naturalist. Some people mistakenly use this same term to describe a hunter who might also have a secondary interest in nature, but for Roosevelt, being a naturalist always came first—and hunting was essential to that role. His seemingly contradictory legacies as both a conservationist and a big-game hunter are perplexing to many today, but we can only understand these legacies when we see how both sides worked together.

Specimen collecting, hunting, and the acceptance of death were the propulsive forces that shaped Roosevelt's maturation as a naturalist. Sensing a growing separation from wildlife and our once strong connection to the land—the consequence of urbanization—Roosevelt strove to counter these trends.

Born in the world of natural-history museums, tempered on wilderness hunting expeditions, and promulgating by his most celebrated executive decisions, Roosevelt never apologized for his honest way of seeing nature. We today have his love of nature to thank for the laws promoting the fair chase of game animals; the land set aside as national parks, wildlife reserves, and bird sanctuaries; and even many individual specimens in our most important natural-history museums.

This is the story of one man's determination to experience nature without sentiment or judgment. "Death by violence, death by cold, death by starvation—these are the normal endings of the stately and beautiful creatures of the wilderness" was one of Roosevelt's retorts to his more saccharine detractors. He may come off as unusually cruel or harsh today, but he understood the reality upon which all life ultimately depends. The most important legacies of Theodore Roosevelt's presidency—the beginnings of the conservation movement and his protection of millions of acres of wilderness—are rooted in his unique brand of naturalism. Roosevelt was a great champion of a certain kind of nature study—one that advocated for, as he put it, "soundness of head" rather than mere "softness of heart."

PART I

The Museum Naturalist

The country is the place for children, and if not the country, a city small enough so that one can get out into the country.

—THEODORE ROOSEVELT

Chapter 1

THE SEAL ON BROADWAY

Along the cobblestone streets of New York City, a small and somewhat pink-faced boy wandered down Broadway, dwarfed by the towering wall of storefronts at his side. Still sporting a full head of baby curls, the child seemed barely old enough to be out in the city alone, and he looked frail, as if he might have been sick.

Horse-drawn carriages rattled by, dropping off elegant women in hoop-skirted dresses and big hats. Gathering their billowing raiments up with their fingers, they floated in and out of stores showcasing velvet gloves, mink stoles, and fancy sweets. This was "Ladies' Mile"— that stretch of Broadway between Union and Madison Squares where New York's fancy boutiques competed for space and well-heeled customers.

Jostled by the swarms of fashionable shoppers, the boy continued along Broadway, glancing through the storefront windows, until he passed a familiar grocery, where something caught his eye. Amid the usual cartons of fruits and vegetables was an object strangely out of place, splayed out on a slab of wood. It was the dull mass of a seal, dead less than a day. Placed on display to attract paying customers, its corpulent body drew the child's attention.

Sliding his hand along the seal's glossy-smooth pelt and peering deeply into its clouding eyes, he was overwhelmed with interest. Its eyes were so big, and they were fringed with delicate eyelashes just like his own. Curious onlookers stood back, only a brave few lean-ing in for a closer look, but the little boy remained transfixed. It was probably a harbor seal, still fairly common in New York Harbor. So transfixed was the boy by this exotic creature that he raced home for a notebook and ruler, returning moments later to measure the carcass and jot down a few notes on its color and appearance. The eight-year-old boy then wrote a detailed natural history of seals based entirely on that one dead animal.

Theodore Roosevelt's life changed forever in that encounter, for it marked, as he later noted, "the first day" of his career as a natural-ist. Recalling the event in his autobiography decades later, Roosevelt wrote that the seal filled him with "every possible feeling of romance and adventure." It was so unlike anything he had ever seen before. Touching that seal, he would have felt the stiffness of its long, grace-ful whiskers, and, gently lifting up its lips, he would have seen the gleaming white teeth. The ears were just tiny holes, barely noticeable in its dense fur. Squeezing the front flippers, he would have felt that they were just like greatly enlarged hands, the individual finger bones completely encased in the flesh of the flipper with tiny claws extend-ing from the tip. Feeling the seal's body with his own hands, he could appreciate all the similarities to his own basic anatomy, but he wanted to get closer—to take the animal home, perhaps to dissect or stuff it. He had read about how naturalists kept animal specimens to study them, and now he had a chance to practice naturalism himself.

BORN ON October 27, 1858, to Theodore Roosevelt Sr. and Martha Bulloch Roosevelt (known as "Mittie"), Theodore was one in a long line of Roosevelts to have lived in Manhattan, the descendant of some of New York's early Dutch settlers. The family had always been well-off, but Theodore's paternal grandfather, Cornelius Roosevelt, amassed an incredible fortune through real estate speculation. From his redbrick mansion on the southwest corner of Broadway at 14th Street, Cornelius settled each of his five sons in nearby homes. Theo-dore Sr. was given a four-story brownstone just a short walk uptown, on East 20th Street. It was here that Theodore Roosevelt Jr. was born and raised with his older sister, Anna (nicknamed "Bamie"), younger brother, Elliott ("Ellie"), and their baby sister, Corinne ("Conie").

Tall, bearded, and with fierce blue eyes beneath heavy brows, Theodore Roosevelt Sr. looked grim, but to those who knew him well, Mr. Roosevelt was benevolence personified. Although he was a partner in the Wall Street investment banking firm Roosevelt & Son, he preferred to think of himself as a philanthropist, and he took great pleasure in championing charitable causes. He especially adored children, even spending Sunday evenings serving meals to destitute newsboys and street urchins.

To his own family Roosevelt Sr. represented strength and courage, tenderness and great unselfishness. He was so admired by his children that they went to great lengths to compete for his attention. Theodore Jr. later recalled that his father was "the best man I ever knew" but added that he was also "the only man of whom I was ever really afraid." What Theodore feared most was his father's stern disapproval—for Theodore, nothing was more important than earning the respect of his father.

Perhaps more than anything, Mr. Roosevelt was shaped by his views as a "muscular Christian." A popular movement with British and American Protestants of the Victorian era, muscular Christianity taught that Jesus was not only morally strong but also physically sturdy. Masculinity—as shown in the will to fight for a cause—was seen as integral to Christian morality. Muscular Christianity was the answer to a growing concern among men that the world was becoming overly feminized, a reaction to the increasing number of sedentary occupations in the industrializing world and women's growing role in the church. The movement stressed physical activity and spending time outdoors, urging cold-water swims and vigorous mountain climbs.

In sharp contrast to the muscular Christians and her robust, rugged husband, Martha Roosevelt was meek and genteel, a southerner who had grown up in a Georgia plantation house. While Mr. Roosevelt worked tirelessly, Mrs. Roosevelt was physically frail and often complained of fatigue. She was obsessively hygienic and had a penchant for immaculate white dresses, which she wore year-round. One acquaintance described her as "the purest woman he ever saw. No matter how dirty, hot, and ruffled everyone else looked, Mrs. Roosevelt seemed so cool and clean. No dirt ever stopped near her." To her children, she was distant, like a delicate china doll—beautiful to look at but fragile and cold.

Young Theodore Jr. inherited his mother's frailty. No amount of money could spare him the almost constant stomachaches, headaches, coughs, fevers, and nausea he suffered. But Theodore's most chronic and persistent struggle was with asthma. He was plagued by the horror of battling for a shallow gasp of air, only to have anxiety trigger still more severe struggles for breath. Theodore's asthma attacks lasted from a few hours to several days of nonstop wheezing, and it was never entirely certain that he would survive to adulthood.

At the time, asthma was a poorly understood condition, which doctors mistakenly attributed to a narrow chest. There were no effective treatments, so the sufferers and their families were often left to devise their own desperate cures. Roosevelt Sr.—so distraught by his son's ill-health—once summoned a horse and rig from a neighboring stable so that he could take young Theodore on a vigorous nighttime ride, attempting to force air into the small boy's lungs.

Fearful of letting the sickly boy out of their sight, his family rarely allowed him far from their watchful eyes, and (except for a very brief period) he never attended school. Although trapped inside all day, fearing his next asthma attack, Theodore sought solace in his father's library—a dark, windowless room on the first floor of their town house. Lined with bookcases of "gloomy respectability" and cluttered with coarse horsehair chairs that scratched his bare legs, the library was, nonetheless, a sanctuary for the young boy. Sitting on his favorite velvet stool or standing with one leg propped against a wall and his neck bent sharply downward, he lost himself in books.

In these tomes, Theodore found adventure. One of his favorites was Scots medical missionary David Livingstone's *Missionary Travels and Researches in South Africa*. Although it was too large and heavy for a small boy such as Teddy to carry properly, he dragged the book around the house, begging people to read it to him. Livingstone had left his native Scotland to devote his life to evangelism in South Africa, but he was much better known for his explorations of the African continent than for his religious work. *Missionary Travels* documented those exploits and was illustrated with detailed engravings. Roosevelt may have been too young to understand the words, but the pictures in Livingstone's book spoke clearly: a desperate man pinned to the earth by a snarling lion; men with spears and shields driving whole herds of zebras, elands, and antelope into giant pitfall traps dug into the earth; a dugout canoe being violently tipped by an enraged hippopotamus, the passengers flailing their arms and leaping to escape.

The man squirming under the lion's paw was David Livingstone himself. He had been trying to help some villagers by shooting one of the lions raiding their cattle corrals. Firing both barrels of his muzzle-loading rifle, he only wounded the lion, which charged him as he hastily reloaded. The animal sprang onto Livingstone, bit into his shoulder, and pulled him down to the ground. "Growling horribly, he shook me as a terrier dog does a rat," Livingstone explained. "It caused a sort of dreaminess, in which there was no sense of pain nor feeling of terror, though I was quite conscious of all that was happening."

Even more influential to young Teddy than Livingstone's writings were the books of novelist and adventurer Captain Thomas Mayne Reid, whose yarns of hunting, animal lore, and natural history were enormously popular during Roosevelt's youth. Described as adventure novels but also as juvenile scientific travelogues, Reid's writing displayed no stylistic pretensions, and he made it very clear that his books were written for boys. His accurate descriptions of the natural world—everything from mammals and birds to plants—became the *mise-en-scène* of all Reid's books.

Reid championed the genre of the hunter-naturalists—those intrepid men of the nineteenth century who were at once avid huntsmen and students of nature, and he counted himself among their ranks. "I have ridden wildly with the hunter and strolled quietly with the naturalist," Reid explained. "I excel not in the chase, I excel not in a knowledge of natural history—but both I *love*." To Reid, the adventure of the hunt and the quiet study of nature were intimately connected.

One of Reid's books in particular must have been especially inspiring to young Roosevelt, presaging much of his naturalist career. *The Boy Hunters* details the lives of three brothers who are sent off by their father on an expedition to shoot a white buffalo for a great museum in Europe. Most important, Reid took the boys and their mission seriously, making very clear from the outset that they were capable of this feat. It's likely that Roosevelt's first impressions of naturalism were formed by countless hours spent with *The Boy Hunters*. Here were children free to roam outdoors in the fresh air all day. They traipsed through the woods with guns and knives; they were crack shots and fearlessly killed charging bears and menacing alligators. They collected gunnysacks full of specimens, preserving them in little natural-history museums of their own making.

Equally significantly for Roosevelt, Reid wrote about the father of these young hunters. Unable to join the hunt because of an old soldiering injury—one that left him with a wooden leg—the father sent his boys off on their buffalo-hunting expedition with a great sense of pride, boasting to his neighbors about his strong "boy men."

How Theodore must have wanted to have such adventures; how he must have wanted his father to be proud of *his* bold and enterprising character. Trapped indoors on East 20th Street, Theodore could only read with rapture the novels of Thomas Mayne Reid and others, the sole antidote to his sickly life indoors. Adventure stories gave him an escape into a world full of exciting possibilities, but the excitement was always out of reach—until he stumbled upon that dead seal on Broadway.

Years later, Roosevelt admitted in his autobiography that the moment he discovered the creature, all the stories he had read sprang to life before him. Adventure suddenly seemed attainable, and, for the first time, Roosevelt thought maybe he could pursue the life of a hunter-naturalist, just like a character in a Thomas Mayne Reid book.

Inspired, Roosevelt returned daily to that storefront to check on the dead seal. He tried to persuade the shopkeeper to give him the whole animal, but since the carcass was already starting to decay, young Theodore had to settle for just the head, which, perhaps together with a few equally pleased flies, he proudly carried home.

Roosevelt wanted to clean the seal head to save its skull, and from his readings he would have been familiar with at least some of the methods used for cleaning skulls. One technique is bacterial maceration, which requires placing the bone in a vat of warm water for days and weeks at a time. Bacteria gradually build up, rotting the meat off and turning the water into a brown mushy soup. This method literally stinks, and it is a slow, disgusting process. If Roosevelt prepared his seal skull using this technique, his parents would have shown unbelievable tolerance, especially in light of his mother's aversion to filth.

Another method involves placing the skull in a chamber of flesh-eating insects. Any invertebrate inclined to eat flesh will do, including ants, woodlice, or even maggots—but flesh-eating beetles of the dermestid family are the most efficient. "Bugging" a skull yields superior results, because all those little mouthparts quickly pull flesh off without harming bone.

But Roosevelt most likely prepared his treasure by boiling it until the meat cooked off. Boiling is the fastest and most intuitive of all bone-cleaning methods, and there is an early reference to Roosevelt once asking a cook to boil a woodchuck carcass for him. The animal can't just be plopped into a pot and boiled intact; first the carcass has to be gutted and skinned, and the major muscle masses have to be carefully removed. Even after boiling, a certain amount of scraping is required to remove the last stubborn bits of gristle adhering tenaciously to bone, and the boiled brain still has to be sloshed out the back of the skull—not an easy job for the squeamish.

Holding the finished skull in his hands, he would have seen for the first time how the seal's teeth worked—lower molars interlocking neatly with the uppers. The suture lines—the places where the different bones of the skull fuse together—would have been obvious, and Roosevelt might have easily learned all the bones' names: frontals, parietals, nasals, occipitals. He could estimate the size of the eyes by placing a ruler across their bony orbits. In the back of each eye socket he would have seen the tiny hole for the optic nerve to pass through to the brain. Inside the nose he would have seen the delicate, scroll-like bone that supports the membranes responsible for the sense of smell. Instead of simply seeing drawings in his favorite books, he could touch the skull, hold it, and look inside it.

What Roosevelt read inspired him to build his own natural-history museum—he had learned how the Reid boys had "artistically preserved by stuffing" the skins of birds and mammals. Roosevelt recruited his brother and sisters to help him, along with his two cousins, Emlen and West. With the seal skull acting as the centerpiece of his budding collection, Roosevelt founded what he ambitiously called "The Roosevelt Museum of Natural History."

All that is known of Theodore's earliest days as a nascent museum curator comes from a brief history recorded on just a few pages of handwritten notes. Roosevelt's *Record of the Roosevelt Museum* begins very officially: "At the commencement of the year 1867 Mr. T. Roosevelt, Jr. started the Museum with 12 specimen . . ." Housed in Theodore's bedroom, the "museum" soon grew to include hundreds of prizes: mice, shrews, and birds. The only organizing principle for the museum's collection was to accumulate as many specimens as possible. The Roosevelt children worked furiously to add to the pile, though it wasn't just the younger family members who were expected to contribute to the eager curator's trove.

Writing to his parents while they were visiting Georgia in the spring of 1868, nine-year-old Teddy stressed that he expected them to collect a few specimens from their exotic southern locality: "In your letter you write to me to tell me how many curiosities and living things you have got for me," he prodded his mother. Writing his father, he was even more direct, goading him to cut off the tail of a "tiger-cat" belonging to a friend, adding that it would be on prominent display in his museum. Even the family nurse was enlisted, as one breathless letter to her reveals: "I have one request to make of you. Press plenty of plants and leaves and get a good many seeds for me, and some beetles and butterflies, get feathers and wood too. Get as many live things as you can."

Though small and frail, Theodore had boundless energy for

building his collection, and although his parents were not especially inclined as naturalists, their delight that their sickly son had found an outlet ensured that his interests—no matter how fanatical or foul-smelling—were never really challenged. The values of the time also dovetailed nicely with little Teddy's keen interest, and Theodore Sr.'s interest in muscular Christianity likely contributed to his encouragement. In the Victorian era, nature study was a moral good. Studying God's word in the Bible and studying His works in nature were considered twin facets of the same truth. British philosopher William Paley's *Natural Theology* had been influential since 1802, arguing that since natural objects showed evidence of design, they also showed evidence of a designing god. Being a very religious man himself, Roosevelt Sr. no doubt saw young Theodore's passion for natural history as a way of bringing him closer to the creating hand of God.

Of course, Theodore's museum ambitions went well beyond what might be considered typical, and he amassed zoological specimens as if they were the sole measure of his self-worth. While other children might have been content with a small collection of seashells or some neatly pressed flowers, Roosevelt's collection included some truly grotesque finds. When he acquired a live snapping turtle—an aggressive pond-dweller covered in algae and decorated with a gruesome frill of leeches—the entire household rebelled. Still, the collection increasingly became the center of his young life. No longer a pastime or mere escape from his dreary existence indoors, he was making meaning out of his fieldwork. As his museum grew, it came to embody his prowess as a naturalist.

But while Roosevelt's naturalist ambitions were openly encouraged, the location of the museum was not as easily tolerated. The housekeepers were the first to protest, and after they received the approval of "the higher authorities" (his parents), it was agreed that Theodore's museum had to be moved, preferably as far away from the family's daily life as possible. In the end, his collection of dead animals was relocated to a far back hallway at the top of a flight of stairs where it would bother no one. For Theodore, the relegation was only a minor setback—not nearly as traumatic as when someone carelessly disposed of some mice he was keeping in a top dresser drawer, an event he perhaps overstated as a "loss to science." At least the reloca-tion of the Roosevelt Museum gave Theodore the assurance that his prized collection was safe from the trash heap.

Ironically, had he been healthy or grown up in the country instead of the heart of New York City, Roosevelt's passion for nature might never have blossomed so extravagantly—for it was the very fact that it offered an antidote to his own limits, one so ripe with complexity, that he was drawn to the natural world. He often felt that he was just a sickly city kid; even when his father took him to the country for his health, Roosevelt was always burdened with the knowledge that he would be returning to the city just as soon as he was well. For young Theodore, his museum provided a measure of assurance that he would always be close to the natural world—he need only go to the top stairs of a back hallway to commune with nature and play the part of the brainy naturalist and muscular adventurer.

⟨ ⟩

COLLECTIONS MAKE MUSEUMS

*I*n gathering animals for study, Roosevelt was participating in a tradition his father could be proud of: one that went all the way back to the Bible, from the second chapter of Genesis, when God brought all the animals to Adam to see what he would name them. If one takes this passage of the Bible literally, animal taxonomy was one of the first responsibilities of man, a duty he was entrusted with even before procreation. It follows that practically everyone has a deep-rooted instinct to collect, an impulse to control and categorize the world around him or her. To collect is human, even spiritual. This fundamental need is perhaps what led to the forerunner of today's natural-history museums—the cabinets of wonders and curiosities.

The word *cabinet* was originally used for a room that might include books, coins, and paintings, in addition to natural-history curios. But even in the early days, there were always a few specialists in *naturalia.* One of the earliest naturalist enthusiasts was the Danish physician and antiquary Ole Worm. A woodcut print from his Museum Wormianum dating to 1655 shows something akin to a natural-history pawnshop, with bins of crystals, corals, and dried puffer fish strewn among other oddments. A stuffed lemur sat on a top shelf in a corner, and on the walls hung dried snake skins, iguanas, and an armadillo. Stuffed birds were suspended from the ceiling alongside benthic fish and a shark. Many of these objects were thought to have medicinal, even mystical, powers, and the Wormianum looks as much like a sorcerer's storeroom as it does a museum.

More than a century later, fascination with these types of collections had only grown. One of the most famous was in London, where the British naturalist Sir Ashton Lever had turned his home into his Holophusicon (meaning, "all nature museum"). Surviving watercolors of the interior show glass-fronted display cases containing thousands of stuffed birds and mammals against clean white backgrounds. Lever loved the exotic, favoring showy birds-of-paradise, colorful parrots, flamingoes, and unusual mammals such as sloths, shrews, and a giant kangaroo. He even had a full-size stuffed Asian elephant in his collection.

The Wormianum and the Holophusicon were just two of many antecedents to Roosevelt's boyhood museum. Traveling through Europe when he was only eleven, Teddy compared some of the Continent's old cabinets to his own collection. After visiting one in Germany, he was pleased to find that out of 101 animals on exhibit there, he already had two of the reptiles and three of the birds in his own collection back home.

Roosevelt was not unique in starting his own museum. Following the Revolutionary War, Americans were quick to imitate the European aristocrats who kept such collections, largely prompted by envy of Europe's cultural primacy and a desire to assert their membership in the same scientific milieu. Even Benjamin Franklin had his own collection. Natural history was a new and popular science on both sides of the Atlantic, but it was especially well suited to Americans, given their easy access to wilderness. Unlike most other cultural pursuits, for which wealth and education were absolutely requisite, anyone with access to the outdoors could participate in natural history, and Americans took to building cabinets of natural curiosities. It was in the early days of this new nation, anchored by democratic ideals, that public natural-history museums were born, beginning with the museum of a patrician Pennsylvanian named Charles Willson Peale.

Soft-spoken and warm, Peale had served with George Washington at Trenton and stayed with him through the long winter at Valley Forge. He was among America's founders and he hoped to make his

living painting portraits of his famous cohorts. Opening a small studio and gallery off to the side of his Philadelphia home, Peale hung
examples of his work for the public to glimpse the visages of famous
Americans, one of few opportunities for the general population to see
the likenesses of their most renowned citizens. But a pile of about
fifty gigantic bones positioned unceremoniously on the gallery's floor
attracted more interest. These were the fossil remains of a large prehistoric creature discovered on the frontier; Peale was making some
drawings of the bones, not realizing that his patrons would be so
taken with them. The fragmented skeleton also awakened in him a
long-simmering passion for natural history, and, seeing the public's
own interest, Peale was inspired to turn his gallery of art into a museum of natural history.

Peale's museum was designed to "diffuse a knowledge of the wonderful works of creation." He was several decades ahead of his time
in anticipating the triple-bore function of a modern natural-history
museum—to keep vast collections of specimens and support scholarly
research in addition to offering popular exhibits. No other museums,
in either Europe or America, had these lofty goals.

To populate his museum, Peale first had to learn how to preserve
his specimens. A few published guides detailed how to skin and stuff
animals, but chemical preservation was still a mystery. The available
books emphasized the use of dubious concoctions of cinnamon, to-
bacco, and pepper, which allegedly preserved animal skins long-term.
One paper even suggested using myrrh and frankincense as preserva-
tives.

Live insects posed great peril to these early museums. Beetles and
moths could devour animal skins with indiscriminate efficiency, and
if these insects were able to access a collection, a curator might be surprised one day to find nothing but a pile of frass (as insect excrement
is called) and some stray bits of stuffing and wire in the place where
prized taxidermy specimens were once kept. But nothing solved the
problem until a French alchemist and naturalist developed a poisonous deterrent.

Ornithologist Jean-Baptiste Bécoeur invented arsenical soap in
the latter half of the eighteenth century. His formula was simple:

arsenic, lime, camphor, and salts mixed into plain white soap that could be moistened and painted on the inside of a skin before the bird or animal was stuffed and sewed up. Even as a child, Roosevelt was allowed to have arsenic for insect-proofing his specimens, but he had to take special care to make sure that the toothbrush he used for applying the poison was kept separate from his own. He had a close call once when someone mistakenly placed his arsenic toothbrush next to the washbasin.

Despite Bécoeur's advancement in collection-related pest control, taxidermy was still very much a crude and imperfect art. Peale struggled to teach himself the basics using the inadequate guides available, and he overcame those limitations in some creative ways. With his artist's eye, he thought that specimens should be displayed in naturalistic poses, grouped together with natural objects in lifelike scenes. In one of the earliest examples of a habitat diorama, he painted scenic backdrops for many of his bird mounts, creating immersive experiences for his viewers.

Eventually, Peale's collection outgrew his home studio, and he moved the museum to the high-ceilinged and bare-wooden-floored rooms of Independence Hall, where the Declaration of Independence had been signed just a few years earlier. He organized his collection to showcase the perfection of creation, and a walk through the museum unfolded as a long march through the animal kingdom.

Despite some early successes—and the expansion of the Peale Museum brand to Baltimore and New York—his family struggled financially. To counter this, and to keep his doors open, Peale had to indulge the whims of his admission-paying visitors, but he did his best to balance monetary priorities with the educational spirit upon which the collection was first founded. Eventually, Peale's sons took over, and they added sensational crowd-pleasers such as a calf with two heads and six legs, a "learned dog" named Romeo who barked out the answers to questions, and Signor Hellene, a one-man band simultaneously playing the viola, Turkish cymbals, tenor drum, Pandean pipes, and Chinese bells.

Attempting to tread a middle ground between serious science and entertainment, the Peales eventually reached the point where they could no longer compete with the rise of a new kind of institution—called the dime museum—that pandered exclusively to the lower levels of popular taste, trivializing museum exhibitions to mere sensationalism. In just a few short decades the Peales were forced to close their museums. Even more tragic, their collections were dispersed, and many specimens were bought by the man whom some considered to be the most notorious dime museum huckster of all—P. T. Barnum.

Phineas Taylor Barnum, of later circus fame, was the genius behind the largest and most outlandish of all the dime museums. Situated in Lower Manhattan at the corner of Ann Street and Broadway, Barnum's American Museum of the 1850s was an immaculate white building festooned with banners and covered with colorful posters on all five stories of the exterior. The main gallery on the first floor was filled with glass cases of stuffed animals. There was even a taxidermy shop where you could drop off a dead pet and have it stuffed and ready to take home by the end of the day. Barnum proudly described his American Museum as an "encyclopedic synopsis of everything worth seeing in the curious world."

By 1864, P. T. Barnum was boasting that he possessed more than 850,000 curiosities. A self-proclaimed proponent of the art of money-making, he was famous for enticing paying customers with outlandish hoaxes, and part of the fun of going to the American Museum was never quite knowing what was real and what was merely a clever trick. Barnum's modus operandi was to turn obvious deceit into a game, baiting the public and the press alike and then sitting back to enjoy the spectacle (and the profits) of a public itching to see his hyped-up exhibits. He also mastered the art of manipulating the press, building suspense so well that people were drawn to his shows even after some of the exhibits were revealed to be bogus.

But Barnum's most outlandish trick played on the tools of the naturalist trade. After obtaining a taxidermy mount of what appeared to be a mermaid, Barnum was careful not to display it right away. Instead, he went on a PR offensive, spinning a yarn about the discovery of the strange specimen he called the "Fejee Mermaid" in the local newspapers. According to Barnum's fiction, the specimen had been recently discovered in the far-off Hawaiian Islands, and a hitherto unheard-of scientist was on his way to exhibit it in the United States for only a very short time. For weeks Barnum craftily fed the newspapers updates about the imaginary scientist and his mermaid, building a great sense of anticipation of their arrival. When the Fejee Mermaid was finally put on exhibit, with placards suggesting a voluptuous feminine creature of outsize proportions, people flocked to Barnum's museum, where, instead of a sea siren, they found an extremely shriveled "mermaid" only eighteen inches long. The mermaid, of course, was an obvious fake—the work of Japanese craftsmen stitching together a monkey torso and a fish tail as a novelty item for sailors.

To Barnum, it was all just fun, but serious naturalists were incensed. Barnum had made a mockery of their science, buying up Peale's prized specimens and turning natural history into a farce. Among those who had been for a long time upset by Barnum's charades were New York City's most respected elites, including Theodore Roosevelt Sr. To these educated men, Barnum symbolized everything that was wrong with America, including the decline of serious scientific inquiry. To their minds, Americans—with their vast reserves of wilderness and wildlife—deserved a grand public natural-history museum. It was a small handful of such individuals—the elder Theodore Roosevelt among them—who played a key role in pioneering serious natural-history museums in America. They sought a return to Peale's original idea of a natural-history museum housing collections of specimens for science, and they were willing to donate substantial amounts to make this kind of public museum a reality; they just needed to find the right flag-bearer.

MUSEUMS *ARE* THEIR collections, and the vitality of a natural-history museum depends on naturalists actively collecting new specimens for science. Without avid specimen hunters, natural-history museums never would have progressed beyond the cabinets of curiosity, those static collections owned by a few wealthy individuals. Through the sheer volume of their findings, it was the specimen collectors who brought natural history to the general population, making museums out of otherwise esoteric groupings. One of the most influential of these collectors was Spencer Fullerton Baird, the force behind the creation of one of America's largest natural-history museums—the National Museum of Natural History at the Smithsonian Institution—and someone who served as an important historical role model for Roosevelt. More than any other naturalist, it was Baird whom Roosevelt looked to for inspiration.

Born to a well-off family in 1823, Baird grew up in the Cumberland Valley in rural southern Pennsylvania, which was something of a naturalist's paradise. His hometown of Carlisle was surrounded by trees so high that he thought it "an almost impossible feat to kill a squirrel or wild pigeon on the top, with one shot." In Baird's time, even very small boys could be experts with shotguns, and they caromed though the brush after school in search of targets. Such shooting was encouraged as a warm-up to the more adult pastime of sport hunting, and since few game laws were in place, the boys killed birds freely. But the songbird slaughter was considered appropriate only up to a certain age. As soon as most boys were old enough to join their fathers and uncles on more gentlemanly game-bird hunts they quit blasting at bluebirds and buntings to hunt waterfowl and partridge. But not Baird. He kept hunting all kinds of diminutive animals well into adulthood. Songbirds and swifts, swallows and wrens—they were all fair game to the fully bearded Baird, and he hunted them relentlessly.

Hunting means different things to different people, but *most* hunters fall into one of two distinct kinds. Most are either meat hunters, who hunt for food, or sport hunters, who hunt for the challenge. These two categories dominate the general public's imagination, but there is a third group whose adherents are more focused on getting as close to nature as possible. This third group of hunters—the least understood of them all—are the nature hunters.

Baird was a nature hunter, and, like Theodore Roosevelt, he tapped these instincts as a very young boy. Typically, these sorts of hunters know much more about wildlife than meat and sport hunters do, and they have a much greater interest in the lives of the animals they hunt. They seek an active, participatory role in the natural world, their goal being intense involvement with wild animals in their natural habitats.

These hunters enter the wild not to dominate nature but to become a part of it. The hunt brings an awareness of nature that never comes from being a mere spectator.

Museum collectors are the ultimate nature hunters. They "hunt" as part of their naturalism. As a young specimen collector, Baird was hooked on gathering specimens for his boyhood collection—"I well remember when a lad of eight, uniting together with two or three friends . . . in combining our joint natural history curiosities into a museum, which attracted a good deal of curiosity." He was entirely self-motivated, for few members of the extended Baird family considered nature study anything worth pursuing.

Baird kept his bird collection in an antique wooden secretary-cabinet that his grandmother—the only family member who supported his ambitions—had given him for that purpose. Much as Roosevelt would do decades later, Baird shot and stuffed birds nearly every day, looking forward to their seasonal migrations the way other children look forward to Christmas. Part of his excitement came from the mystery and surprise of nature. Hundreds of different bird species passed through the Cumberland Valley, and, in addition to the thrill of adding something new to his collection, there was always the chance of making his own scientific discovery. So little was known of the birds of the eastern United States in Baird's time that stumbling upon a species that had not yet been formally identified was a real possibility for a young boy.

One evening, while staying up late to prepare some study skins, Baird noticed that two of his birds were unlike any he had seen before. He had shot them in a swampy place, and although they looked somewhat like little tyrant flycatchers (then called *Muscicipa pusilla*), there was something not quite right about them. Puzzling over the birds for days and checking all the published sources, he excitedly concluded that the birds must be new to science.

Baird understood the steps for describing a new species: discuss what makes it different, compare it to other named forms to make sure it was not already identified by someone else, propose an original scientific name, and publish the findings in a peer-reviewed journal. But he was hesitant, intimidated at the prospect of authoring a scientific paper. The process was especially daunting for Baird, who had been birding in academic isolation. All the specimens, notebooks, and theories he had collected were kept locked up in his grandmother's cupboard in Carlisle, Pennsylvania. But Baird must have known that this was his best—perhaps only—chance to really move his career forward, and so, with much trepidation, he decided to draft a letter to none other than John James Audubon, the famed ornithologist.

Audubon's name was, and still is, synonymous with birds, and Baird penned his first letter to him with great tact, emphasizing that he was "but a boy, and very inexperienced." He continued with detailed descriptions of every species of bird in his collection that he thought Audubon might be interested in: "This letter is already too long, yet perhaps you will pardon me for adding a few remarks about some of the Birds found around Carlisle." If Baird convinced Audubon of anything, it was that he had a deep and abiding passion for bird study.

Audubon, like many other nineteenth-century American ornithologists, was entirely self-taught. There were no schools offering training in ornithology, and Audubon had learned by experience. He shot birds and then propped them up on twigs in his studio so that he could paint them while still fresh. He also made hundreds of study skins, building up a large reference collection to use when painting.

Baird was just fifteen when he first wrote to Audubon, and, although forty-three years his senior, Audubon was impressed. "Although you speak of yourself as being a youth," he wrote, "your style and the descriptions you have sent me prove to me that an old head may from time to time be found on young shoulders!" Baird's timing was perfect. Audubon and his colleague, John Bachman, were in the middle of preparing *The Viviparous Quadrupeds of North America*—a book that was to include descriptions and illustrations of every mammal on the continent. There were hundreds of species, and Audubon needed to secure the corresponding number of specimens to produce accurate renderings. To accomplish this mass collecting, he was planning to outsource the task, recruiting an army of boy hunters. Responding to Baird, he revealed his grand plan: "Assisted as we hope and trust to be, by numerous friends and acquaintances in different portions of our Wide Union, we expect to collect, not only new species, but much of the valuable matter connected with their geographical range, and particular habits. . . . You may be able to send us valuable intelligence respecting the Shrews, Mice, Rats, Squirrels, etc., found in your immediate vicinity . . . and by saving and forwarding specimens to us, be able also, in all probability, to place into our hands, objects never before known to the World of Science. . . . Please collect all the Shrews, Mice, (field or wood), rats, bats, Squirrels, etc., and put them in a jar in common Rum, not whiskey, brandy or alcohol. All of the latter spirits are sure to injure the subjects."

Thus deputized, Baird spent the next year collecting specimens and exchanging letters with the famous artist. When he finally made the trip up to New York to meet his epistolary mentor, though, Baird found Audubon "very unlike my preconceived idea of him." Audubon was an eccentric obsessed with collecting specimens, although brilliant when it came to painting them. He became a mentor to Baird, giving him bird specimens and teaching him how to draw. The generous Audubon also brought him to the taxidermy shop of John Bell—a naturalists' hangout and the place where a young Theodore Roosevelt himself would one day learn the art of specimen-stuffing. He also introduced Baird to all the important players in the nascent field of American ornithology.

Baird's family probably looked at Audubon as a bad influence, luring the boy further from an occupation that might one day secure him a decent livelihood and deeper into the unprofitable world of natural history. Baird wanted nothing more than to be the curator of some great museum, to the exclusion of all other pursuits. Borrowing Audubon's idea of employing teams of eager young boys in specimen collecting, in 1846 Baird published a twelve-page pamphlet outlining techniques for preserving plant and animal specimens, embedding in the pages an invitation to send any specimens to Baird himself.

In a life-changing decision, Baird spent two months in Washington, D.C., volunteering to help sort the zoological collections of the United States Exploring Expedition. Spanning the years 1838 to 1842, the "Ex Ex squadron" (as it was called) was the U.S. government's first survey of the Pacific Ocean and surrounding lands. Several naturalists were included as part of the expedition, among them William Peale's son Titian, who collected barrels of botanical and zoological specimens that were ultimately sent back to Washington. It was Baird's job to curate and identify all these specimens before their ultimate transfer to the nascent Smithsonian Institution.

The Smithsonian was also out to prove itself. The institution had only recently been founded when James Smithson—the bastard son of a noble Englishman who had great admiration for America's democratization of science—bequeathed his entire fortune to the United States of America, "to found at Washington, under the name of the Smithsonian Institution, an Establishment for the increase and diffusion of knowledge among men." Valued at more than half a million dollars in 1838, Smithson's fortune was shipped to New York in ten heavy wooden crates filled with a thousand pounds of gold apiece. Meeting them on the dock were just two U.S. Treasury agents, who accompanied the crates down to Washington.

The money secured, it was time to get to work. But just what kind of institution Smithson had in mind was open to interpretation. Joseph Henry, first secretary of the Smithsonian, insisted on founding the institution solely for scientific research, and he fought vigorously against spending Smithson's money to establish a museum, believing them mere collections of junk. Baird (now a respected naturalist with strong ties to the leaders in the field) very strongly disagreed and, after being hired as its first curator in 1850, Baird spent the first decade of his tenure at the Smithsonian advocating for a museum. Secretary Henry eventually relented on the condition that if any collections were made, they should be of a purely scientific kind—a collection available for scholarly research.

The Smithsonian Institution came to be dominated by its natural-history museum, which had everything to do with Baird's enthusiasm; he entered the position with unmatched zeal. One of his first orders of business was to donate his entire boyhood natural-history collection to the institution. When the precious cargo was finally packed up and loaded for transport, the collection filled two freight cars to the roof.

Building the Smithsonian collections, Baird wrote: "My object is to make the Smithsonian Museum eminent above all others American."

But Spencer Fullerton Baird was only one of America's early museum builders, and just as the Smithsonian's museum was getting on track, another curator-to-be, tall and ambitious, approached the Roosevelt residence on East 20th Street, where he was met at the front door and ushered into the parlor.

Chapter 3

THE MIND BUT
NOT THE BODY

*A*s the most formal space in the Roosevelt home, the front parlor was generally reserved for receiving the most distinguished guests. On the night of April 8, 1869, it was dazzling under the light of its great cut-glass chandelier, with some of the wealthiest philanthropists in the city milling about below. To the Roosevelt children peering in from the hallways, it was clear that this was an important night, and if one of the guests seemed a little more anxious to them than the others, it was probably Albert S. Bickmore. Unlike the other men in the room—all New York elites—Bickmore had no prestigious pedigree, little money, and only average academic credentials. But he did have unbounded enthusiasm for the dream that had carried him into the Roosevelt home that night: he wanted to found a natural-history museum in the heart of New York City.

Bickmore hailed from Maine, where he lived an idyllic life nestled between the forest and the sea. He grew up watching great schools of mackerel and herring swim each spring, and in summer he gathered bushels of giant lobsters at low tide. Fall brought basking seals almost to his doorstep, and all year long he explored the old Penobscot trails that meandered through the woods behind his house. Like Spencer Baird before him, he always knew he wanted to be a naturalist, ultimately making his way to Harvard to study under an influential professor named Louis Agassiz. A Swiss biologist and geologist, Agassiz had brought to America a very different kind of naturalism that tended to reduce animal study to the animal's component parts. This was a much more European style of nature study—one that used microscopes to zero in on minute anatomical complexities. While American naturalists looked to the frontier for new species to discover, Agassiz lost himself in the infinite details of animals, especially of fish and sea creatures found not far from his home. The professor was eager to study more specimens than he could ever hope to personally collect, and he printed thousands of copies of a pamphlet describing how to preserve fish for study. Sending these out, he received specimens from hundreds of amateur naturalists all over America. The Agassiz team's findings began to pile up at Harvard, filling the basement to the point that Agassiz needed the university to build him his own museum. Agassiz's new museum—later named the Museum of Comparative Zoology—finally opened its door to the public in November 1860.

Arriving at the Museum of Comparative Zoology as a Harvard student, Albert Bickmore found Agassiz amid a jumble of amber jars full of dead animals. The broad-shouldered, square-jawed Agassiz barely looked up from his work as he handed Bickmore a jar with a sea urchin in it and told him to make a study of it. This was the eccentric Agassiz's standard entrance exam. "You will either become utterly weary of the task, or else you will be so completely fascinated with it as to devote your whole life to the pursuit of our science," he told Bickmore as he waved him out of the room. Of course, the young student passed the test.

But Bickmore found life at Harvard more oppressive than enlightening. Agassiz told his students they were forbidden to publish, barred from seeking employment, and could not even plan a simple field trip without his permission. Agassiz controlled everything, stifling his students, and after two years of languishing in Agassiz's shadow, Bickmore let his mentor know he was looking for a way out. Infuriated by what he perceived to be a lack of gratitude and loyalty, Agassiz refused to consider Bickmore for a permanent position in his own Museum of Comparative Zoology, essentially shutting him out of any gainful museum employment.

But his experience with the domineering professor was not wholly without value. In addition to studying *under* Agassiz, Bickmore had been making his own independent study *of* Agassiz. As he watched him charm Boston's wealthy elite for donations, Bickmore realized that Agassiz had made a mistake building his museum in the sleepy town of Cambridge, as all the important museums of Europe were centered in major cities. If a museum is to become great, Bickmore thought, does it not need to be near the heart of a nation's wealth and power? And yet no such museum existed in New York City, the commercial capital of America. He became increasingly certain that he could found his own museum; all he needed were enough specimens to convince the bankers and philanthropists of the country's biggest city to back him. So Albert Bickmore left Harvard intent on founding his own museum in New York, one that he insisted would be run on "democratic principles," in sharp contrast to the "dictatorial methods" employed at Cambridge. Bickmore, like Peale before him, held strongly to the distinctly American belief that museums needed to be accessible to everyone.

Inspired, he drafted a proposal for his museum and sailed off to collect specimens in remote Asia. Armed with his two most valuable possessions—his Bible and his plan—Bickmore spent the next three years collecting birds and shells throughout Borneo, Java, and the Spice Islands. His main purpose was to amass "the beautiful shells of those seas," and he followed this trip with a year-and-a-half-long sojourn through China, Japan, and Siberia. On his return he wrote a book about his adventures called *Travels in the East Indian Archipelago*—one that matches David Livingstone's *Missionary Travels* in its thrilling illustrations, especially the drawing depicting Bickmore clinging to the deeply rooted fern that saved him from falling into a volcano.

Albert Bickmore returned home, a robust specimen collection in hand, just as the nation was rebuilding after the Civil War and its captains of industry were amassing great wealth. Wealthy men began thinking and talking about millions of dollars instead of mere thousands. Some of these same Americans were also painfully aware of their inferiority to Europeans in matters that ranged from architecture to the arts and the sciences, and they hoped that their money and influence could correct that. All these circumstances coalesced to create the perfect climate for speculation in the world of museums.

Theodore Roosevelt Sr. was among those seeking to elevate America's cultural heritage, and together with Albert Bickmore he hoped to do his part by founding a great natural-history museum. American scientific advancement (and his son's interest in the subject) aside, the widespread Victorian belief that nature had a strong moralizing effect was also a motivating factor. Being a very moral man himself, Roosevelt considered the construction of a natural-history museum one of his greatest endeavors.

Bickmore also shared some of Roosevelt's belief in muscular Christianity. Both men saw nature as a link to a simpler and more honest time, before the corrupting influence of urban life, and they valued natural-history collecting for the virtues of manly struggle it embodied. They even shared a similar visage, with full beards and serious eyes, and young Theodore likely saw in Bickmore the ideals of his father.

The 1869 meeting in the front parlor of the Roosevelt home was the culmination of months of discussions in which Roosevelt Sr. played a lead role. The men had gathered on East 20th Street to draft a charter and elect the museum's first officers. More contentious than the parliamentary plans was the selection of a name befitting such a grand institution. In the end, it was Bickmore who came up with one they would all agree upon. Their new institution would be called the American Museum of Natural History—and although P. T. Barnum's dime museum bearing the same name was still fresh in the minds of New York citizens, this uptown establishment would be something completely different.

Theodore was but ten years old when the American Museum of Natural History was officially founded, yet he was already keenly interested in the subject. The elder Roosevelt even ensured his son was present to watch as Bickmore unpacked the museum's first specimens. Besides the Spice Islands specimens, the collection included more than three thousand items from the cabinet of the late French naturalist Édouard Verreaux, with hundreds of birds and small mammals.

Also among Verreaux's collection was the first specimen officially entered in the museum's catalogue book—a snarling lion.

The holdings of the early museum soon doubled when the museum purchased more than four thousand mounted birds, six hundred mounted mammals, and two thousand fishes and reptiles from the heir of the Prussian prince Alexander Philipp Maximilian of Wied-Neuwied. Maximilian's explorations of southeastern Brazil and travels in the American West in the first half of the nineteenth century had brought him international renown as a naturalist and ethnographer. He had had all his specimens expertly mounted, and at the time of their purchase, the American Museum bragged that "the cost of mounting this collection exceeds the price we paid for it." There also came a flood of many smaller donations, including a fur seal, a giraffe, and a baboon from P. T. Barnum, along with a number of animals from the nearby Central Park Menagerie. Wishing to contribute, Theodore made an early donation of his own, and an annual report records the acquisition of one bat, twelve mice, one turtle, a red-squirrel skull, and four birds' eggs.

Once the museum was fully operational, Theodore visited regularly. The American Museum of Natural History was at first temporarily housed on the top floors of the old Army Arsenal Building on the southeast corner of Central Park, not very far from the Roosevelts' home. It would be five more years before the collection would move farther uptown to its permanent home on Central Park West. There, in 1874, President Ulysses S. Grant laid the cornerstone for "building one" of the American Museum of Natural History, a quaint Victorian structure that would eventually grow into a campus of more than thirty buildings.

Being so well-connected, Theodore could have aimed for a respectable career as an "armchair naturalist" at the American Museum. He easily might have taken one of the high-ceilinged offices on the top floor and from one of its arched windows peered out across Central Park in the direction of his home, describing new species from the comfort of a study. But Theodore was motivated to pursue his passion in a way that challenged him—thanks, in no small part, to his father.

. . .

MR. ROOSEVELT WAS deeply bothered by his son's poor health, and he resorted to desperate measures to make the boy well. He found that caffeine sometimes helped ease Theodore's asthma, so Teddy started drinking coffee at a very early age. Nicotine was also thought to help, and there are sadly comical accounts of little asthmatic Theodore smoking fat cigars in bed. After years of failed treatments, Roosevelt Sr. was persuaded by doctors that perhaps the one thing Theodore needed most was a change of scenery.

In the span of just a few months in the spring and summer of 1870, the Roosevelts traveled all over the Northeast in search of the perfect conditions to alleviate young Theodore's health problems. Based at the family's summer home in the Bronx's Spuyten Duyvil, Theodore visited relatives in Philadelphia, went to water-cure spas in Saratoga Springs, and then ventured to Oyster Bay on Long Island before heading back up to central New York State, enduring more water-cure spas in Richfield Springs. "Of course I came here because I was sick," he wrote to his beloved sister Anna, adding that he had been "several times sick" that season.

Theodore was always happy to get out of New York City and into the country, where he had the freedom of the great outdoors. There he could swim, ride his pony, and play in the woods. Always the naturalist, he dabbled in studying wild mice, outsourcing some collecting to the townsfolk by announcing that he would pay ten cents for every mouse and a whopping thirty-five cents for every family of mice delivered in good condition. Unfortunately, Theodore had to leave for another stop on his cure tour before he could make good on his promise, leaving Anna to deal with the droves of "clamoring country people" who "demanded their ten-cent pieces or the larger sum irrelevantly offered by the absentee young naturalist."

In the end, Theodore's summer travels were no more effective in curing his asthma than caffeine, nicotine, or brisk midnight rides. He returned to Manhattan just as sickly as ever. A doctor examining him found the boy still short, frail, and with a chest that seemed too small for his body. This news was a blow to Roosevelt Sr., who once again attempted to take charge of a situation that he increasingly felt was out of his control.

In the fall of 1870, on the eve of Theodore's twelfth birthday, his father sat him down for a talk that would completely reframe the younger Roosevelt's life. Rest cures weren't working; water spas did nothing. There seemed to be no effective treatment that would improve his son's health. Drawing on his background as a muscular Christian, Mr. Roosevelt gravely explained, "You have the mind, but you have not the body, and without the help of the body, the mind cannot go as far as it should." The conversation was a last resort, and, knowing that Theodore was a determined little boy, he insisted: "You must *make* your body. It is hard drudgery to make one's body, but I know you will do it."

It was a challenge, and one that had been building up slowly over the years, although never expressed with the same force as it was then. Struggling with his asthma, his diarrhea, and his constant headaches and fevers, young Theodore was acutely aware of how his father felt about his physical shortcomings. He knew that his father loved him—that he would do anything to ease his discomfort—but he also keenly felt his disappointment. As the years went by, Theodore's health was not improving, and the unspoken tension between father and son exacerbated the problem, culminating in this stern warning.

Theodore was determined to build up his physical strength. There would be no more excuses and no more accepting the fate of an invalid—he could transform his body, and he was determined that he would. But his father's words profoundly affected him in another way as well. His whole outlook changed: no longer would Theodore tolerate weakness in anyone.

Determined to make his father proud and prove to himself that he could be physically fit if he willed it hard enough, Theodore enrolled in Wood's Gymnasium on Manhattan's Upper East Side. The gym was known for turning out heavyweight fighters, but little Theodore was escorted to his first session by his mother. Seated on a big settee at one end of the gym, Mrs. Roosevelt watched as her son wended his way through a roomful of sweaty men. He headed straight for the chest weight machines, and, standing with his left foot planted well forward, he pumped a featherweight's load of iron. Slowly at first, and with a slight tremor in his arms, he raised and lowered the weights until he was able to lift them with a machinelike rhythm.

The workouts were pure toil, but by the end of his first session Theodore's determination was enough to convince his father to install a complete set of exercise equipment on the open-air porch of their home's second floor. Now Theodore could work out whenever he pleased—which, evidently, was often. He wanted desperately to become strong and prove himself to his father. Favoring the parallel bars, he continued his exercise regime all winter and into spring, and as the girth of his chest increased, the severity of his asthma attacks appeared to Roosevelt Sr. to have diminished. (In truth, though, Theodore still suffered periodic asthma attacks—he simply got better at hiding them.)

Whatever their effects on his illnesses, Theodore's workouts did have the undeniable effect of transforming him from a frail and timid boy to one full of courage and vitality. No longer content merely reading Livingstone's and Reid's adventure stories, he now looked forward to actually having a few adventures of his own. His chance came soon enough, as the family was already making plans to visit the Adirondack Mountains.

THE ADIRONDACKS COVER much of the northern part of New York State, forming a mosaic of rocky hills and boggy valleys so impenetrable that they remained virtually unexplored wilderness until well into the nineteenth century. Mountainous only in the high-peaks area of the Northeast, most of the region consists of gently rolling hills forested with patchworks of red spruce, yellow birch, black cherry, and maple that shimmer with color in the fall—not a true mountain range so much as a vast, eroded dome of uplifted rock. What make the Adirondacks so impassable are the valleys, with their berry-choked bogs and dense mats of elfin moss beneath spindly tamaracks and cedars. This is where the black bears come down to feed after emerging from their dens in springtime. Beaver dams intersect cool, hemlock-lined brooks, creating a vast network of shallow ponds where an occasional moose can be seen knee-deep in the water.

The Roosevelts left New York City on August 1, 1871. Their party included Theodore, his parents, his two sisters and brother, two sets of aunts and uncles, and his cousin West, who was just about the same age as Theodore. They began with a leisurely stay on Lake George in New York, and the three young boys quickly demonstrated their unbridled enthusiasm for the outdoors by exploring the rural paradise. They searched the ruins of Fort George, took turns shooting an air gun, visited a Native American encampment, rowed to an island in the lake, swam offshore, ascended a small mountain, and climbed some trees atop that mountain—all in one day. If Roosevelt Sr. had any reservations about his son's readiness for a camping trip, he almost certainly didn't after that first day.

Continuing north up Lake Champlain to Plattsburgh, the visitors hired two stagecoaches and turned west, away from the settled lowlands of the Champlain Valley and deeper into the true wilderness of the Adirondacks. Theodore and cousin West rode with the driver up top, who regaled them with stories of wolves and bears before they strategically changed their seats to the rear storage rack. Dangling their feet off the back of the stagecoach, they could easily jump off to investigate anything interesting they saw along the way—animal tracks, birds, and even unusual mosses and ferns. Ultimately the boys exhausted themselves, and after they were summoned inside the stagecoach, they promptly fell asleep, not waking until they had arrived at the family's destination, Paul Smith's lodge.

Paul Smith's was the leading Adirondack resort hotel, still run by its namesake—a large jovial man with a hearty laugh. Smith spoiled his guests with home-cooked meals of fresh game he had hunted himself. Surrounded by dense conifer forest, the lodge offered spectacular views of St. Regis Lake. Giant pileated woodpeckers hammered in the treetops, and curious gray jays chuckled in the understory; these were nothing like the birds Theodore was used to seeing, and he must have been raring to get out into the woods.

But the Roosevelts began their first day in the mountains in another sort of spiritual communion—attending a wilderness church service, as it was a Sunday when they arrived. Teddy sat through the sermon, likely fidgeting as he thought about all that awaited him outdoors. It had been a full week since their departure from New York City, and Theodore was eager for his first adventure. After the services let out, the family "went to a sort of half swamp," where Theodore caught and killed a common snake and several species of frogs for his collection, classifying all of them in his diary using their appropriate Latin names. His real adventure would begin the next day.

Adirondack mornings are serene, and at an hour when the streets of New York City were already baking in the hot summer sun, Theodore found the shores of St. Regis Lake surprisingly chilly. The last of the morning mist was dissipating over the water's surface as the Roosevelt boys, together with Mr. Roosevelt and their guides, slid their three birchbark canoes into the water. Loons cried out eerily in the distance. As he gently paddled south, Theodore could look over his shoulder and watch the rustic outline of their lodge diminishing against a backdrop of seemingly limitless white pines.

After hours of water travel came an overland carry, and the party dragged their canoes through the woods behind horse-drawn sledges. They traveled miles through the forest and ate lunch under their upturned canoes when a thunderstorm hit.

Theodore was in heaven. Later, he would refer to his Adirondack days as his introduction to and first inspiration for preserving wilderness. The fact that such wilderness existed so close to his home was especially moving. The remote wilds of Africa that he often read about in books seemed impossibly far off, but in the Adirondacks he found a wilderness that felt very much his own.

Canoeing farther down the forest stream, they passed through two small rapids, bringing them to the junction of a much larger stream, where they pitched their tents. The campers had to live off the land, and the Roosevelts did a great deal of fishing. (Although the guides hooked trout, Theodore caught nothing, thus beginning his lifelong aversion to the sport.)

The Roosevelts depended wholly on their guides. Part practical helpmate and part wilderness sage, the best Adirondack guides en-

thralled their clients with the majesty of nature, leading them effort-
lessly through the wilderness by day and keeping them amused with
tales of the animals that roamed the forests by night. One of the Roosevelt guides, a man named Mose, told a particularly chilling story
of a winter hunt that had ended with an encounter with a mountain
lion. For young Theodore, campsite tales like this—ones of sudden
danger—only increased the wilderness's allure. Later in life, Roosevelt's own experience would prove that the North American mountain lion is not nearly so threatening, but that day in the Adirondacks,
he was sure Mose was just like David Livingstone, narrowly escaping
the jaws of a big cat.

As the Roosevelts traveled through the wilderness, Theodore,
his brother Elliott, and his cousin West tipped their canoe, drench-
ing themselves and all their gear. Their spirits, however, were hardly
dampened, and they spent most of the rest of the day reenacting
Mose's encounter with the mountain lion. Playing the part of the lion,
the guide climbed a tree, but the boys chopped it down. When he
dashed to a second tree, the boys pulled him down by his feet, and
from a third tree they jabbed at their prey with sharpened sticks until
Mose could take no more. When finally it was too dark for playing
games, Theodore wrapped himself in a thick wool blanket in front of
the campfire and struggled to stay awake as his father read aloud from
his copy of *The Last of the Mohicans*.

The days came and went, each full of adventure and opportunity.
Theodore Jr. kept a meticulous diary of his time "in the bush," as
he called it, and what is most impressive about the account, besides
the group's ambitious itinerary, was the boy's precocious knowledge
of the fauna and his expert command of scientific names. Covering
the entire month of August, Roosevelt's accounts of his trip included
references to no fewer than thirty species, ranging from the ham-
ster mouse to wolves, from bald eagles to salamanders, all with Latin
identifiers meticulously transcribed in boyish scrawl; Roosevelt had
made such a study of his father's library that most sightings were aug-
mented by supporting descriptions of the creatures' natural history.

The trip was Theodore's first taste of the real wilderness, and although he didn't wrestle any bears the way the boys in his books did,

he saw the tracks the bears made. He didn't have any near-escapes from mountain lions, but he skulked around the mountains they wandered. He was finally having his own wilderness adventure. Young Roosevelt had not only survived the endurance tests of the Adirondacks, but he had proven himself more than capable of handling the outdoors' physical challenges—all while compiling a notebook full of data. The whole experience instilled him with a new confidence. He now felt he could embody the adventurous naturalist who lived between the covers of his favorite books—books that captured the spirit of what his father considered an ideal son.

Chapter 4

---◄ ►---

FULL-BORE BIRDER

$\mathcal{B}$y the time Theodore Roosevelt was a teenager, his passion for natural history had turned into an all-out obsession for birds. Other animals still interested him, but the feathery ones captivated his imagination the most. Brightly colored and twittering by day, birds were both conspicuous and abundant. Whereas herpetologists needed to turn over logs in search of snakes and salamanders, and ichthyologists needed to fuss with nets in the water, all that was required of Roosevelt as an ornithologist was a stroll outdoors. The birds came to him, even in the middle of a bustling city.

Roosevelt was also distinctly advantaged in having an ornithologist in the family. In the brownstone next door lived his uncle Robert Barnwell Roosevelt, author of the classic ornithological text *The Game Birds of the Coasts and Lakes of the Northern States of America* and one of America's pioneering conservationists. As was true of so many naturalists of his time, Robert Barnwell Roosevelt's interest was rooted in his passion for hunting and fishing, and he traveled the northeastern United States in pursuit of sport.

In his uncle, Theodore had an early mentor and role model who in later years influenced his own conservation ethic. Robert Barnwell was among the first American naturalists to really appreciate that the nation's fish and fisheries were being destroyed. Sawmill dams and gristmills were blocking spawning migrations; factories and municipalities were already dumping unhealthy loads of waste into once-productive fisheries. Setting what would be an example for his young nephew, Robert Barnwell worked tirelessly for conservation, lobbying the New York State legislature to create the New York Fisheries Commission in 1867, of which he was later appointed chair. He established fish hatcheries to replenish lakes and streams depleted due to fishing during spawning seasons and the use of seines and gill nets of fine mesh. These practices decimated entire breeding populations—adults, fingerlings, fry, and all. In Robert Barnwell's experience, entire waterways could become devoid of fish if these went unchecked.

But while he fought to protect fish, birds were his other great passion, and he was devoted to their fair chase. He advocated tirelessly against the shooting of birds without first giving them a chance to take flight, and he was a staunch supporter of restricting hunting to non-breeding seasons and implementing sensible bag limits. Although he deplored the meat hunters who hunted and fished in excess, he recognized that, with proper management, certain lesser-quality fish and game could be managed as a sustainable source of food for those too poor to buy their own. Robert Barnwell's work in this area set a profound example for his nephew, and it encouraged the younger Roosevelt to pursue naturalism with great zeal.

Like any teenager with an obsession, Roosevelt had a certain arrogance and was eager to show off his exhaustive knowledge. In diary passages where *snow bunting* would have sufficed, he took care to also note its scientific name, *Plectrophanax nivalis.* Gulls were *Larus,* and terns were *Sterna.* He memorized the names of all the local birds and, after a relatively brief period of study, could confidently identify any species by both sight and sound. He knew where to find their nests and could mimic a great variety of birdcalls. Touting his bona fides as a naturalist, Roosevelt wanted everyone to know that *he* was a bird expert.

Although Roosevelt was at a self-conscious age, he would have found nothing to be embarrassed about in his fascination, given Victorian attitudes. Ornithology was considered a more masculine pursuit then, and there can be no real comparison with bird enthusiasts of today. Equipment was different, and good binoculars were decades away from being widely available, the best substitute being a pair of opera glasses, hardly adequate for the task. Field guides were also still in their infancy and most often illustrated with simple woodcut prints. But the differences were ideological, too. There was an unquestioned belief that being in nature was about direct experience, not about being a spectator. The spirit of the frontier was still alive and well in America, and that legacy deeply influenced how people interacted with nature. Nineteenth-century Americans romanticized the wilderness, inspired to emulate the hardy perseverance of their pioneering forebears.

Ornithology as a practice was rapidly evolving when Roosevelt was growing up. While John James Audubon set an early tone for collecting that carried into Theodore Roosevelt's day, it was Spencer Fullerton Baird who really transformed ornithologists into hard-core field collectors. Just as soon as Baird had convinced Joseph Henry to let him build a natural-history museum as part of the Smithsonian, he launched a full-bore effort to fill it. So obsessed was Baird with adding specimens that he could no longer be satisfied with his own efforts. Borrowing an idea from Audubon, Baird became what one of his biographers described as a "collector of collectors," enlisting an army of adjunct naturalists to build his museum.

Baird found his zoological foot soldiers in an actual military organization—the United States Army. The Army was an ideal choice for Baird, as it had in its ranks thousands of men already stationed to some of the least-explored territory in North America. Conducting boundary surveys in the newly annexed Southwest or scouting out railroad routes to the Pacific, these soldiers had unprecedented access to the American frontier. Many soldiers signed on, realizing the work could be as enjoyable as sport hunting, and some even reenlisted just so that they could continue collecting for the Smithsonian. Baird's plan was genius: these soldiers were already familiar with guns, and many of them were even amateur naturalists, so popular was the field with men of the outdoors. Moreover, Baird made a special effort to recruit Army medics, whose familiarity with dissecting flesh and stitching wounds made them especially adept at preparing specimens.

The Smithsonian's collections swelled to more than 150,000 specimens in its first decade alone. Baird even evoked the power of Thomas

Mayne Reid and was so impressed with *The Boy Hunters* that he sent a copy off to one of his collectors in the field, adding that "It will always give me much pleasure to stimulate your tastes for natural history by means of such works as these." Thanks to Baird's soldier-naturalists, the public perception of ornithology became even more masculine, just as young Theodore set his sights on joining their ranks.

From his urban post in New York City, Roosevelt idealized these adventurous birdmen who helped establish the fledgling American field of ornithology, and he longed to be a scientific man of the Audubon or Baird type. Still haunted by his sickly past but already seduced by outdoor adventure, Theodore saw ornithologists as the embodiment of everything he hoped to become—hardy, erudite, and courageous. To become a bird naturalist, though, he would need more than Latin names and field notebooks. He would need to learn all the necessary hands-on skills of a museum field naturalist, beginning with taxidermy.

Taxidermy shops were once important meeting places for scientists. For more than fifty years one of the most important of these was run by John Bell. A tall, white-haired gentleman with piercing blue eyes, John Bell had been Audubon's field assistant out west. Bell's shop on the corner of Worth Street and Broadway—not far from the Roosevelts' New York City home—was a regular ornithologists' haunt, with Audubon and Baird among the most famous patrons. Through his shop, Bell had come to know all the great naturalists of his time, becoming the most "connected" person in that rarefied community. If an expedition was about to set off for some remote corner of the American West, or if someone had just collected a new species of bird, Bell's shop was the place one would go to hear about it first.

Like most Victorian taxidermy shops, Bell's was festooned with all kinds of trophy heads, stuffed birds, and drying bones. The air was laced with the odors of acrid chemicals and desiccated flesh. An early firsthand account of Bell's shop gives us some sense of the mischievousness with which Bell practiced his art. "As I entered the room, I observed an old red fox chained to a bolt in the wall, but lying down with his head between his forepaws and eyes upturned in my direction. On the floor in his immediate neighborhood were a number of beautifully mounted birds on stands, and fearing lest the animal should suddenly arise if I came farther into the apartment, and do some damage, I started to pass 'round and give him as wide a berth as possible. The room was small, and Mr. Bell was engaged with a couple of students at a window opposite where I entered, but he turned in time to see my detour around the fox and did not spare me in his merriment at my thinking the animal was alive."

Bell was notorious for wooing prospective students with the mysteries of taxidermy, setting before them exquisite, lifelike examples of his work before offering his services for an exorbitant fee. To Theodore's father, though, this evidently seemed money well spent, as it was in Bell's shop that Theodore received his first formal training in the art of taxidermy.

The practice is surprisingly simple, and animals today are skinned essentially the same way that they were in Roosevelt's day. As Roosevelt learned from Bell, all taxidermy jobs begin with getting the skin off the body of the animal. With a small mammal, for example, this is done by making an opening incision down the midline of the abdomen, allowing for the separation of the skin from the body. Skin pulls off an animal in much the same way that one might peel off a tight-fitting shirt; the trick to this is learning just how hard to pull on the skin without stretching or tearing it. For most of the operation, pulling on the skin suffices, but often a taxidermist will encounter tough spots where the connection of skin to muscle must be loosened with a knife (most common around the ears, eyes, and nose and down around the wrists and ankles). But the skillful skinning of an animal should always involve more pulling and tugging than cutting. It is also a surprisingly bloodless process; if it is done correctly, the body cavity is never cut. An animal can be completely skinned without ever exposing its internal organs.

As the taxidermist loosens the skin in this way, it is usually the very tip of the nose that is the last point attached, and once that is severed, the artisan's focus shifts to preserving the skin and sewing it up in a lifelike fashion. In the early days of taxidermy, the skin of an animal was, literally, stuffed. While this is still true for scientific specimens, exhibit-quality taxidermy more properly involves the fitting of the skin over an artificial mannequin. These artificial bodies better replicate the details of an animal's form and muscles than stuffing ever could.

Besides learning how to mount animals in lifelike poses for display, Roosevelt learned the finer points of making proper scientific specimens. Unlike those in traditional taxidermy, scientific specimens are prepared to be uniform and compact. Preserved by the thousands and stored in tidy museum drawers, study skins provide scientists with a wealth of information about the external characteristics of an animal. Collect enough, and the range invaluably shows how species can vary with geography, age, the changing seasons, and time. Until his lessons with Bell, Roosevelt had added specimens to his collection haphazardly—a seal skull here, a turtle shell there, some mice caught in the pantry. But after his training, he aimed to build a serious bird collection, one that would include many examples of each species collected and all the subtle changes in their plumage over the seasons. Roosevelt had great ambitions for his collection; he simply needed to get out and shoot some birds so that he would have animals to stuff.

Roosevelt also learned more at this time about how to acquire those species. Guns were the most essential tool, and every ornithologist must be an expert with shotguns. Theodore was just fourteen years old when he got his first gun in the summer of 1872. It was a simple, double-barreled, 12-gauge shotgun that had been recommended by his naturalist uncle, Robert Barnwell Roosevelt, who had dedicated a whole chapter to shotguns for bird hunting in his book on northern game birds. Robert Barnwell had suggested one model in particular for Theodore because of its relative simplicity and durability. With its solid breach-loading construction and exposed hammers, it was the perfect gun for a "clumsy and often absent-minded boy," and, as Theodore later explained, if the mechanism ever became rusty, he could "open it with a brick" without serious damage to the instrument.

Unlike rifles, which fire a single bullet across potentially long distances with great accuracy, a shotgun typically fires a cloud of pellets, or shot, a relatively short distance. Bird collectors typically use break-action shotguns, single- or double-barreled implements that break open at a hinge in the middle of the gun where it is loaded and unloaded. Shotgun shells are filled with different-size pellets, and the collector chooses a shell with bigger pellets for bigger birds or when making a longer-distance shot; shells with smaller pellets are used for smaller birds at close range. Since the bird collector is never entirely certain what he might encounter, it's imperative to be able to quickly swap out the shells in a shotgun depending on the circumstances.

Newly armed, Roosevelt hunted in the countryside outside the family's new Dobbs Ferry summer home but never very successfully, despite blazing away at anything that moved. It was while hunting with a few friends that it finally occurred to him that there was something wrong with his vision—the others were hitting targets that he never even saw. Roosevelt learned that he was profoundly nearsighted, and it seemed the only things he could hit were those he "ran against or stumbled over." It was a crushing realization. Without the benefit of clear vision, it was practically impossible to be a good field naturalist, as the profession depends on careful observation.

But the setback didn't deter the intrepid Roosevelt. Determined to make a go at ornithology, he raised the issue with his father, who took him to the optometrist for a set of glasses. Although he was enamored with nature before, Roosevelt had no idea how beautiful it was until he tried on his first pair of spectacles. Trees were now intricate assemblages of branches and leaves. For the first time he could see the tiniest warblers twittering in the treetops. The improvement in his vision only further solidified his conviction that he needed to be a naturalist.

Gun-toting, bespectacled, and confident in his taxidermy skills, Roosevelt was ready to take his naturalist career to its next step. He wanted to be like his father's friend Albert Bickmore and found his own museum; he wanted to be like Spencer Baird, who'd filled a freight car full of specimens. Now with clear vision, he dreamed of spending his summer shooting birds in the New York countryside. Just as he was soaring highest and best prepared to make a serious study of the natural world, though, his dreams of long, rural summers were dashed when it was suddenly announced that the family was planning a year-long tour of Europe. Theodore was crushed. He remembered the Continent from a vacation the family had taken two years prior, and he hated the idea of returning, believing it would be "another terrible trip." And now that he had settled into the serious business of his museum, the thought of a prolonged delay of his naturalist work was doubly devastating.

But there was one redeeming aspect: it was decided that Europe would only be a stopping-off point as the family made their way to Egypt and the Middle East. Even better than the promise of more exotic locales was his father's permission to take along his shotgun. The trip was suddenly an opportunity to collect birds he had only ever seen in books. Encouraged, Roosevelt prepared as if he were embarking on a museum expedition. Drawing on his observations of the professional naturalists he encountered in John Bell's taxidermy shop and from working at the American Museum with Bickmore, he had several hundred specimen labels printed in anticipation of all he would capture. These, in keeping with standard museum practice, were for affixing a catalogue number to each specimen so that he could cross-reference them with the detailed notes in his field journal. The tags were about one inch high and three inches wide with ROOSE-VELT MUSEUM printed in all caps across the top:

Theodore stuffed into his suitcase the accoutrements of his craft: taxidermy kit, pocket lens, writing paper, and enough ammunition to get him started.

Chapter 5

EGYPT, LAND OF MY DREAMS

$\mathcal{T}$he air must have been heavy with anticipation as Theodore crossed the gangplank onto the SS *Russia*. On deck, gruff seamen exchanged yarns of thick fogs and wave-swept decks within deliberate earshot of the apprehensive landlubbers plodding aboard. Soot was already billowing from the enormous center stack, sending burning coal cinders up through the rigging while well-dressed women leaned over the railings waving white handkerchiefs to the crowds gathered on land. At last came the final *"All ashore!"* and with the touch of a bell the commanding officer signaled full steam to the engineer belowdecks. In a wake of roiling seawater, the Roosevelts embarked upon their journey.

At 358 feet long, the *Russia* was large enough to offer private cabins but still small enough for the passengers to feel the ups and downs of every crest and trough across the Atlantic. After watching the low hills of Staten Island and Sandy Hook disappear over the horizon, Theodore felt the first symptoms of seasickness. Confined to his cramped cabin and unable to write more than a line in his diary, he lay in his berth longing for the end of the eleven-day crossing to Liverpool.

It was only toward the end of their journey, a few days shy of port, that Theodore felt well enough to emerge, and immediately he was on the lookout for seabirds. The ship had never really been all that far from land, having traveled up the Eastern Seaboard of North America to Newfoundland before jogging out across a short stretch of open ocean, which meant that good numbers of birds still hovered around the ship. Gulls followed closely in the ship's wake, swooping down for scraps thrown overboard, while terns plunged into the schools of tiny fish attracted to the cover of the ship's hull. He observed kittiwakes, truly pelagic birds and lovers of storm-tossed seas. They are rarely seen near shore but occur in incredible numbers farther out, following ships when no land is in sight. Despite his serious nausea, an eager Theodore identified every bird by scientific name: *Larus, Sterna,* and *Rissa*. When a snow bunting alighted on deck, he made a special note of the fact that it "was captured," perhaps added to his growing collection.

Landing in Liverpool, the family had hardly settled into their hotel when Theodore was out on a frantic ornithological errand. He had forgotten to pack the arsenic he needed to preserve the birds he would shoot. Roaming the streets of the English city, looking very much a Yankee, the young, undersize teenager quickly attracted a swarm of hecklers. When he finally found a drugstore, he was so agitated by the abuse hurled at him that he demanded a full pound of the deadly poison with such force that the druggist at first refused to sell it to him. After producing what was essentially a character witness (whose name is lost to history), Theodore got his poison.

The real thrills of the European leg of the journey, though, were trips to the meat markets, which were full of dead game animals that Theodore could purchase and skin. Traveling south through Europe, he stocked up on local delicacies in each place. He bought game birds in England, rabbits in Germany, and songbirds in France, all of which he dutifully stuffed and added to his collection. Paris was an especially good place to source wild birds, and he did so almost every day of his visit there, as he recorded in his diary:

Paris. November 14th 1872. Thursday

In the morning I went out and bought some larks and buntings, which I returned home and skinned.

Paris November 15th 1872 Friday

I bought and skinned a bunting in the morning. In the afternoon I bought all my christmass presents. We dined out at a Café. Rainy.

Paris. November 16th 1872 Saturday

Rainy. I skinned some birds in the morning. We dined at Theodore Bronsons', where we had a good deal of fun.

Paris November 18th 1872 Monday

I skinned some birds in the morning. Rainy in the afternoon.

Paris. November 20th 1872. Wednesday

Out to the market as usual and skinned some birds. Read in the afternoon.

As a fourteen-year-old boy with a habit of skinning bird carcasses before breakfast, Theodore likely sported fingernails caked with dried bird blood, and stray downy feathers probably clung to his woolen trousers through the afternoon. "I suppose that all growing boys tend to be grubby; but the ornithological small boy, or indeed the boy with the taste for natural history of any kind, is generally the very grubbiest of all," he wrote of himself.

When the Roosevelts reached the heel of southern Italy, they changed ships, boarding the *Poonah* for Alexandria. A relatively swift two-day journey across the Mediterranean was now all that separated Theodore from his long-awaited Egyptian adventure—one that would lead him back in time all the way to the archaeological ruins of the dawn of civilization, the hinterlands of primordial Africa. Little did Theodore know that much later in his life he would complete this journey in reverse, drifting down the Nile after a lifetime of adventure that would culminate in his African safari. But as a teenager, he could only wonder at the excitement that awaited him in the wilds of a continent he didn't yet know well.

Rising long before breakfast, Theodore joined his family on deck to witness the first glimmers of dawn over Alexandria. Ships were not allowed to enter the port until daylight because smugglers and pirates infested the waters, so the Roosevelts had the pleasure of watching the sun rise over the harbor. As the morning fog burned away, Pompey's Pillar slowly came into view amid a jumble of whitewashed buildings on the distant shore. For once Theodore put aside all thought of birds to wax poetically on the view. "How I gazed on it! It was Egypt, the land of my dreams; Egypt, the most ancient of all countries! A land that was old when Rome was bright, was old when Babylon was in its glory, was old when Troy was taken! It was a sight to awaken a thousand thoughts, and it did."

The family's tranquil morning proved short-lived, as Mrs. Roosevelt, unaccustomed to foreign ports, recorded in her diary: "The green water was alive with water craft—boat upon boat filled with savages tattooed—and, oh, the dresses! And the wild jabbering, screaming at everyone—and when they gained admittance to the ship, the scene was absorbingly awful." To Theodore's eyes, the strangers boarding the *Poonah* must have seemed something akin to a pirate attack, as the local men vied frantically for the chance to pilot them into harbor. It was a wild scene, and Mrs. Roosevelt began to prickle all over with what she imagined to be fleas or maybe lice. "When I undress tonight, I shall find out," she noted dryly.

The region where the Roosevelts landed was brooding with rebellion and violence, and they were planning to trek right through the middle of the conflict, with two weeks in Cairo before a two-month river trip up and down the Nile. Moving quickly on to Cairo after a brush with Alexandria's usual chaos, Theodore spent most of the six-hour train ride with his nose pressed against the window, fully absorbed in his first opportunity to observe the wild fauna of the Nile Valley. "Numerous birds of various species arose, while herds of buffalos and zebu cows grazed quietly in the marshy fields. Among the birds were snipe, plover, quail, hawks, and great black vultures."

Since leaving New York, Theodore had been trying to find a book about Egyptian birds. After having no success in Europe, in Cairo he finally got hold of Reverend Alfred Charles Smith's *Attractions of the Nile and Its Banks, a Journal of Travel in Egypt and Nubia*. While not exactly a field guide, it included an appendix of sixty-eight pages listing the names and descriptions of 108 species and was invaluable to Theodore's ornithological work in Egypt.

The family had only just arrived in Cairo when Theodore was once again on a mission. Along the narrow, dusty streets of the city he threaded his way through a maze of donkey carts, hopped over piles of drying lentils, and brushed up against carriers hauling overflowing goatskins of water. Virtually everything was for sale in Cairo—if only it could be found—and walking down Mooskee Street, the market, Theodore was struck by the hundreds of narrow side alleys, each leading to its own specific bazaar. There were silk bazaars, gold bazaars, and spice bazaars; Persian bazaars, Turkish bazaars, Algerian bazaars. Bazaars selling nothing but fruit or teapots or incense. Entire alleys were devoted to the purveying of red slippers, tin boxes, or a particular kind of fruit or flower. But Theodore was seeking something very specific. Wandering the narrow streets, he ignored the wary glances of the shopkeepers squatting and smoking in front of their stalls until he found what he was looking for—the bird market.

Almost immediately he spotted a quail laid on a makeshift table. Theodore seized the bird and asked for a price. When the shopkeeper held up eight fingers, Theodore responded with two, but the shopkeeper shook his head and put up seven fingers. Theodore raised three, followed by the shopkeeper's six, at which Theodore thrust forward four fingers, his final offer, which was accepted—half the original asking price.

Dead quail in hand, it was business as usual for Theodore back at the hotel. He had become so fixated on collecting birds that his sister Corinne complained that whenever he entered the room, she unfailingly heard the words *bird* and *skin*. Even his younger brother, Elliott, who was normally mild mannered and accommodating, revolted at sharing a room with someone who frequently filled the washbasin with the guts of the animals he was dissecting.

Theodore took at least some time away from his birds to be a tourist in Cairo, climbing one of the pyramids at Cheops stone by stone. Surveying the vast Sahara desert from above, he may have gazed at the valley of the Nile a little longer, knowing that his family was soon to ascend its waters nearly six hundred miles to the ruins of Karnak,

Thebes, and Luxor. There was no way to reach the ruins except by boat, but his father had already secured a fine *dahabeah*—a shallow, bargelike watercraft with lazy lateen sails that would be their home for the next two months. It was named the *Aboo Erdan* (Egyptian for *ibis*), and Theodore found it "the nicest, cosiest pleasantest little place you ever saw."

Sailing up the Nile, Theodore was at first disappointed. Its west banks were so high above the river that it was impossible to see very much of the land except for the tops of the date-palm trees growing in groves along the shore. But in places where the banks were unusually eroded, he managed to make out fields of wheat and barley extending off into the distance all the way to the Mokattam Hills, ranging south of Cairo for nearly fifty miles. Here and there were little collections of mud hovels, each roofed over with cornstalks, and, in scenes unchanged for millennia, he spotted men plowing behind oxen and groups of women gathering water in enormous jugs. Everyone wore dark trousers, their garments flowing in loose sheets around them as they sang, chattered, or scolded each other. Their voices carried well over the waters of the Nile, and Theodore watched as the women filled their big jars with water, put them atop their heads, and carried them back up the steep bank to their village. To the east the land was low and silted, with scattered trees and only a few inhabitants at long intervals. The fertile topsoil of these eastern flats had already been washed away by the river, as the Nile gradually eroded its way westward through the land.

On the boat, Theodore was allowed to open his Christmas present a few weeks early. He was delighted to find a new shotgun inside the wrapping. Craving more birds to skin, he set out the next morning to do some shooting in the fields and groves adjacent to the river. On a short walk of just a few hundred yards, he shot two small warblers and "blew a chat to pieces." These were the first birds Theodore killed in Egypt, and he was "proportionately delighted."

Theodore hunted whenever he got the chance, venturing out again later that first evening to bag a yellow wagtail, followed by still more bird hunting the next day. He was amazed at the sheer number of birds, spotting no fewer than fifteen species in an hour's walk. They were all unafraid of humans, and he had an excellent opportunity to observe their behavior up close before collecting them. At one point he spotted a white-tailed plover, which he described as one of the rarest and best-marked birds in all of Egypt. He noted its calls and was satisfied with just a glimpse of the rare bird, refraining from even taking a shot.

The Roosevelts sailed up the Nile at a time when the prevailing northerly winds were unreliable, and the *dahabeah* made frequent stops, enabling the crew to pull it along with ropes from the shore. Every time they stopped, Roosevelt jumped out of the boat to explore the Nile's crocodile-infested shores. Sometimes he would sling his gun over his shoulder, mount a barely controllable donkey, and "ruthlessly lope after whatever object he had in view, the donkey almost invariably crowding between any other two who might be riding together." Few dared ride with young Roosevelt, for he had a habit of allowing his loaded gun to bump and bounce about freely on his cantering donkey.

Theodore never shot more than one or two birds a day. Sitting under the cloth canopy on the deck of the *Aboo Erdan*, he skinned and stuffed while the curious boatmen stared over his shoulder. It's time-consuming to make a bird study skin, and Roosevelt made sure he never collected more birds than he could prepare in a single day. As soon as he shot a specimen, he had to carefully clean any blood off the feathers and quickly stuff a wad of cotton down the bird's throat to prevent any more body fluids from leaking out and spoiling the plumage. Theodore had only a few minutes to record the color of the eyes before they faded forever. Next he took a series of standard measurements, described the habitat where he shot each bird, and then tagged each with his ROOSEVELT MUSEUM labels so he could cross-reference it to his field notes. As he knew from his readings and his own practical experience, decomposition sets in quickly in tropical climates, and he worked especially fast to preserve all his birds before they spoiled.

The procedure used to prepare a bird study skin varies from collector to collector, but it always begins with skinning. One of the most challenging steps in the whole process is skinning the back of the head. The skin is most delicate there, and any slips of the knife or tears to the skin are noticeable and difficult to mend. During the preparation procedure, a bird's skin (unlike the skin of a mammal) is never completely removed from the head. Instead, the back of the skull is exposed, so a series of cuts can be made to scoop out the brains and eyes. A stick is then thrust through the empty cranium and rooted in the spongy bone inside the bill to support the skull; the wings and legs are stripped of flesh and the bare bones left in place to provide structural support. Before being sewn up, the skin is usually treated with that all-important naturalist tool, a concoction of arsenic suspended in soap.

Free of brains, eyes, muscles, and guts, the skull, eye sockets, limb bones, and body cavity are then wrapped or filled with stuffing to give the bird's skin a natural-looking form. This is a difficult step to get just right. Too much stuffing, and it's difficult to sew up the skin; too little stuffing, and the skin will slacken, failing to sufficiently show the plumage. Finally, assuming the preparatory work has not taken so long that the skin dries out, the initial incision is sewn up, and the specimen is neatly pinned to a board for drying.

The very best ornithologists, working as efficiently as a machine, might be able to finish a bird skin in as little as ten minutes. But little Theodore likely needed at least an hour to painstakingly prepare each of his specimens. An especially large bird, such as the crane he shot as it rose from a lagoon near Thebes, probably took him all day. Slowly his Egyptian collection grew, until his haul included "between one and two hundred specimens" as a tally of birds recorded in his "Zoological Record" confirms: two partridges, three quail, thirty-seven doves, eighty-one pigeons, eighteen large plovers, thirty-six little shore birds, eight hoopoes, eight cow herons, one gray heron, and two squirrels.

Theodore filled five notebooks on the trip, giving each of them a unique title: *Remarks on Birds, Ornithological Observations, Ornithological Record, Catalogue of Birds,* and *Zoological Record.* Totaling nearly a hundred pages of detailed natural-history data, they show that he was faithful to the ornithologist's credo of studying the behavior of living birds in the field and killing them only when it was necessary for his collection. Though Theodore may have been holding a dead bird in hand as he described the physical attributes of a green bee-eater (*Merops orientalis*), he recorded his reverence for the living creature in a prose account of its behavior:

Bill long, without bristles, except around the rictus, where there are a few short ones, decurved, making the culmen convex, the gonys concave. Nostrils small and round. Tarsus extremely short. Toes slender, outer one longer than inner, reaching beyond the centre of middle claw. Wing long, 2d primary longest, tertiaries slightly longer than secondaries. Tail long, nearly even, the two central tail feathers with attenuated and much elongated tips, reaching three inches beyond the rest of tail.

Colour green. Legs brown. Bill, stripe through eye, band on throat, and tips of central tail feathers black. Primaries and secondaries rich golden brown, the latter with deep, the former with faint brownish tinge. The green colour is deepest on the back and wing coverts. Just below the eye there is a bright blueish green spot.

This beautiful little bird is very common on the Nile, and adds greatly to the beauty of the Egyptian scene, its vivid coloring and quick movements rendering it very conspicuous. It haunts especially the palm and sont [Acacia arabica] groves, but I have often seen it on the open ground. Its manners resemble to a great extent those of the flycatchers. Sitting on some lofty palm, it surveys the surrounding neighborhood with a quick, vivacious eye. Suddenly it swoops off through a glade of trees with such quickness as to remind one of a hummingbird and returns with an insect in its bill. This, if small, is swallowed immediately, but a large beetle usually needs a good deal of battering against the branch before it can be safely swallowed.

From his notebooks, it is clear that Theodore Roosevelt spent as much time observing birds alive as he did preparing specimens after they were dead. It was in Egypt that he became a focused and determined naturalist, furthering his knowledge as a bird specialist, acquiring a fine collection of specimens, and (armed with John Bell's training) mastering the precise art of formal taxidermy.

. . .

BY THE END of his Egyptian trip, Theodore had been physically transformed. Deeply tanned and threadbare, he likened himself to Robinson Crusoe—bony wrists and ankles sprouting from frayed cuffs and
sleeves, sun-bleached hair so long and ragged that everyone laughed
and called his new style "à la mop." His shoes were caked thickly
with Nile muck, his pants smeared with grease and blood. He emit-
ted such a rancid fetor, it was best to stand upwind of him. His voice
was changing, too, and he had developed such a hideous adolescent
laugh that his own mother described it as a sort of "sharp, ungreased
squeak" that hurt her ears.

It had been a long year in Africa, and after a brief jaunt through
the Middle East, the family prepared to split up. His sister Bamie accompanied their mother to the spas of Carlsbad, while Roosevelt Sr.
returned to New York. The three younger children (which included
Theodore) were placed in the care of a family in Dresden, where the
young naturalist's attempts to add to his specimen collection were
thwarted by his hosts.

Back in New York, Roosevelt Sr. spent the five-month separation
from his family anxiously supervising the construction of a dream
house, just south of Central Park at 6 West 57th Street. The family
of six had long since outgrown the cramped quarters of East 20th
Street, and the downtown neighborhood had become very commercial, blighted by sweatshops and immigrant labor. The area around
Central Park had a distinct residential appeal, and, more important
to Theodore, the park meant more convenient and varied bird sightings. Their new home, at Roosevelt Sr.'s insistence, also had a fully
equipped gymnasium on the top floor. And in a generous paternal
gesture, the attic turret was reserved exclusively for Theodore's museum.

When the rest of the Roosevelt clan arrived at 57th Street, the
front entrance was unfinished, but the house still felt impossibly
grand. Theodore unpacked his Egyptian specimens upstairs and
eagerly gave a report of his new acquisitions to his cousins Emlen
and West—the boys with whom he had, six years earlier, formed the

Roosevelt Museum of Natural History. Technically, the three were equally vested in the museum, and while they were still willing to play along with Theodore by attending his "trustees meeting" over Christmas, the teenage Emlen and West likely snickered at the seriousness with which their cousin read the minutes, which were full of grandiose proclamations and resolutions. When the trustees met again in April, it was with much-diminished ceremony. The spring meeting's minutes consisted of a single sentence stating that Theodore would spend eight dollars and fifty cents to buy some more bird specimens. Emlen and West, it seems, had backed their way out of their earlier childhood commitment to the museum, and with their departure the "Record of the Roosevelt Museum" came to an unceremonious end.

Nevertheless, Theodore was undeterred in perfecting the museum itself, and he settled into his new home with a distinct purpose. He wanted to go to Harvard—the alma mater of Albert Bickmore and arguably the best school in America for the study of natural history. The famous naturalist Louis Agassiz had died a few years before Roosevelt applied, but his Museum of Comparative Zoology was still a real draw. Although Theodore's enthusiasm was unbridled and he was very knowledgeable about some topics, there were still significant asymmetries in his education. He was, for example, unusually strong in history, science, and literature, but his knowledge of Greek, Latin, and mathematics—all required on the Harvard entrance exam—was abysmal. Theodore knew that if he was to enter the school's hallowed halls in another two years, he would have to teach himself those challenging subjects. It seemed an almost impossible task, but Roosevelt had a tremendous capacity to remake himself—rushing headlong into challenges simply because they seemed impossible. After triumphing at his physical transformation and improved health, Theodore felt confident that he would have little trouble cramming the requisite knowledge into his mind and thus obtain entry to the school that would carve out his naturalist path.

THE ROOSEVELT TOWN HOUSE on West 57th Street was one of two new homes that Theodore returned to in 1873. The second was in

Oyster Bay, Long Island, where the Roosevelt family had already established an enclave. Less than thirty miles from New York City, Oyster Bay was easily reachable by train or steamboat, yet it remained a quiet and mostly rural community of rolling hills and woods. The Roosevelt family rented a big white house with colonnades and a wide veranda, and they christened their new summer home Tranquility.

For Theodore, summers at Tranquility meant birds—watching birds, listening to birds, shooting birds, and stuffing birds. The home's location on Long Island Sound meant plentiful shore birds in addition to the woodland dwellers he already encountered in the city. The area was still wild enough that Theodore could roam the coastal woods with his shotgun, and he could fire without having to worry about shattering a neighbor's window. It was, in short, the perfect place for a budding ornithologist to practice his craft.

One book that likely had an influence on his studies at Oyster Bay was *The Birds of Long Island* by J. P. Giraud Jr., which was published in 1844. Like all early ornithologists, Giraud was a hunter and believed that the shooting of animals was prerequisite to their study. He encouraged his readers to make collections but not to despair if these never focused on more than just the local fauna. He advocated for collectors to study the birds of their home region first and to branch out after mastering the local species. By "pursuing this plan, they would be enabled to obtain such species of birds as visit their section and also have an opportunity of studying their habits, which affords greater pleasure than labeling a dried skin received from a distance." He believed that from these collections "interesting facts would be acquired relative to the migration and habits of many species of which at present we know but little; and it is highly probable that new species would be discovered even in those sections supposed to be thoroughly explored. . . ."

Through books like Giraud's and his own accumulating experience, Theodore had grown to become a more seasoned naturalist. Unlike in boyhood, when his collecting was obsessive and haphazard, he was now more focused, shooting only the birds he needed for his collection. He observed and meticulously recorded bird courtship, nest building, and migration, precisely documenting the spring arrivals and fall departures of every migrating species. His dedication was reflected in his own migratory patterns: since the family occupied the house only in the spring and summer, he had to make regular day trips from Manhattan to continue recording his migration data into the fall.

The most noteworthy of Theodore's bird observations at Oyster Bay was that of a passenger pigeon, a species already in decline in the 1870s. Theodore collected one specimen, noting that "now and then one is seen." The birds had once filled the skies of North America in vast migrating flocks, their population hovering in the billions, but the species was now on its way to extinction. In what would become part of a lifelong pattern, Theodore collected a few of these as specimens, knowing how valuable they would become, scientifically, if the species ever went extinct.

Perhaps because of his poor eyesight, Theodore developed a good ear for birdsong, and as he grew as a naturalist, his hearing became even more attuned. He easily identified the "guttural joch joch" of the fox sparrow and the "rather jingling trill" of the dark-eyed junco, the "rollicking, bubbling notes" of the bobolink or the "sweet and plaintive song" of the white-throated sparrow. Theodore was also a critic. He thought the chipping sparrow a very poor singer because of its "exasperatingly monotonous notes," which usually continued for hours on end. Worse was the catbird, which he described as making "such horrible noises," complaining that you could not walk in a woods where there were catbirds without "promptly being informed of their presence by the monotonous and exasperating 'pay, pay.'"

Theodore delved into some of his most creative onomatopoeic prose when describing his favorite birdsongs. The Maryland yellow-throat had, according to the young Roosevelt, "a very bright, short song, sounding like *wit-te-weet, wit-te-weet, wit-te-weet, wit-te-wee.*" The American redstart, with its loudly and quickly repeated *"tseet-see-tseetsee,"* was another favorite. There was also the ovenbird's song, which consisted of "the repetition of a note of two syllables, somewhat like *tchea, tchea, tchea, tchea, tchea,* growing louder, shriller towards the end, so that while the first repetitions are full and distinct, it ends in a sort of shriek."

Sometimes Theodore had trouble inventing words to describe the sounds of certain birds, such as the song sparrow: "Its song is loud and cheerful, if not very musical, and is uttered freely from March to October. It is short, and may be represented by *cheet, cheet, cheet, chirr, che, che, che,* or *cheet, cheet, cheet, cheet, chirr, che* (—-^^^ UUUUUU or—-^^^)." But more than that of any other bird, Theodore savored the melody of the wood thrush: "Its delightful song—by far the sweetest bird music in our woods—is most often heard in the evening twilight, when it is all the more noticeable because it is the only sound to be heard, for the thrushes sing later than any other diurnal bird of the neighborhood. In the early morning its song is given forth just as freely, but at that time it is almost drowned out by louder, although far less melodious voices of the hosts of robins, catbirds and the like. After about the middle of August they stop singing, and during autumn are perfectly silent." All these observations Theodore recorded in his "Remarks on the Zoology of Oyster Bay, L.I." The account included a few notes on mammals and other animals but was, for the most part, a treatise on his favorite birds.

Theodore Roosevelt was a self-made ornithologist, and by the time he reached adulthood, he had amassed a museum of hundreds of bird specimens. He could identify the birds of the Adirondacks and coastal New York by sight and sound and he had compiled reams of detailed notes on avian behavior. He knew precisely when migrating birds would return in the spring and when they were likely to leave again in the fall. On the cusp of adulthood, Theodore Roosevelt was a walking field guide to the birds he had known—and even the ones he hadn't. Confident as he was in his interest, the only thing keeping him from becoming a truly professional naturalist was a formal education. Although Louis Agassiz had left no intellectual heir in Cambridge, Massachusetts, Roosevelt nonetheless followed in the footsteps of Albert Bickmore and readied himself for Harvard.

Chapter 6

ALONE AT HARVARD

On a cool September evening in 1876, Theodore Roosevelt walked the narrow streets of Cambridge, Massachusetts, and strained his eyes to bring into focus the address numbers on the tidy row houses. He was looking for 16 Winthrop Street. After locating the simple clapboard residence, he ascended a flight of stairs to his new home—a single but sunny room with an alcove sleeping area in the back. It was furnished with sturdy wooden pieces, masculine curtains, and a rich wool carpet. A fire was burning in the hearth. Eventually, the walls would sport his favorite bird lithographs, and the shelves would be filled with stuffed birds and his favorite books—John James Audubon's *Birds of America,* Spencer Baird's *Catalogue of North American Mammals,* and Elliott Coues's *Key to North American Birds.* A month shy of his eighteenth birthday, Roosevelt was about to experience total independence for the first time in his life.

Nineteenth-century Harvard was still a small sleepy college. Its students were, for the most part, sons of Boston elites—Brahmins who considered their four years of college more a sojourn of worldly pleasure than serious work. Not Roosevelt. He was astonished by how few of his peers had any intention of actually gaining an education at the school. Irrevocably shaped by his father's sense of morality, Roosevelt was initially worried about falling into the moral trap of hedonism, and he kept his father's words of wisdom close to his heart: "Take care of your morals first, your health next and finally your studies."

Aside from the unspoken culture of the "sporting" male, which mostly played out across the river, in a seedier part of town, Roosevelt also had to deal with the unwritten code as to how a Harvard man was to present himself in life—so bored as to seem on the verge of sleep. There was a lazy saunter called the "Harvard swing" and a yawnlike manner of speaking called the "Harvard drawl." But even as a freshman Theodore could not conform to such ennui, so overflowing with enthusiasm that he actually *ran* to his lectures. In his high-pitched, frazzled voice, he sputtered out words faster than he could enunciate them, ending his sentences with a menacing snap of his large square teeth. So peculiar was his manner of speaking that some of his classmates assumed he had a speech impediment. But misfits have a way of finding like-minded people, and while Theodore may have been the only student to include a full taxidermy kit in his essential school supplies, he was not the only student interested in becoming a naturalist.

The day after Roosevelt settled in at Winthrop Street, Henry Davis Minot came to pay him a visit, hoping to strike up some ornithological conversation. The son of a wealthy Boston lawyer, Minot learned of Roosevelt's arrival from family connections. He shared Theodore's all-consuming passion for birds, and although he wasn't quite as avid a collector as Roosevelt, he already had an ornithological book to his name called *The Land and Game Birds of New England,* which was a comprehensive treatise on the entire avifauna of the northeastern United States, numbering hundreds of pages. It was on this footing that the freshmen naturalists initiated their friendship.

When it came to making friends, Roosevelt was something of a novice, as he had spent most of his youth socializing within the milieu of his extended family. Cousins, a brother, and sisters had always smoothed Theodore's social interactions—and, being privately tutored his whole life, Teddy had never before faced the social pressures of a school setting. At Harvard, however, with the exception of Minot, he got off to a socially isolated start and began to notice that his odd manners put his classmates off. He made up his mind to reinvent himself (a talent of his), and by the winter of his first year, Theodore was transformed yet again. In an attempt to adopt an air of sophistication, he grew side whiskers and parted his hair down the middle. He wore expensive English suits and an elegant felt hat. He completed his new look with a walking stick (including the accompanying swagger) and soon found that he had suddenly become a star on the Harvard social scene.

At the first sign of spring, however, Roosevelt's attention was again focused on birds as he wrote home describing his warm-weather plans: "By the way, as the time when the birds are beginning to come back is approaching, I wish you would send on my gun, with all the cartridges you can find and my various apparatus for cleaning, loading, etc. Also send on a dozen glass jars, with the rubbers and stoppers (which you will find in my museum) and a German dictionary if you have one." Roosevelt was planning a collecting trip to the Adirondacks with his new friend Hal Minot. His previous forays to that region had been in the summer, after the birds had stopped nesting and singing, but now he wanted to return at the peak of the breeding season, when all the birds were in full plumage and song. With his style upgrade complete, he may well have been trying to eliminate another deficiency—since naturalists of note eventually made their reputations by writing research papers and presenting new information. His buddy Hal had penned a thick book, but all Theodore had to show for his efforts was a large collection of dead birds. He had published nothing, and he felt he was in danger of becoming a mere technician who collected and stuffed birds for someone else to study. Comparing himself to Hal, Roosevelt seemed a mere dabbler—and underachiever—and that rankled him. He had taken extensive notes during his three previous visits to the Adirondacks and was now hoping to shape his field notebooks into something publishable. He had two notebooks to work from: "Journal of a Trip to the Adirondacks" for the years 1874 and 1875 (accounts of family trips made when he was between the ages of fifteen and sixteen), and the more substantial "Notes on the Fauna of the Adirondack Mountains," which was filled with anecdotal accounts of animals made from the time he first visited the site at age twelve. Entries from these notebooks show that he had already made a good start:

Zonotrichia albicollis [White-throated Sparrow]—No. 575. Aug. 6th 1875 [referring to the catalogue number Roosevelt had assigned to the specimen and the date he collected it] *. . . It becomes very fat in August and is at all times insectivorous. . . . It has a singularly sweet and plaintive song, uttered with clear, whistling notes; it sings all day long especially if the weather be cloudy, and I have frequently heard it at night but its favorite time is in the morning when it begins long before daybreak; indeed, excepting the thrushes, it sings earlier than any other bird. . . . It sings all through the summer.*

Anorthura troglodytes [Troglodytes troglodytes, Winter Wren]—No. 585. Aug. 11th 1875 . . . Rather common in the dense woods, but rarely seen. . . . It is often heard, however, for it possesses a gushing, ringing song, wonderfully loud for so small a creature; excepting the thrushes it is the sweetest songster of the Adirondac [sic] *woods. . . . It moves by jerky hops and short flights, the tail being held perfectly erect. . . .*

Roosevelt and Minot set off for the Adirondacks just as soon as the spring semester came to an end. For a week, they tramped the shores of the lakes St. Regis and Spitfire, shooting birds. Their timing was perfect. The birds were in their finest plumage, singing their sweetest songs. But even this beauty wasn't enough to keep Hal Minot in the field, and he left after just one week—the first signs of his chronic, debilitating depression. Working alone in the Adirondacks, Theodore carried on, writing detailed notes on the breeding behavior of some ninety-six species. The experience was transformative for him, and he found something akin to spiritual communion there. One such reckoning came after he heard a particular bird, and taking pen to paper he waxed poetic:

Perhaps the sweetest music I have ever listened to was uttered by a hermit thrush. It was while hunting deer on a small lake, in the heart of the wilderness; the night was dark, for the moon had not yet risen, but there were no clouds, and as we moved over the surface of the water with the perfect silence so strange and almost oppressive to the novice in this sport, I could distinguish dimly the outlines of the gloomy and almost impenetrable pine forest by which we were surrounded. We had been out for two or three hours but had seen nothing; once we heard a tree fall with a dull, heavy crash, and two or three times the harsh hooting of an owl had been answered by the unearthly laughter of a loon from the bosom of the lake, but otherwise nothing had occurred to break the deathlike stillness of the night; not even a breath of air stirred among the tops of the tall pine trees. Wearied by our unsuccess we at last turned homeward when suddenly the quiet was broken by the song of a hermit thrush; louder and clearer it sang from the depths of the grim rugged woods, until the sweet, sad music seemed to fill the very air and conquer for a moment the gloom of the night; then it died away and ceased as suddenly as it had begun. Perhaps the song would have proved less sweet in the daytime, but uttered as it was, with such surroundings, sounding so strange and so beautiful amid these grand desolate wilds, I shall never forget it.

Returning to Oyster Bay in mid-July 1877, Roosevelt published his first ornithological work, *The Summer Birds of the Adirondacks in Franklin County, N.Y.* More of a pamphlet than a book, it was just a few sheets of unbound paper that Roosevelt paid to have privately printed and distributed. Although probably no more than a few hundred copies were issued, one made its way to prominent naturalist Clinton Hart Merriam, head of the U.S. Biological Survey, which was closely tied to the Smithsonian Institution. Merriam had been asked to review a number of recent amateur works on the birds of New York State. Writing in the *Bulletin of the Nuttall Ornithological Society* in the spring of 1878, Merriam criticized many of the other papers for numerous errors and inconsistencies but made an exception for the paper submitted by Roosevelt and Minot. In fact, he singled out their work as one of the finest lists of its kind by any amateur naturalist:

By far the best of these recent lists which I have seen is that of *The Summer Birds of the Adirondacks in Franklin County, N. Y.,* by Theodore Roosevelt and H. D. Minot. Though not redundant with information and mentioning 97 species, it bears prima facie evidence of reliability—which seems to be a great desideratum in bird lists nowadays. Based on the sound principle of exclusion, it contains only those species which the authors have themselves observed there, and consequentially furnishes that which was most needed, i.e., exact and thoroughly reliable information concerning the most characteristic birds of the limited region (Franklin County) of which they treat.

Two years later, after spending the summer break from Harvard at Oyster Bay, Roosevelt wrote what would become his second published work, *Notes on Some of the Birds of Oyster Bay.* It consisted of a few brief notes on just seventeen species of birds that he considered particularly rare or noteworthy for the region. Years later he half-mockingly laughed at his youthful energy: "Along with my college preparatory studies I carried on the work of a practical student of natural history. I worked with greater industry than either intelligence or success, and made very few additions to the sum of human knowledge; but to this day certain obscure ornithological publications may be found in which are recorded such items as, for instance, that on one occasion a fish-crow, and on another an Ipswich sparrow, were obtained by one Theodore Roosevelt Jr. at Oyster Bay, on the shore of Long Island Sound."

As a Harvard sophomore, Roosevelt was finally free to take some science courses, and he chose to study anatomy, vertebrate physiology, and botany. He was committed to becoming a "scientific man" and wished to emulate his heroes of American descriptive natural history—John James Audubon and Spencer Fullerton Baird especially—both of whom gained their fame discovering new species in unexplored territory. These were the real-life adventurers, facing outdoor hardships and danger in pursuit of scientific advancement, who had so captivated Theodore as a boy.

Following Minot's lead, Roosevelt joined Harvard's Nuttall Ornithological Club, where some of the more senior members thought him a bit too cocksure for his age. But his arrogance was earned, as Roosevelt always ended up on the right side of prevailing science. He gained particular notoriety for his denigration of the English sparrow. Recently introduced and rapidly displacing native species such as bluebirds and wrens, the English sparrow was at the center of what was called the "sparrow wars"—an intensely heated argument between hard-core scientific naturalists who saw these birds as an invasive species, and a softer, more sentimental group that opposed killing them even knowing they were harmful to native birds. Roosevelt was a vocal antagonist of this invasive species, as it was squeezing out the native fauna and causing irreparable harm. He gave an impassioned presentation at the Nuttall Club for the English sparrow's extermination in America. Speaking out against the sparrow, Roosevelt was showing his colors as a fact-driven scientist, one motivated not by sentiment but by the laws of the natural world. The English sparrow did not belong in North America, and Roosevelt knew it had to be eradicated immediately, before it further disrupted the native ecosystem. In response to this hard-nosed approach, the newspapers were flooded with letters and editorials debating Roosevelt's credentials, and it was only after some of the nation's most prominent ornithologists finally intervened—among them Joel A. Allen, who would later be appointed the first Curator of Birds and Mammals at the American Museum of Natural History—that the matter was settled in Roosevelt's favor.

Although he was taking a leadership role at Harvard, and was as eager as ever to get into the field, during his sophomore year Roosevelt still found himself somewhat adrift. None of his professors noticed or cared much about his passion for natural history, which had gone largely untended since his arrival at Harvard. Without the mentorship so vital to a burgeoning scientist's development, at times it seemed he was carrying on with naturalism solely to please his father.

More distressing than his rudderless pursuit of naturalism, news that his father was ill reached Theodore in mid-December. It made him uneasy, but he didn't immediately realize the seriousness of the elder man's condition, or was simply in denial of this fact. Writing home, he was almost jocular in suggesting that maybe a traveling trip would help, teasing his father that he would give him "a good rowing up for not taking better care of himself." But within just a few days of his first serious symptoms, Roosevelt Sr. collapsed in pain.

He had acute peritonitis, brought on by advanced stomach cancer. For days he was in agony, managing to rally only briefly when Theodore arrived home for Christmas. Although Theodore seemed to willfully ignore it, the man who had stood as the very symbol of physical strength was dying.

Theodore returned to school on January second, still seemingly unaware of the seriousness of his father's illness. A month later, Roosevelt Sr.'s condition had steadily worsened—his hair turning gray almost overnight, though he was just forty-six. With Theodore's midterm exams coming up, his parents thought it best to not inform him of how grave things were, and the letters their son soon sent home—letters describing how he had aced those very exams—were the ones that cheered his father the most. But on the morning of February 9, when the bad news could no longer be postponed, an urgent telegram was sent to Harvard calling Theodore home.

In shock, Roosevelt hurried back to New York City and arrived to find a crowd of mourners already gathering in front of the house. He was too late. His father had died at exactly one hour past midnight, February 10, 1878. "Thirteen and a quarter hours of agony it took to kill a man broken down by three months of sickness," Elliott Roosevelt wrote of the final hours of his father's life. All Theodore could record in his diary was that it was the "blackest day" of his life. Everything he had ever done had been wrapped tightly in his father's wise counsel, his example, and a need for his approval. Whom would Theodore confide in and look up to now? He loved his mother, but she was never someone the children could depend on before, and now she had been leveled by grief, besides. His caring sister Anna, already comfortable in a maternal role, received a desperate appeal from her brother: "My own sweet sister, you will have to give me a great deal of advice and assistance now that our dear Father is gone, for in many ways you are more like him than any of the rest of the family." But Anna was only three years older than Theodore and could never be the hero to him that his father had been.

Back at school, Theodore tried to turn to his friend Hal Minot, but Minot was in the throes of his own personal crisis after suffering a nervous breakdown brought on by the stresses of Harvard. "Old

Hal Minot has left college; his father has taken him away and put him in a big office to study law. I am awfully sorry and so is he," Roosevelt lamented in a letter home about his former Adirondacks traveling companion.

The young Roosevelt's support system was rapidly crumbling around him. Feeling acutely alone, he thought much about the loss of his father and about the man's legacy. He constantly replayed one of their last conversations, when the older man had told his son that if he really wished to become a scientific man—an "out-of-doors" naturalist, as Theodore put it—he could do so, but he must be sure that he "really intensively desired to do scientific work." Roosevelt Sr. warned that Theodore "must not dream of taking it up as a dilettante."

Remembering his father's words, Roosevelt dealt with his grief by pushing himself, working to the limits of his physical and mental strength, burying himself in a steady stream of anatomy, botany, literature, and rhetoric. He declined every social call and made every effort to avoid the frothy amateurism that his father cautioned him against, "grinding like a Trojan" until he had passed all his exams.

Summer came, but Roosevelt was still in mourning. He distracted himself with relentless rowing, hiking, and horseback riding at Oyster Bay. Everywhere he turned, he saw his father. "Every nook and corner . . . every piece of furniture . . . is in some manner connected with him," he wrote. Roosevelt felt even more alone and adrift in the world, fearing for the first time about his own future, and after a romantic entanglement with his childhood sweetheart ended suddenly, Theodore seemed closer than ever to a breakdown. Rowing furiously in Long Island Sound, he shot at anything that caught his eye, including dolphins. He needed to get away from his family, away from polite society, to go someplace where he could immerse himself in raw physical exertion—somewhere with no reminders of his father.

Theodore got the idea of going to the North Maine Woods from his adventurous cousins and former Roosevelt Museum co-trustees Emlen and West, who had made the trip a year before with local guide William Sewall. Sewall lived in Island Falls—the state's northernmost county and a place of intense wilderness. By comparison, Island Falls made Roosevelt's previous trips to Paul Smith's Adirondack lodge seem cushy. The few inhabitants of the North Maine Woods depended completely on their own prowess for survival, and they spent most of their time hunting food and cutting firewood for winter. But Sewall, being somewhat savvier than the typical Maine woods-man, had a different livelihood in mind when he turned his home into a hunting lodge for out-of-towners.

Just getting to Island Falls was an expedition in itself—the last stop on any train was still thirty-six miles from the town. Travel-ing by horse-drawn wagon, Roosevelt finally reached Sewall's home on the Mattawamkeag River near dusk of his journey's second day. Roosevelt found in Sewall all the personality traits he had admired in his father. He was physically imposing, the quintessential Maine backwoodsman—a man six feet tall, with a reddish-brown beard and "warm friendly eyes." He read the Bible every day and never drank alcohol or smoked. Like Roosevelt, he, too, had fought childhood ill-ness to build up his body. Roosevelt also found Sewall surprisingly literary, and the two men shared an interest in the writings of Scott, Whittier, and Longfellow.

Rising early in the morning, they canoed down the Mattawamkeag River, which was lined by deep stands of spruce spreading out in all directions. After making camp along the rocky shore, Roosevelt spent a week wandering up and down the river with his gun. He was hoping to bag a deer or maybe even a bear. Sewall marveled at this Harvard boy's fortitude. It was obvious to the guide that he was undersize for an eighteen-year-old, but what he lacked in size, Roosevelt made up for with pure grit. Sewall had never had a hunting guest with quite the drive of this particular young man—someone who could walk for miles all day despite his obvious asthmatic "Guffle-ing."

Roosevelt stayed with Sewall for nearly three weeks, but he was not a very successful hunter. He managed to bag some small game for the cook pot—rabbit, duck, and partridge—but he couldn't kill any-thing bigger, although he was certainly captivated by the larger ani-mals. Roosevelt may have remembered his formative first trip to the Adirondacks—woods that were very similar to what now surrounded him in northern Maine—and he recalled his father reading to him by the light of a fire. Deep in the heart of the wilderness, Roosevelt may have felt as if his father's presence was still very much with him, and for the first time since his death, he felt as though he could come to terms with that loss.

Returning to school in the fall of 1878, Roosevelt was surprised to learn that he had been offered membership in the prestigious Porcellian Club—Harvard's highest social honor. In accepting the offer, he joined an elite social circle, and one of the first to welcome Roosevelt was Dick Saltonstall. Saltonstall invited the newest Porcellian to spend the weekend at his home in the wealthy Massachusetts suburb of Chestnut Hill. Riding to the end of a long, tree-lined drive, Roosevelt was led to an immense lawn boasting two large houses. One of the houses belonged to the Saltonstalls, the other to their relatives, the Lees.

As Theodore rode up to the two houses, the sun lighting up the red and orange and green of a spectacular New England fall, he saw a beautiful girl strolling down a garden path to greet him. She was Alice Hathaway Lee, Dick Saltsonstall's cousin. At five feet seven inches, she was tall for her time, with fair skin and honey-colored hair that she wore in fashionable curls. Like his mother, she carried herself gracefully and often wore white—but her most attractive feature was her eyes, which varied from pale blue to a dreamy dove gray depending on the light. Roosevelt was dumbstruck and "loved her as soon as he saw her sweet, fair, young face."

Seeking a picture of his new love, Roosevelt proposed an outing to get tin-types taken, an early form of photography, but Alice effectively used the excuse of needing her mother's permission to delay the event until the following spring. Undeterred, and with the compliance of his friend Dick, Theodore made regular calls on Alice. He studied less that fall semester and had his horse brought up to school so that he could make the trip to Chestnut Hill in better time. Roosevelt rode that horse so hard, it went lame after just one month.

Perhaps to cool his passions, Roosevelt returned to Bill Sewall and the North Woods of Maine in the winter of 1879. He knew that tromping through the region and being forced to depend on his own fortitude for survival would invigorate him, and his fellowship with Sewell and their wilderness immersion helped fill the void left after his father's death. In fact, these trips may have been a sort of path back to his father, who would have been so proud to see how strong Theodore had become.

The snow was three feet deep when he arrived, and, wearing snow-shoes for the first time in his life, he and Sewall trudged six miles to a remote lumber camp. When they arrived, Roosevelt got along well with the lumberjacks, seeing in them kindred spirits and probing them for knowledge of the forest. Roosevelt was captivated with the desolate wilderness, and, writing home to his mother, he declared that he had never seen a more beautiful sight than these northern woods in winter.

The real joy of nature, at least to Theodore, was the chance to engage with it. In his diary he noted everything he saw there: the tracks of mice in the snow, the flocks of snow buntings, a red crossbill, and a party of grosbeaks. Despite the fact that it was a hunting trip, Roosevelt remained as observant a naturalist as ever. He spent several days in that isolated camp, and whether by barter or by his own prowess, he obtained specimens of fox, lynx, raccoon, and deer for his museum—not a bad haul for an asthmatic city slicker.

But upon returning to Harvard, Roosevelt once again trained his hunter's instincts onto Alice Lee. Now though, instead of threadbare shirts and mud-covered boots, Theodore wore his very best suits, tracking his prey during polite afternoon teas and dances. The hunt eventually blossomed into a romance and by the end of his junior year he proposed marriage. Alice neither accepted nor refused, leaving the infatuated Roosevelt determined and anxious. To burn off some of his exuberant energy—and perhaps also to top the challenge of his winter snowshoeing hikes—Roosevelt made a third and final trip to Maine in the late summer of 1879. He had a clear goal in mind—to climb Mount Katahdin, at 5,268 feet, the second-highest peak in New England. Here was a supreme challenge, and preparing for the ascent, Roosevelt donned a flannel shirt, duck trousers, flannel under trousers, and a heavy woolen jacket. He carried a blanket for sleeping, both a rifle and a shotgun, and a small bag of necessities that included two complete changes of clothes and wool socks.

The expedition to Katahdin took eight days, and, carrying a forty-five-pound pack, Roosevelt hiked ten miles to a base camp at Lake Katahdin below the summit. The journey was a strenuous one. Although he lost one of his shoes in the current while fording a stream, he managed the climb in a pair of flimsy moccasins, undeterred even by this loss of suitable equipment. The group hunted for a couple of days around the lake, shooting small game while preparing themselves mentally for their eventual dash to the summit. During their ascent, some of his traveling companions collapsed before they reached the top, but Roosevelt found that he could "endure fatigue and hardship pretty nearly as well as these lumbermen." He was in "beautiful condition" and very much satisfied with his physical stamina.

No sooner had Roosevelt conquered Mount Katahdin than he asked Sewall to join him on a pirogue trip to Munsungan Lake, a wild and isolated part of Maine accessible only by canoe. They camped there for several days, hunting and living off the land, but even this was not quite enough to satisfy Roosevelt's exuberance. With just three days left before he had to head back to Harvard, Roosevelt went on one last hike, and by the end of the trip he had covered more than a hundred miles through the North Maine Woods. Despite the pouring rain and treacherous conditions, Roosevelt enjoyed himself tremendously. Finally, after more than three weeks of constant physical exertion in the wilderness, Sewall guided Roosevelt back to the main railroad station to send him back to Harvard. Here was a young man who, despite all his physical shortcomings, was determined to prove to the world that he could reinvent himself. As he boarded the train, Roosevelt thanked his Maine friends one last time for making him feel "as tough as a pine knot."

THEODORE ROOSEVELT GRADUATED magna cum laude on June 30, 1880, and ranked twenty-first in a graduating class of 161. Harvard had been good for him. Although he claimed to have gained little of specific value from his coursework, he had learned much from the Harvard social scene. This enabled him to transform from a misfit with a monomaniacal obsession for birds to one of the most interesting and dynamic men on campus. On the eve of graduation he opened his diary and penned his expectations for the future: "With Alice to love me, life will always seem laughing and loving."

Roosevelt was constructing a narrative of seeming storybook happiness, but his infatuation with Alice also marked a period during which he questioned a career as a naturalist. After he'd toiled for years to transform himself into someone of whom his father could be proud—a strong man paired with his ideal version of a mate and a career of his own choosing ahead—the thought of spending several more years at school getting the necessary degrees to become a proper university naturalist made him "perfectly blue." He also struggled with the concerns of a man insecure in his beloved's affection. Would sophisticated Alice have any interest in marrying a man who reeked of rotting flesh and who insisted on keeping hundreds of stuffed birds and pickled snakes in his house? So, although he was still an avid amateur naturalist, his determination to transform his life to meet his own ideal of perfection was even greater than his desire for scientific credentials. On the cusp of manhood, young Theodore was still very much driven by a need to prove himself, and he wasn't quite convinced that the laboratory brand of naturalism popular in the universities was the best he could aspire to.

In February of his senior year he wrote to his old pal Hal Minot with an important declaration: "I write to you to announce my engagement to Miss Alice Lee; but do not speak of it till Monday. I have been in love with her for nearly two years now; and have made everything subordinate to winning her; so you can perhaps understand a change in my ideas as regards science, etc." Later in life, he insisted that the ultimate blame for his decision to leave academia rested not with Alice but with Harvard, which "utterly ignored the possibilities of the faunal naturalist, the outdoor naturalist and observer of nature. They treated biology as purely a science of the laboratory and the microscope, a science whose adherents were to spend their time in the study of minute forms of marine life, or else in section cutting and the study of the tissues of the higher organisms under the microscope."

He went on to explain: "There was a total failure to understand the great variety of kinds of work that could be done by the naturalists, including what could be done by outdoor naturalists. . . . My taste was specialized in a totally different direction, and I had no more desire or ability to be a microscopist and section cutter than to be a mathematician. Accordingly I abandoned all thought of becoming a scientist." And, thus, the determined Theodore—who accomplished every task he set his mind to—decided he would marry Alice Lee and put aside his long-harbored plans to become a naturalist.

PART II

All Hunters Should Be Nature Lovers

It is to be hoped that the days of mere wasteful, boastful slaughter are past, and that from now on the hunter will stand foremost in working for the preservation and perpetuation of the wild life, whether big or little.

—THEODORE ROOSEVELT

Chapter 7

ROOSEVELT REBELS

*H*aving built up the muscles in his chest through exercise, all but extinguishing his asthma, Roosevelt was immensely proud of how he had improved his body. He was fit, confident, and vigorous. But, seeing a physician before his wedding to Alice Lee, Roosevelt received grim news. His heart was weak—so much so that he had to change his lifestyle or face early death. No more hunting up north, no more rowing on Long Island Sound. Even the simple act of running up a flight of stairs could kill him. He had to lead a quiet life of minimal exertion or risk a heart attack. The news stood in direct contradiction to his father's formative advice, and, having spent his adolescence living as strenuously as possible, Roosevelt faced the specter that he might have overexerted himself and done his heart irreparable harm.

A lazier man might have welcomed the diagnosis as an excuse for a life of sloth, but to Roosevelt that would have been tantamount to a living death. He (perhaps foolishly) had greater faith in his father's wisdom than in the words of any medical doctor, no matter how well schooled. And he knew his own body, having personally experienced the debilitating effects of inactivity. After the prognosis, Roosevelt was quick to retort: "Doctor, I am going to do all the things you tell me not to do. If I've got to live the sort of life you have described, I don't care how short it is."

Theodore's first act of defiance was to join his brother, Elliott, on another hunting trip. The American Midwest was the latest destination for young men seeking adventure, and, using Chicago as a base, the men planned to spend six weeks exploring and hunting the surrounding countryside in the late summer of 1880. The jaunt was intended to fortify Roosevelt before his wedding and, with his history of nervous diarrhea, perhaps also to calm his stomach. The Adirondacks and Island Falls, Maine, were no longer the training grounds where hardy men built themselves, as tourists had overrun these regions and ravaged the native wildlife.

Two years younger, Elliott was, on first impression, the more accomplished and likable of the two Roosevelt boys. Angel-faced and soft-spoken, Elliott was stronger, more athletic, better-looking, and more charming than Theodore. Unlike his sputtering, ball-of-energy brother, Elliott was suave, and he never showed weakness, even though he also suffered from asthma. To combat his own condition, Elliott had been sent off to Fort McKavett in the rugged hills of central Texas to live with the 10th U.S. Infantry. There he had mingled with hardened veterans of the Mexican and Civil Wars—picking up an assortment of bad habits during his stay. Writing home, Elliott had described how he'd resisted the urge to drink or smoke, yet, he'd admitted to his father, he "wanted to very much" and it was hard for him to say no when "asked about every five minutes during the day."

Theodore envied his brother's adventurous life in Texas—adventures that had included his joining in the melee of buffalo hunting. At just seventeen years of age, Elliott had already killed several buffalo and on one occasion was almost trampled by a stampeding herd. Still, the brothers had remained close, and their Midwest trip was intended to be one last hurrah before Theodore's wedding. Theodore and Elliott organized everything for the trip, this time without their father's informed planning. However, they quickly discovered that the Midwest could not quite satisfy their quest for adventure and abundant game.

Hiring a guide with a team of bird dogs, they made three separate forays into the surrounding prairies—first around Illinois, then Iowa, and finally Minnesota, each time venturing farther afield in the hope of finding game, and each time returning to Chicago disappointed.

Rising early each morning, they tramped for miles across open fields, and Theodore could not help but feel vaguely uneasy about the alien, barren landscape. It was nothing like the woods he was used to, where steep hillsides gave way to dense bogs, sunny meadows, and old-growth hardwoods. There was almost no distinguishing topography on the prairie and only scattered trees. It was a vast sea of open wheat and cornfields coating everything to the horizon. Most disturbing of all, there were no longer any mammals left on this plain to hunt: no deer, no bear, no buffalo. Years earlier, while climbing the Pyramid of Cheops in Egypt, Roosevelt had gazed out across the Sahara and likened it to how he imagined the North American prairies would look. Now, seeing the region for the first time, he was reminded of that trip and felt as though he was scanning the boundless sands of a desert. Indeed, the early explorers of the American prairies and plains felt much the same way when they described these areas as being good for nothing more than buffalo.

"Buffalo" is something of a misnomer for this American bovine, as the true buffalo are the water buffalo of Southeast Asia and the Cape buffalo of Africa. The American variety—*Bison bison*—is best called "bison." It is the largest and most distinctive land mammal on the North American continent. Full-grown bulls stand between five and six feet at the shoulder, and they can be nearly nine feet long, weighing in between 2,000 and 2,600 pounds. At the time of the European discovery of North America, bison covered one-third of the continent, ranging from central Mexico to the Canadian subarctic, as far east as western New York and Pennsylvania, and as far south as the northern half of Georgia. As grazers, their range was restricted to the western grasslands and to the narrow belts of open land along rivers and streams in the East. Woodlands cleared by Native Americans were also readily invaded by these animals, and before the settlement of the continent's east coast, bison probably penetrated every patch of grassy land. Roosevelt's hero and respected naturalist Spencer Baird reported finding their bones in the bogs and caves near his home in Carlisle, Pennsylvania, and there are early accounts of the species making it as far east as the eventual site of Washington, D.C.

The number of bison roaming across North America was once as high as fifty million, but those numbers started to decline soon after the arrival of Europeans. The bovines were quickly extirpated from east of the Appalachians and thereafter from the regions east of the Mississippi; by the early 1800s vast herds persisted only on the Great Plains of the West. So numerous were the bison there that early accounts describe them as blackening the plains as far as the eye could see. Their grunts and the collective sounds of their hoofbeats often traveled farther than the sight of the herd, and clouds of dust rising on the horizon often forewarned of a rapidly approaching herd. Witnesses describe herds of these powerful creatures literally drinking small streams dry, the water not resuming its flow until after the animals moved on.

Prior to humans, wolves were the only real threat to the bison, and early explorers wrote of solitary bison surrounded by packs of the hungry canines. The predators would follow the bovines for days, waiting for them to become sufficiently exhausted before launching their attack. One graphic account from 1877 described "a huge bull, encircled with a gang of white wolves," which, after being chased off by the men who stumbled upon the scene, revealed the wounded but still-living bison: "his eyes being entirely eaten out of his head, the gristle of his nose mostly gone, his tongue half eaten off, and the skin and flesh from his legs torn almost literally into strings. In this tattered and torn condition, the poor old veteran stood bracing up in the midst of his devourers, who had ceased hostilities for a few minutes to enjoy a sort of parley, recovering strength and preparing to resume the attack in a few moments again."

The cornfields west of Chicago may not have been quite so tooth-and-claw when the Roosevelt brothers were there, but with the help of their guides they flushed up a variety of game birds—sharp-tailed grouse, greater prairie chicken, bobwhite quail, common snipe, plovers, doves, and ducks. The grouse and prairie chickens exploded from the thickets and tussocks, and Theodore's heart jumped when they flew off in all directions like missiles. This was wing shooting at its best, and while Roosevelt had killed plenty of birds in his childhood, he had always been more of a bird *collector* and had never really shot birds for pure sport.

Sport hunters and scientific collectors have different motivations. Sportsmen seek challenging shots, and they concentrate their energies exclusively on fast-flying birds. Their sport is a ritual, repeating the process of finding, flushing, and firing at game birds. Bird collectors are focused on scientific discovery; their goal is to acquire specimens of all kinds of birds—even slow-flying birds—in order to document species diversity. As a bird collector, Roosevelt had shot at songbirds perched in hedgerows and targeted wading birds standing motionlessly in Oyster Bay. He had always been more focused on the biological diversity of his catches, and it didn't really matter to him whether they offered a challenging shot or not. But now, accompanying his brother, Theodore was beginning to shoot at birds solely for sport rather than for serious scientific inquiry.

Bored with the lack of animal diversity, Roosevelt turned his inquisitiveness to the human landscape. Like a naturalist recording the diversity of animal species, he described the unusual people all around him. There was a quiet, intelligent Yankee, a reformed desperado, a good-natured German boy, a clumsy and giggly Irish girl, and a hard-featured backwoods woman who swore like a trapper. Roosevelt was just waiting for the trip to end.

ON THIS TRIP, Roosevelt had come west but not quite far enough to encounter what he considered to be real wilderness. Hardly any of the western mammals he had read about could be found here—no buffalo, no pronghorn, and no elk. Commercial hunters had killed most of the game, and settlers had uprooted most of the prairie for crops. If Theodore wanted to see the West at its wildest, he would have to follow the example of the museum naturalists who had come decades before him—to take the railroads to their very end and then keep going, for with the railroads soon came a taming of the land. Wilderness remained a constantly westward-moving target, and for naturalists such as Roosevelt, the trick was to get ahead of human progress.

Decades before Roosevelt set out on his westward trek, Spencer Baird had found his way to the lines' end. When the United States Congress authorized the Pacific Railroad Surveys of 1853–1855, the principal goal was to discover and plot the best possible routes for a transcontinental railroad across North America. Led by the United States Army, the surveys' ranks included hundreds of engineers and surveyors under the protection of thousands of soldiers. Also accompanying the military men was a sizable cadre of naturalists, whose mission it was to collect massive quantities of natural-history data and museum specimens along the way. These were the railroad naturalists, the brainchild of master museum builder Baird. Tapping his close connections to the Army—Baird's father-in-law was a high-ranking officer—he organized his railroad naturalists under the aegis of the newly formed Smithsonian Institution, and with full military escort they marched west even before the first railroad ties were laid down.

Official reports on the railroad surveys list more than a dozen major expeditions, which followed the course of what ultimately became the four main east–west transcontinental railways: the Central Pacific passing through the Rocky Mountains and across the Great Basin to the Sierra Nevada range; the two Southern Pacific lines transecting the deserts of the Southwest; and the Northern Pacific passing through the Badlands of the Dakotas. Baird could not have devised a more efficient way to survey the western fauna. The railroads were paths through otherwise inaccessible terrain, snaking their way deep into the continent at different latitudes and thus offering the opportunity to acquire specimens from dramatically varied habitats and faunas—plus, an easy way to send specimens back to the Smithsonian.

Baird seized on this opportunity and hired dozens of naturalists, seeing to it that "all the parties were fitted out in the most complete manner; the natural history apparatus and material prepared under the direction of the Smithsonian Institution, which also furnished the necessary instructions as to the objects most important to be collected."

The Pacific Railroad Surveys resulted in the collecting of thousands of museum specimens and thousands of corresponding pages of scientific results in a formidable set of thirteen quarto volumes under the imposing title *Reports of Explorations and Surveys, to Ascertain the*

Most Practicable and Economical Route for a Railroad from the Missis-sippi River to the Pacific Ocean. Made Under the Direction of the Secre-tary of War, in 1853–4, According to the Acts of Congress of March 3, 1853, May 31, 1854, and August 5, 1854. Weighing in at more than eighty pounds, the thirteen volumes of the Railroad Surveys were the richest store of information then available on the natural history of the American West. Written in large part by Spencer Baird himself, they included comprehensive accounts of every species of vertebrate known at the time of the surveys, and they quickly became the single most important reference on the fauna of the American West; volume 8 (1857) in particular was considered a book for naturalists—a must-have reference that young Theodore owned.

THE UPPER MIDWEST may not have been quite the frontier Theodore and Elliott had envisioned, but they still had fun playing the roles of rugged westerners with their "cropped heads, unshaven faces, dirty grey shirts, still dirtier yellow trousers and cowhide boots." Strutting in and out of the saloons, they acted like cowboys and, in the case of Elliott, even indulged some of their more notorious bad habits.

It was a last wild fling for the two unwed brothers; despite get-ting lost in an early snow squall, being bitten on the boot by a ven-omous snake, and breaking two of his guns, Theodore managed to shoot an impressive tally of birds—more than thirty species includ-ing coots, rails, four different kinds of plover, three different snipe, a goose, doves, and quail. This was especially remarkable for someone not known to be a particularly good shot, and he most certainly had to work hard to attain this bag. His competitive instincts are evident in the final page of his journal, where he makes a great show of the fact that, all told, he shot a grand total of 203 animals—two more than his brother. Satisfied with himself, Theodore summed up his midwestern experience on the last page of his diary, noting that the work he had done had freed him up to devote more of his obsessive energy to his future bride: "The trip was great fun; but how glad I am it is over and I am to see Alice!"

. . .

ON HIS TWENTY-SECOND birthday, just four months after his Harvard graduation, Theodore Roosevelt stood at the altar of the First Unitarian Church in Brookline, Massachusetts, and married Alice Lee. It had been just over two years since he'd first met her—two years of solid courting, strutting, and wooing. Because she had always been coy, the oh-so-eager Roosevelt could never be fully certain he had really secured her affections until they were actually wed. For the highly competitive and obsessive Roosevelt, Alice was (to a certain degree) a highly coveted trophy in his eyes—his natural feelings for her notwithstanding. *Win* was the word he used when describing his need to be with her, and on October 27, 1880, Roosevelt finally won.

A proper honeymoon was postponed until the following summer, when they would tour Europe, so Alice and Theodore spent their first weeks as husband and wife at the Roosevelt summer home in Oyster Bay. There they enjoyed long walks in the woods and quiet evenings reading books aloud in front of a warm fireplace. The summer house, which the family still rented, was not far from where Roosevelt and Alice had recently purchased 155 acres of land on which they planned to build their own home. Alice helped draw the layout of its twenty-two rooms and the three wide verandas from which they could enjoy expansive views of the sea. Roosevelt (ever the avian enthusiast) recognized that the verandas commanded excellent views of the many bird species that flew over their property. Construction had not yet begun, but Roosevelt had already decided to call their future house Leeholm, in honor of his wife's maiden name. Life certainly looked cozy for the newlyweds, and after moving back into his mother's home at 6 West 57th Street in the autumn of 1880, Theodore began studying law at Columbia University.

Law is an entirely different pursuit from natural history, but Roosevelt felt that the shift was necessary, not only to keep his new wife happy but also to support both of them financially. Naturalists' salaries (if they are lucky enough to have any salary at all) are notoriously abysmal—not nearly enough to support a wife and future family.

Moreover, at Harvard Theodore had developed a taste for finery in everything from the clothes he wore to the guns he carried afield.

Theodore was devoted to Alice, and as if to prove to her that he was through studying birds and mice and ready to pursue a more lucrative profession, he dissolved his boyhood museum. Painstakingly accumulated over the course of a decade, his collection included hundreds of scientific specimens representing thousands of hours of dedicated work, and getting rid of them was a potlatch of sorts—the deliberate dispersal of property as a demonstration of his commitment.

Looking at the labels on the various specimens as he packed them away, Roosevelt could recall the many milestones of the past several years of his life. There were the Brewer's voles he had collected on Muskeget Island, Massachusetts, just after the founding of his Roosevelt Museum of Natural History, the flying squirrels from the Adirondacks, and weasels from Island Falls. Even the study skin of the slit-faced bat from the pyramids in Egypt had to go. From Oyster Bay alone, there were hundreds of bird specimens. All these treasures were unceremoniously packed up and shipped off to Washington, D.C. This decision was a powerful symbol, for, in giving up his specimens, he was essentially severing his ties to the field to which, until now, he had so painstakingly devoted his life.

Most of the specimens were sent to the Smithsonian Institution, and a few years later he donated the balance (about twenty specimens) to the American Museum of Natural History, where they reside today. Museum specimens are sometimes passed around from institution to institution, but as long as their specimen tags remain intact—tags bearing such valuable information as the date and place at which the specimen was collected—they remain valuable to science. At that time, no one could have predicted that these specimens might one day gain a degree of cultural value as well, thanks to their collector. At the time, Theodore Roosevelt was just another amateur naturalist—one of the many thousands who routinely donated their specimens to these museums.

As with all his pursuits, Roosevelt studied the law with all of his energy. Columbia Law School was then located in Lower Manhattan on Great Jones Street, some fifty-four blocks south of Theodore's residence, and yet he insisted on walking it regularly (and, in all likelihood, briskly). He studied hard and won the praise of his mentors, but he was still restless and impatient—often interrupting class to question his professors. His mother described him as "a caged lynx who just needed to go off with his gun instead of immersing himself in the tedious details of legal cases."

Despite his seemingly enthusiastic class participation, Theodore was becoming disillusioned with law, regarding it as something socially unjust and even repellant. He was already gearing up to become the kind of lawyer who could only defend someone he knew was innocent—one who could only represent a cause he thought was just. Over time any zeal he might have had for his studies quickly fizzled. He rationalized law as something he might find himself pursuing only if he was really desperate for a living. Law was a fine occupation, but it didn't supplant the passion he had for naturalism. Although he had only just started law school, he was itching for something new.

ROOSEVELT MAY HAVE marched a full fifty-four blocks to school, but a far more intriguing destination lay just outside his front door. Occupying the upper floor of a saloon, Morton Hall was the headquarters of the 21st District Republican Association. Barnlike in construction despite being a seat of political power, the hall was crudely furnished with wooden benches and a large prominently positioned spittoon. The place was full of foulmouthed men, and, as someone who was always drawn to power, Roosevelt felt pulled to join their ranks. But these Republicans were more akin to a gang than to a political party.

At first the men he encountered there didn't accept him, laughing Theodore off as a runaway from his "silk stocking" class. As a friend of Roosevelt's later described it, he "had to break into the organization with a jimmy." Up until this time he had consorted exclusively with "the men in the clubs of social pretension and the men of cultivated taste and easy life," and when he asked these men for advice on how to get into politics, they laughed at him, telling him that politics was lowbrow—certainly not a vocation befitting a gentleman. They assured him that politicians were "rough and brutal and unpleasant."

All of this suited Roosevelt fine. He had already developed a decided affinity for ruffians. Furthermore, his own father had previously taken on a number of corrupt politicians in the years before his death, seeing it as a noble cause, and Roosevelt likely picked up this cudgel as an expression of the morals that had been instilled in him. Besides, he liked being the center of attention, in the middle of all the power and action. Roosevelt reasoned that if it really was true that politicians were an unsavory lot, then it "merely meant that the people he knew were not a part of the governing class, and that other people were." Ever confident in his abilities to transform himself, to meet any challenge, taking on thugs was merely continuing his tradition of confronting adversity head-on.

His timing could not have been better. When Theodore Roosevelt entered politics, the Republican Party was embroiled in bitter internal divisions, with everyone on the lookout for an eligible young man untainted by any long-standing partisanship. As a fresh new face from a long-established elite New York family, Theodore must have seemed to some of these men a perfect candidate, and in 1881 the party asked him to run for State Assembly. Roosevelt was easily elected, becoming the youngest member of the State Legislature.

Hedging his bets, though, Roosevelt was adamant that politics would not be his sole career path. He considered it a "dreadful misfortune" for a man to stake his entire livelihood on remaining in office. He dabbled with the idea of being a professional writer but met with only marginal success. (His *Naval War of 1812*, which he began writing while a student at Harvard, consumed years of his time, but the reviews were mediocre and sales even less impressive.) Ultimately, none of his interests came close to satisfying the hunger for adventure that still brewed inside him. Ever since the death of his father, Roosevelt had been locked in a struggle to transform himself from a boy with dreams of adventure into a man intent on securing the accoutrements of adulthood—a degree, a wife, and a solid career.

While Theodore grappled with his conflicting instincts, his

brother, Elliott, pursued a more intrepid lifestyle—traveling the globe and acquiring hunting trophies that lined the walls of the Roosevelt home on 57th Street. Teddy observed his brother's adventures jealously, hoping to one day have his own. Months would pass before he got the chance, but when the opportunity presented itself, Theodore seized upon it.

HUNTING WAS IN the midst of a resurgence, as increasing numbers of well-to-do easterners discovered the sport and found it enjoyable. Before the Civil War, people hunted only when it was necessary to survive, but these attitudes began to change with the opening of the American West. As men returned from their time in the wilderness, not only was hunting no longer considered a vice, but it became a virtue, thanks to the hypermasculinity it promoted. The Army, for example, considered sport hunting so conducive to being a soldier that it outright encouraged it. Under General Order No. 9 of August 1879, General William Tecumseh Sherman declared that time taken by an officer for a hunting excursion should not be charged as a leave of absence, the sport being "in so many ways advantageous to the Service." Even Roosevelt would go on to weigh in on the close links between hunting and the military. "The qualities developed by the hunter are the qualities needed by the soldier. . . . No training in the barracks or on the parade-ground is as good as the training given by a hard hunting trip in which the man really does the work for himself, learns to face emergencies, to study the country, to perform feats of hardihood, to face exposure and undergo severe labor. . . . Big-game hunting tends to produce or develop exactly these physical and moral traits."

The fact that Roosevelt came to see hunting as a moral good is telling. For the first time large numbers of Americans were openly and avidly hunting for sport, and as these "hooked-on-hunting" military officers returned to civilian life, they introduced eastern gentlemen to the sport. As it became fashionable, more Americans accepted sport hunting, and a hunting craze gripped the nation.

An opportunity for Roosevelt to profit from this new fervor came on a warm May evening in 1883. He was the keynote speaker at a meeting of the Free Trade Club. The meeting was convened in Clark's Tavern on West 23rd Street, and it had a partylike atmosphere, stocked with ample bumpers of wine and sparkling cider. More than a hundred men attended the event, and among them was Henry Honychurch Gorringe, a retired naval commander just returning from the Dakota Badlands. While he and Roosevelt probably discussed their shared interests in the Navy—Roosevelt had just published his tepidly received *Naval War of 1812*—the conversation inevitably turned to the West and to hunting.

The noise in Clark's Tavern grew louder, and Theodore leaned in closer to hear Gorringe over the din explaining his money-making scheme. New railroads offered cheap and easy access to remote areas, and advanced repeating firearms were now widely available. A novice hunter could be out west in as little as five days, and he no longer had to fuss with ramming black powder, wad, and shot down a muzzleloader. The newer guns, firing metal cartridges and using smokeless powder, were cheap and forgiving; if one missed the first shot, a second and third could be fired off quickly. The West was teeming with big game and even an inexperienced hunter could expect success.

With all this in mind, Gorringe had purchased an old military cantonment in the Dakota Badlands with the intent of turning it into a hunting lodge. The lodge was relatively new, having been constructed by the 6th Infantry only a few years prior to house the fifty-odd soldiers stationed there to protect the construction crews building the Northern Pacific line. Overlooking the cottonwoods that grew along the well-watered banks of the Little Missouri just below, the garrison, with its rough-hewn boards and new tin roof, was the nucleus around which the small town (affectionately called "Little Misery" by the locals) soon grew. Location was what mattered, and at the time that Gorringe purchased the cantonment, the town of Medora sat at the edge of the frontier in the Dakota Badlands. Deer, elk, bighorn sheep, pronghorn, and even bears were still present in that place. Perhaps Theodore would like to be one of the first to arrange a hunt there?

The sales pitch was too good for Theodore to resist. Of course he was interested, and although Gorringe's camp was not quite ready for clients, Medora already had a hotel, a general store, and a few dusty saloons that would accommodate visitors just fine.

Leaving Clark's Tavern later that evening, Roosevelt could not stop thinking about his prospects for a western hunt. The designs for his new Oyster Bay home were nearly complete, and he needed something to hang on its bare walls—deer antlers and perhaps the head of a bison. The grandest of all North American trophies, the bison was of supreme interest to Roosevelt. As a signifier of the rugged American frontier, the bison reigned as king; however, it could not persist much longer against the onslaught of civilization. Before accepting Gorringe's offer, Roosevelt remarked that he intended to shoot an American buffalo "while there were still buffalo left to shoot."

Chapter 8

HELL WITH
THE FIRES OUT

$\mathcal{T}$he American buffalo, or bison, once migrated in the millions, traveling thousands of miles in roughly circular routes across the Great Plains. From preventing the encroachment of trees to cycling soil nutrients through their dung, the bovines were at the fulcrum of an entire ecosystem. For years the region's indigenous tribes had hunted these animals, but never to the detriment of entire populations of them. The introduction of horses (and, later, repeating firearms) made it far easier to kill bison in greater numbers, but it was the advent of railroads that led to their near-total annihilation. Rail tracks cut through the heart of the bisons' migration routes, giving commercial hunters easy access to the herds while at the same time allowing for the transport of bison products east.

Meat was not the primary objective. Pound for pound, bison hides were easier to preserve and transport, and they brought a much better price. Buffalo robes were used by both eastern carriage drivers and western frontiersmen to keep warm. But at the height of the slaughter, given the sheer number of bison being killed, even hides were too much trouble to preserve, so hunters economically harvested only the most valuable part of the animal—the tongue. Smoked and pickled, hundreds of bison tongues could be packed in a single barrel for sale in Atlantic-coast cities, where they were considered a delicacy.

Almost no bison survived in the vicinities of the thousands of miles of rail track that coursed westward across the continent, thus

cutting the once-massive population into distinct northern and southern herds. With the completion of the railroad in the early 1870s, the
southern herd was quickly destroyed. As for the northern herd, extreme cold and the fierce resistance of the Sioux and Cheyenne kept
these animals safe—at least for a time. Inevitably, though, even these
herds were conquered, and in the years leading up to Roosevelt's introduction to the West, the bison there were all but eliminated.

As the time of his western hunt with Gorringe drew near, Roosevelt wrote him a series of letters to fix the date of their departure.
He needed to squeeze the trip in around his busy political schedule,
but he made it clear that he would give it top priority, explaining that
he was "fond of politics, but fonder still of a little big-game hunting."
Adding to the sense of urgency was the fact that Alice was now pregnant, and he most certainly couldn't slip away to the wilderness in the
weeks around her due date.

But Gorringe, knowing something of the plight of the bison, was
having second thoughts about the hunt. Since first proposing the trip
to Roosevelt, he himself had witnessed the decimation of the bison—
and with their decline went all his hopes for a successful hunting-
lodge business. When he finally responded to Roosevelt, it was to
suddenly withdraw from the trip. Undeterred, Roosevelt decided to
complete the venture on his own. Leaving a pregnant Alice behind
with her parents, he boarded a train heading west into what would
become yet another life-changing experience.

CHUGGING WESTWARD, ROOSEVELT watched the landscape change
from the familiar woodlands of the East to rolling brushland and then
to the prairies, where he had only recently hunted with Elliott. It was
the middle of the night when Theodore finally reached his destination
in the Badlands, on the western edge of what is today North Dakota.
He had been traveling for five days straight, and he fumbled with
his gun cases and duffel bag as the train finally screeched to a halt.
He was, however, in no danger of missing his stop—he was the last
remaining passenger, and the crew was eager to be rid of this eastern
dude so that they could finally return home.

Roosevelt stepped out of the carriage into frigid darkness. There was no platform, just one long step onto bare earth. All around him there was nothing but sagebrush and grass. As the locomotive steamed off into the darkness, even the fearless Roosevelt might have suddenly felt a pang of regret as the sound of rolling steel gave way to the quiet of the prairie. Roosevelt stood all alone in what the Northern Pacific Railway travel guide called the most dangerous stop along the line: the settlement of Little Missouri in the heart of the Dakota Badlands.

As his eyes adjusted to the dim light, Roosevelt spotted a large darkened mass against the starry horizon. It was the Pyramid Park— the only hotel in town. After dragging his baggage through the sagebrush, he banged on the door until the owner appeared, looking angry and as if he had been drinking. The man led him upstairs to "the bull pen," where fourteen beds were scattered about here and there. Thirteen were already occupied, and Roosevelt accepted the last one without complaint.

After just a few hours of sleep, Roosevelt wiped the thick prairie dust off the lenses of his glasses and set out to find himself a wilderness guide. The innkeeper's son introduced him to Joe Ferris. But from Roosevelt's pale looks to his rather excited and jerky movements, the easterner didn't seem the hunting type to Ferris. After some convincing and perhaps a gratuity, however, Ferris agreed to take him as a client. Ferris was about the same age as Roosevelt but stockier, and he sported a long, drooping moustache. Despite his strenuous occupation, he had the reputation of being a lazy fellow, one who often slept in rather than working outside on a rainy day. He agreed to guide the tenderfoot fifty miles up the Little Missouri River to a cattle ranch on the Little Cannonball Creek belonging to a man named Gregor Lang.

It didn't matter that Lang had no idea they were coming; they would simply drop in and use his place as a base of operations for hunts into the surrounding countryside. Lang's place was a two-day ride away from the Little Missouri, but Joe Ferris had a brother named Sylvane who lived in a cabin up that way with his partner, Bill Merrifield, so Joe reckoned they could all bunk there as they trekked on toward Lang's.

The taciturn Sylvane and Merrifield greeted Roosevelt icily. As far as they were concerned, he was just another Yankee—and one with funny glasses, at that. They led him into their cabin. With its sod roof and dirt floor, it was more like a burrow than a house. Inside was a stove, a table and chairs, but with just three bunks, Roosevelt would have to sleep on the floor.

None of the men were tired yet, so the group decided to pass the evening with a game of cards. The mood was tense. The frontiersmen didn't quite know how to act around this assemblyman-turned-hunter from New York City, glaring at one another in relative silence. It was an awkward beginning, but everything changed when a sudden, furious squawking erupted from a nearby henhouse. A bobcat had managed to get at the chickens, and everyone, including Roosevelt, grabbed nearby rifles and ran outside to chase off the varmint. They never got off a shot at the cat, but in all the excitement the tensions eased and soon the men discovered they had more in common than initially thought.

The three stoic westerners sharing the cabin with Roosevelt had actually come west from New Brunswick, Canada, to work as wood-cutters for the railroad. Merrifield had later taken up hunting, supplying the railroad with fresh meat, while Sylvane drove mule teams and Joe became a part-time guide. Having some familiarity with the New Brunswick region from his trips to Maine, Roosevelt kept pace with the conversation, soon convincing his hosts that he wasn't a complete novice when it came to the outdoors.

Early the next morning the men readied for the second leg of their journey to Gregor Lang's camp, but Roosevelt ran into what he considered a serious problem. In lieu of a horse, the new man was asked to ride in the back of the wagon with all the gear. He immediately balked at the humiliation. Having come west for adventure, Theodore insisted on having his own steed and when the men didn't acquiesce, he grew livid. In the end, Roosevelt was so insistent that he ended up buying his guide's horse and saddle with cash on the spot.

They arrived at the camp near dusk, just as the owner was sitting down to dinner. Like the Sylvane Ferris and Bill Merrifield house, Lang's cabin was simple—clay roof, dirt floor—but it had a window, which was something of a luxury. A stocky man with bespectacled blue eyes and muttonchops, Lang lived in the cabin with his young son Lincoln. Roosevelt spent this first night talking animatedly with his host about everything from cattle and politics to literature and geology.

Everyone was tired from the long ride, and a late-night rain carried on steadily into the next morning—but, inclement weather or not, Roosevelt intended to hunt. In a bit of a role reversal, Roosevelt roused Joe, and they set out at dawn to cross the Little Missouri and ride across miles of rugged terrain. Roosevelt got a shot at a mule deer but missed, only to watch Ferris drop it on the run with a single lucky shot. Compounding Roosevelt's disappointment, they saw little else that day, returning to Lang's well after dark, soaked and covered in mud. Ferris immediately wrapped himself in his bison robe and went straight to bed, but Roosevelt remained alert and energetic. This pattern continued for the next five days: Roosevelt insisted on getting an early start and then stayed up late to engage in lively discussions with Gregor Lang after the hunt. Joe Ferris was amazed at how woefully he had misjudged Roosevelt and underestimated his stamina, finally admitting that this new eastern tenderfoot was a "plumb good sort."

The rain continued. Sometimes Ferris and Roosevelt caught fleeting glimpses of bison, spooked and running well out of rifle range. Other times they found old tracks but not the animal. Toward the end of the trip, though, they caught a glimpse of three brown specks in the distance. Realizing the futility of attempting to run them down on horseback, they dismounted while still a half mile from their quarry to begin slowly and carefully stalking on their hands and knees. Clumsy Roosevelt blundered into a cactus and came out with a handful of spines but was undaunted. Pressing on, they crawled up to within 150 feet or so of the bison.

Once they were within range, Roosevelt fired. The bullet hit the side of one animal with a loud smack and kicked up a little puff of dust from its hide, but the animal ran off, seemingly unscathed. Disgusted with his poor shot placement—he had clearly missed the animal's "vitals," the heart and lungs—the party ran back to their horses and chased the bison for approximately seven miles, until finally, as the sun was just about to set, they saw the shaggy bull standing in a sheltered hollow. There was no cover, no time for stalking it. In a last-ditch effort they decided to spur on their tired horses in a risky charge.

Night was closing in, and the full moon rose out of the darkness on the horizon as Roosevelt and Ferris drove their horses to a gallop. Finally, they came upon the wounded animal, which stood silently, holding its ground. Suddenly, and at a distance of only twenty feet, the bull began his charge. Roosevelt's pony panicked, rearing up violently and smashing Roosevelt's rifle into his forehead, where it cut a deep gash that bled down into his eyes. "Don't mind me!" Roosevelt cried out to Ferris. "I'm all right!" The bison barreled past Roosevelt's swerving horse in a blur and sped on toward Ferris, chasing him a short distance before lumbering off into the night. Just as quickly as they had found their bison, the bull was gone.

Standing in the dark, bleeding, and unsure of their whereabouts, the two hunters stumbled across the prairie under the light of the moon. It was an hour before they found a fetid source of water for their horses. Exhausted, they didn't bother to build a fire as they made camp and tied their horses to their saddles, which served both as anchors for the horses and as pillows for the men. No sooner had they fallen asleep than their makeshift head supports were yanked out from under them, their horses spooked by wolves. In a further stroke of bad luck, it started to rain, leaving the already unhappy hunters cold, wet, hungry, and—most notably—without their bison prize.

Despite this confluence of miseries, Roosevelt was still captivated with the land. At Lang's cabin he continued his late-night discussions, admitting to his host that he was considering going into the cattle business. He had been suppressing his boyhood reverence for the outdoors, convincing himself that a respectable career in a sedentary field such as law was his only option. But in the Badlands he found a way to combine this urgent need to be in the natural world with an opportunity to make real money, thus supporting his wife and still managing to spend time in the wilderness he so loved.

Ranching was hard work, but Roosevelt was hoping to enter the business as an investor, hiring others to do most of the hard labor while making regular visits west to check in and do a little hunting. He propositioned Lang to take charge of his future herd, but Lang was already committed as caretaker to another wealthy cattle owner. Undeterred, Roosevelt signed contracts with Sylvane Ferris and Bill Merrifield instead—big contracts, committing a sizable portion of his inheritance. He and Merrifield were to purchase a few hundred head of cattle that fall in addition to the fifty Roosevelt was already agreeing to buy out from their current employer. Thoroughly convinced of his plan, Roosevelt simply removed a checkbook from his pocket and, sitting at a log in the open Dakota air, wrote a check for $14,000 for Sylvane. To the astonishment of both Ferris and Merrifield, Roosevelt did not ask for a receipt, coolly exclaiming, "If I didn't trust you men, I wouldn't go into business with you."

A COUPLE OF days after making that deal, Roosevelt was riding over a ridge of broken buttes just over the border in Montana, when both his and Joe Ferris's ponies suddenly reacted to a scent from below. Slipping off his horse, Roosevelt climbed down into a creek bed, there finding a fresh set of bison tracks. He soon spotted the animals that had left them, now grazing up the ravine. Roosevelt would later, in one of his books, describe stalking the bison: "The wind was just right, and no ground could have been better for stalking. Hardly needing to bend down, I walked up behind a small sharp-crested hillock, and, peeping over, there below me, not more than fifty yards off, was the great buffalo bull. He was walking along, grazing as he walked. His glossy fall coat was in fine trim, and shone in the rays of the sun; while his pride of bearing showed him to be in the lusty vigor of his prime." It seemed an almost impossible shot to miss. Here was his second chance, and, aiming just behind the bison's shoulder, Roosevelt fired.

At the sound of the blast the bison ran, but when the men continued up the gully, they found the bull dead.

Roosevelt was so excited at his conquest that he performed a celebratory dance around the carcass. "I never saw anyone so enthused in my life," Ferris recalled, "and by golly, I was so enthused myself for more reasons than one. I was plumb tired out, and, besides, he was so eager to shoot his first bison that it somehow got into my blood; and I wanted to see him kill his first one as badly as he wanted to kill it."

After his buffalo dance, Roosevelt presented his guide with a hundred-dollar tip. He then began the messy business of caping the trophy, as skinning the head of an animal for mounting is called, and removing the rest of the hide and sun drying it so that it would keep long enough for him to get it tanned into a supple robe. The head was taken to a taxidermist in Bismarck so that it could be mounted before his journey home. He said his good-byes to the guides who had made it possible for him to claim such a prize, and he proudly surveyed the landscape just before boarding his train. Lang, watching his impressive guest ride off on his way back east, muttered that Roosevelt was "the most extraordinary man I have ever met."

IN 1886, ONLY three years after Roosevelt shot his bison, Spencer Baird called the Smithsonian's chief taxidermist, William Temple Hornaday, into his office. Having previously been asked to go into their collections to compile an inventory of their *Bison bison* holdings for Baird, Hornaday was dismayed to report that, after rummaging through some dusty cabinets, "the American people's own official museum was absolutely destitute of good bison specimens of every kind." He could find only a few tattered robes and some incomplete skeletons, but nothing that could ever go on exhibit to help educate the American public on the plight of this iconic species.

By then, it was generally assumed that the extermination of the bison was nearly complete and that probably fewer than a few thousand of the animals remained across the remote northwestern portion of the United States. Baird now told Hornaday that he was being sent off at once on a special mission to the Montana Territory. His sole purpose would be to secure bison specimens for exhibition—before the species disappeared entirely. It was to be a three-man expedition, and as its head, Hornaday arrived at Fort Keogh seeking the military escort that Baird had promised would be waiting for him. When he finally found the fort's commander and informed him that he was there on behalf of the Smithsonian Institution for the purpose of collecting museum specimens, the Army commander laughed. "There are no buffalo anymore."

But Hornaday headed into the badlands of easternmost Montana, the last best place to look for bison, and it was here that he found them—in a way. The first was an enormous bull sprawled in the prairie grass. It lay exactly as it had fallen, its head still topped with its dense, woolly mane, the rest of its body but a weathered skeleton. Riding up to the scene, he saw another bison and then several more, until a whole plain of these "ghastly monuments of slaughter" stretched out before him all the way to the horizon. He was too late. At least for the moment, the most the Smithsonian Bison Expedition could hope to find were old bones. Hornaday had come west to shoot a buffalo at a time when there were no longer any buffalo left to shoot.

"HURRAH! . . . I will bring you home the head of a great buffalo bull," Roosevelt wrote to Alice from the field. He had just shot the animal and was flush with adrenaline, excitedly recalling close encounters with rattlesnakes and quicksand before giving her a play-by-play of how he'd killed his bison. Three days later Roosevelt sent a second letter with equally exciting news—her husband was now a cattleman. He had invested in cattle—"very cautiously," he assured her—adding that it would supplement his income as an assemblyman and author. Besides, he reasoned, his trips to the West might also inspire new books, thus bringing in additional money for his growing family.

But even Alice knew that cattle ranching—the get-rich-quick scheme of the early 1880s—was a risky business. Ever since the publication of General James S. Brisbin's book, *The Beef Bonanza, or How to Get Rich on the Plains*, inspired young men of means had been flooding the northern plains, hoping to add to their fortune. Roosevelt knew he was taking a serious gamble by spending as much on Dakota livestock as he had spent on his new Oyster Bay home. But he also knew he could never expect to support his wife and the baby they had on the way as an honest politician.

Roosevelt didn't have much time to think through the decision;

their baby was due in a few months, and, true to form, he acted on impulse. "But, my own darling, everything will be made secondary to *your* happiness, you may be sure," he assured his wife. Despite those words, it was clear that Roosevelt was setting up things so that he could get away from the tedium of domestic life on a regular basis. He was growing somewhat bored with his life at home—still in love with Alice but needing more action than a well-bred, delicate young lady could ever provide. Cattle ranching would allow him a periodic, and very likely adventurous, escape under the pretext of running his cattle business.

Roosevelt had grown accustomed to regular outings in the country to heal himself when he'd suffered from severe asthma, and even as his ailments diminished, he still found that he needed outdoor escapes and the challenge of physical exertion to remain whole. In the Badlands, Roosevelt had found his new retreat. Still sunburned and callused, he headed back up to Albany to begin his third term in the New York State Assembly, but his mind was never far from the Dakotas.

ROOSEVELT WAS AMONG the last cadres of people to shoot a wild bison for sport. He had reached the Little Missouri just before the last great northern herd was completely destroyed. Like most Americans, at the time he considered this the inevitable reality of human progress. The fact that he was also hunting the bison (and contributing to its demise in at least a very small way) didn't occur to him, as the commercial hide hunters were responsible for decimating the herds en masse, oftentimes killing dozens of animals in just one day. In a way, the bison's fate encouraged men like Roosevelt to hunt them while they still could. There was even a name for the phenomenon of shooting the last of something—it was called a "final trophy," and the hunter who shot one held a special distinction among his peers. The importance of conservation—something that seemed so unnecessary in a country of plentiful wilderness—was still far from most Americans' minds.

America was at the peak of its hunting frenzy in 1889. Rapid industrialization, urbanization, and the development of the railroads along with other forms of transportation and communication all combined to effect the speedy development of a wildlife industry. Hunting was not only more accessible but also profitable, and the systematic, commercial exploitation of American wildlife was evident everywhere. Any animal that could be converted into cash was shot and sold.

Also culpable in the destruction of wildlife was the non-hunting urban upper class, whose taste for the exotic was reflected in the bird feathers in their hats, in the buffalo robes draped over their laps in elegant carriages, and on the fancy menus of hotel restaurants. The culinary tastes of America had shifted, making wild game more desirable, if only for its novelty.

Back in New York City, the pregnant Alice had hardly seen Theodore, except for short intervals and weekends, and she was rightly feeling lonely and neglected. They had sublet their brownstone at West 45th Street to Elliott so that Alice could move in with Mrs. Roosevelt, Corinne, and Anna at 6 West 57th Street for more companionship and assistance during the final months of her pregnancy. Here these three rallied around Alice, comforting her and making her feel a part of the family. The Roosevelt women clearly adored her; yet for much of her pregnancy, Roosevelt felt that his work in the legislature was just too important for him to wait by Alice's side, even with her due date mere days away.

Roosevelt learned of the birth of his daughter by a telegram sent to his Albany office. She was born on the evening of February 12, and her mother named her Alice. As word spread through the hall, Democrats and Republicans alike gathered around Roosevelt to congratulate the new father, who was already busy shaking hands and passing out cigars. It was only hours later, though, after receiving a second telegram, that he rushed to catch the next train back home. The message was as short as it was horrible: his mother and wife were both gravely ill.

A great fog enveloped the northeastern states that next day. All transportation came to a near standstill, turning what was normally a five-hour train ride from Albany to New York City into an all-day trip. The locomotive crept along, stop-and-go, painfully slow. Roosevelt couldn't even gaze at the majestic landscape from the window as a distraction, there being nothing but swirling white vapor all around.

The house was already dark when he finally arrived. His brother, usually cheerful and energetic, was solemn when he met Theodore at the door. "There is a curse on this house," he said. Alice was only semiconscious, and she scarcely recognized her husband as he knelt beside her. She had suffered kidney failure, complicated by her pregnancy. A floor below, his mother lay dying of typhoid fever.

Mrs. Roosevelt died at three that morning, and by two o'clock that same afternoon Alice was also dead.

February 14, 1884—Valentine's Day. Roosevelt could do nothing more than ink a thick black *X* in his diary, followed by the single sentence: "The light has gone out of my life." It would be the last entry in his diary for four months as he completely shut down. His despondency was so great that he all but abandoned his newborn daughter, placing her in the care of his sister Anna. A week after the funerals, the residence at 6 West 57th Street was sold, its contents divided among the remaining family.

Emotionally distraught, Roosevelt sought his usual cure, hard labor, and returned to work at once. Heading back up to Albany, he threw himself into the State Assembly, drafting legislation and ferociously arguing his points. Nobody wanted to cross him, and because of this he was unusually successful in getting things done. Those working with him on the Assembly floor recalled a man who refused to talk about his personal tragedy. Despite having seemingly abandoned Alice in the last months of her life, Roosevelt remained as much in love with her as he had been during his college days. "How I did hate to leave my bright, sunny little love yesterday afternoon!" he wrote to her just the week before her death. "I just long for Friday afternoon, when I shall be with you again."

But, as at least one biographer has suggested, Theodore's love for Alice was deeper than simply romance. He had met his wife-to-be in the months shortly after the death of his father six years earlier. The loss of the man who was his most important role model and confidant had hit Roosevelt hard, but he eventually overcame his grief in part through the wilderness exertions he immersed himself in at that time, but also by channeling some of it into affection for a pretty young woman. In Alice, he had found someone to serve as "an emotional replacement for his father," a repository for all his deep feelings and emotions. He was devastated by this second loss, and the emotional damage was so severe that, for the rest of his life, he refused to speak of Alice. His pain was "beyond healing," and when others tried to comfort him with promises of the soothing effects of time, Roosevelt was adamant that it would never get better. Two days after he buried his wife and mother in Green-Wood Cemetery, he summed up his feelings: "For joy or for sorrow, my life has now been lived out."

Chapter 9

CHANGE IN THE WEST

*T*en years before Roosevelt shot his lone bison, before he performed his victory dance and wrote home with the triumphant news of his kill, the man who would one day change Theodore Roosevelt's attitude about wildlife first traveled west into the American frontier. George Bird Grinnell was only about a decade older than Roosevelt, but that made all the difference in how he experienced the West.

Born in Brooklyn, Grinnell had much in common with the younger man. His parents were wealthy New York elites, the principal Wall Street agents to Cornelius Vanderbilt, and George was sickly. When he was eight, Grinnell's family moved to the countryside of Upper Manhattan on account of his health. "The city" proper did not extend much farther north than 23rd Street, yet the Grinnells relocated all the way up to Audubon Park, a tract of land bounded by what is today West 158th and 155th Streets between Amsterdam Avenue and the Hudson River. The land was part of the estate of the great naturalist John James Audubon, and his widow was still living there with her sons and grandchildren, gradually selling off subplots in order to survive.

For the young Grinnell, Audubon Park was heaven. The land was fields and woods, left in a wild state of nature. Their house stood at what is today 157th Street and Riverside Drive, with a cow pasture just a block north; what is now the subway entrance on Broadway marks the former Grinnell garden plot. George freely roamed the stands of oak and chestnut that cloaked Upper Manhattan and followed hemlock-shaded brooks down to the Hudson.

Before this move to the country, Grinnell's most formative connection to nature had come from his uncle Tom. An avid hunter and taxidermist, Tom had shot and stuffed enough birds to make a little museum in his home. The so-called "bird room" was kept in Grinnell's grandfather's house, and George marveled at the collection every time he visited. Like Roosevelt, Grinnell had been an avid reader of Thomas Mayne Reid's books, many years later citing their influence on him. "I had been brought up, so to speak, on the writings of Captain Mayne Reid. . . . His stories had appealed to my imagination, and I had always been eager to visit the scenes he described." To Grinnell, Uncle Tom seemed like a character out of *Boy Hunters*, and he reenacted the stories his uncle told him while stalking through the woods near his home.

Grinnell had been drawn to guns at an early age, but, unlike Roosevelt, he did not have his parents' permission to use one. He and another boy convinced the village tailor to secretly lend them an old British muzzle-loader, though neither Grinnell nor his companion could hold up the long musket on their own. Instead, they took turns resting the gun on each other's shoulders, which gave them the leverage to wield and aim the massive musket. In the shadow of John James Audubon, Grinnell found bird hunting to be his avenue into serious natural-history study, and he avidly pursued all kinds of songbirds. Audubon's own grandson even became his hunting partner, and in later years they would together try out some of the famed naturalist's old muskets along the Hudson River, shooting muskrats as the rodents emerged through holes in the winter ice.

Visiting the various Audubon kin surrounding him, Grinnell was impressed by how their houses were so full of things belonging to the great naturalist—from racks of deer and elk antlers supporting rifles and shotguns, to old powder horns and shot pouches. There were quite a few big-game trophies from his early western expeditions, bookcases stocked with natural-history books, and hundreds of

Audubon's paintings and drawings. One of Grinnell's favorite boyhood play areas was Audubon's old barn, the loft of which was being used by one of his sons for his own natural-history pursuits.

John Woodhouse Audubon was as much of a naturalist as his father and as such he was in regular communication with naturalists stationed across the country. This led to a constant stream of boxes containing freshly collected specimens, which George Grinnell and the Audubon grandsons all helped unpack. It was there in the barn, working with the extended Audubon family, that Grinnell got his earliest and most important exposure to the mysteries of taxidermy and museum specimens.

Early on, Grinnell had been schooled by "Grandma Audubon"—the great birdman's widow—who ran a small classroom for the neighborhood children out of her bedroom. By then well into her seventies, Lucy Audubon had a reputation for allowing boys to discover themselves, and while this might have fed Grinnell's passion for the hunt, it left him ill-prepared academically. As Grinnell later described Lucy, she was "a beautiful, white-haired old lady with extraordinary poise and dignity; most kindly and patient and affectionate . . . of whom all the children stood in awe."

Despite good family connections at Yale, Grinnell struggled to meet the university's minimum admission requirements, but he was eventually accepted. He was "perpetually in trouble" and was even suspended for a time during his sophomore year. By his own admission, Grinnell "wasted" his years in college. All he wanted to do was hike through the woods with his gun, looking for adventure. He kicked about Yale, dreading the date of his graduation, knowing that his father was eager to set him down to a life of desk-bound misery in the family stockbrokerage firm on Wall Street.

The obvious parallels to Theodore's life—the city where he grew up; his childhood illness; ready access to the countryside, guns, and hunting; an interest in taxidermy and Captain Thomas Mayne Reid—would one day solidify the bond between the two men. But Grinnell and Roosevelt were not unique in this regard; many boys shared a similar set of interests. Hardy rural life had long been the norm in America, but rapid urbanization brought with it a pronounced backlash effect, essentially shocking society into retreating to nature. At the same time, rapid westward expansion was sending a steady flow of new and unusual animal specimens back east, where naturalists such as Spencer Baird and Louis Agassiz were busy describing them. Charles Darwin's relatively recently published *On the Origins of Species by Means of Natural Selection* created a growing awareness of evolution, also making nature study all the rage in mid- to late-nineteenth-century America. Natural history was a rapidly advancing, cutting-edge science, and it was considered important to a child's development.

Like Roosevelt a decade later, Grinnell longed for his chance to have some real adventures in the outdoors. He was also looking for an escape from having to work in his father's company. Salvation came in the spring of 1870, just a few months before his graduation from Yale. A rumor was spreading that Professor Othniel Charles Marsh was planning a fossil hunt out west and was looking for Yale graduates to help him dig. Short and stocky, with a receding hairline and full beard, Marsh had the studious look of a formidable academician. He had only recently assumed the post of curator of paleontology after his rich uncle George Peabody donated the money to found Yale's Peabody Museum of Natural History in 1866. The Peabody was a significant addition to America's growing body of natural-history museums, led at that time by Spencer Baird's Smithsonian collection and Louis Agassiz's Harvard museum. After his western digs, Marsh returned to his museum with the remains of a tiny primitive horse. Naming his find *Equus parvulus,* Marsh described the horse as "scarcely a yard in height, each of his slender legs was terminated by three toes." The find added key support to the theory of evolution and reaffirmed to Marsh the West's enormous potential as an untapped fossil bed.

Grinnell, having finally found a career worth pursuing, suddenly felt a pang of regret for squandering his college years. He wanted to join Marsh's upcoming expedition but feared he would never be considered, thanks to his terrible school record. It took the nervous Grinnell days to approach Marsh and explain his interest. Marsh was apparently not impressed and discouraged him at first, but after a second meeting he revised his opinion, deciding that pluck, native intelligence, and a free-spirited wanderlust—qualities Grinnell had in abundance—were more important on an expedition than school grades. He invited Grinnell to join his expedition. Moreover, he asked him to invite friends—as many as a dozen. The group left New Haven on June 30, 1870, bound for a West that, as Grinnell described it, "was really wild and woolly."

Theodore Roosevelt was only twelve years old when George Grinnell joined the Marsh Expedition in 1870. It was the peak of the Wild West, with Native American intertribal conflict and bison hunting rampant. In this dangerous climate, the expedition could proceed thanks to the backing of two powerful men: General William Tecumseh Sherman, head of the Army, and General Philip Sheridan, head of western forts. Using the newly constructed Union Pacific rail line to access a string of frontier forts, Marsh hoped to trace a path through western Nebraska, Colorado, and Wyoming in search of fossils.

Arriving at their first stop, Fort McPherson on the banks of the North Platte River, they were met by three antelope hunters straggling back to the fort, one with an arrow sticking out of his arm. The hunters had been attacked by a band of Sioux warriors but managed to kill one before beating a hasty retreat. It was a rather shocking way for the Yale neophytes to begin their western jaunt, and, not wanting to take any chances with his life—or, perhaps, not wanting to *miss* any chances for adventure—Grinnell made a point of always carrying a rifle, a bowie knife, and a revolver in addition to the requisite geological rock hammer.

Trailed by six Army wagons full of provisions, feed, tents, and plenty of ammo, Grinnell found adventure along the trail. He wandered off to hunt ducks with a companion one day, only to suddenly realize they had gotten lost. Stopping to smoke their pipes and regroup, they touched off a massive prairie fire. Fleeing just ahead of the roaring flames, they realized that the blaze had most certainly given away their position to the hostile Sioux watching from the surrounding bluffs. In a bit of subterfuge, they dismounted and lit a campfire to give the appearance of making camp for the night, then left the fire burning and made a hasty retreat after darkness fell, eventually retracing their steps to the safety of the real camp.

After five months in the field, the Marsh expedition brought back to the Peabody an impressive trove of fossils. These specimens were of interest not only to the scientific community, but to the American public at large. Over one hundred species of extinct vertebrates new to science were discovered, including toothed birds, fossil horses, and a flying reptile called a pterodactyl. All were excellent proof of the validity of Darwin's evolutionary theory—which was then a hotly contested argument. Furthermore, there were enough fossils to sustain Marsh's career for decades.

As Grinnell discovered on the trip, the West was a hodgepodge of rocky outcrops from different geologic ages, and while some yielded dinosaurs from tens of millions of years ago, other formations yielded the remains of more recently extinct species. Keeping all these fossils in proper context required making careful notes on the geology and the particular layers of rock in which the specimens were found. In this way scientists could separate the truly ancient fossils. Of the more recent fossils, Grinnell dug up specimens of the extinct, long-horned bison that had once roamed the western plains along with the lion, cheetah, hyenas, and even rhinos. The North American fauna was at one time very reminiscent of the modern-day fauna of East Africa—a revelation that fascinated Grinnell, opening his eyes to the methods of serious scientific inquiry.

The Marsh expedition marked a turning point in the exploration of the West. Previous expeditions had focused more on charting unfamiliar mountains and plotting river courses, and natural-history specimens had been collected on only a catch-as-catch-can basis. After the Marsh expedition, natural-history exploration took on a decidedly more systematic approach, as naturalists thought more about the bigger picture, collecting their specimens to inform an overarching context about the diversity of life.

George Bird Grinnell was part of this vanguard of sophisticated naturalists who saw specimen collecting as more than merely filling museums' drawers; he used specimens as clues to understanding the plight of the fauna in the West. Regardless of whether he was looking at the disappearance of North America's megafauna over geological time or at the more pressing extinction of the bison, the Marsh expedition made Grinnell keenly aware of nature's constantly changing landscape.

Back from his five-month western jaunt, with no other plans and little means for supporting himself, Grinnell very reluctantly settled into working at his father's brokerage house on Wall Street. The life of a stockbroker hardly compared to the adventures he had known out west. Longing for his next chance to be employed as a naturalist, he roamed the woods and fields of Audubon Park at night, keeping his instincts sharp. He also visited local taxidermy shops on weekends—including John Bell's, where young Theodore Roosevelt would learn the craft of stuffing and preserving—in the hopes of finding specimens to send to Professor Marsh at Yale's Peabody Museum of Natural History in New Haven. For several years Grinnell supplemented his late-night walks with a hobby in taxidermy; as he later recalled, he would spend "two or three hours in the evening down in the cellar, where I had an excellent outfit for mounting birds." But bird stuffing alone could hardly satisfy his quest for adventure, and he was "anxious again to go out West."

Theodore Roosevelt was just fourteen years old as George Bird Grinnell galloped across the plains of northern Kansas in 1872. Grinnell had heard through contacts at the Peabody Museum that the Pawnee tribe was about to embark on a massive buffalo hunt, and he was desperately trying to catch up to them in time to get in on the action. Confined to a small reservation along Nebraska's Loup River, twice a year the Pawnee were permitted to pursue buffalo on their traditional hunting grounds. For Grinnell, the hunt was a valuable window into the quickly vanishing Native American way of life, a return to the "old free life of earlier years, when the land had been all their own, and they had wandered at will over the broad expanse of the rolling prairie."

Grinnell caught up with the grand procession, led by eight men carrying buffalo poles—flags of red and blue cloth used to guide the hunters to the buffalo herd. "Here was nature," he marveled at the scene.

Grinnell galloped across the plains of Kansas with more than eight hundred Pawnee intent on marauding a herd of more than a thousand buffalo. The strategy was for every man to ride directly into the herd, with some of the faster riders double-timing to the opposite side of the herd, where they hoped to turn it, driving the bison directly into the main body of hunters following. Approaching in a long, crescent formation, they got to within half a mile before some of the animals rose to their feet. Those men leading the hunt then gave the *Loo-ah* cry and started galloping toward the herd in unison. Grinnell, among the main body of slower riders, found himself "in the midst of a throng of buffalo, horses, and Indians." Shooting at stampeding targets, dodging the bison horns appearing and disappearing in the clouds of dust, he watched massive buffalo tumble and fall to the ground all around him.

In 1874—a year when George Bird Grinnell seemed to be everywhere the action was taking place out west—Theodore Roosevelt was still traipsing around Oyster Bay, trying to convince his cousins to take his museum seriously. Grinnell ran with George Armstrong Custer and an army of hundreds of men. True, he was simply tagging along to collect fossils for Yale's Peabody Museum, but he also eagerly joined the ranks of the expedition's meat hunters, which on certain days killed "100 deer or more."

While Roosevelt was taking his first classes at Harvard, further adventures unfolded for Grinnell. He was invited to be the naturalist on the 1875 expedition to explore Yellowstone National Park, led by Captain William Ludlow. The park had been created only three years earlier, and Ludlow's mission was to discover exactly what had been preserved when the land was set aside. It was generally known that there were geysers, hot springs, and spectacular geological formations in Yellowstone, but nobody was seriously thinking about protecting the land yet. The park had been created in large part as a place where geological oddities could be on exhibit—a kind of outdoor museum of curiosities and wonders rather than a sacred space for nature.

However, when Grinnell and the Ludlow expedition finally reached Old Faithful, they discovered something very disturbing: a large party of whiskey traders was already set up for business. Additionally, the park was overrun by poachers. Incensed, Grinnell focused his expedition report on the plight of the park's animals and wildlife, issuing a stern warning: "It is certain that, unless in some way the destruction of these animals can be checked, the large game still so abundant in some localities will ere long be exterminated."

Perhaps more than any other naturalist at that time, Grinnell understood the delicate dynamics of the western big-game fauna. From his fossil digs he knew that the land had once supported lions and cheetahs and hyenas, and he had held the skulls of now-extinct dire wolves in his hands. Like that of few other naturalists in the 1870s, Grinnell's mind was uniquely trained to think of the western fauna in terms of extinction. In a time when few Americans believed that the modern buffalo could ever disappear, his viewpoint would become incredibly valuable.

Publishing the first of what would become many articles in the influential sporting journal *Forest and Stream*, Grinnell issued a prescient warning about the bison: "[T]heir days are numbered, and unless some action on this subject is speedily taken not only by the States and Territories, but by the National Government, these shaggy brown beasts, these cattle upon a thousand hills, will ere long be among the things of the past." Although the response to this call was mixed, Grinnell was not deterred from arguing his point, instead becoming much more vocal about the plight of big game in the American West.

Around this time, *Forest and Stream* needed an editor for its natural-history page, and Grinnell was the obvious choice for such a job. In exchange for ten dollars a week, Grinnell started writing a page or so for the magazine. His audience was sportsmen—hunters and anglers—and it was this constituency that emerged as the first real champions for the conservation of wildlife. Their collective voice continued to call for a halt to the slaughter of the buffalo, as well as pronghorn antelope and the elk. It also argued for the implementation of sensible game laws that could be enforced. It was a movement that had never been so well organized, and its voice of conscience would soon reach the ears of a young Theodore Roosevelt.

AFTER THE LONG and sullen spring of 1884 and what seemed an equally long train ride back to the Little Missouri, Theodore Roosevelt opened his diary for the first time in months and wrote, emotionless: "Arrived at my cattle ranch."

Roosevelt had never felt so alone in the world. The nearly simultaneous deaths of his wife and mother had left him so dazed that everyone close to him feared he would lose his mind. "He does not know what he does or says," remarked one acquaintance. To escape his internal demons, he needed the kind of solitude found only in the deepest nature of the Badlands. A landscape of desolate buttes and scorched mesas, the Dakota landscape was aptly described as "hell with the fires out"—the perfect place for an intense man to grieve.

He arrived in the summer of 1884, but any emotional healing was postponed as he toured his ranch and took stock of his herd. Roosevelt was new to ranching, and he had good reason to be concerned about his investment; the year prior had seen a spectacular financial meltdown in the United States. Thousands of financial institutions collapsed overnight, shutting down the entire banking system and paralyzing credit. But Roosevelt had $62,500 at his disposal—his inheritance from his mother's estate—and that gave him enormous purchasing power, especially given the economic climate. To his mind, the prevailing panic in the financial world was an opportunity to make a fortune by buying cattle cheaply.

Riding across the Badlands once again with his newly minted business partners, Bill Merrifield and Sylvane Ferris, Roosevelt learned that most of his herd had made it through their first winter. He had lost only 25 of his 440 cattle to wolves and the cold—a number more than offset by the birth of 155 new calves. Although it had been an unusually mild winter, the local newspaper—the *Badlands Cowboy*—had convinced him that the sheltered canyons and coulees of the terrain were uniquely suited to protecting the herds from even the harshest winters. Encouraged by this, he decided to double his investment.

Three days later Roosevelt, Merrifield, and Ferris rode down to Gregor Lang's ranch to draw up a contract committing $26,000, close to half of Roosevelt's inheritance. Sending the two cowboys off with his money to buy cattle in Minnesota, he trusted them to invest it wisely, as managing money was not among his talents. He was too much of a romantic dreamer, evidenced by the two things he wanted more than anything else—a buckskin suit with all the fancy cowboy embroidery work, and the chance to shoot the quintessentially western game species, the pronghorn antelope.

The pronghorn, this speedy runner of the American West, with its short, stocky body and peculiar, backward-hooked horns, was unlike any other mammal Roosevelt had seen, truly native to the land. Even that most iconic of American mammals, the bison, was a relatively recent invader, only appearing in the North American fossil record during the last interglacial period, or roughly within the last half million years. The pronghorn (*Antilocapra americana*), however, had evolved in North America, its lineage going back tens of millions of years, and it was the sole survivor of a diverse radiation of American antelope that had once shared the plains with mammoths (*Mammuthus columbi*), giant ground sloths (*Megalonyx jeffersonii*), and lions (*Panthera leo atrox*).

Lincoln Lang, in whom Roosevelt had confided these wishes for a cowboy costume and a chance at a pronghorn, came up with a plan that he thought would satisfy both desires. He knew of a woman called Old Lady Maddox living some twenty-five miles to the east who still knew how to make such suits. As a further incentive, the Deadwood trail to her place passed through excellent pronghorn habitat. They left the next morning, and Lincoln later recalled that their journey was one of almost constant "lopes and pauses," since Roosevelt was always seeing something out of their way that he wanted to investigate. They stopped to take a shot at a prowling coyote, to kill a rattlesnake, and to enjoy a spectacular view from a commanding eminence, racing their ponies hard between pauses to make up the lost time. They examined peculiar rock formations, watched a belligerent king-bird harry a hawk, and paused to ponder odd-looking fossils. Roosevelt was again completely captivated and would have seemed almost boyish in his enthusiasm were it not for the fact that he actually knew things about some of the species they were observing, reciting their scientific names to Lincoln with delight.

One encounter in particular impressed Lincoln. Riding through a bottomland, they were drawn to a commotion in the sagebrush, a loud squeaking of an animal in distress. Turning sharply, they rode over to investigate and found a half-grown jackrabbit struggling desperately in the coils of a large bullsnake. Hastily dismounting, the two men "basted the life out of" the snake and proceeded to administer first aid to the panting bunny. Carefully picking it up, Roosevelt set it in the crook of his arm; he felt it over gently for broken bones, but it was barely injured. Satisfied that the rabbit was able to take care of itself, he released it "beamingly while expressing joy over the happy outcome. 'There goes a sore but wise rabbit,' Roosevelt said as the animal made off stiffly through the sage-brush."

Arriving at Old Lady Maddox's, Roosevelt found her to be strong, fearless, and deadly accurate with a rifle—vital for a woman living alone in the Dakota Badlands. Heavyset, muscular, and rather short of stature, she had years ago evicted her scoundrel of a husband with an iron poker, no doubt threatening worse if he ever came back. But to Theodore and Lincoln, she displayed a warm affection, serving them a hot meal before measuring Roosevelt for his suit. She would have it ready for him in a couple of weeks, she said. To Roosevelt, the fringed-buckskin hunting garb was "the most picturesque and distinctly national dress ever worn in America"—the quintessential western costume. Every one of his heroes had worn buckskin suits, going all the way back to the musket-toting trappers and mountain men who had first penetrated the wilderness. It was "the dress in which Daniel Boone was clad when he first passed through the trackless forests of the Alleghenies" and "the dress worn by grim Davy Crockett when he fell at the Alamo."

Thanking Old Lady Maddox for her hospitality, they hastened back to the ranch. On their way to her, they had passed a few pronghorn feeding in a depression, and, peering down from a hillock,

Roosevelt could see that the animals were still there, not more than a hundred yards below. It was an easy shot, and Roosevelt raised his rifle and dropped one where it stood. At once, his calm composure was lost, broken by the thrill of bagging that all-American specimen, and with wild enthusiasm he launched into another impromptu victory dance, his rifle in one hand, waving his hat with the other. "I got him! I got him!"

Roosevelt insisted on gutting the animal himself, and, with dried bloodstains on his hands and forearms, and two hindquarters of meat draped over his saddle, he took a long, circuitous route back to his ranch. As he basked in the glory of his successful hunt and the beautiful surroundings, Roosevelt's mind quieted enough to reflect. The wild, open country was good for him. Riding hard across the lonely plains, he thought about the past year's events. So much had happened, much of it tragic but some of it sublime. He loved the wide-open country but was still not entirely sure of himself in the West. He could look forward to donning his buckskin cowboy suit, but could he really consider himself a man of the wilderness? Shooting and gutting a pronghorn was one thing, but could he really survive out in this harsh landscape on his own? More to the point, would he ever overcome the tragic losses of his father, his mother, and his wife and make a fresh new start in life? Had his life really been "lived out" on Alice's death, or was he merely on the cusp of a new opportunity in the West? Ever pushing himself, testing his mental and physical resolve, Roosevelt was determined to find out, despite the inherent risks. He was going to take a solitary hunt across the Badlands in an effort to prove to himself that he could do it all on his own and survive.

Packing little more than his rifle, a book, a tin cup, and a few other essentials, he set out on horseback early the next morning. He rode silently, enjoying the songs of the shy woodland thrushes in the gray dawn. As the morning sunshine cast pink and then brilliant red tints against the distant buttes, the awakening prairie was bursting with birdsong. The spring migration was under way, and the thickets and groves were alive with the winged creatures. For the first time in a very long while, Roosevelt took time to listen to them: the sad and "inexpressibly touching" call of the meadowlark, the "sweet, sad songs" of the hermit thrush, and the soft melancholy cooing of the mourning-dove, "whose voice always seems far away and expresses more than any other sound in nature the sadness of gentle, hopeless, never-ending grief."

He rode for hours over the seemingly limitless plains and ever-changing landscape. "One day I would canter hour after hour over the level green grass, or through miles of wild rose thickets, all in bloom; on the next I would be amidst the savage desolation of the Badlands, with their dreary plateaus, fantastically shaped buttes and deep, winding canyons." And through every landscape he experienced an incredible feeling of solitude. "Nowhere, not even at sea, does a man feel more lonely than when riding over the far-reaching, seemingly never-ending plains."

Roosevelt wanted to see if he could go it alone in the wilderness, and he succeeded beyond his expectations, feeling perfectly at home in this alien landscape. Much the way he had wandered in the Adirondacks or the deep woods of Maine, Roosevelt rode through the Badlands in search of game by day, and at night he lay wrapped up in his blanket, looking at the stars until he fell asleep, perhaps reflecting back on the time when his father had first read aloud from *The Last of the Mohicans* on a starry night in the Adirondack wilderness. It had been just three weeks since Roosevelt returned west, and already he felt transformed. Having arrived a grieving and confused widower with little knowledge or experience of the West, in a whirlwind of action, he had not only expanded his cattle holdings significantly, but also learned how to ride with cowboys, proved himself with a solo hunt on the prairie, and made plans for a second ranch house. Emboldened by his time on the frontier, Roosevelt penned a final tribute to the wife he had lost:

She was beautiful in face and form, and lovelier still in spirit; as a flower she grew, and as a fair young flower she died. Her life had been always in the sunshine; there had never come to her a great sorrow . . . loving, tender, and happy as a young wife; when she had just become a mother, when her life seemed to be just begun, and when the years seemed so bright before her—then, by a strange and terrible fate, death came to her. And when my heart's dearest died, the light went from my life for ever.

Despite this dramatic proclamation, the wilderness proved a salve to Roosevelt's wounds. He had been leveled by grief, but that sorrow brought him full circle, back to the naturalist roots of his childhood, and he used his love of that world to build himself back up. No longer just a hunter, he heard more clearly the very birdsong that had first stirred his passions as a naturalist so many years before, as if calling him back to a life in nature that he had too hastily abandoned.

———— ⤙ ⤚ ————

Chapter 10

WINCHESTER NATURALIST

At his Chimney Butte Ranch, Roosevelt wore a fringed buckskin suit, a loosely knotted silk bandanna, oversize sealskin chaps, and pointed alligator boots. A pearl-handled Colt rested on his hip, and he gripped an ornately engraved Winchester rifle. Clearly, he felt every inch a westerner, but to any cowboy passing by in the Badlands, the dapper dude must have seemed crazy, his getup more like the costume of someone playing at the cattle business than that of a practical rancher. Had he not just purchased a couple hundred head of cattle? And had he not just begun building an even newer ranch house?

Despite his performance-worthy outfit, Roosevelt still managed to get important work done. His men would soon finish building his second ranch, which he named Elkhorn in honor of the two skulls he had found on the site with antlers interlocked. "Theirs had been a duel to the death," Roosevelt remarked. That the eponymous elk had been all but shot out in the immediate vicinity of his ranch was unimportant; there were still plenty farther out west, and that was exactly where he was heading to write a western hunting book.

Roosevelt was a compulsive writer who, at the age of twenty-three, had already published a naval history with G. P. Putnam's Sons. He saw the West as a place fertile with stories, its people, somehow larger than life, living in extremis amid a rugged terrain and, more important to Roosevelt, with plenty of opportunities for hunting game. Roosevelt was trying his best to stitch himself into this scene, using his garb as one entry point. He could rightly claim to have lived and worked as a cowboy and to have successfully hunted deer and antelope, but so, too, had hundreds of other easterners.

What Theodore now wanted most was to bag an immense elk or maybe even a grizzly bear. These were the frontier's most iconic species, trophies that would mean something to the people back in Oyster Bay. Of even greater interest than this, though, was the rare opportunity to observe firsthand how the animals of the West behaved— something he had been reading about since he was a little boy. To see them at their wildest, he'd have to go deep into the frontier, so he set off for the remote Bighorn Mountains of northern Wyoming.

The Bighorns were hundreds of miles southwest of his ranch. The railroads had not yet reached them, and since there were no roads or signposts to guide them, his party—which consisted of himself, Bill Merrifield, and a man named Lebo, who was their French-Canadian teamster and cook—simply set off with a wagonload of gear in the general direction of the mountains. It would be four weeks before they even spied the Bighorns in the distance.

This was to be no mere hunting trip—it more closely resembled an expedition. Roosevelt and Merrifield rode ahead while their canvas-covered supply wagon rumbled behind. They traveled west across the hot plains of southern Montana for days, shooting birds and jackrabbits for meat. When they finally reached the foothills of the Bighorns along the banks of Crazy Woman Creek, Wyoming, the group abandoned their wagon and rigged up a pack train to carry them up into the mountains. Roosevelt recalled the hard work of the journey, writing, "No one who has not tried it can understand the work and worry that it is to drive a pack train over rough ground and through timber. We were none of us very skilful [sic] at packing, and the loads were all the time slipping; sometimes the ponies would stampede with the pack half tied, or they would get caught among the fallen logs, or in a ticklish place would suddenly decline to follow the trail, or would commit some one of the thousand other tricks which seem to be all a pack pony knows."

The men traveled light, each riding a stout horse while distributing their packs on four other animals. Besides the elaborate costume he was wearing, Roosevelt packed a coon-skin overcoat, an otter fur robe that buttoned into a sleeping bag, oilcloth slickers, moccasins, overalls, a jersey, two flannel shirts, three suits of light and heavy underclothing, heavy socks, "plenty of handkerchiefs, soap, towels, washing and shaving things," and rubber blankets. He packed three rifles, a shotgun, and a revolver along with 1,700 rounds of ammunition for them all. Having no tent, they strung up the canvas wagon cover instead. For food they brought enough flour, bacon, beans, coffee, sugar, and salt to last them the four months until Christmas, if necessary. The frontier was unpredictable, and they needed to be ready for any contingency.

Swift-flowing brooks of clear, icy water flowed down from the rocky peaks of the Bighorns, and the men found it pleasant to climb up through the cool and shadowy pines—a respite from the burning prairie. Upward they climbed, reaching a parklike mosaic of dense woods and open glades, the perfect place for stalking game. Moving noiselessly in his soft moccasins, Roosevelt recorded his glimpses of the "inner life" of the mountains: "Each animal that we saw had its own individuality. Aside from the thrill and tingle that a hunter experiences at the sight of his game, I by degrees grew to feel as if I had a personal interest in the different traits and habits of the wild creatures . . . and it was pleasant to watch them in their own homes, myself unseen, when after stealthy, silent progress through the somber and soundless depths of the woods I came upon them going about the ordinary business of their lives." Although hunting these animals with a rifle, Roosevelt understood the potential for marrying hunting with naturalism. Becoming a predator himself, Roosevelt stalked his quarry while still very much intent on learning its natural history. "The true still-hunter should be a lover of nature as well as of sport, or he will miss half the pleasure of being in the woods."

Despite these musings, the group's first day of hunting was a bloodbath; they shot more elk than they ever could have used. Roosevelt killed a mother and calf, and Merrifield shot two others. Even Lebo shot two mule deer. Yet none of these was a trophy bull, and

Roosevelt was determined to keep hunting until he shot one. Eventually he got his chance. He had been advancing with the usual caution, keeping the wind in his face so that his scent drifted away. Making as little noise as possible, he stepped out into a patch of open ground and there came upon a great bull elk "beating and thrashing his antlers against a young tree." The bull stopped and faced him for a second, "his mighty antlers thrown in the air" as Roosevelt sent a bullet tumbling through his flesh just behind the shoulder. "No sportsman can ever feel much keener pleasure and self-satisfaction than when, after a successful stalk and good shot, he walks up to a grand elk lying dead in the cool shade of the great evergreens, and looks at the massive and yet finely molded form, and at the mighty antlers which are to serve in the future as the trophy and proof of his successful skill."

His trophy elk secured, Roosevelt shifted his attention to grizzlies. Pursuing a grizzly bear was especially dangerous (and, thus, especially interesting to Roosevelt) and something he had previously only read about in his boyhood books. Merrifield was, at the time, hunting about ten miles from camp and returned after a week with news of definite grizzly signs. Shooting another elk for bait and setting it out for the bear, Roosevelt waited impatiently for his first close encounter. Grizzly bears are some of the largest land predators in North America, attaining weights of well over one thousand pounds. Normally active at night and in twilight, they can be ill-tempered and dangerous if surprised during the day, and they have been known to attack without provocation. The hunters, however, had tipped the scales in their favor. Laying out an enticing pile of meat, they knew exactly where to expect their quarry and could approach it with caution. Quietly sneaking up to where they had laid out the dead elk, they discovered that, indeed, a bear had fed off the bait that first night, tearing large chunks out of it. Roosevelt and Merrifield tracked the bear to a tangled thicket of spruce:

I saw Merrifield, who was directly ahead of me, sink suddenly to his knees and turn half round, his face fairly ablaze with excitement. Cocking my rifle and stepping quickly forward, I found myself face to

face with the great bear, who was less than twenty-five feet off, not
eight steps. He had been roused from his sleep by our approach: he
sat up in his lair, and turned his huge head slowly towards us. At that
distance and in such a place it was very necessary to kill or disable him
at the first fire; doubtless my face was pretty white, but the blue barrel
was steady as a rock as I glanced along it until I could see the top of the
bead fairly between the two sinister looking eyes; as I pulled the trigger
I jumped aside out of the smoke, to be ready if he charged; but it was
needless, for the great brute was struggling in the death agony . . .

That brown bear—a fine specimen and a symbol of North American game—would remain forever emblazoned in Roosevelt's mind. That it had made some move to attack before falling to his gun meant a great deal to him, for there could be no greater challenge to his courage. The encounter, as Roosevelt described it, might just as well have been a chapter in a Thomas Mayne Reid adventure novel. Captain Reid had, indeed, described a very similar grizzly-bear encounter in his *Boy Hunters*, in which the adventurers shot three grizzly bears, not just one, coming to their bait.

Altogether the hunters shot six elk, three grizzly bears, seven deer, and 109 small-game animals, always making a special effort to get the most impressive animals. Two weeks into their hunting, the first snow flurries of winter began to fall. It was an ominous sign. In the Bighorns such snows could portend a blizzard lasting days, and the group thought it best to pack up their trophies and start off for home. In all, Roosevelt and Merrifield spent seven weeks on their Bighorns hunt—a length of time in the field Roosevelt would not match until his future expedition to Africa.

When Roosevelt returned to his sister Anna's New York apartment just a few days before Christmas, he was surprised to see that his baby daughter had sprouted soft blond ringlets in his absence. She was so like her mother that, for Roosevelt, the reminder of his wife was painful. He sought solace in his writing, and, with memories of the Bighorns still fresh, he began to pen his observations on the American West. He opened with a warning: "After the buffalo, the elk are the first animals to disappear from a country when it is settled. . . ." From there he worked so furiously that in just nine weeks' time, the book was done.

Hunting Trips of a Ranchman represented a departure for Roosevelt, his first western big-game hunting book. Lavishly bound, it was replete with triumphant details of his hunts, but it also included lengthy passages on the natural history of the game he bagged. Part adventure story, part natural history, the book was a unique mélange, and Roosevelt eagerly awaited the first reviews.

THE EDITOR OF *Forest and Stream* magazine, fellow New Yorker George Bird Grinnell, was one of the first to personally review Roosevelt's *Hunting Trips of a Ranchman*. His comments were mixed: "Mr. Roosevelt is not well-known as a sportsman, and his experience of the Western country is quite limited, but this very fact in one way lends an added charm to his book. He has not become accustomed to all the various sights and sounds of the plains and . . . mountains, and for him all the differences which exist between the East and the West are still sharply defined. . . . Mr. Roosevelt's accounts of life on a ranch are delightful from their freshness."

Roosevelt was less than pleased by the suggestion that he was inexperienced, but as the review went on, the criticism grew even more pointed: "Where Mr. Roosevelt details his own adventures he is accurate, and tells his story in simple, pleasant fashion, which at once brings us into sympathy with him. We are sorry to see that a number of hunting myths are given as fact, but it was after all scarcely to be expected that with the author's limited experience he could sift the wheat from the chaff and distinguish the true from the false."

By the time he finished reading, Roosevelt was livid. All this talk about his "limited experience" and "simple fashion" was tantamount to calling his naïveté charming, but it was the damning accusation that he was perpetuating myths that was most offensive. Just a few days after the review was published, the ever-impulsive Roosevelt stormed into the Broadway office of *Forest and Stream* and confronted Grinnell face-to-face.

George Bird Grinnell's soft-spoken and rather sagelike demeanor calmed Roosevelt's ire shortly after they met. Grinnell had been acquainted with Roosevelt's good work in the New York State legislature, but he had not otherwise known him as a naturalist. He did know Theodore's uncle Robert Barnwell Roosevelt, already a well-known sportsman and future contributor to *Forest and Stream*. As Grinnell later recalled, they talked rather freely of Roosevelt's inexperience. Grinnell had spent years in the American West, engaging in nearly every facet of western life; and, unlike Roosevelt, he was a professional naturalist, with a Ph.D. in zoology from Yale. Although he may have felt more accomplished in the field than he actually was, Roosevelt was at best still a relative newcomer, someone seeking adventure in the closing days of the Wild West.

As the two men spoke, Roosevelt learned that Grinnell had actually lived with the Plains Indians in their teepees for months at a time. He had been adopted into the Pawnee tribe as "White Wolf" and was variously known across the plains: "Fisher Hat" by the Blackfeet, "Grey Clothes" by the Gros Ventres, and simply "Bird" among the Cheyenne. He was with George Armstrong Custer when gold was discovered in the Black Hills in 1874 and had joined in General Ludlow's historic first reconnaissance of the Yellowstone region. He was also the naturalist on several western exploring expeditions before the encroachment of the railroads, when vast herds of bison still roamed the plains. Grinnell, Roosevelt realized with awe, had years of experience in the real Wild West and no need to sensationalize his adventures.

As they exchanged stories, Roosevelt finally became convinced that he might have something to learn from this soft-spoken editor, whose crisply starched collar and flaring moustache belied his true identity as a tough veteran of the West and whose experiences captivated the younger man. Settling into the chair in the *Forest and Stream* office, Roosevelt listened to the editor's conservation efforts, which Grinnell favored over his more swashbuckling adventures. No mere raconteur, Grinnell shared one of his articles describing the wholesale destruction of big game due to the commercialization of wildlife, explaining that it was the market hunters who were the greatest threat. He feared the destruction would spread from the railroad lines that continued to spread across the country.

Grinnell had been editorializing about this problem in the pages of *Forest and Stream* for quite some time but with little effect on the public imagination or on policy. In Roosevelt, though, he found an eager ear. The meeting in Grinnell's office was Roosevelt's first real education in conservation and an introduction to what was at stake for America's natural landscape.

Roosevelt immediately agreed with Grinnell's rallying cry for a more organized effort. Their best hope for success was to form an association of powerful men bound together by their interest in protecting big game and ready to take legislative action if necessary. Grinnell had already founded a similar organization, specifically for the protection of birds. It was called the Audubon Society, named as much for Lucy Audubon, Grinnell's boyhood teacher, as it was for the great naturalist. To found a similar organization for the protection of big-game mammals, Grinnell needed the help of someone with Roosevelt's drive, energy, and willingness to learn.

Grinnell preferred to remain on the other side of the spotlight, and he was all too happy to have Roosevelt play the role of charismatic flag bearer. He could see that the young man was primarily interested in hunting, but he also saw in him a burning desire to gain credibility as a naturalist. Grinnell had a knack for organizing master plans while at the same time tapping the energies of younger, more passionate men to lead his cause. He was careful not to tell his new friend what to do—he knew that wasn't an effective way of leading men like Roosevelt. Instead, he simply planted the seed of a big-game-mammal society in the younger man's mind, knowing Roosevelt would soon make the idea his own.

THEODORE ROOSEVELT AND his former neighbor in New York, Edith Kermit Carow, had been playmates since their earliest childhood and they had never really lost their affection for each other. As teenagers the pair had smoothly transitioned into sweethearts, until one summer day after Theodore's return from Harvard, when they had a serious falling-out. In a fit of temper, Theodore said something to Edith that had, evidently, "not been nice," and this outburst terminated their relationship, at least for a time. However, even as Edith watched him court and marry the beautiful Alice Lee, she grasped at the notion that he might eventually grow bored with her, a hope encouraged by the fact that, with each passing year, Roosevelt seemed to be spending less and less time with his wife. Between his legislative duties in Albany and extended hunting trips out west, Theodore barely had the time to see Alice for more than a few days each month and those close to her noted how lonely she had become. Ultimately, of all the emotions bedeviling Roosevelt after Alice's death, the guilt of not spending enough time with her may have been the most heartwrenching.

In keeping with the mores of his time, Roosevelt shunned second marriages and wished to honor the memory of his departed wife by remaining a widower unto his own grave. "I have always considered that they argued weakness in a man's character," he wrote of second wives to his sister Anna. It was a view Roosevelt's moralistic father might have staunchly upheld, but in reality, Roosevelt was torn between traditional views of morality and his continued and strong affection for Edith. As if to reinforce this stubborn sense of morality, upon returning to New York Roosevelt made it clear to Anna that he wished to avoid all contact with his former flame.

Roosevelt needed to make such an explicit request because he was living with his sister in her Madison Avenue apartment, and Edith Carow was friendly with both his sisters. Thus, she was liable to stop by at any time. Since Roosevelt wanted to minimize the risk of a chance encounter, weeks of artful dodging ensued. In the fall of 1885, however, Roosevelt's skill at evasion experienced a setback as he came face-to-face with Edith coming down the apartment stairs. It had been years since they'd last seen each other, and certainly both of them had changed. To Edith, Roosevelt was brawnier and more rugged; to Roosevelt, Edith seemed less girlish, more mature. Roosevelt was smitten enough to ignore his guilty conscience, and soon the two were meeting every day.

Having known each other since childhood, they had no need for a lengthy courtship, yet their easy reunion seemed somehow scandalous. Because of this they kept their relationship secret. Nevertheless, news of their engagement ultimately leaked to the press, even before Roosevelt had a chance to tell his family. Theodore and Edith were married quickly in England on December 2, 1886.

Following their wedding there was a grand tour of Europe (Roosevelt's fourth), and Edith proved a most stimulating intellectual companion. Whereas Alice had once questioned how zookeepers managed to shave the lions so that they looked like French poodles, Edith was interested in more substantial subjects, such as history, art, and literature. Still, the honeymoon was not all bliss; although the Dakotas seemed impossibly remote, Roosevelt received news of the terrible blizzards that were enveloping the American West, threatening his business in the Badlands.

The winter of 1886 started early and would prove to be one of the harshest ever on record for the northern plains. The first snow fell in November, about a month earlier than expected, then swelled into a blizzard that raged nearly nonstop until January. Temperatures plummeted. Winds blew. The grass, of course, was completely buried, and, unable to paw through the deep snow for food, cattle weakened and died. The Roosevelts had to cut their honeymoon short so the new groom could attend to his cattle.

As soon as they were back in New York, Roosevelt set out for his ranch, but he was unprepared for what awaited him. "It is even worse than I feared," he wrote home to Anna. His herd was ravaged. "I wish I was sure I would lose no more than half the money I invested out here." Things were so bad that the high-spirited Edith suggested closing their new home on Long Island so that they could move out west and rough it together. Certainly that would have cut down their expenses, but with little Alice a mere toddler and another baby now on the way, the move was unthinkable; Roosevelt would have to attempt to salvage his snowbound business from a distance.

Edith and Theodore settled into their new home in Oyster Bay in the spring of 1887. Roosevelt had originally intended to name his estate Leeholm in honor of Alice Lee, but the couple rechristened it

Sagamore Hill, after the Matinecock chief Sagamore Mohannis, who had signed away his tribe's rights to the land two and a half centuries before. Opening up the house, which had been shuttered through winter, they found it cold and drafty, with all the furniture still under white sheets. They moved the heavy oak table and chairs that they had picked out in Florence into the dining room, organized their substantial collection of books on the shelves of the first-floor library, and hung trophy heads—including Roosevelt's prized bison—on the empty walls.

Nearly every room at Sagamore Hill reflected the very core of Theodore Roosevelt's being. He had a habit of turning all of his residences into private museums, from his boyhood room on East 20th Street to his apartment at Harvard, and Sagamore Hill would be no exception. The Roosevelt décor had always been equal parts trophy room, library, and armory—an admixture of animal heads, books, and guns. Roosevelt spent most of his time writing in his third-floor "gun room," which afforded him an excellent view of the vistas and shorelines that had inspired him as a boy.

For all its grandeur, though, Sagamore Hill was a money pit, and Edith worried about paying for its upkeep. With his cattle business in ruins, and his new wife now pregnant, Roosevelt had to ramp up his writing career as never before. All through the summer of 1887, he struggled to finish manuscripts while Edith grew noticeably larger. He was working on *Gouverneur Morris*, an installment in the American Statesmen series, which an old friend, Massachusetts politician Henry Cabot Lodge, had arranged for him to write on contract. The writing went "drearily on by fits and starts," and to break up the work, Roosevelt chopped wood "vigorously" or took Edith rowing until at last he was able to cobble together something for his publisher. He submitted the final manuscript just two weeks before both of their due dates.

Suddenly free of looming book deadlines, Roosevelt was left with all his attention focused on Edith. Latently fearful of the prospect of losing yet another wife in childbirth, he was so stressed that he had a relapse of asthma—the worst case he'd suffered in years. To make matters even more nerve-racking, Edith went into labor early, and

Theodore had to quickly call on his cousin West—who happened to be a doctor—to assist with the delivery. But this time, after the commotion came a happy ending. Theodore Roosevelt III was born in the early-morning hours of September 13, 1887, to a healthy mother.

Although the new father was relieved that Edith had delivered the eight-and-a-half-pound boy without incident, Roosevelt wanted to give the new mother and baby some space. With his son just a few weeks old, he went off to his ranch in the Badlands, imagining all the things he hoped to do with his newborn once he was grown. They would ride across the open plains, perhaps shooting a pronghorn for meat, and he would show little Teddy how to cook it "cowboy style" over an open fire while recounting all his adventures from the days when bison still roamed the land. Everything Roosevelt loved about hunting in the wide-open West he hoped to share someday with his new son.

Despite dealing with a failing business and the collapse of the cattle market, Roosevelt spent the weeks happily roaming the rough country between the Little Missouri and the Beaver River. The bison and elk had been shot out of existence in this area long ago, but Roosevelt was surprised to find that even the pronghorn and mule deer were becoming scarce. It seemed that everything George Bird Grinnell had recently told him about the imminent extermination of big game was coming true.

Roosevelt had always accepted that the largest of the noble western animals—bison, grizzly bear, elk—could not survive the advance of civilization, but he *was* surprised by the speed of their decline. Theodore was haunted by the idea that by the time his newborn son was grown, there would be nothing left of the West's great natural majesty. Unlike Grinnell, Roosevelt hadn't spent enough time in the wilds to get a real sense of the rapid pace of the change that was taking place. Wealthy big-game hunters generally came and went in a matter of weeks, a time span that made game appear plentiful. What none of these sporadic hunters could appreciate was just how much more abundant the game had been the year before. Only men like George Bird Grinnell, who witnessed the changes year by year, could really comprehend the magnitude of the decline. But now Roosevelt was beginning to feel the loss too.

Something needed to be done to change the ethics of hunting in America. Left unchecked, gluttonous practices meant that many species were facing extinction. The problem, as Grinnell saw it, was that in almost every other developed country, hunting was the exclusive privilege of the wealthiest elites, but in the United States anyone with a gun was free to hunt, and game was considered the property of whoever could kill it. Indeed, the places with the most fertile hunting grounds were the regions that most embodied American ideals of democracy. Hunters there believed they had an absolute right to take as much as they pleased, and they extirpated game at a frenzied pace, trying to outdo one another. Any effort to regulate hunting was seen as an attempt to impose an elitist, Old World ethic upon them, which the vast majority of Americans viewed as a threat to their basic liberties.

For years Roosevelt had hunted without much restraint, taking a fatalist view. Now, though, it was only a matter of time, he thought, before the steady march of civilization completely decimated the American wilderness. Roosevelt's conversations with Grinnell had shifted his earlier perspective, and he began taking these ideas seriously as he considered the kind of world his children would grow up in. Grinnell promised that Theodore could still look forward to hunting with his son, but only if he made immediate, activist changes. The country needed an ethical code that would allow some big-game animals to survive. The animals must be carefully studied in their natural habitats and data compiled to identify meaningful harvests that were strictly enforced. Americans needed to learn to regard these animals less as trophies and more as living specimens worthy of study and protection. Taking his cues from George Bird Grinnell, Roosevelt realized he needed to reshape the way America thought about the wilderness in general. To draft a long-term solution for protecting the natural world, Americans had to see their unspoiled landscape as their greatest treasure.

Chapter 11

REAL MEN AND MOUSERS

*E*ver since assuming the editorship of *Forest and Stream* magazine in 1876, George Bird Grinnell had argued that the field of naturalism needed the voices of people other than academic zoologists, who rarely interacted with animals in the wild. Hunters, Grinnell argued, made the best naturalists. And getting the nation's hunters to see their role in nature—and their obligation to protect it—would be key to preserving the American West.

So impressed was Roosevelt with Grinnell's approach that he adopted the older man's philosophy, and the two began to work together, advocating for sportsmen to study the animals they hunted, set reasonable limits on hunts, and establish a strict moral code to ensure compliance even when no game warden was present to provide enforcement. Vaguely at first, Roosevelt and Grinnell formulated their ideas: "We regretted the unnecessary destruction of big game animals . . . we wanted the game preserved, but chiefly with the idea that it should be protected in order that there might still be good hunting which should last for generations." However, it was not until the September 1876 issue of *Forest and Stream*, when Grinnell reported an especially devastating scene of carnage—no fewer than three thousand bison slaughtered in Yellowstone—that Roosevelt was finally motivated to take serious action. Combining forces with Grinnell, Roosevelt proposed to found an organization to unite his own ethics of outdoor adventure with Grinnell's approach to conservation.

Gathering a small number of like-minded men at his apartment on Madison Avenue in late 1887—among them his brother, Elliott, and his cousin West (former "trustees" of his boyhood Roosevelt Museum of Natural History)—Roosevelt hosted a dinner at which they proposed the new club's objectives:

1) to promote manly sport with the rifle.

2) to promote travel and exploration in the wild and unknown or but partially known portions of the country.

3) to work for the preservation of the large game of this country, and, so far as possible, to further legislation for that purpose, and to assist in enforcing the existing laws.

4) to promote inquiry into and to record observations on the habits and natural history of the various wild animals.

5) to bring about among the members the interchange of opinions and ideas on hunting, travel, and exploration, on the various kinds of hunting-rifles, on the haunts of game, animals, etc.

Roosevelt called his new organization the Boone and Crockett Club in honor of two of his greatest heroes: Daniel Boone, the "archetype of the American hunter," and frontiersman Davy Crockett, who was "perhaps the best shot in the country."

As a requirement for membership, inductees had to have killed "in fair chase" one adult male of at least three North American big-game species—bear, bison, mountain sheep, caribou, cougar, musk ox, mountain goat, elk, wolf, pronghorn, moose, and deer. In Roosevelt's own words, the club was for men who believed that "the hardier and manlier the sport . . . the more attractive it is." The club soon boasted seventy members—all men of wealth and status; in banding together, they consolidated enormous power.

Of the club's original objectives, promoting manly sport with the rifle and the exploration of unknown parts of the country proved too difficult to meet. Busy members occasionally killed "a head or two of game," but there really wasn't very much unmapped terrain left on the continent. Those loftily worded goals were put aside in favor of a more urgent and practical need: preserving suitable refuge for America's bison and elk through protected land. Born of this, the club's first major achievement was successfully lobbying for the protection of Yellowstone National Park.

Established by an Act of Congress in 1872, Yellowstone was supposed to protect a geologically unique area from desecration; however, without any provision for enforcement, the Northern Pacific Railroad was able to extend its line directly to Yellowstone's border. Developers quickly followed, and, uniting themselves under the umbrella of the "Yellowstone Park Improvement Company," they obtained leases for more than six thousand acres of the park's most scenic land, which they were plotting to transform into a sprawling resort-hotel destination. The Yellowstone Park Improvement Company monopolized the park, brazenly cutting timber to build their monstrous hotels and contracting teams of gunners to shoot wild game for their kitchens. Poachers and pillagers operated freely, taking every valuable thing in the park. Someone even chopped out a wagonload of geyser formations, only to dump them on the prairie when they proved too heavy to transport. Conditions had deteriorated so rapidly that in the spring of 1883 the U.S. secretary of the interior asked the secretary of war to detail a force of troops to protect the park. The stakes were especially high, because Yellowstone was home to the last large herd of wild bison—if Yellowstone was not protected, the very animal that symbolized the West and America's natural bounty could go extinct.

Members of the Boone and Crockett Club spent years lobbying Congress for greater protection of the park, with very little success. Then, in 1894, the issue reached a boiling point after an Army scout caught a poacher skinning a bison cow and surrounded by the carcasses of several other freshly killed animals. The soldier arrested the man, but, technically, there existed no law under which he could be charged. The scout had no other option but to set the man free. Angered by his release, the Boone and Crockett Club members seized on the incident to lobby their cause in the pages of *Forest and Stream* magazine. Grinnell wrote impassionedly in a March 24, 1894, editorial: "This occurrence calls public attention again and most forcibly to the criminal negligence of which Congress has been . . . guilty for all these years in failing to provide any form of government." Less than a month later, in the April 14, 1894, issue, he rallied his readers around the cause again: "Congress has put a premium on the head of every one of these great beasts. Any man is free to enter the national park and kill them and knows that even if taken in the act—no punishment can be inflicted on him." While Grinnell was generating support from the public, other club members were getting to the business of drafting legislation, and the Yellowstone Protection Act was introduced and pushed through Congress by John F. Lacey, himself a Boone and Crockett Club member. Grinnell excitedly reported to his readers on April 21 that change was beginning on Capitol Hill: "At least Congress has taken action. On Tuesday of last week a bill . . . to protect the birds and animals in the Yellowstone National Park, and to punish crimes in said park . . . passed the House of Representatives."

Finally, on the front page of the May 12 issue of *Forest and Stream*, came the news Grinnell's readership—and the American people—were longing for: "The bill for the protection of the Yellowstone Park, which for some time has been before Congress . . . passed both houses and received the signature of President Cleveland last Monday." The 1894 Lacey Act, pushed through Congress with the help of George Bird Grinnell and other members of the Boone and Crockett Club, established Yellowstone as a protected wildlife refuge—America's first.

HIS SPORTSMAN'S ETHIC now codified in the tenets of his own Boone and Crockett Club, Roosevelt became a more discriminating hunter. No longer did he simply bluster off into the Badlands to blast away at deer and antelope; he now carefully planned his hunts to expand his knowledge of natural history. He sought mountain caribou in Idaho (1888), grizzly bear in Montana (1889), and peccary in southern Texas (1892) for the purposes of informing his next natural-history books. His trips resembled scientific expeditions, aimed at observing and recording animal behavior. He wanted to become an expert on North America's largest mammals and gain a more intimate understanding of these animals through hunting them.

Taking Grinnell's original critique of his *Hunting Trips of a*

Ranchman to heart, Roosevelt wrote with a new purpose, publishing *Ranch Life and the Hunting-Trail* in 1888, followed by *The Wilderness Hunter* in 1893. Through this trilogy, Roosevelt found his voice as a hunter-naturalist: "I wanted to make it a plea for manliness and simplicity and delight in a vigorous outdoor life, as well as to try to sketch the feeling that the wilderness, with its great rivers, great mountains, great forests, and great prairies, leaves on one. The slaughter of the game, though necessary in order to give a needed touch of salt to the affair, is subsidiary after all."

From his caribou hunt in Idaho, he described the difficulty with which he traveled through "the tangled, brush-choked forest, and along the boulder-strewn and precipitous mountain sides." He recorded the sounds of the night—the wind moaning "harshly through the tops of the tall pines and hemlocks" and "the clatter of huge rocks falling down the cliffs, the dashing of cataracts in far-off ravines, the hooting of owls." Of his grizzly hunt, he treated his readers to experience how he had been "lulled to sleep by the stream's splashing murmur" while snug in a buffalo robe by the fire. "A little black woodpecker with a yellow crest ran nimbly up and down the tree trunks for some time and then flitted away with a party of chickadees and nut-hatches." And from his peccary hunt, we are told of how the hoofed mammals were once found in parties of "from twenty to thirty, feeding in the dense chaparral," preferring to shelter for the night "in a cave or big hollow log, one [pig] invariably remaining as a sentinel close to the mouth, looking out."

Roosevelt came to believe that he could make a significant contribution to science simply by noting, in detail, his experiences with animals in the wild. As far as he was concerned, too few naturalists went out into the field, and too few hunters described the things that they saw. Hardly anyone was taking advantage of the opportunity to study these magnificent creatures while they still roamed free. Pitifully little was known of the mammals of North America in the early 1880s—not much more than had been known to John James Audubon and John Bachman thirty years earlier—and there were only small and spotty collections of mammals in the American Museum of Natural History and the Smithsonian Institution. Mammalogy as a discipline was not merely neglected; it was considered unworthy of attention—except by men like Roosevelt, who liked to hunt big game.

Empowered through his Boone and Crockett Club association and confident in his abilities to describe the secret lives of America's big-game mammals in stirring prose, Roosevelt sought to embody the ideal of a faunal naturalist. But just as he was getting his footing in the world of serious naturalism, another young mammalogist was making a name for himself in the field, one who was taking an entirely different approach—and with whom Roosevelt would soon lock horns.

BORN IN LOCUST GROVE, on the fringes of New York's Adirondack wilderness, Clinton Hart Merriam began his naturalist's career with the acquisition of a shotgun when he was about thirteen years old. His father—the congressman Clinton Levi Merriam—had given it to him with encouragement to collect specimens from the dense woods and bogs surrounding their home. As a man of considerable influence, he arranged to take his boy down to Washington, D.C., so that he could meet Spencer Fullerton Baird in his office at the Smithsonian. Merriam was just fifteen years old at the time, but he had already stuffed a small collection of bird skins. Baird gave him some suggestions on how he might improve his taxidermy (Merriam had been self-taught and eventually took formal lessons) but otherwise found the boy bright and enthusiastic. Young Merriam evidently made a strong impression, for soon after their meeting, Baird invited him to join the upcoming Hayden Geological Survey, the latest government exploration of the Yellowstone region.

Merriam joined the 1871 expedition—which was full of high adventure—and the experience proved formative, for he harkened back to it throughout his life. That survey had two principal field parties, with Merriam assigned to the Snake River Division under the title of ornithologist. As Merriam proudly noted for his section of the expedition report, he had personally collected 121 birds and 52 nests with eggs out of a total 313 birds and 67 nests gathered during the entire expeditionary effort. Although no mammalogist was specifically designated for the trip, Merriam reported on a large number of mammals, having catalogued some sixty-four specimens ranging from black-bear and grizzly-bear skulls to a least weasel, a wolverine, several skunks, and a total of forty-two rodents representing at least a dozen different kinds, plus three bats, a moose, and a pronghorn antelope. In addition, Merriam took special pride in capturing examples of "Baird's rabbit": "I was fortunate enough to secure five specimens of this rare and remarkable rabbit. Heretofore but one specimen of this species has been brought before the scientific world, and it (No. 4263) is now on exhibit in the Smithsonian Institution."

As Theodore Roosevelt would later discover, very few naturalists cared much for mammals. There was no real "culture" or circle of naturalists taking a serious interest in these animals, and if mammals were ever written about, it was most often in the spirit of a Thomas Mayne Reid adventure. There was, however, quite a large community of bird enthusiasts who formed university clubs, the most important of which was the Nuttall Ornithological Club at Harvard (an organization that would later count a young Theodore among its members). Merriam had just begun his undergraduate studies at Yale, which in 1873 offered a much more rigorous course of science than anything Roosevelt would encounter at Harvard a few years later. Merriam contributed to the Nuttall Club's news bulletin from New Haven, and it was this kind of ready exchange of ideas among bird enthusiasts that kept ornithology a vibrant field of study while mammalogy languished.

Merriam was also one of those naturalists who seemed especially drawn to the smaller and more obscure species; the mice and shrews scurrying through the mossy understory around his Adirondack home had always caught his attention. Perhaps he was looking for a wide-open field, a study animal to claim as his own specialty, or maybe he simply wanted to distinguish himself from the ornithological obsessives, but Merriam's early interest in birds gradually made room for his growing interest in mammals, leading to the 1882 to 1884 publication of his two-volume *The Mammals of the Adirondack Region, Northeastern New York*. The work was remarkable for its time in that it focused almost entirely on the lives and habits of these particular animals. There were no fantastic tales and nothing of the detailed

morphological descriptions that had come to characterize ornithological literature. As Merriam explained in his preface, "It is in no sense
a technical treatise, and technical matter will but rarely be found in
its pages." But he more than made up for this deficiency with his own
expert knowledge. He knew the fauna intimately, and his accounts are
so vivid that they place the reader deep within the Adirondack woods
with Merriam as a most knowledgeable guide.

But there was another reason why mammalogy took longer to pop-
ularize. From the early days of Audubon and Bachman right up until
the late 1880s, the study of small mammals was severely handicapped
by technological limits. While leg-hold traps and guns were used to
take larger mammals, smaller specimens, shrews and mice, were not
only difficult to observe but impossible to capture without traps of the
proper size. Only after the introduction of the first mass-produced
mousetraps did the study of small mammals became possible. One
kind of trap in particular transformed the science of mammalogy: the
Cyclone trap, patented in 1883. For decades ornithologists had been
shooting birds and filling up museum drawers. The Cyclone allowed
mammalogists to study the great diversity of even the tiniest furry
species for the first time.

On the heels of the Cyclone trap's invention, Merriam was usher-
ing in what was later called the American School of Mammalogy,
whose steady streams of expeditions systematically collected hundreds of thousands of specimens in order to discover new species,
reveal the patterns and limits of variation, plot species' exact distribu-
tions, and elucidate broader patterns of the diversity of life across the
American landscape. As far as Merriam was concerned, specimens
were like data points, and he could never have quite enough of them.
He thought museum collections could never reach a point where they
could be considered complete; the addition of more specimens only
uncovered more complex scientific questions that, in turn, required
still more specimens. It was a rigorous, methodical, and distinctly
scientific approach to putting together the complex puzzle of natural
history.

Working his teams of collectors, Merriam developed a system of
mammal study that focused on using large numbers of small traps—

hundreds at a time—to bring in big catches of mice, rats, and other small mammals. These traps were set out in long lines, targeting one particular natural habitat or another. Generally, the collectors didn't set traps for specific species; rather, they trapped in certain locations with the intent to document all of the species that lived there. The exact placement of these traps was always a compromise between maintaining proper spacing—say, five or ten paces apart—and reading the habitat for signs of small mammals. The sign could be anything from an obvious rodent runway to features such as hollow logs or tufts of dense grass or anything else with a "mousy" look.

Traps were always checked at first light, all captured animals being brought back to camp for immediate processing. The specimen was tagged with a label indicating the precise location where it was caught, the date it was collected, details of its habitat and capture, and the collector's name. This information (together with lengthy field notes) made it possible for mammalogists to readily recognize and interpret the variations that denoted different species and subspecies. Another hard-and-fast rule was that the tag always remain affixed to the study skin.

This was a much more meticulous system than the one used to collect elk and grizzlies out west. Roosevelt and Merriam thus represented flip sides of the nascent field of mammalogy: Roosevelt observing the life histories of showy big-game mammals and rallying popular attention through his wilderness hunting stories, Merriam adhering to a stricter scientific regimen, collecting small mammals with machinelike efficiency.

Though they took different approaches, the two men's ideas dovetailed nicely in other ways. Both considered it imperative that aspiring naturalists get out into the wilds, and Merriam was one of the staunchest advocates for personal specimen collecting. "I do not believe that a naturalist was ever made without the actual field experience of collecting specimens. The idea that a man can become a naturalist by studying specimens in the museum and books in the library is to me altogether preposterous. Without the enthusiasm generated by actual collecting and the exhilaration and thrills incident[al] to the capture of a rare specimen, how can one even hope to become more than the mere vacant shadow of an amateur?"

Two years before Roosevelt and Grinnell created the Boone and Crockett Club, Merriam founded something he later called the U.S. Biological Survey. Technically a part of the U.S. Department of Agriculture, "the survey" had originally been authorized by Congress as an agency for finding and exterminating agricultural pests—sort of a gopher- and sparrow-killing operation—but Merriam essentially hijacked the office and transformed it into a platform for launching scientific collecting expeditions.

Much as had Spencer Baird with his railroad surveys a generation before, Merriam found no shortage of bright young naturalists eager to get out into the field. And every one of them had to be, at heart, an adventure-seeker. Not only were they required to work hard while camped out for months on end on strange land with few comforts, but museum collectors were paid very little, if anything at all. Thus, the opportunity for adventure had to carry serious weight for these recruits.

The collecting efforts of the Biological Survey were always a race against time. Hundreds of traps had to be tended to and perhaps dozens of animals skinned and stuffed each day before they started to decay. (Trap-success rate varies according to environment. In tropical rain forests, mousetraps typically have a trap-success rate of 2 to 3 percent, meaning two or three animals per hundred traps set; in desert environments, the trap-success rate can be considerably higher, perhaps 20 percent or more.) In the afternoon, traps are generally checked again for diurnal species and baited as necessary so that the process can be repeated day after day. After a week to ten days, the whole trapline is picked up and moved to sample a slightly different habitat of interest, and the entire process is repeated. Working in this way, and supplementing their trap captures with animals shot at all hours of the day and night, a collecting party can quickly amass large numbers of specimens, each invaluable to understanding particular species in their habitat.

Roosevelt himself had even tried to collect some small mammals for Merriam while on his caribou hunt in Idaho. Camped beside a little brook for a lunch of "cold frying-pan bread," he was sitting by a great rock at the edge of the brook, when "suddenly a small animal swam across the little pool at my feet. It was less in size than a mouse, and as it paddled rapidly underneath the water its body seemed flattened like a disc and was spangled with tiny bubbles, like specks of silver. It was a water-shrew, a rare little beast." He sat motionless, watching the scene, and in a minute or two the shrew again caught his eye. "It got into a little shallow eddy and caught a minute fish, which it carried to a half-sunken stone and greedily devoured, tugging voraciously at it as it held it down with its paws. Then its evil genius drove it into a small puddle alongside the brook, where I instantly pounced on and slew it; for I knew a friend in the Smithsonian at Washington who would have coveted it greatly."

Quickly skinning the animal, Roosevelt turned its hide inside out and kept it stretched using a little bent twig. Not prepared to make a proper museum study skin, he set the half-prepared specimen down on a log in front of the fire to preserve it by drying. Unfortunately, his efforts were all for naught, as someone in camp later absentmindedly took that same log and threw it into the fire. "That was the end of the shrew," Roosevelt lamented dryly.

Apparently, despite his affinity for big-game hunting, Roosevelt's interest in small mammals was growing. At the same time he felt a more pressing need to study the big-game species first, since their habitats and numbers were in much steeper decline. He was actually something of an expert on shrews, as a boy having kept several short-tailed shrews (*Blarina brevicauda*) alive over a period of weeks in order to make careful drawings and notes before going to study at Harvard and collecting specimens during trips to Maine. And after reading Merriam's Adirondack-mammal monograph, he wrote him to tell him how closely their observations on this shrew matched and to share some observations on the character of the animal. Although it was a diminutive species, Roosevelt found shrews ferocious, and in his letter to Merriam he blatantly revealed his rather tooth-and-claw view of the animal world: "In proportion to its size, the male shrew is as formidable as any of our beasts of prey." Roosevelt knew

This snowy owl, now on permanent display at the American Museum of Natural History, was stuffed by Roosevelt when he was just twelve years old.

Young Theodore Roosevelt, at age six or seven. A few years later he discovered the dead seal that inspired him to become a naturalist.

The American Museum of Natural History as it looked shortly after the completion of the first building. The museum was chartered in the front parlor of Roosevelt's boyhood home.

Theodore Roosevelt, during his awkward Harvard years, holding a snowshoe hare he shot while hunting in Maine in 1879.

TOP RIGHT: *Theodore Roosevelt—the determined suitor—poses with his future wife Alice Hathaway Lee (far left) and her cousin Rose Saltonstall.*

BOTTOM LEFT: *Edith Kermit Carow Roosevelt, Theodore's childhood friend and second wife, photographed in 1885, the year before they were married.*

BOTTOM RIGHT: *Theodore Roosevelt in his favorite western hunting gear.*

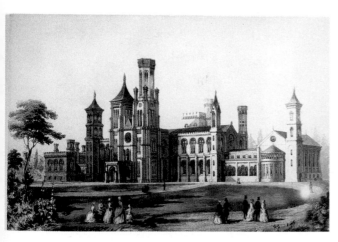

This engraving of the original Smithsonian building, called "the castle," reflects the relatively small size of the Institution when Spencer Fullerton Baird was appointed its first curator and assistant secretary.

LEFT: *Spencer Fullerton Baird, the Smithsonian naturalist responsible for creating a natural-history museum within the Institution. As a young man, Theodore Roosevelt aspired to become a scientist of the "Baird type."*

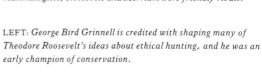

ABOVE: *Clinton Hart Merriam led an effort to systematically collect museum specimens across the American West. As mammalogists, Roosevelt and Merriam were friendly rivals.*

LEFT: *George Bird Grinnell is credited with shaping many of Theodore Roosevelt's ideas about ethical hunting, and he was an early champion of conservation.*

Theodore Roosevelt (front right) rides in a horse-drawn sleigh, Yellowstone National Park, 1903. Roosevelt jumped from this sleigh to capture a vole, which he stuffed and sent to the Smithsonian. The Institution catalogued it in the mammal collection (USNM 126419)—a rare example of a scientific specimen collected by a sitting U.S. president.

The American Museum of Natural History during an expansion in 1907. The original building is obscured behind the completed 77th Street façade; the Columbus Avenue wing is still under construction. During Roosevelt's lifetime, natural-history museums' collections grew so quickly that their rapid expansion demanded the construction of massive new buildings.

At the turn of the century, the Smithsonian's natural-history collection had long since outgrown the original museum buildings. In 1903, Congress appropriated funds for the construction of the Smithsonian's new United States National Museum (now called the National Museum of Natural History). The museum opened to the public on March 17, 1910, just as Roosevelt was finishing his Smithsonian African Expedition.

Theodore (right) and Kermit Roosevelt with their first African buffalo. Roosevelt had originally conceived his African safari as a father-and-son hunt, but early in the trip's planning he approached the Smithsonian about supporting a scientific collecting expedition.

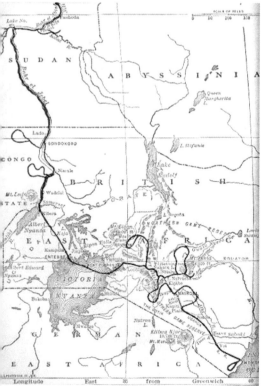

ABOVE: *Theodore Roosevelt (left) on the cowcatcher of a train used by the Smithsonian African Expedition in Kenya. R. J. Cuninghame (center) was Roosevelt's professional hunting guide, and Dr. Edgar Mearns was the museum naturalist in charge of the men's scientific surveys.*

LEFT: *The route of the Smithsonian African Expedition, from Mombasa on the coast, through Kenya, across Lake Victoria, and down the Nile.*

A major undertaking of the Smithsonian African Expedition was the preparation of large mammal specimens. Here, men work on preparing the skeleton of a hippopotamus that has already been skinned.

The Smithsonian's taxidermy studio after Roosevelt's return from Africa. The lion cubs in the foreground were the first ones taken by Theodore and Kermit.

Theodore Roosevelt's lions on display at the Smithsonian Institution's newly opened United States National Museum.

Taxidermist Carl Akeley sculpts an early version of the model over which he would mount the skin of a bull elephant shot by his wife on Mount Kenya. This bull will be the centerpiece of his elephant group at the American Museum of Natural History, which includes a total of seven animals. Theodore and Kermit Roosevelt each contributed to the collection.

Completed elephants in the Akeley Hall of African Mammals at the American Museum. The cow was shot by Theodore Roosevelt, just to the northeast of Mount Kenya. The tiny male calf entwining its trunk around the large female's was shot by Kermit while he and his father hunted with Carl Akeley on the Uasin Gishu Plain.

Theodore Roosevelt collected and prepared these two study skins of voles, representing pivotal points in his naturalist career. He was only eleven years old when he collected the specimen (bottom) from Muskegat Island, Maine, on June 30, 1870. More than thirty years later, as president of the United States, he jumped from his touring sleigh to collect and prepare the specimen (top) in Yellowstone National Park.

this to be true because he had conducted experiments with one of his caged shrews. He had been feeding it insects over the course of several weeks, which it always devoured, but one day he had the idea of introducing a much larger pine mouse to the cage, which it immediately killed and devoured despite its being several times the size and weight of the shrew.

Later, Roosevelt repeated his experiment by presenting the shrew with a seven-inch garter snake, and his account merits recounting in detail not just because it is a remarkable example of his powers of observation and description, but also because it reveals his proclivity for action:

The little snake at first moved slowly about and then coiled itself up on a piece of flannel. The shrew had come out from its nest, but did not seem to see the snake and returned to it. Soon afterwards it came out again and quartered across the cage; while doing so it evidently struck the scent (the snake all the time was in sight), raised its nose, turned sharply round, and ran rapidly up to the flannel. It did not attack at once as with the mouse but cautiously smelt its foe, while the little snake moved its head uneasily and hissed slightly; then with a jump the shrew seized it, low down quite near the tail. The snake at once twisted itself right across the shrew's head and under one paw, upsetting him; but he recovered himself at once and before the snake could escape flung himself on it again and this time seized it by the back of the neck, placing one paw against the head and the other on the neck, and pushing the body from him while he tore it with his sharp teeth. The snake writhed and twisted, but it was of no use, for his neck was very soon more than half eaten through and during the next twenty-four hours he was entirely devoured.

The duration of this battle between shrew and snake could not have taken more than a minute or two—at high speed and with very tiny shrew feet flying—yet Roosevelt could recall the play-by-play blows with perfect clarity, so intense was his concentration on a good animal fight. "Certainly a more blood-thirsty animal of its size I never saw," Roosevelt concluded.

The other naturalist might have been amused by Roosevelt's dramatic descriptions of this death match, though Merriam stressed a highly rational, ordered approach to his studies. In fact, Merriam's insistence on the systematic study of large series of uniformly prepared small-mammal specimens from all available localities in an environment—indeed, across the North American continent—became his legacy to the field. Roosevelt, however, felt that the science could use a little less scientific regimen and a little more of the naturalist's passion for the animals as they lived and died each day.

AS SOMEONE WHO was increasingly recognized as an expert on American big game, Roosevelt longed for a comprehensive book on their natural history. Clinton Hart Merriam was one of the few naturalists qualified to write one, but he had become preoccupied with describing new species of pocket mice and gophers—a practice Roosevelt deplored as a misplaced priority. Roosevelt thought there would always be time for the scientists to study the smallest and most obscure species, none of which was in any danger of extinction, but the opportunity to study big mammals in their natural habitats was quickly evaporating.

Roosevelt went on to vent his frustrations with those he called "half baked" scientists: "I know these scientists pretty well, and their limitations are extraordinary, especially when they get to talking of science with a capital S. They do good work; but, after all, it is only the very best of them who are more than brick-makers, who laboriously get together bricks out of which other men must build houses. When they think they are architects they are simply a nuisance."

Since publishing his works on Adirondack mammals, Merriam had slowly moved away from prosy natural-history accounts and embraced a more straightforward approach to naturalism that focused on collecting and describing new species of mammals through a series of dry, technical pamphlets that seemed to come out as fast as his collectors could trap specimens. More distressing to Roosevelt, Merriam was arguing for a more liberal interpretation of what constituted a species, setting himself up to describe potentially thousands more new ones based almost entirely on his interpretations of the subtle variations among the teeth and skulls in his collection.

Roosevelt had first started to grow concerned after Merriam presented a lecture at the March 1896 meeting of the Biological Society of Washington, during which he espoused his thoughts on the big bears of North America. According to Merriam, a study of more than two hundred bear skulls in the National Museum of Natural History led him to conclude that there were far more species than anyone had previously suspected. He split what was formerly known as the grizzly bear into five species, and he divided the black bear into four. The "Louisiana black bear" (*Ursus americanus luteolus*), with its slightly bigger teeth and elongated skull, was suddenly distinguished from something called the "everglade black bear" (*Ursus americanus floridanus*), which was nearly identical to the Louisiana bear but with a slightly more domed cranium. Merriam argued that there was not just one grizzly bear, but also Yakutat bears, Sitka bears, and Sonora bears. He even resurrected from taxonomic obscurity something called the Barren Ground Grizzly Bear, which had been described by Thomas Mayne Reid in the region of the Great Slave Lake in Canada's Northwest Territory in 1864. Each of these bears, Merriam claimed, should be classified as a distinct and separate species. None of Merriam's proposed species is considered valid today; all are mere variations of the same species first described from a specimen brought back by the Lewis and Clark Expedition, but at the time of his postulations, these were earthshaking claims.

Shortly after presenting his astonishing discoveries, Clinton Hart Merriam published his results in the prestigious journal *Science*, thus formalizing his new methods for discriminating among species. Shortly thereafter, Roosevelt, who was furious, published a counterargument in the same journal. Not one to stop before his point had been thoroughly pounded home, he then challenged Merriam to a public debate at the next meeting of the Biological Society of Washington. A total of fifty-seven people attended the event on the evening of May 8, 1897. Merriam arranged a large number of wolf and coyote skulls from the Smithsonian in front of him, then used the specimen samples to argue his case, pointing out what he considered to be an array of morphological differences between his various species.

At first the audience seemed to take Merriam's arguments as fact—there really *were* obvious differences in the skulls of bears from different parts of the country. But when it came time for Roosevelt to present his side of the argument, he used the very same specimens to show how animals can exhibit a wide range of morphological variation even among those taken from the same population. Roosevelt echoed the understanding of most other taxonomists that certain character-istics were more informative of species than others. The fur color, for example, was a highly variable characteristic subject to all kinds of environmental conditions and liable to change even with the changing seasons. Looking just at the skulls before him, Roosevelt might have argued how the molar teeth were much more reliable as diagnostic characters of species than, say, the precise shape of the nasal bones, which tended to vary dramatically even among animals taken from the same population.

What Roosevelt was trying to explain to Merriam was that he had to take all this into consideration and weigh it accordingly, using personal judgment to disregard certain differences in the skulls that seemed uninformative, while giving greater weight to the charac-teristics that were valuable. To Merriam, though, it all seemed very subjective and he would have none of it. As far as he was concerned, measuring and quantifying the differences between specimens was all that mattered, and he took special pains to keep subjectivity out of his equations. Merriam went on to explain: "It is not the business of the naturalist to either create or suppress species, but to endeavor to ascertain how many nature has established."

The debate brought up a larger and pervasive thread of naturalist thought: Roosevelt and Merriam were arguing opposite extremes of a long-standing difference of opinion between what are known as taxo-nomic "lumpers" and "splitters." The former tend to recognize fewer species by "lumping" together a greater variety of kinds under one scientific name, while the latter tended to "split" off new species from what was previously regarded as a single, variable species. Roosevelt tended toward lumping, whereas Merriam was a consummate splitter.

In the end, neither Merriam nor Roosevelt was willing to change his own views, and the debate only served to steel each man's resolve. The impasse meant that all Roosevelt could do was write Henry Fairfield Osborn, the president of the American Museum of Natural History, to explain his perspective:

> *I believe that with fuller material Dr. Merriam could go on creating new "species" in groups like the bears, wolves and coyotes until he would himself find that he would have to begin to group them together after the manner of the abhorred "lumpers" . . . I think it would be merely cumbrous to lumber up our zoological works by giving names to all as "new species." . . . Dr. Merriam has shown that there are different forms of wolf and coyote in many different parts of the country. When he gets a fuller collection I am quite sure he will find a still larger number of differences and he can add to the already extensive assortment of new species. Now, as I have said before, it is a very important and useful work to show that these differences exist, but I think it is as only a darkening of wisdom to insist upon treating them all as a new species. . . . I firmly believe that he will find that with every new locality which his collectors visit, he will get new "species," until he has a snarl of forty or fifty for North America alone.*

Summing up his feelings to George Bird Grinnell, Roosevelt explained that he just couldn't bear to see "an old familiar friend suddenly cut up into eleven brand new acquaintances."

But Merriam was no fool, and although history (and DNA analysis) reveal much of his work to be a classic example of taxonomic over-splitting, his ultimate scientific goal went beyond individual descriptions of species. Merriam was in the middle of what would become a decades-long effort to elucidate what he called the "life zones" of North American wildlife. Having specimens pouring into Washington, D.C., from all across the American West and, indeed, extending his hair-splitting taxonomic methods to all kinds of mammals—everything from weasels to pocket mice—he was hoping to methodically discern and ultimately map out the precise patterns by which species were distributed across the continent. It was a long-view approach that only a rigorously objective scientist such as Clinton Hart Merriam could adopt.

Chapter 12

A TIFFANY KNIFE
TO THE HEART

*F*rom the time he married Edith Carow until his years in the White
House, Theodore Roosevelt worked feverishly to support his growing
family. In addition to his eldest daughter with Alice Lee, Theodore
and Edith would have five children together, which meant he was always scrambling to make money. He continued to write and publish
(books, articles, reviews), but the income was never sufficient on its
own. To add to that modest salary, he went through a decade-long
period of working his way up through a number of political appoint-
ments.

He spent the fall of 1888 campaigning for Benjamin Harrison, and
when Harrison won the presidency, he rewarded Roosevelt with a seat
on the Civil Service Commission. Ironically, given how he won the
post, the job involved countering favoritism and corruption in government. While Roosevelt felt that the appointment was beneath him,
he needed the money and so accepted it. Moving his family to Washington, D.C., he took residence in a small house near Connecticut Avenue, where for the next eight years Roosevelt worked to reform the
spoils-ridden civil-service system. He removed thousands of federal
jobs from political patronage, and although he continued his tradition
of an annual fall hunt, his life began to feel static without his naturalist pursuits. Toiling in his office each day, Roosevelt grew tired of
Washington, D.C., and in 1895 he jumped at the chance to become
the police commissioner of New York City.

Delighted to be back in his hometown, Roosevelt was, neverthe-less, surprised by the levels of corruption and graft he found within the force. As commissioner, he crusaded tirelessly to reform the in-stitution, and he was so obsessed with expelling vice within it that he roamed huge sections of the city at all hours as part of an effort to catch delinquent officers. Despite his best intentions, Roosevelt was essentially powerless and only succeeded in annoying everyone. In 1897, and after only two years on the job, Roosevelt resigned his posi-tion to become assistant secretary of the navy (ASN).

During this stage of his political career, Roosevelt also completed a second trilogy of hunting books. They were co-edited with George Bird Grinnell and served as part of their Boone and Crockett Club series on hunting and conservation: *American Big-Game Hunting* (1893), *Hunting in Many Lands* (1895), and *Trail and Camp-fire* (1897). These were more than just hunting narratives—they were an early formulation of Roosevelt's conservation approach, one that combined a naturalist's appreciation for the vulnerability of wildlife with a busi-nessman's sense for managing natural resources and a strong hunt-ing ethic. As one historian has pointed out about their collaborations, Roosevelt absorbed and articulated not only Grinnell's ideas about conservation, but also his paleontologist's appreciation for extinc-tion, a businessman's grasp of the idea that natural resources could be managed for future use, and a sportsman's ethic that there was but one proper way for a gentleman to pursue game—through fair chase. All these ideals came to Roosevelt through Grinnell, who had been promulgating them in the pages of *Forest and Stream* but who also found in Roosevelt a much more effective voice.

Although still only in his third decade of life, Roosevelt com-plained that he was becoming "a most orthodox middle-aged indi-vidual." Jumping from one government appointment to another, he had not quite lived up to the visions of a life of adventure that he had imagined as a boy. Theodore was, in fact, itching for more excitement, and he soon found it, splashed across the headlines of daily news-papers rife with sensational stories of Spanish atrocities against the people of Cuba. These papers fed an American public eager to force the Spaniards out of the Western Hemisphere. For his part, Roosevelt, who sensed that a conflict with Spain was inevitable, began making plans to build up the Navy. Then, on February 15, 1898, the U.S. battleship *Maine* mysteriously blew up in Havana Harbor, killing 260 sailors, and the United States was set on the path to war.

The jingoistic Roosevelt angled to participate in the Spanish–American War from the moment it was declared. He resigned his post in the Navy—as ASN, he was too high-ranked to go into battle—and was determined to get into the fight. Through his contacts in the War Department, Roosevelt had himself appointed lieutenant colonel of the First United States Volunteer Cavalry, soon to be nicknamed the "Rough Riders." Under the capable leadership of Colonel Leonard Wood, a career military officer, Roosevelt was second in command of a varied group of New York elites and dust-bitten cowboys. Armed with some of the best repeating rifles then available, they were raring for a good fight.

America's "splendid little war," as the then Secretary of State John Hay called it, was over in a relative heartbeat—just four months—and Roosevelt's heroics on the battlefield followed him home, making him a rising star in the Republican Party. Just days after the victorious Rough Riders landed at Montauk Point, Long Island, Roosevelt was asked if he would accept his party's nomination for governor of New York. He agreed, and after an easy victory, he was sworn in on January 2, 1899, a day that was so cold that the welcoming brass band refused to play, out of fear that their lips would freeze to their instruments.

As governor, however, Roosevelt failed to please anyone. Reformers saw him as a disappointment, while the party-line Republicans regarded him as a loose cannon. After he'd proved himself a bit of a maverick, the party wanted nothing more than to push him out of politics.

The solution was to put the rogue politician in a dead-end job. When the Republican Party nominated Roosevelt for vice president under William McKinley, it was supposed to mark the end of his political career, there being little opportunity to push any agenda in the role of VP. Roosevelt, ambitious and fiery, vehemently opposed his own nomination, adding that he would "rather be anything, say, professor of history, than Vice-President" and that he would find the job "a bore." But boredom was exactly what the Republican Party bosses wished for Roosevelt, having grown wary of his progressive tendencies. When McKinley was elected in 1900, Roosevelt was sure his days in politics were numbered. Making matters worse, becoming vice president precluded him from participating in one of the most important natural-history expeditions to be launched in that decade.

The lavishly funded Harriman Alaska Expedition, conceived by the millionaire railroad magnate Edward Harriman, undertook a comprehensive survey of coastal Alaska. Harriman was one of the most powerful men in America, but when his health began to fail, he decided to fulfill his desire to hunt the big brown bears of Kodiak Island. Never one to think small, Harriman turned his hunt into a scientific expedition, with the idea of inviting America's best naturalists to help him explore the whole Pacific Northwest coastal region, from Seattle to Siberia. Contacting Clinton Hart Merriam, Harriman explained that he would cover all the costs for a team of artists and scientists to join him; he just needed Merriam to select the best participants. Merriam, in a flurry of planning, organized all kinds of arctic experts—botanists, geologists, artists, and a photographer—to join the expedition, which was to be based off a repurposed steamship, the *George W. Elder*. Harriman had the ship specially refitted for the expedition, adding lecture rooms, a specially stocked library of more than five hundred books covering the natural history of Alaska, stables to hold the men's hunting steeds, a full taxidermy studio, and luxurious quarters for every member of the team.

Those invited on the project were a veritable who's who of American naturalists, though Theodore Roosevelt was not among them. Merriam was the ship's chief naturalist; George Bird Grinnell and conservationist and essayist John Burroughs were also aboard as writers. As the expedition took shape, and as Roosevelt heard news of the various naturalists who were going, all he could do was prepare to assume his official duties as vice president. Receiving regular reports on their progress through the newspapers, Roosevelt paid particular attention to Merriam, the mammalogist and, thus, the naturalist whose interests were the closest to Roosevelt's own. That there was a bit of rivalry between these two men is clear—and Roosevelt did not hold back from saying so at times when he felt Merriam's methods misguided. He must have seethed with jealousy, however, knowing that Merriam was positioned to make a whole slew of new discoveries in Alaska while he merely sat in the White House.

But Vice President Roosevelt was able to find other adventures while in office. Just weeks after he was sworn in, and having very little responsibility in the office, he headed off for the wilds of northwestern Colorado, arriving in the middle of January and with the temperature dipping to a dangerous eighteen degrees below zero. Theodore was there to hunt mountain lions, and he hired a local guide named John B. Goff, who had a pack of trained hunting dogs. With the help of Goff and the dogs, the restless vice president hoped to kill as many of the big cats as he could find. Nineteenth-century mountain lions were considered pests, and Roosevelt saw hunting them as an important step toward protecting the lives of their big-game prey, such as elk. The hunts were literally cat-and-dog fights—savage battles to the death:

This kind of hunting was totally different from that to which I had been accustomed. In the first place, there was no need of always being on the alert as it was the dogs who did all the work. . . . Leading our horses, we slid and scrambled after the hounds. . . . It was the first time I had ever seen dogs with a cougar, and I was immensely interested. . . . After running a couple of hundred yards, the dogs seized it. The worry was terrific: the growling, snarling, and yelling rang among the rocks; and leaving our horses we plunged at full speed through the snow down the rugged ravine in which the fight was going on. It was a small though old female . . . and the dogs had the upper hand when we arrived. They would certainly have killed it unassisted, but as it was doing some damage to the pack, and might at any moment kill a dog, I ended the struggle by a knife-thrust behind the shoulder.

Some days after this first cougar encounter, Roosevelt got into a situation in which he almost became the victim of another big cat, and his breathless description is reminiscent of some of his earlier observations on the ferocious short-tailed shrew. The dogs were on a cougar, and one of them grabbed the cat by the tip of its tail:

She was a powerful female . . . and made a tremendous fight; and
savage enough she looked, her ears tight back against her head, her
yellow eyes flashing, and her great teeth showing as she grinned. . . .
Just as I was about to strike her . . . she turned upon me . . . I
jammed the gun-butt into her jaws with my left hand and struck home
with the right, the knife driving straight to the heart.

But while these fights were exciting to Roosevelt, he was most looking forward to debunking some of Clinton Hart Merriam's claims about the delineation of species. Years earlier, on hearing that Merriam had described two new species of cougar from Nevada, Roosevelt once again chuffed in a letter to the president of the American Museum of Natural History about the ridiculousness of Merriam's claims:

I almost broke the heart of my beloved friend Merriam,
however. He felt as though he had been betrayed in the house of his
friends; but he really goes too far. He has just sent me a pamphlet
announcing the discovery of two new species of mountain lion
from Nevada. If he is right I will guarantee to produce fifty-seven
new species of red fox from Long Island.

Now that he was on a hunt in mountain-lion country, he had a chance to finally disprove Merriam's theory through the scientific study of real specimens.

Roosevelt understood the wide range of variability in animals. For example, just because one cougar is large and grayish and another small and reddish does not necessarily mean that they are different species. Any number of individuals might intergrade between these two extremes. By collecting a large number of specimens from a single locality, Roosevelt hoped to demonstrate a wide range of morphological variation within what was obviously one species, forever proving that Merriam's "species" were really nothing more than the extremes of normal morphological variation. Spurred on by his firm respect for scientific truth (and a little bit by his need to be right), Roosevelt took careful measurements of every specimen he shot, jotted down notes on their various pelage colorations, and sent every skull back to Merriam for further study.

In sending his specimens back to Washington, of course, Roosevelt also wanted to add his own account to the bank of knowledge about mountain lions. Hunters were responsible for much of what was known of the big-game species, but Roosevelt was disgusted with how little the cougar hunters in particular set down in writing: "Astonishingly little of a satisfactory nature has been left on record about the cougar by hunters, and in most places the chances for observation of big cats steadily grow less." He was also dismayed at the prevalence of sloppy writing among hunters. "No beast has been the subject of so much loose writing or of such wild fables as the cougar . . . the average writer, and for the matter of that, the average hunter . . . knows little or nothing of them, and in describing them merely draws upon the stock of well-worn myths which portray them as terrible foes of man, as dropping on their prey from the trees where they have been lying in wait."

IT WAS MID-SEPTEMBER 1901, and the sugar maple and birch were just turning red and yellow. Theodore Roosevelt was taking in the view from Lake Tear of the Clouds, just down from the top of Mount Marcy, New York State's and the Adirondacks' highest peak. He was on vacation, but his mind was clouded with recent news. A crazed anarchist had shot President McKinley as he greeted the crowds at the Pan-American Exposition in Buffalo the week prior, and although Roosevelt had been quick to join McKinley at his bedside, he felt it was his duty as a high-ranking member of the president's administration to remain publicly calm, to carry on as if nothing too serious had just happened—and in the hope that things wouldn't get worse. The vice president hiked back up into the mountains.

Wandering around the tranquil lakeshore now, Roosevelt was hoping for some quiet reflection to soothe his nerves, but his solitude was interrupted by a messenger running up the steep mountain slope with an urgent telegram: "McKinley's wounds gangrene. . . . No longer expected to live. . . . Return to Buffalo at once." Scrambling down the mountainside, Roosevelt reached the foot of Mount Marcy after dark and found a horse and wagon waiting to take him the fifty miles to the North Creek railroad station. In the middle of the night and on dark, unpaved roads, the wagon driver pushed through the wilderness, with Roosevelt lending a hand to help change horses several times along the way. He could not have known it at the time, but at precisely 2:15 on the morning of September 14, 1901, President William McKinley died. Theodore Roosevelt was now president of the United States.

JUST FORTY-TWO YEARS OLD, Roosevelt was America's youngest president. Of course being elected president and being elevated to that office by the act of an assassin were two entirely different things. Roosevelt now faced the daunting task of proving his own worth to the government and the American people. His ascension coincided with America's rise as an industrial power, and he spent most of his time trying to strike a balance between the often conflicting needs of industry and society. Capitalism was, to his mind, in constant danger of barbarism, the spirit of the banker, the broker, and the manufacturer "unhappily prominent" in the United States. Roosevelt's task was to see to it that the "right kind" of civilization—a just one, fair to all society's classes—developed from "these wonderful new conditions of vast industrial growth."

Roosevelt might have preferred to spend his first term pushing conservation measures, but his political instincts kept him from making too many bold moves. He would go on to designate his first national park at Crater Lake, Oregon, as well as the first of fifty-one National Wildlife Refuges. But he also understood that the nation was still in shock over the assassination of McKinley, and he knew better than to force an aggressive conservation agenda. Besides, he was facing too many pressing emergencies to be pushing pet projects: the Philippine insurrection and accusations of American atrocities, the Panama Canal and a revolution in Colombia—all while an ongoing coal strike threatened to freeze the American economy. This would become the well-known backdrop of Roosevelt's first presidential term. But through it all, the founder of the Roosevelt Museum of

Natural History remained deeply engaged in a personal struggle to find and assert his views as a naturalist.

During his years in the White House, Roosevelt remained a man desperate to tout his bona fides as a naturalist. Despite a precocious start, Roosevelt had to cut short his natural-history career too soon. Few among his politician peers had any knowledge of his past obsession, yet he craved recognition of his early—and continuing—naturalism, and he feared losing his grasp on such an important aspect of his self-identity.

Roosevelt surrounded himself with naturalists, kept up on the details of their research, and worked hard to cultivate their friendship. What he enjoyed most about his job as president was the chance to help along the work of other scientists, and throughout his years in office he nurtured his personal friendships with every leading naturalist of his time—George Bird Grinnell, writer John Burroughs, zoologist William T. Hornaday, ornithologist Frank Chapman, British explorer Frederick Courteney Selous, taxidermist Carl Akeley, field naturalist Edgar A. Mearns, and, of course, Clinton Hart Merriam. As an honorary member of their ranks, he felt comfortable with them in a way few other politicians would. He entertained more naturalists in the White House than did any other president, and they were amazed by his erudition. "Very few people are aware of Roosevelt's knowledge of mammals and their skulls," explained Merriam, who kept about five thousand mammal skulls in his home for ready reference and was perhaps the best person to judge whether or not someone was an expert in such subjects. "One evening at my house he astonished everyone—including several eminent naturalists—by picking up skull after skull and mentioning the scientific names of the genus to which each belonged." Although occupying the nation's highest office, Roosevelt still felt the pull of the comparatively less glamorous fields of science and natural history—from the country's highest office, a part of him still longed to be a naturalist.

Roosevelt was vocal about the need for scientists and naturalists to write with scientific accuracy and readability. "There is no use in having a book scientific in its accuracy if no one will read it, and it is worse than no use to have a book that is readable and at the same time false." He was generous with other naturalists, quick to praise any work that met his high standards. To Frank Chapman of the American Museum of Natural History he wrote: "I wonder how I ever got on without your *Birds of the Eastern United States* and your book on warblers," and of Chapman's later book, *Camps and Cruises of an Ornithologist,* he remarked, "Not only shall I enjoy the book, I feel the keenest pride in your having written it. . . . I like to have an American do a piece of work really worth doing." But more than merely offering praise of a completed work, Roosevelt was equally renowned for goading naturalists to write, as he believed this was the best way to advance this particular scientific discourse.

Among the many natural-history books tracing their origins to Roosevelt's nudging, the most famous is the work of the London-born African explorer and sportsman Frederick Courteney Selous. Through years of big-game hunting and careful natural-history observation Selous had amassed a treasure trove of knowledge on African big-game mammals. Regarding these accounts as largely uninteresting personal anecdotes, Selous squirreled them away in a desk drawer. During a White House visit in 1903, the president learned of Selous's unpublished notes, and, having read some of the man's earlier writings, Roosevelt encouraged him to put forth the new material: "You have the most extraordinary power of seeing things with minute accuracy of detail, and the equally necessary power to describe vividly and accurately what you have seen." Roosevelt knew that the Africa Selous had known would soon be gone forever (the wilds there were changing just as they were in the American West), and he urged Selous to set his experiences to print. Selous published *African Nature Notes and Reminiscences* five years later, with a dedication to Theodore Roosevelt, "not only because it was entirely owing to his inspiration and kindly encouragement that it was ever written but also because both in private and public life he has always won the sincere admiration and esteem of the author."

Although many of Roosevelt's naturalist friends heeded his call to write books, Clinton Hart Merriam was not one of them. He remained obdurate, fixated on accumulating and publishing an endless train of new species descriptions. As far as Merriam was concerned, the big natural-history books that Roosevelt so revered were just so many collections of anecdotes, observations, and impressions—all of them purely subjective. Merriam, on the other hand, was devoted to the meticulous accumulation of data. Keeping his eyes close to his museum specimens, Merriam stayed focused on his long-term plan to slowly but surely unravel the puzzling patterns of animal speciation in North America: in other words, not only where species delineated themselves on the map of the continent but, just as important, what environmental and geographic forces were driving these patterns. It might take years or even decades to accomplish, but Merriam believed that the payoff would be worth the trouble.

As for Roosevelt's imploring him to write a comprehensive book describing the lives of wild animals, Merriam believed he had already written just such a book—*The Mammals of the Adirondack Region*. And now he wanted no more part in such unscientific endeavors. He had higher aspirations, if only Roosevelt would understand.

Roosevelt finally realized that Merriam would never give in to his cajoling, and he vented his frustration in typical fashion: "Oh, Heavens! How I wish I could make you really appreciate what I said the other day, and sit down in good faith and all solemnity and write the great formal natural history of the mammals of North America, life histories and all, which you alone can write." In the end, though, Merriam never wrote the comprehensive tome that Roosevelt so desired.

Hunting also remained an important part of President Roosevelt's expression as a naturalist. Out in the wilderness with his rifle, he was reminded of his place in the natural world. To Roosevelt, the sport symbolized the foundational structure of all life, for, without exception, animals must be either predators or prey. It was only among *Homo sapiens*—whose societal constructs can prohibit such things—that this essential truth sometimes broke down. As a hunter, Roosevelt was always deeply in touch with his own predatory instincts, but not everyone understood these to be fundamental to the human experience. Others sought to view nature as something detached from human existence. To these preservationists, humans were not really a part of the natural world, at least not to the extent that Roosevelt believed, and they held to the idea that nature should be left in a pristine state devoid of human interference. Thanks in large part to such attitudes, Roosevelt could never enjoy a hunting expedition as president. Even in the remote wilderness, journalists hounded him relentlessly, and his hunts made great newspaper copy.

One incident in particular illustrated just how problematic such trips could be. Early in his first term Roosevelt planned a six-day bear hunt in Mississippi. This would be his first high-profile hunt as president, and as such it was carefully monitored by the press. He was camped along the banks of the Little Sunflower River, where the terrain was a dense tangle of thick underbrush, stunted pines, and canebrake. For this particular hunt, Roosevelt depended on the skill of his guide, the hunter Holt Collier. Collier had killed his first bear when he was just ten and worked as a bear-hunting guide for more than thirty years. By the time Roosevelt met him, he had killed more than three thousand bears. There was no better companion for the Mississippi trip.

Collier hunted with hounds, and though the dogs picked up the scent of a bear early in the morning on November 14, 1902, the chase went on for hours, and Roosevelt was called back to camp to wait for a predetermined signal. Just as he was sitting down for a picnic lunch, the hounds caught up to the bear. They had cornered it in a low, swampy hollow where they could circle around the bear, keeping it at bay. But not for long.

Collier bugled for Roosevelt to come at once, but suddenly the bear lunged forward and grabbed one of the dogs, crushing it to death with a bite to the neck. Frustrated with his absentee client but without permission to kill the bear himself, Collier did the only thing he could under the circumstances—he whacked the bear with the barrel of his gun, stunning it so that it was technically still alive but no longer a danger to his dogs. He then lassoed the bear around the neck and secured it to a nearby tree while he waited for the president of the United States.

When he finally arrived, Roosevelt was dismayed to see the scene of the struggle, clearly a violation of the important sportsman code he had worked hard to write with the Boone and Crockett Club. One dead dog lay in the dirt, two injured dogs stood by, and the stunned bear was still tied to the tree, groaning. The press was gathered, pencils poised, waiting for the president to shoot the bear.

But he couldn't do it. He had shot plenty of animals at bay before, but the idea of having another man incapacitate a bear so that he could hustle on to the scene and blast it was anathema to him. The papers would have a field day, but, more crucially, such an act would violate the "fair chase" laws and his own personal ethics. According to Roosevelt's sportsman's code, the hunt should always be a pitting of one man's skill against his quarry—an animal-to-animal contest that left some room for the nonhuman to escape. But this business of tying a wounded bear to a tree was an entirely different matter. Roosevelt would have no part of it. Offering his ivory-handled knife, he asked one of the onlookers to put the animal out of its misery, but no one dared to take the president's Tiffany dagger. They quickly dispatched the animal, slung it over a horse, and trudged back to camp.

While most reports spun the details of the hunt into a chivalrous story of a good sportsman refusing to shoot a subdued bear, the episode was a devastating blow to Roosevelt, who was forced to acknowledge that he would never be able to experience the full thrill of nature while in office. The potential for some misstep that would give both the presidency and the sport of hunting a bad name was just too high. Among the press were those just waiting for the president to make a mistake. The hunting trips of heads of state were simply too high-profile, and Roosevelt made the difficult decision to all but hang up his rifle while he remained in office.

Chapter 13

WHO'S A NATURE FAKER?

*I*n the spring of 1903, President Roosevelt was to embark on a grand western tour to include a stay at Yellowstone Park. It was supposed to present an opportunity for him to trumpet his conservation agenda—something he finally felt confident enough to do—before the 1904 election, but he couldn't resist the lure of the park's pristine wilderness and had been quietly trying to arrange a hunt. Through the Boone and Crockett Club, Roosevelt had played a part in helping to protect Yellowstone's ungulates (hooved animals such as deer and elk) from market hunting and commercial development. He had a vested interest in the park, believing it to be an important sanctuary and breeding ground from which the surrounding wilderness could be repopulated after so many years of exploitation. More than anything, Roosevelt wanted to ensure the continuation of hunting. As a naturalist, he firmly believed that by curtailing predation on elk by cougars, he could help these tenuous deer populations recover. He was not simply being altruistic, though—he wanted to hunt—but the premise of thinning out the predators gave him a degree of political cover. It was one of the few scenarios in which Roosevelt could envision having an opportunity to hunt while he was president without the usual dangers of public outcry.

However, many of Roosevelt's political confidants warned him that if the public found out about his activities in Yellowstone, it would create a scandal—hunting was forbidden in the park. Even though the park's superintendent had personally written Roosevelt to tell him that the cougars "have simply got to be thinned out," Roosevelt grew increasingly worried that the need to bring in a pack of trained dogs to help him find the cougars would draw too much public attention. Still wary after his fiasco in Mississippi, he abandoned all ideas of a Yellowstone hunt.

As an alternative, Roosevelt invited the great naturalist John Burroughs to be his traveling companion at Yellowstone. Burroughs was a natural-history celebrity in his day. Tall, unassuming, and with a full snowy-white beard, he was widely revered by the American people as a popularizer of a simpler life closer to nature.

Of course, word of the possibility of a hunt leaked out—such a big operation couldn't be kept a secret—and as news spread, some of those opposed to hunting voiced their dissent, calling the president a hypocrite for even considering the idea of a Yellowstone hunt, as he had worked tirelessly to establish the park in the first place. Yellowstone National Park was supposed to be a place where animals could live without fear of being hunted, at least by humans. Many of these "mushy sentimentalists," as Roosevelt dubbed them, assumed that the sagelike Burroughs was in sympathy with them, but this was hardly the case. Burroughs actually supported Roosevelt's hunting, knowing that the hunter-naturalists had more respect for and knowledge of nature than some of the public decrying the hunt did.

Some of our newspapers reported that the President intended to hunt in the Park. A woman in Vermont wrote me, to protest against the hunting, and hoped I would teach the President to love the animals as much as I did,—as if he did not love them so much more, because his love is founded upon knowledge, and because they had been a part of his life. She did not know that I was then cherishing the secret hope that I might be allowed to shoot a cougar or bobcat; but this fun did not come to me. The President said, "I will not fire a gun in the Park; then I shall have no explanations to make." . . . I have never been disturbed by the President's hunting trips. It is to such men as he that the big game legitimately belongs,—men who regard it from the

point of view of the naturalist as well as from that of the sportsman, who are interested in its preservation, and who share with
the world the delight they experience in the chase.

Roosevelt and Burroughs set off largely alone in the park, with
only a small party of guides accompanying them. As Burroughs explained: "He [Roosevelt] craved once more to be alone with nature;
he was evidently hungry for the wild and aboriginal—a hunger that
seems to come upon him regularly at least once a year, and drives him
forth on his hunting trips for big game in the West."

Roosevelt and Burroughs spent two weeks in the park together,
occupying camps on the Gardiner River before moving higher up
into the geyser region. The snow was still five or six feet deep, and
as they were making their way in a horse-drawn sleigh, something
caught Roosevelt's eye. He leapt from the sled and dove for a mouse
scurrying across the ground, saying to Burroughs that it would make
an excellent specimen for Merriam—and perhaps even reveal a new
species. On the lakeshore that afternoon, the president skinned the
mouse and prepared its pelt with the skill of a professional taxidermist. It was the only animal that Roosevelt killed in the park.

EVEN FROM THE presidential residence, Theodore Roosevelt found
ways to engage with his beloved nature. The White House, with its
patchwork of trees, shrubs, and open lawns, was a perfect songbird
habitat. The president often walked the grounds after breakfast in the
hope of perhaps seeing a red-headed woodpecker or maybe to hear the
distinct "creaking gurgling" of the blackbirds. During a number of
hot June evenings he enjoyed the company of a pair of saw-whet owls,
"little bits of fellow, with round heads . . . I think they are the young
of the year; they never uttered the saw-whet sound, but made soft,
snoring noises." The owls appeared each evening as Theodore and
First Lady Edith sat on the south porch under the stars. "They were
fearless and unsuspicious. Sometimes they flew noiselessly to and fro,
and seemingly caught big insects on the wing."

Roosevelt sometimes paid more attention to the birds perched outside the White House windows than to the statesmen seated inside. One morning he burst into a Cabinet meeting with startling news. "Gentlemen, do you know what has happened this morning?" he squawked. Every man in the room feared national crisis, but, to their surprise, the president chirped, "I just saw a chestnut-sided warbler—and this only in February!"

The arrival of migrating birds each spring was cause for writing to the Roosevelt children, who were away at school, and in his dorm room Roosevelt's son Kermit read a letter from his father: "The birds have come back. Not only song-sparrows and robins, but a winter wren, purple finches and tufted titmice are singing in the garden." Identifying migrating warblers, however, proved challenging for Theodore— especially without having a specimen in hand. Even with the best binoculars, sight identification was difficult. And some birds, such as the dull-colored females of the various warbler species, were simply impossible to identify by sight alone. There were myrtle warblers, magnolia warblers, chestnut-sided, bay-breasted, and Blackburnian warblers along with black-throated blues, Canadians, and, later in the season, blackpoll warblers. Roosevelt grew frustrated at how difficult it was to spot these birds—especially when, after listening for a full half hour to a fine, wiry little song, the elusive singer would fly away without Roosevelt's having a firm idea what the bird was.

But when he was able to hold specimens in his hand, Roosevelt proved frighteningly perceptive of the natural world, as during a morning walk with his younger sister, Corrine, along the great circle behind the White House. As they walked through the gardens, a tiny object on the path caught his eye. It was a minute brown piece of fluff that anyone else might have missed, but, stooping to pick it up, Roosevelt squinted to examine it closely. "Very early for a fox-sparrow," he said, dropping the feather back onto the path.

Just as Roosevelt had come to speak out against the market hunters' slaughter of mammals, he used the power of his office to protect his beloved birds. He specifically targeted the plume hunters who were slaughtering millions of beautifully feathered birds for hat ornaments, a cause Roosevelt had earlier championed in a much more limited way as governor of New York, signing legislation (at the behest of ornithologist Frank Chapman) making it a crime to kill non-game birds for commercial purposes in New York State.

Chapman, bird curator at the American Museum of Natural History, was another outspoken critic of the widespread practice of using birds for hat ornaments. He once took to the streets along New York City's Ladies' Mile shopping district and on just two afternoons recorded 542 hats sporting feathers from more than forty different kinds of native birds. Impressed with Chapman's dedication, Roosevelt wrote to the man, telling him how personally he took the loss of any bird species: "When I hear of the destruction of a species, I feel just as if the works of some great writer had perished."

Roosevelt then tasked Chapman to keep checking up on some of New York's millinery factories to confirm that the law was being followed. Roosevelt had previously let it be known that certain undercover "Audubonists" were being deployed, and he threatened a state-sanctioned factory shutdown if any illegal feathers were found.

Now, as president of the United States, Roosevelt was in a position to enact change on a national level. The frontlines of the "feather wars" were being waged in a place called Pelican Island in Florida. It was just a tiny patch of land on the Indian River, but it was a nesting area for countless egrets, ibises, and spoonbills, and the plume hunters were shooting them as they sat on their nests—a situation that was unsustainable. Ornithologists, in an effort spearheaded by Chapman, had been fighting to stop the slaughter on Pelican Island for years with little traction, but now there was a naturalist in the White House.

Roosevelt declared Pelican Island a federal bird reservation on March 14, 1903, thereby establishing the country's first National Wildlife Refuge. From that declaration, all birds on the island were free to breed unmolested. It was a modest start as far as conservation efforts go, but it was a success that encouraged Roosevelt to take even more robust action. By the end of his presidency, he had created a total of fifty-one such wildlife refuges.

WHILE ROOSEVELT MAY not have been the first president to pen a book, he was the first to have one published while in office. *The Deer*

Family was the first of an intended ten-volume series proposed for the American Sportsman's Library. Roosevelt wrote the introduction and the first half, which included chapters on elk, white-tailed deer, mule deer, and (although technically not a deer) pronghorn, while three prominent mammalogists contributed chapters for the remainder of the book.

Unlike in many of his earlier writings, Roosevelt scarcely mentioned his hunting exploits in *The Deer Family.* Instead, he focused on animal behavior. He was much less sensational than before, striving for the book to be as factually accurate as possible. He was also meticulous, and on reviewing his first copy in the White House, Theodore immediately noted small inaccuracies with two of the illustrations. One was labeled "The Black-tail of Colorado," but, as Roosevelt could clearly see, it was "on an animal with a head of the Colorado blacktail, but with the tail of the blacktail of Columbia. There is not and never has been any kind of Rocky Mountain blacktail or mule deer, which has such a tail as that carefully and prominently pictured in the illustration." The second error related to an illustration labeled "The Whitetail in Flight," except "both the head and the tail are those of the Colorado or Rocky Mountain blacktail, or mule deer." These were, of course, minor errors that the general population was sure not to notice, but facts were important to Theodore. Roosevelt published *The Deer Family* at a time when nature study was extremely popular.

As a reaction to a period of rapid urbanization, the country was in the midst of an environmental awakening. Nature books were frequent best sellers, and Roosevelt had dreams of launching a series of successful natural-history books that would both edify and entertain. But popular taste was swinging in the other direction. Writers were penning anthropomorphic wild-animal stories, which in no way reflected the natural world, and American readers favored them over anything Roosevelt wrote. The market for such books was enormous, and, with money to be made, authors rushed to get titles to print. Many of these writers had no background or experience with natural history, instead drawing on personal sentiment and producing what one reviewer called a "whole lot of goody-goody books of the natural history kind."

One of the worst offenders was Reverend William J. Long. His immensely popular stories were narrated in his own voice, in an attempt to transmit to the reader a feeling of harmony with the world's creatures. The works of Long and other like-minded authors riled experienced naturalists, who felt that these authors were either innocently or maliciously deceiving their readers. In their view, the sheer emotional power of Long's stories made his writings particularly dangerous. They were worried that the general readership would take his sentimental misrepresentations for natural-history truth.

In protest, Roosevelt's Yellowstone companion John Burroughs published an open letter to the *Atlantic Monthly* explaining why such drivel was harmful. Reverend Long rebutted, saying that he was simply trying to make points about the diversity of animal behavior and that no single person had any right to condemn the observations of another. The mere incredibility of a single incident was no proof that it hadn't happened, Long claimed. "I have never read such nonsense in my life," Roosevelt wrote to Burroughs when he saw Long's response.

At first Roosevelt vented his frustrations to Burroughs privately, but as the controversy boiled, he could no longer contain himself and jumped into the fray. Roosevelt's opinion was printed in the June issue of *Everybody's Magazine* in a piece titled "Roosevelt on the Nature Fakirs": "I don't believe for a minute, that some of these men who are writing nature stories and putting the word 'truth' prominently in their prefaces know the heart of the wild things. They don't know, or if they did know, they indulge in the wildest exaggerations under the mistaken notion that they are strengthening their stories."

It is not often that a private citizen is singled out for attack by a sitting president, let alone a clergyman writing treacly stories about cute, furry animals. Of course, the incident meant that Long's popularity only skyrocketed. He was the "dove shot at by an elephant gun," and he insisted on fighting back. He wrote another open letter—this time to the president—explaining how unfair it was for the most powerful politician in the country to attack a little man he had never met and that he had used his high office to cowardly effect. Two weeks later, Long issued a third open letter arguing that President Roosevelt was nothing more than a "big bully" who took delight in "whooping through the woods killing everything in sight." Long thought it absurd for Roosevelt to consider himself a naturalist. "He is a hunter and nothing more."

Roosevelt then made a major gaffe, reiterating that Long "didn't know the heart of a wild thing." Long fired back: "Every time Mr. Roosevelt gets near the heart of a wild thing, he invariably puts a bullet through it."

Long went on: "From his own records I have reckoned a full thousand hearts which he has thus known intimately. In one chapter alone I find that he violently gained knowledge of eleven noble elk hearts in a few days." He was referring to *Hunting Trips of a Ranchman* and *The Wilderness Hunter* with dramatic effect. He did a page-by-page accounting of all the animals Roosevelt had killed and made a special effort to quote some of Roosevelt's most gory discourses. After painting such a bloody picture of Roosevelt, Long concluded, "If it is charged that I do not understand nature as Mr. Roosevelt does, I stand up and plead guilty; yes, guilty in every page, every paragraph, and every sentence."

The American people tended to sympathize with Long, even if his accounts were inaccurate and misleading. They considered him less guilty of wrongdoing, especially compared to the belligerent Roosevelt, who had not only slaughtered so many animals but who was also on record as saying he wanted to "skin Long alive."

The whole controversy came to a dramatic conclusion when it was proposed that the nation's top professional naturalists publish their views in a symposium, which appeared in the September issue of *Everybody's Magazine* under the title "Real Naturalists on Nature Faking." The symposium was led by William Temple Hornaday, director of the New York Zoological Society, who had written a rather snarky takedown of the clergyman. Also weighing in was Roosevelt's good friend Clinton Hart Merriam, and, as chief of the U.S. Biological Survey, he commanded tremendous prestige. Merriam cuttingly declared, "The Reverend Dr. Long is possessed of that rare gift of a creative memory . . . a nature writer blessed with the Creative Memory does not have to go about wasting valuable time waiting and watching for animals to appear and do something. . . ." Joel A. Allen, curator of mammalogy and ornithology at the American Museum of Natural History, also lashed out at Long for accusing scientists of attacking him out of jealousy of his book sales, when, in fact, they were reacting to his injustices to science.

That same issue of *Everybody's Magazine* included another stand-alone article by President Roosevelt titled "Nature Fakers." Roosevelt's barbs were now thrown at the editors who accepted Long's work, rather than faulting only the clergyman. "We abhor deliberate and reckless untruth in this study of natural history as much as in any other and therefore we feel that a grave wrong is committed by all who . . . encourage such untruth."

In the end, Roosevelt and the naturalists won a Pyrrhic victory— although they were technically correct, they had irreparably tarnished their reputations by ruthlessly attacking the elderly and nationally beloved Long, who soon afterward went both blind and insane. Roosevelt could not have cared less and was now more than ever determined to force his own brand of naturalism upon the public. Frustrated with critics jabbing at his hunting, and determined to upend sentimental attitudes, Roosevelt squared off to deliver the knockout punch of his own brand of naturalism, laying bare for all to see the harsh realities of animal life as it truly existed in the wild.

PART III

Roosevelt's New Naturalism

Most big-game hunters never learn anything about the game except how to kill it; and most naturalists never observe it at all.

—THEODORE ROOSEVELT

Chapter 14

I AM GOING TO AFRICA

*E*ver since his Harvard days, when he received the grim news about his fragile heart, Roosevelt knew that he could drop dead at any moment. He expected his life to be short and relished the thought of having an especially heroic demise. Whether during his close encounter with an enormous grizzly in the Bighorns or his bullet-zinged charge up Kettle Hill in the Spanish–American War, Roosevelt enjoyed the temptation of bringing his life to its grand finale.

Visions of death and legacy were likely swirling through Roosevelt's head when, after winning the White House in 1904, he abruptly announced that, after completing his next term, he would never run for office again. Official presidential term limits did not yet exist, so Roosevelt technically could have stayed in power for the rest of his life. But, having finally been elected by the people instead of by an assassin's bullet, Roosevelt wanted to end his career as a winner. To anyone who asked, he explained that he was merely following the two-term tradition set by George Washington, but his advancing age was likely closer to the truth. At forty-six, Roosevelt was already feeling the onset of rheumatism and his expanding waistline, and he could not bear the thought of spending his last healthy years sitting in the White House. That was not how he wanted the story of his life to end.

He also knew that he was missing out on a great deal of fun. The rough-and-tumble world of Washington, D.C., politics certainly had its appeal, but it was no substitute for real outdoor adventure. "I am fond of politics, but fonder still of a little big-game hunting," he wrote before the start of his first western buffalo hunt in 1883, and the same still applied more than a quarter century later. But being president was an impediment to Roosevelt's ability to hunt. The job demanded his full attention, and the constant presence of newspapermen since his disastrous Mississippi bear hunt kept him cautious. Writing to his son Kermit, he explained how "all kinds of people crowd after me, and it is too much like hunting with a 4th of July procession." As president of the United States, Roosevelt had little choice but to wait until he was out of office before contemplating any serious hunting.

Retreating to the leather-bound chairs of his study, he found respite in books, and these remained an important part of Roosevelt's nature experience—the adventures on the pages coming alive for him almost as vividly as if he were there. Just as he had when he was a boy, Roosevelt found himself drawn to stories of East Africa. The railroads were opening up the continent, as had happened years earlier in the American West, and many hunters were writing books about their adventures on the far continent. Paving the way was Lieutenant Colonel John Henry Patterson's best-selling *The Man-Eaters of Tsavo*, which tracked the predations of a pair of lions ravaging the railway workers constructing the new Uganda line. In Patterson's book, it was the hunter who played the role of hero, finally taming the ferocious beasts standing in the way of progress. From British conservationist Edward North Buxton's *Two African Trips* to Winston Churchill's *My African Journey*, Roosevelt voraciously consumed the adventures of these hunters. He even read African hunting stories to his children, so much so that they grew up unusually knowledgeable of African fauna. As far as Roosevelt was concerned, East Africa was "the greatest of the world's great hunting grounds."

Hunters from all regions were also regular visitors in the Roosevelt White House. If Roosevelt could not travel to the hunt, he could, at least, bring the hunters to him. Sometimes these were of the "backwoods" type; for example, in 1907 he hosted a "bear hunt dinner" that was attended by a number of his especially rugged chums. "We had bear meat as the main course, as well as wild turkey, I think it was about as nice a dinner as we have ever had in the White House.

Nobody wore dress suits, for I think most of the bear hunters did not have any." More often, though, the hunters were of the refined British type, and of these Roosevelt especially enjoyed the company of fellow African enthusiast Frederick Courteney Selous. Tall, fit, and with a neatly trimmed snow-white beard and clear blue eyes, Selous was the picture of a dashing British sportsman. Any time Selous came to visit the White House, the affairs of state were set aside for the occasion, freeing the friends to discuss African animals and hunting well into the night.

Like Roosevelt and many other naturalists, Selous started out with a love of birds, and he, too, was influenced early on by the writings of hunters. As a child, he was captivated by William Charles Baldwin's *African Hunting from Natal to the Zambezi*, which planted in him the resolve to one day become an African hunter-naturalist. Once caught sleeping on the bare floor instead of in his bed, he explained that he was merely trying to harden himself for his future life in Africa, exclaiming, "I mean to be like Livingstone."

Leaving England for South Africa at the age of nineteen, Selous set out to make his fortune hunting ivory in a land where elephants were already scarce. He had to trek far inland and got off to a bad start when someone stole his prized double-barreled rifle. Forced to make do with a clumsy muzzle-loader that fired a four-ounce ball of lead, he was badly burned by an accidental gunpowder explosion, nearly died of thirst in the bush when lost for days there, and when he finally found the chief of the Matabele people to ask permission to hunt elephants on his turf, he was mocked for his hubris and small stature: "You are only a boy; have you come to hunt tiny antelope?"

Unlike most ivory hunters, who pursued their quarry on horseback, Selous hunted on foot. This allowed him to penetrate deep into tsetse-fly areas, where horses could not survive due to the rinderpest disease these flies carried. Here, the elephants had learned that they were safe from hunters, a false security that Selous exploited. He spent years killing elephants this way, becoming an African legend. Roosevelt must have seethed with envy every time he read of another of Selous's adventures. "Who could wish a better life," he mused many years later. But Roosevelt's life was full of commitments, none of which related to elephant hunting. In a letter to Selous, he voiced his frustration:

> *I have found it more and more difficult to get away; for the last eight years, indeed, my hunting trips have merely been short outings. . . . I cannot say how I long at times for the great rolling prairies. . . . I also long for the other wilderness which I have never seen, and never shall see, excepting through your books. . . . It may be that some time I can break away from this sedentary life for a hunt somewhere; and of all the things possible to me, I should like to take this hunt among the big bears of Alaska. . . . But I don't know whether I shall ever get the chance.*

Nearing the end of his presidency, Roosevelt was hungry for a good hunt, and although seriously considering Alaska, he had confided to Selous that an African safari was still one of his greatest ambitions, even if it always seemed more dream than reality. Alaska was certainly the more feasible destination, and the chance to hunt dangerous game in North America was a real draw. Ever since the Harriman Alaska Expedition made hunting in the territory popular, quite a number of Alaskan hunter-naturalists had been sending their bear skulls back to Washington, D.C., where Clinton Hart Merriam was busily describing some of them as new species and subspecies. But despite the efforts in Alaska, the numbers of bear skulls available in the Smithsonian's National Museum of Natural History were still inadequate, and Roosevelt wondered if he needed to go to Alaska to shoot more bears for the collection, much as he had done with the Colorado cougars. As he approached his last year in the White House, Roosevelt had not yet made up his mind about his next destination. Hardheaded devotion to America pushed him closer to hunting in Alaska, but he could never completely quiet his boyish passion for Africa.

He finally made up his mind in the middle of a presidential dinner party. Seated next to Roosevelt was Carl Akeley, a museum taxidermist and African explorer who was getting a lot of attention for the new ways in which he was preparing specimens. Roosevelt had previously admired one of Akeley's works, an especially expressive deer head Akeley had entered in the Sportsmen's Show in New York in 1895. Roosevelt, who was the state's governor at the time, was one of the taxidermy judges, and he awarded Akeley a prize. Back at the Field Museum of Natural History in Chicago, Akeley had started working on a more ambitious project called *The Four Seasons*, which displayed not only heads but entire deer standing in exquisite, re-alistic settings representing all four seasons. What made Akeley's taxidermy especially lifelike was his training as a sculptor; he had perfected a technique that not so much stuffed animals as, rather, arranged their skins over sculptured mannequins that conveyed the spirit of the living animal. The specimens were placed in detailed, three-dimensional reconstructions of their habitats; the scenes were groundbreaking. Roosevelt later visited the Field Museum as vice president, and he was so impressed with the *Four Seasons* exhibit that he invited Carl Akeley to the White House, an event for which Akeley was required to get a new "store bought" suit.

Akeley had just returned from a Field Museum expedition to Af-rica, and, sitting next to the president, he hardly had a chance to eat. Roosevelt aggressively hounded him to tell of his adventures, mining his guest for vicarious thrills. One of Akeley's most vivid stories was of being jumped by a wounded leopard—which attack he survived only because he had the presence of mind to choke the animal to death by shoving his fist down its throat after it bit his hand. Perhaps rolling up his sleeves to show off his scars, Akeley went on to tell another story, of how he was left for dead in the Somali desert, living only by demanding at gunpoint a lifesaving drink from a passing caravan.

But the story that most captivated Roosevelt was about the sixteen lions emerging from the mouth of a cave Akeley once counted at a place just outside Nairobi called Juja Farm. Lions were known to pop-ulate the area around that cave in great numbers, and they had a repu-tation for being especially bold and fearless. Roosevelt was transfixed. Although earlier that evening he had seemed determined to hunt in Alaska—the North Woods hunter at the table already congratulating himself for winning the president's favor—Roosevelt capped off the evening with a sudden change of mind. He turned to Akeley and with great resolution proclaimed: "As soon as I am through with this job, I am going to Africa."

Africa! It had been decades since Roosevelt had set foot on the continent, and he had little idea how to begin planning his trip. Writing to Frederick Courteney Selous to prepare, he could hardly contain his enthusiasm. "How would it do for me to try to go in somewhere from Zanzibar and come out down the Nile, or vice versa? What time ought I to go? That is, what time ought I make my entry into the country? Is there anyone who could give me an idea of how much the trip will cost; and, finally, could you tell me whether there are people to whom I could write to ask about engaging porters, or whatever it is I would travel with? I hope I am not asking too many questions."

This breathless note was followed by a flurry of similar letters to about a half dozen other prominent hunters, all nearly identical in their tone of earnest questioning. Writing to Kermit at Harvard, he asked his son to come along. "You blessed fellow, I do not think you will have to wait until your ship comes in before making that African trip. If all goes well I intend to make it soon after I leave the Presidency, and unless there is a very real reason to the contrary, you will go with me. It ought to be a very interesting trip." Like his father, Kermit was manly and athletic—he had even taken up boxing—and Roosevelt hoped to add a little African hunting to the boy's repertoire.

Edith, meanwhile, was wringing her hands over the thought of her husband and son traipsing across the African plains for a year. Anticolonial sentiment was still a source of great tension, and there had just been an epidemic of sleeping sickness in the region. Transmitted by the bite of the tsetse fly, the disease had no known cure, and most cases resulted in death. Roosevelt took it all with humor, reminding everyone that *sleeping* sickness was of no concern, because it did not suit his active personality. But even minor scrapes and cuts can be potentially dangerous in the tropics, as they are especially prone to infection in the tropical environment. The dangers facing Roosevelt on the safari were not lost on the general public, and some of his detractors seemed to genuinely hope for his speedy demise, quipping that every lion should "do its duty."

Edith's concerns were not allayed by some of the mail delivered to Oyster Bay that summer, as Roosevelt corresponded with politicians and naturalists in preparation for his upcoming trip. Some of these men couldn't help but make light of the dangers the president would face. Theodore's old friend, British diplomat Cecil Spring Rice, sent him a pamphlet on sleeping sickness but joked that there was no reason to worry because he would no doubt escape the dreaded disease on account of having previously been eaten by a lion or crocodile or mauled by an enraged elephant or buffalo. More alarming—and perhaps more personal—were some of the pieces that ran in the papers. An article in the Philadelphia *Ledger*, for example, remarked that since Roosevelt had already had a very colorful career, and as it was probably now at an end, it would be a fitting and wholly happy conclusion if he were to die in bold and dramatic fashion on safari. Roosevelt found it all very amusing (if anything, the articles actually fueled his obsession with a heroic death), and even Edith finally admitted that the dangers of Africa were really no worse than the dangers of being president, the target of crank assassins.

More than disease and dismemberment, Roosevelt dreaded the specter of being trailed through Africa by tourists or, worse, a horde of reporters. Roosevelt had long resented the press for its interference in his hunts, and he entertained the idea of getting the colonial authorities to intervene on this trip, perhaps buying him some time to elude the reporters in the wild. He also went to great lengths to make it widely known that he would not say anything to the press while on safari, so that any quotes published would be known to be without authority and foundation. He even appealed to the Associated Press, telling its general manager that it would be a "wanton outrage" for them to send reporters to follow a private citizen into the bush.

At first, Roosevelt was planning nothing more than a father-and-son hunt—something he had been dreaming about since his earliest wanderings in the West. For years he had been writing to Kermit about the possibility of their taking such a trip. Of his four sons, Kermit was the one most interested in the sport, and Roosevelt hoped to share with him a bit of true wilderness—to ride across unfenced plains and to hunt vast herds of game in a land where the onslaught of the railroads had only just begun. When a younger man himself, Roosevelt was "just in time to see the last of the real wilderness life and real wilderness hunting" in the American West; now he hoped to share a bit of the same spirit with Kermit on the plains of East Africa.

To bankroll the trip, Roosevelt accepted a $50,000 advance from *Scribner's Magazine* to write a series of twelve articles detailing his safari even as it unfolded, the plan being to finally publish them all in book form at the end of the expedition. Other magazines had made more lucrative offers, but Roosevelt didn't think them "dignified and appropriate" enough to publish his work, and the $50,000 was more than enough to cover the party's expenses, with some left over for Edith's trip through Europe (she was to be reunited with her husband at the end of the expedition in Khartoum—"lions, mosquitoes and the tsetse fly permitting").

Two British hunters—Frederick Courteney Selous and Edward North Buxton, both Boone and Crockett Club members—helped Roosevelt plan his trip, and through dozens of exchanges the three men carefully considered routes, personnel, and equipment. Sometimes the Brits gave Roosevelt conflicting advice. One of the most serious points of contention related to the type of guide he should rely on in the bush. Selous felt very strongly that Roosevelt needed a "white hunter," while Buxton countered that he should "trust to the native." Roosevelt was puzzled over what to do; he trusted the opinions of both but eventually sided with Selous and hired the same professional hunter Carl Akeley had recently used. Following Buxton's advice on another matter, though, he arranged his trip as a series of smaller two-month-long safaris that would set off from points along the Uganda Railway. Roosevelt figured that two months was sufficient time to get him into "good game country and out of the ordinary tourist infested areas."

Roosevelt gave serious thought to the nature of his trip. For plenty of moments in his past he had been caught up in the thrill of the hunt, yet he always remained a naturalist at heart. It was not lost on him that his upcoming African trip was very much like one that medical missionary David Livingstone might have taken, and this certainly brought up feelings from his earliest stirrings as a naturalist. From the beginning Roosevelt had identified with museum collectors and shared the need to build up natural-history collections. Although certainly at moments in his adolescence his zeal for hunting got the better of him, ever since meeting George Bird Grinnell and founding the Boone and Crockett Club, Roosevelt had strived to marry the finest qualities of both museum collecting and sport hunting. As a naturalist, he hoped that the chief value of the safari would be his observations "upon the habits of the game, and to a lesser extent of birds, small mammals, etc." Hunting was only part of what motivated him, and he was eager to have more than a "mere holiday after big game." So just three months into the planning, Roosevelt came up with a far more ambitious plan, and one that took into consideration his earliest boyhood passions as a museum collector—to turn his hunting trip into a full-scale natural-history expedition. He wished to have along a team of naturalists to study the non-game fauna while he and Kermit collected big mammals for museum exhibits.

There was a precedent for what Roosevelt was proposing. The American Museum of Natural History's Tjäder Expedition to East Africa of 1906 had recently traveled much the same route that Roosevelt was contemplating. That expedition had consisted of one hunter and one naturalist with a special skill for preserving specimens. Together they had brought back just over two hundred large mammal specimens for the museum—a fine haul, but Roosevelt hoped his expedition would do even better. A bold expression of his lifelong dedication to naturalism was what the president had in mind. Roosevelt aspired to write himself into the annals of natural history by leading what he envisioned to be the grandest collecting expedition of all time.

FOUNDED IN 1846, the nucleus of the Smithsonian's natural-history collection was at first crammed into a castle—the institution's original Gothic Revival building on the National Mall. Some relief, in terms of a more appropriate space, came with the construction of the new Arts and Industries Building next door, but within a year the museum was again pleading for additional room. America's hunger for knowledge, and the accumulation of specimens and artifacts in the warrenlike recesses of these museum buildings, was outpacing the physical space available. Materials were pouring in faster than new buildings could be constructed.

It was during the first years of Roosevelt's presidency that Congress appropriated the funds for a new and sufficiently large building. Roosevelt gleefully signed the legislation authorizing construction of the massive neoclassical building (which still houses many of the museum's collections today) on Constitution Avenue, just a short walk from the White House. With its towering rotunda and impressive storage wings, the new museum building was conspicuous, broadcasting the vast amounts of empty space it now had to fill. Conveniently for the outgoing president, the building was expected to be completed just in time for his planned return from Africa. Roosevelt approached Charles Doolittle Walcott, the administrator of the Smithsonian Institution, with an idea:

> As you know, I am not in the least a game butcher. I like to do a certain amount of hunting, but my real and main interest is the interest of a faunal naturalist. Now, it seems to me that this opens up the best chance for the National Museum to get a fine collection, not only of the big game beasts, but of the smaller animals and birds of Africa; and looking at it dispassionately, it seems to me that the chance ought not to be neglected. I will make arrangements in connection with publishing a book which will enable me to pay for the expenses of myself and my son. But what I would like to do would be to get one or two professional field taxidermists, field naturalists, to go with us, who should prepare and send back the specimens we collect. The collection which would thus go to the National Museum would be of unique value.

The "unique value" Roosevelt was referring to, of course, was the chance to acquire specimens shot by him—the president of the United States. Always a tough negotiator, Roosevelt put pressure on Walcott by mentioning that he was also thinking about posing his offer to the American Museum of Natural History in New York—but that, as president, he felt it was only appropriate that his specimens go to the Smithsonian in Washington, D.C.

Compared to those of other museums, the Smithsonian's African-mammal collection was paltry back then. The Smithsonian had sent a man to explore Kilimanjaro in 1891 and another to the eastern Congo, but the museum still held relatively few specimens. Both the Field Museum in Chicago and the American Museum in New York had been sending regular expeditions to the continent, bringing home thousands of African specimens. Eager not to fall farther behind, Walcott took up Roosevelt's offer and agreed to pay for the preparation and transport of specimens. He also agreed to set up a special fund through which private donors could contribute to the expedition. (As a public museum, the Smithsonian's budget was largely controlled by Congress, and Roosevelt worried that politics might get in the way of his expedition—the fund solved this sticky issue).

As far as Walcott was concerned, the expedition was both a scientific and a public-relations coup. Not only would the museum obtain an important collection from a little-explored corner of Africa, but the collection would come from someone who was arguably one of the most recognized men in America—the president of the United States. Under the aegis of the Smithsonian Institution, Roosevelt's proposed safari had been transformed from a hunting trip to a serious natural-history expedition promising lasting scientific significance. An elated Roosevelt wrote Frederick Courteney Selous to tell him the good news—the trip would be conducted for science, and he would contribute to the stock of important knowledge being accumulated on the habits of big game.

Roosevelt saw the trip as perhaps his "last chance for something in the nature of a great adventure," and he devoted the last months of his lame-duck presidency to little other than making preparations. Equipment needed to be purchased, routes mapped, guns and ammo selected. He admitted that he found it very difficult to "devote full attention to his presidential work, he was so eagerly looking forward to his African trip." Having studied the accounts of other hunters, he knew that the Northern Guaso Nyiro River and the regions north of Mount Elgon were the best places to hunt, and that he had to make a trip to Mount Kenya if he was to have any chance at getting a big bull elephant. He made a list of animals he sought, ordering them by priority: lion, elephant, black rhinoceros, buffalo, giraffe, hippo, eland, sable, oryx, kudu, wildebeest, hartebeest, warthog, zebra, waterbuck, Grant's gazelle, reedbuck, and topi. He also hoped to get up into some of the fly-infested habitats of northern Uganda in search of the rare white rhino. Winston Churchill had shot one the year prior, and, after reading all about Churchill's safari—which was serialized in *Strand Magazine* and later released as a book, *My African Journey*— Roosevelt was inspired by the Brit's feat.

Roosevelt did use the power of his office to open doors for himself in Africa, but when the colonial officials suggested a hunt in the reserves, he demurred, making it clear he did not want to shoot in areas that were entirely closed. Roosevelt had developed a strong aversion to hunting in protected enclaves. "I shall leave Mombasa just as soon as I can after reaching there; go straight to Nairobi, stay there as short a time as possible. . . . I particularly wish to avoid going on any hunting-trip immediately around Nairobi or in the neighborhood of the railroad, for that would be to invite reporters and photographers to accompany me, and in short, it would mean just what I am most anxious to avoid."

Assembling a crack team of field naturalists for the expedition proved challenging. The American university system had long since abandoned outdoor study in the natural sciences in favor of laboratory work, and professional naturalists were hard to find. Experimental biology was deemed more "scientific" than mere wanderings in the wilderness, and university presidents seemed to prefer the look of crisp lab coats and bubbling beakers to that of dead animals and dusty trappers. This new crop of histologists and embryologists sneered at the outdoor naturalists, and, as Roosevelt put it, the result was to "crush out the old school of faunal naturalists." Roosevelt resented how the universities were transforming otherwise vigorous naturalists into hunched-over microscopists, and he still harbored a grudge from his own frustrations as a young naturalist at Harvard. Roosevelt called these laboratory scientists "little scientific men," and he wanted none of them on his African expedition.

Instead, he would populate his party with men of science who had experience in the field. At Walcott's suggestion, Roosevelt selected a retired Army physician with ample experience in the tropics named Dr. Edgar A. Mearns to lead the scientific team. Mearns was touted as the "best field naturalist and collector in the United States." Short of stature, slight of build, and with an imposing walrus moustache, Mearns—who, at 52, was just two years older than Roosevelt—had spent years collecting zoological and botanical specimens and had already collected thousands for both the Smithsonian and the American Museum. While serving in the Philippines during the Spanish–American War, he had sometimes put himself in the line of fire to collect particularly valuable specimens (and rumor had it that he also liked to collect human skulls after skirmishes in the jungle). Given this robust résumé, Roosevelt had full confidence in Mearns and left it to him to recruit the rest of his scientific team. Mearns selected the two best men to join him on the trip—American zoologist Edmund Heller and American mammalogist and field naturalist J. Alden Loring.

Heller was just returning from a trip in Alaska when he was asked to join the expedition. At thirty-four, Heller was rather dapper, with his hair parted neatly just off the centerline of his scalp. But he was also experienced, having traveled throughout the Southwest, Mexico, and Central America as a professional collector for the Field Museum. He had also been Carl Akeley's accomplice in Africa, and it was Akeley who recommended Heller for the Roosevelt expedition.

At age thirty-eight, Loring sported a full moustache to offset his thinning hair. A seasoned hunter and outdoorsman from upstate New York but with considerable experience in the American West as a member of Clinton Hart Merriam's Biological Survey, he had already been sent abroad to collect small mammals in Sweden and northern Europe, where he set an unofficial record by trapping nearly a thousand specimens in just three months' time. His job on the Roosevelt trip was to target the smallest of species—to be the catcher of thousands of African rats, bats, and shrews.

Gathering some of these naturalists together at Sagamore Hill, Heller developed a firsthand appreciation for the president's expertise in mammalogy; he was struck by Roosevelt's encyclopedic knowledge of obscure animals. "He is well aware of the distinctions between the different genera of rodents and also with the characters of the northern species notwithstanding the extreme obscurity of many of them," he marveled in a letter to Merriam.

As Roosevelt's venture grew to the size of a military expedition—and at Selous's protestations that if Roosevelt didn't stop adding to it, he would end up spending all his time managing logistics instead of enjoying his trip—Roosevelt reluctantly agreed to contract an outfitter. Newland, Tarlton & Co. was the very best at planning lavish East African safaris, but they were caught off guard when the swashbuckling Roosevelt rebuked them for thinking him effete after they made the mistake of suggesting that he pack some pâté de foie gras and other French delicacies. The president struck these items from the list, penciling in practical canned beans and tomatoes in their place. Cracking open a can of beans brought back fond memories of his many outdoor adventures, lifting his spirits in a way that no French delicacy ever could. His only luxury was to be a selection of homegrown strawberry, raspberry, and blackberry jams for those rare occasions when he craved a sweet treat.

Selous was curious to know how much liquor Roosevelt wanted to bring along, but on this matter he was clear. "I do not believe in drinking while on a trip of this kind, and I would wish to take only the minimum amount of whiskey and champagne which would be necessary in the event of sickness." Later he would eliminate all the whiskey except for three flasks, but he kept a case of champagne handy "in case of fever." Roosevelt made an exception for brandy, which was also brought along for medicinal purposes. By the end of the trip Roosevelt would have drunk no more than six ounces of the stuff.

The president of the United States took pride in choosing mostly American-made firearms, favoring his military-style .30 1903 Springfield Sporter, "a sturdy, reliable bolt-action rifle of perhaps a somewhat light caliber for the larger African game but perfectly ideal for smaller antelope." For heavier game—buffalo, hippopotamus, and rhinoceros—he ordered a Model 1895 Winchester .405, but the rifle did not quite pass muster when it first arrived. Test-firing it in a makeshift rifle range that he set up in the basement of the White House, Roosevelt was incensed when he discovered that the sights were entirely off mark. Writing an angry letter, the president shipped it back to Winchester, demanding that it be fixed at once.

A very fine 12-gauge Fox shotgun was sent from the company as a gift. When Roosevelt first saw it, he thought it the most beautiful gun he had ever seen. He was "exceedingly proud" that it was of American manufacture, and was "almost ashamed" to take it to Africa, where it would be subjected to very rough use. The gun was intended for the gentlemanly pursuit of game birds, and Roosevelt no doubt horrified Mr. Fox when he spelled out his intentions for the gun: "I should like in case of an emergency to have it loaded with ball and use it as a spare gun for lion." Such a special gun was not meant to be a backup lion slayer.

But by far the most magnificent gun in Roosevelt's arsenal was of strictly European origin—an exquisite, double-barreled, .500/450 Holland & Holland royal-grade elephant rifle that was presented to him at the White House. It came with a list of the names of more than fifty prominent donors, led by Edward North Buxton, along with a note stating that it was "In recognition of his [Roosevelt's] services on behalf of the preservation of species by means of national parks and forest reserves, and by other means." It was an obvious gesture of respect, and Roosevelt was relieved to have received it—fine double-barrels were exceedingly expensive but absolutely essential for hunting Africa's biggest game. As for Kermit, he had his own Winchester .405, a .30/40 Winchester, and a borrowed .450 Rigby double-barreled elephant gun, though it was not nearly as impressive as his father's.

Clothing was something Roosevelt had always taken very seriously (and there was always a performer's element to his naturalist costumes). After much consideration, he settled on heavy, hobnailed boots with rubber soles, khaki trousers with leather-faced knees, tan army shirts, and a sun helmet instead of his usual slouch hat. He had a slicker for wet weather, an army overcoat, and a mackinaw for the cold African nights.

Everything the hunters might need to live in the wild for a year had to be packed and carried—axes and matches, ladles and lanterns, saddles and shovels, candles and bridles, gun-cleaning rods and sewing needles. Every specimen they collected and prepared, from tiny mice skins to enormous hippopotamus skulls, had to be packed in paint cans, barrels, or waterproof metal boxes and carried around on the expedition until they could be shipped back to America.

Supply quantities had to be exact. Bringing a little extra, out of caution, would quickly bog down the safari. Even the lantern Roosevelt would use when writing up his notes in the evening folded down into a compact four-inch square. Still, a few exceptions were made. Kermit packed his mandolin, and one item Roosevelt would never skimp on was his glasses. Without them he was practically blind, and their loss would have brought the entire safari to a standstill. Roosevelt took no chances. He packed nine pairs.

Also, perhaps considered extraneous by some explorers was the library Roosevelt brought along. He could not go anywhere, "not even into the jungles of Africa," without a fine selection of books, and he made a list of about sixty he wished to take. Titles were chosen to span the full history of Western literature and included the Bible, Homer, Shakespeare, Poe, Twain, Longfellow, and Dickens. Roosevelt passed this list to his sister Corinne, and she obtained the books in the smallest possible sizes, trimming them down at the margins so that they would fit in a good-size overcoat pocket. She then had them bound in durable pigskin—a move that marked the beginning of Roosevelt's famous "pigskin library." Specially packed in an oilcloth-lined aluminum case that weighed in at just less than a pound per book, Roosevelt's portable field library was light enough for one porter to carry it on his back yet durable enough to withstand the toughest conditions imaginable. Corinne presented the library to her brother as a parting gift, adding that she hoped he would think of her when "reading in some little mosquito cage far off in Africa." On the hunt, Roosevelt carried a volume from the collection wherever he went, and the leather covers became so stained with dust, sweat, and gun oil that they began to look and feel like a well-worn saddle.

As his departure date neared, Roosevelt reflected on the hazards that lay ahead. Africa was a dangerous place, and he suddenly grew apprehensive about bringing along Kermit. Having lived for more than fifty years with vainglorious ideas of death crowding his mind, he was perfectly content to die himself, but Kermit was just nineteen—a tender age for hunting African lions. In the weeks leading up to the safari, Roosevelt constantly reminded his son of the danger: "It is no child's play going after lion, elephant, rhino and buffalo. We must be very cautious; we must be always ready to back one another up, and probably we ought each to have a spare rifle when we move in to the attack."

Roosevelt warned Kermit that his favorite .30/30 deer rifle was too light for African game and that he had better leave it behind. He was also worried about Kermit's marksmanship; a charging lion offers just one or two shots, with no margin for error. Roosevelt was experienced enough to know that it took regular practice to develop what he called "rifle sense," and he expected that both he and Kermit would be fairly "rusty" after their month-long transatlantic voyage.

Finally, on the morning of March 23, 1909, Roosevelt and Kermit said good-bye to Edith before riding a carriage down the hill from Sagamore to the Oyster Bay train station. Newspapers reported an emotional farewell, the father and son fighting tears as they waved to their wife and mother. Arriving at the train station, the Roosevelts again welled up as they bid farewell to Quentin, the youngest Roosevelt child, before continuing on to New York City. A subway ride under the Hudson River took them to Hoboken, New Jersey, where they worked their way through a jubilant crowd to board the *Hamburg* for Naples. An estimated three thousand well-wishers converged on the scene to wave them off, and a brass band blared "The Star-Spangled Banner." Roosevelt worked the crowd, shaking hundreds of hands, even as some of those same hands clamored to snatch the gold buttons off his overcoat.

Once across the Atlantic, they changed ships, boarding the *Admiral*—another German-flagged ship, chosen because it was among those allowing transport of large volumes of ammunition, bound for the East African port city of Mombasa. The seasickness that at first troubled Roosevelt eventually subsided, and he eagerly greeted his old friend Frederick Courteney Selous, who had boarded the *Admiral* en route to his own safari. Intending to pass through many of the same parts of Kenya as Selous, Roosevelt had previously joked about the fortuitous timing of their two trips. "Three cheers! I am simply overjoyed that you are going out. It is just the last touch to make everything perfect. But you must leave me one lion somewhere! I do not care whether it has a black mane or a yellow mane, or male or female, so long as it is a lion; and I do not really expect to get one anyhow."

Life aboard the *Admiral* settled into a routine of daily anticipation interrupted only by the occasional departure of the naturalists as they made brief bird-collecting forays ashore at Suez and Aden. These birds were later skinned and stuffed in Roosevelt's own room, as it was the largest and most suitable for this task. Looking at all the taxidermy specimens being stuffed in his cabin, Roosevelt reminisced about his long-ago family trip to Egypt, dashing off a letter to his sister Corinne to tell her that the bird skins they had just collected from Suez were "drying in my room at the moment, just as if we were once more on the Nile." By the time they reached Mombasa, the Smithsonian naturalists would have collected 102 "nicely prepared" birds for the museum.

In the morning, they prepared to go ashore, and although dark storm clouds threatened, enough sun streaked down on the green hills of Mombasa to give the whitewashed buildings dotting the landscape an eerie luminosity. Roosevelt gazed at the scene from the *Admiral,* still anchored offshore. Poised to begin his adventure, it was the perfect opportunity to mentally jog through the events of his life leading up to this point—from his childhood weakness and earliest attempts at being a naturalist, to his hunts in the Dakota Badlands, and to the assassin's bullet that put him in the White House. The adventure ahead of him had been a long time coming. As it started to rain, Roosevelt gripped the deck railing, his eyes bright with excitement as he looked toward Mombasa and uttered, "That's a wonderful sight."

Chapter 15

A RAILROAD THROUGH
THE PLEISTOCENE

By evening, the day's rain had turned into a torrential downpour, and everyone was soaked as a surf boat sidled up to the *Admiral* to take the expedition ashore. It had been thirty-seven years since Roosevelt first set foot in Africa, eagerly playing the role of a museum naturalist by shooting pigeons along the banks of the Nile. This time, instead of to his bedroom collection, his specimens were going directly to the Smithsonian Institution. Having long since traded his boyhood scattergun for a big-bore rifle, Roosevelt dressed the part of an African hunter in his smart khakis and broad sun helmet. Signs of the dangers that awaited them were evident on the face of the lone man sent to row them ashore—he had been mauled by a lion the year before and was only just recovering. Perhaps even more terrifying to Roosevelt was the pack of marauding reporters who had gathered to accost him as he took his first step ashore. As swiftly as he might have shouldered a rifle, he blasted out three curt retorts—he was happy to be ashore, excited about the hunt, and in splendid health.

Waiting for him on shore was British ornithologist and administrator Lieutenant-Governor of the East African Protectorate Sir Frederick John Jackson and his local entourage, the latter of whom stared solemnly with their spears at their side. Among them stood R. J. Cuninghame and Leslie Tarlton, the two professional hunters Roosevelt had hired for the expedition. A sinewy and thickly bearded Scotsman, Cuninghame was a former arctic whaler, professional elephant hunter, and collector of animal specimens for the British Museum. As for Tarlton, he was a redheaded Australian who had fought in the Boer War and stayed behind in Africa to hunt. That first night they were treated to a lavish dinner at the Mombasa Club, although Edgar Mearns so dreaded having to wear a dinner jacket that he asked to be excused. Preparing their equipage was more important, he implored. Still miles from the nearest hunting ground, the next morning Roosevelt boarded a special train on the famous Uganda Railway—the so-called Lunatic Express—which chugged westward across hundreds of miles of barren land through what is now Kenya. Roosevelt and Selous took their seats in "first class," which in this case was an open-air bench specially affixed to the front of the locomotive just above the cowcatcher. Excluded from this prime seating, Kermit Roosevelt rode on the roof of his coach instead. Selous and the senior Roosevelt had perfect views, but at first there was hardly anything worth seeing. For miles all around there was nothing but endless palm trees and dense, thorny bushes. Here and there Roosevelt caught glimpses of guinea fowl, and a black-and-white hornbill feeding on the tracks flapped upward so close, he could almost catch it in his hands. The only indication that there might be mammals in the area came with the news that a small herd of giraffes had knocked out the telegraph lines. It was only toward dusk that Roosevelt got his first good look at a carnivore, when they nearly plowed over a hyena.

On awakening in his coach the next morning, however, Roosevelt was surprised to see an entirely different landscape—a vast panorama of grassland dotted with flat-topped acacia trees and seemingly limitless game. Long-faced hartebeests stood everywhere, zebras were scattered across the plains, and a straw-colored monkey scampered through the trees as the train chugged by. Roosevelt recognized the dark silhouettes of ostriches in the distance, and toward the horizon he could see herds of giraffes loping along. It was all a prelude to the great diversity of species he would encounter when he alit from the train: bushbuck, wildebeest, kudu, eland, reedbuck, waterbuck, duiker, dik-dik, klipspringer, pygmy antelope, and gazelle.

Roosevelt likened it to a ride through the Pleistocene—an era when big game abounded not only in Africa but all around the world, as giant mastodons, hairy rhinoceros, and lions roamed the wilds of temperate Europe, Asia, and North America. Now though, on these continents, only fossils record the former presence of these giants, so Roosevelt's comparison to a prehistoric environment was an apt one. East Africa was one of the few places on Earth where such a diverse megafauna had remained since the Pleistocene.

The reason these animals seemed so free and abundant became clear as the train rolled along. The game was protected on either side of the rail line, part of a reserve intended to give paying passengers a pleasant view. Roosevelt called it "a vast zoological garden" and a "naturalist's wonderland." For as far as he could see, the wildlife thrived in the sanctuary, and this was perfectly fine with him, even though he planned to hunt many of these same species elsewhere. Roosevelt believed wildlife conservation was a matter of common sense. He found "mushy sentimentality" repugnant and was outspoken against those "well-meaning persons" who, as a matter of principle, felt that all shooting was wrong. He was referring, of course, to the preservationists, who held firm to the belief that nature should be left alone, without human interference, even if a certain amount of game harvesting had no appreciable effect on animal populations. Sticking to *his* principles as a Boone and Crockett Club man, Roosevelt upheld game reserves as a perfect example of how the middle course was best. "There should be certain sanctuaries and nurseries where game can live and breed absolutely unmolested; and elsewhere the laws should so far as possible provide for the continued existence of the game in sufficient numbers to allow a reasonable amount of hunting on fair terms to any hardy and vigorous man fond of the sport . . . but to protest against all hunting of game is a sign of softness of head, not of soundness of heart." Always a realist, he believed it impossible to preserve the larger wild animals in regions better fit for agriculture, and he was staunchly against preserving the larger carnivores for "merely aesthetic reasons."

THE WORD *SAFARI* refers as much to the personnel and equipment of an expedition as it does to the expedition itself, and as Roosevelt's

train steamed into the Kapiti Plains station, he found his safari standing tall and attentive on the parched land. There were no fewer than
265 personnel, plus horses and wagons, arrayed before sixty-four
canvas tents—eight for the museum collectors, fifty for the porters,
and six for the horses—and hundreds of wooden equipment crates
with THEODORE ROOSEVELT painted prominently on the outsides. The
amount of equipage required by the scientists to collect and preserve
all the anticipated specimens was enormous. A full two hundred of
their porters were dedicated to carrying just this equipment—some
four hundred animal traps along with bales of stuffing, coils of wire,
and assorted dissection tools needed to prepare the study skins of the
specimens collected. Preserving big-game specimens for museum exhibit also required that the men carry at least four tons of salt for
curing the hides. Roosevelt remarked that it looked as if "some small
military expedition was about to start."

As befit a Newland, Tarlton & Co. safari, the porters were more
sharply dressed than those of most other outfits; they were issued
navy-blue jerseys with the scarlet initials NT embroidered on the
front. Each man was also issued a blanket and a three-pound bag for
his daily *posho* (a staple food) ration, which was tied around his waist
along with a water bottle. One large cook pot was allocated for each
four porters. Most prized among their issuance were the obligatory
new boots; these were still considered something of a novelty, and
most of the porters hung them around their necks while on the march,
saving them for when they could parade around in them back in town.

Besides the porters, who were essential for carrying supplies where
wagons could not go, there were also gun bearers, tent boys, horse
tenders, and fifteen *askaris*—native soldiers dressed in a uniform of
white knickerbockers and loose-fitting blue shirts, all topped with a
smart red fez. Each carried a rifle and enough ammunition to protect
the expedition from warring tribesmen in the area. A kind of military police, the *askaris* were also tasked with keeping law and order in
camp, and as further insurance against a possible mutiny, the Roosevelt party chose their porters from several different tribes so as not to
favor one over the other. All were standing in formation in front of an

oversize American flag marking Roosevelt's quarters as he stepped off the locomotive at the Kapiti station.

Roosevelt appreciated the flag, and he also loved the fact that his tent was the grandest and most elaborate. It was nine feet by twelve feet inside and had a large green canvas fly, or outer layer, to deflect both rain and the heat of the equatorial sun. It also boasted a little canvas awning to create a shady "porch" out front. Inside was a canvas ground cloth, folding armchairs, a folding bed, and a mosquito-net canopy. Best of all, though, was the privy, with a folding rubber tub in a special back room so that he could have a shave and hot bath in private before dinner each evening. Roosevelt had two gun bearers, two *saises*, or grooms, to tend to his two horses, and two personal attendants, or tent boys, named Bill and Ali. Ali spoke a little English, and it was he who ensured that a framed picture of Edith was always carefully dusted and positioned so that Roosevelt could see it when writing at the little table that was set up under the awning in front of his tent.

Roosevelt admitted to being somewhat embarrassed by all the luxuries. He felt almost too comfortable after spending so many years sleeping on the bare ground in the American West. But he could also appreciate the inherent dangers of working in the tropics, far from his usual environs of "pine and birch and frosty weather."

One peril that became immediately apparent was that the Kapiti Plains were infested with ticks and jigger fleas. The former transmitted disease, and the latter burrowed painfully into the flesh beneath fingernails and toenails, but both were repulsive. The game brought into camp was so covered with ticks that the arachnids formed a plate-like armor over any exposed skin. Roosevelt was appalled to see the animals so afflicted, and he described how the ticks swarmed around the creatures' eyes, making complete rims, "like spectacles," and how in the armpits and groin they were massed "like barnacles on an old boat." The horses had to be picked clean of hundreds of ticks each night, and one wonders how many the safari men had to remove from themselves in the privacy of their tents. "Nature is merciless indeed," Roosevelt reminded himself.

Nature itself was also being mercilessly ravaged in Africa. Drought had scorched the plains to the point of cracking the ground, withering the grass to short, strawlike stubble. Laying his eyes on the physical enormity of the equipage and the boisterous swarms of natives that comprised his safari, Roosevelt was finally grateful for Selous's insistence that he hire a professional outfitter to run the expedition. Even with that help, it would take days to unpack the crates and organize the safari. "Few laymen have any idea of the expense and pains which must be undergone in order to provide [to museums] groups of mounted big animals from far-off lands," Roosevelt explained in one of his earliest accounts for *Scribner's Magazine*. Despite the outfitters, everything was scattered about as they unpacked the crates, and, "owing to the enormous masses of stores and boxes and cases of ammunition," it would take time before they could hope to move the unwieldy camp. Making matters worse, Cuninghame had somehow forgotten to order any bread or flour.

Wishing to get away from the clamor of the camp beside the train station, Roosevelt left everything in the hands of his outfitters. Together with Kermit, the naturalists, their gun bearers, horse tenders, and a small contingent of porters, they split off and rode sixteen miles north to the comfortable ranch house of British pioneer settler Sir Alfred Pease, leaving the rest of the safari behind. On the ride out Roosevelt shot some of his first game, including a bull and cow wildebeest, which, with their shaggy manes and humped forequarters, reminded him of the bison of western America. It was a humble beginning to an ambitious expedition, but Roosevelt was in no hurry. He had planned for a slow and deliberate start in order to grow accustomed to the strange landscape, and, indeed, the first several weeks saw him hunting the more settled portions of the Kapiti Plains, moving from one ranch house to another while the outfitters ironed out the functional aspects of the safari.

Sir Pease's ranch was called Kitanga, and although his house and the surrounding hills looked tranquil enough, the pastoral scene was somewhat blighted by the fact that the compound was built on the site where a man had been mauled and killed by a lion only a few years prior. Roosevelt was shown the man's grave behind the new ranch house—a one-story structure with a veranda running around three sides overlooking the surrounding valleys of flat-topped acacia trees. On a clear day one could see the snow-capped summit of Kilimanjaro far off in the distance. Situated on the Athi River and comprising seven thousand acres, Kitanga reminded Roosevelt of his own ranch on the Great Plains of the American West, and he was taken with the abundance of birdlife flitting about the front porch. Not knowing the names of many of the winged creatures, he described them in detail: a "little red-billed finch with its outer tail feathers several times the length of its head and body," a big, parti-colored shrike with a "kestrel-like habit of hovering in the air over one spot." Eared owls flew up from the reeds and grass, and, overhead, little pipits sang like Missouri skylarks.

Roosevelt also recorded some of his first impressions of the more common plains game. Thomson's gazelles were "pretty, alert little things" that he noted were half the size of the pronghorn from western America. The larger Grant's gazelle was "among the most beautiful of all antelope, being rather larger than a whitetailed deer . . . the old bucks carry lyre-shaped horns." Unlike the Thomson's gazelles, which always kept their tails in a constant "incessant nervous twitching, never being still for more than a few seconds at a time," the larger Grant's gazelles hardly moved their tails at all. Less conspicuous but just as prevalent were the many different kinds of small mammals the naturalists were already trapping and cataloguing. Roosevelt noted these in reference to their North American counterparts: "mole rats with velvety fur, which burrowed like our pocket gophers; rats that lived in holes like those of our kangaroo rat; and one mouse that was stripped like our stripped gopher." They saw hyrax among the rocks on the hills, which Roosevelt likened to "heavy woodchucks" but with teeth somewhat like those of a "wee rhinoceros." Most interesting of all was a brilliantly colored yellow and blue bat, which they flushed one day while beating through a ravine. "It had been hanging from a mimosa twig, and it flew well in the strong sunlight, looking like some huge, parti-colored butterfly."

On starting his safari, Roosevelt made it clear to Pease that he was "absolutely out of condition, not only grown fat, but also a little gouty" and that he would have to begin "with great moderation." The semi-settled nature of Kitanga made for a charming and relatively safe landscape for adjusting to African hunting, and Roosevelt was almost never out of sight of game. Most days he rode off with just his gun bearers, and many times he passed through herds of game with no inclination to shoot anything at all. At least in these early weeks of the safari he was more intent on observing the landscape before moving into ardent hunting. Accordingly, his dispatches to *Scribner's Magazine* were more prosaic accounts of animal behavior and quaint stories of ranch life than the action and adventure that some of his readers were anticipating. A typical day had him riding off on horseback at dawn, stopping during the heat of the day to have lunch under a tree, the men lying in the shade and dozing in the heat, and then mounting up again for an afternoon trek before riding home in a red sunset.

Roosevelt was pacing himself, but even in the early weeks of the expedition, when he was deliberately restrained in his shooting, it was clear that he was hardly an expert shot. He usually fired off more ammunition than was considered respectable, dutifully recording each miss and botched shot in his writings. He rarely had the patience to painstakingly stalk animals, preferring instead to fire a volley of shots at longer range. Few people knew that Roosevelt was practically blind in his left eye (the result of a friendly boxing match in the White House in 1908) and, thus, handicapped at judging distance. He adjusted his aim by way of the little clouds of dust kicked up around the fleeing animal. He wounded many animals this way, and Kermit was often obliged to chase them down to deliver the *coup de grace*.

Roosevelt's rather hasty shooting can perhaps be forgiven in light of the many goals of the expedition. Primarily, of course, it was a scientific expedition aimed at documenting—with actual scientific specimens—the fauna of East Africa, which at that time was very poorly known. One important part of the expedition was to be conducted primarily by Loring and Mearns; bird and small-mammal collecting was most of what they did, but the work of large-mammal collecting championed by Roosevelt, Kermit, and Heller was equally important in a time when there were huge gaps in the scientific community's knowledge of these larger species.

The men's first goal was to build up their scientific collections—the specimens intended for science, not public exhibit. Many thousands of cabinets and drawers were being installed in the new museum for this purpose, and the more specimens the scientists added to these drawers, the better the scientists were able to discern the often subtle distinctions among species. Just as Mearns and Loring needed to collect thousands of mice, bats, and shrews to fully document the diversity of life in East Africa, Roosevelt and his party needed to collect relatively large numbers of the bigger game.

A second goal of the expedition was to collect larger mammals for public taxidermy displays, with luck at least one each of an adult male, adult female, and different ages of young for each major species (hunters had long had a bias for shooting only the most impressive animals, but Roosevelt was intent on collecting a more representative sampling of each species). Museum taxidermy was enjoying a renaissance led by Carl Akeley, and Roosevelt was eager to bring some of this energy to the empty halls of the Smithsonian's new natural-history museum building. Akeley had agreed to share his new methods of taxidermy—which relied on using sculptures of animals to create accurate models over which to mount the tanned skins, rather than just stuffing the skins with excelsior—with a young sculptor at the American Museum of Natural History named James L. Clark, who had been hired for precisely that purpose. Through the talents of Akeley, the Field Museum and the American Museum were creating exquisitely lifelike examples of African and North American animals; Roosevelt did not want the Smithsonian's exhibits to be inferior.

The meat of any large animals shot for taxidermy was distributed and eagerly eaten by all the porters and scientific staff, but this was not so much an objective of the expedition as it was necessary for survival. Despite all the game being shot for specimens, Roosevelt was often obliged to shoot additional game just to satisfy the hunger of his helpers. Add to this mix the few exceptional trophies that Roosevelt wanted to hang over the fireplaces at Sagamore, and the various motivations for his kills become blurred.

One purely practical matter animated the trip—the writing that Roosevelt was obliged to do for *Scribner's Magazine,* so that he could pay for it all. In fact, Roosevelt was equally concerned with preserving for posterity—in writing and in specimens—all that he saw in the great game land of East Africa. As a young man he had rued missing the chance to see the American West before the catastrophic decline of its megafauna. When he first went west, the bison were virtually extinct, with elk and brown bears exceedingly rare. For all the greatness of the conservation measures he had helped put into place, they preserved only a shadow of what they might have if only they had been implemented earlier. But in East Africa, the game was still fairly abundant, and although his descriptions of the great herds of big mammals are tinged with the likelihood of their eventual decline, Roosevelt was eager to do what he could to promote their protection.

Following Roosevelt's example with the Boone and Crockett Club, it was Edward North Buxton—Roosevelt's expedition advisor—who first proposed founding a similar group of British sportsmen and museum naturalists to protect exotic African game. The Society for the Preservation of the Wild Fauna of the Empire was founded in 1903 and included American Theodore Roosevelt as an honorary member. Its ranks quickly grew to include one hundred of some of the most powerful men in Britain with the goal to incite and encourage the conservation of big game. With mostly sportsmen comprising its membership, the group was quickly lampooned as "penitent butchers," and, indeed, the society issued a rather painful admission shortly after its founding that its members were "men who, having in earlier days taken their fill of big-game slaughter and the delights of the chase in the wild, . . . now, being smitten with remorse, and having reached a less strenuous term of life, think to condone our earlier bloodthirstiness by advocating the preservation of what we formerly chased and killed." Roosevelt could certainly appreciate this sentiment.

IF ANYONE WANTED to win Roosevelt's favor, all he needed to do was affirm his conviction that lions were the most dangerous game in Africa. Some thought elephant or buffalo more formidable; others believed the rhino most deadly. To Roosevelt, these were merely the opinions of men whose powers of observation were obviously flawed.

Lions reigned supreme as the most dangerous game as far as he was concerned, and his great ambition was to kill a large and ferocious male charging straight toward him with bared teeth.

Shooting the grizzly bear at close range in the American West was the one time he'd had this kind of hair-raising encounter, but the memory of that bear was fading to the point that it seemed the experience did not even belong to him any longer. "If I can only get my lion, I shall be happy," he declared aboard the *Admiral*, still weeks away from his first chance to kill one. Since antiquity, the lion has symbolized strength and masculine power—qualities of supreme importance to Roosevelt's ego—making it the ultimate safari prize, one that would symbolically crown him king of his own expedition.

At first, Roosevelt was confident he could command any face-to-face encounter with a lion; after all, he was an experienced hunter with the best available firearms. But as the group drew nearer to the hunting grounds, he started to get agitated, spurred on by the seemingly inexhaustible supply of lion stories he had heard since landing in Africa. It suddenly dawned on Roosevelt that he might want to get in a little more rifle practice before going after any lions.

Hundreds of men had been killed by big game in the years leading up to Roosevelt's safari, and nearly all those deaths were at the paws and jaws of lions. The most famous were the man-eaters of Tsavo: two lions that nearly brought the construction of the Uganda Railway to a halt by systematically hunting, killing, and eating workers on the line. More than a hundred men were killed over the course of a year before the engineer in charge of construction finally found the lions and gunned them down. Roosevelt thought Lieutenant Colonel Patterson's account, *The Man-Eaters of Tsavo*, was the most thrilling book of true lion stories ever written, although Sir Alfred Pease had some stories that rivaled even these—stories of men being stalked by lions as they walked about their farms, and being chased while on horseback.

One man was yanked from his saddle by a pursuing lion, which started trotting off with his prize in his mouth. The man was saved only because he managed to slip his knife out of his belt and stab the animal in the heart, killing it almost instantly. It was as if some of the wild adventure stories Roosevelt had read as a boy—in particular about David Livingstone's being mauled by a lion—were still playing out on the plains of East Africa. Roosevelt slowly came to the realization that these were not mere storybook beasts, but hungry, flesh-and-blood opponents.

Roosevelt had arrived on African shores at a time when lion attacks on the human population were on the increase. Some attributed this to a recent rinderpest epidemic, a viral disease of cattle that had leveled the local prey population. Others pegged it as the result of an especially dry summer, which they figured drove the lions closer to human encampments. Still another theory pointed fingers at the burial tradition of certain tribes, in which the bodies of the dead were left out in the open, making enticing meals for lions and hyenas roaming the grasslands. Whatever the reasons, lions were considered to be a menace, and the laws of the land allowed a hunter to shoot as many of them as he could find.

Roosevelt trusted Sir Alfred Pease to lead him to a lion. As Pease later recalled, "Roosevelt had mapped out his time and allotted me three days for him to get his lion." But before going for just any lion, Pease wanted to first give Roosevelt a crack at an especially magnificent, black-maned lion he had recently seen, which meant passing up more certain chances. Fortunately, Pease was an old pro at lion hunting—he had tracked them alone on foot, flushed them out with dogs, waited for them at night while lying beside water holes, and ambushed them at freshly killed bait. He had mastered all the techniques common in bagging a lion, but his favorite technique was coursing lions on horseback—something he felt was decidedly the most sporting way to hunt. He would ride to a lion hideout, such as the dense brush that grew along the edges of small watercourses, or dongas, and, using a combination of dogs and native beaters, he would flush out the lions and chase them down on horseback until they turned to fight. Then he dismounted and shot them as they charged. To Pease it was great fun, and he liked to share in the chase. "It can be done alone," he said, "but is much more amusing in the company of one or two friends, and it is a diversion in which ladies can share the excitement whilst avoiding serious risks."

Their first full day of lion hunting was a bust, in part because Roosevelt and Kermit were so easily distracted. "Away went Kermit after a Hyena—he had a most desperate and long gallop, but shot him at last after about a 10-mile run. This delayed us," Pease wrote in his diary. Later that same day, while pushing through a thickly vegetated donga in search of lions, Pease walked into a 13-foot python. Did Roosevelt want it? Yes, came the reply, "so we went back and took it home," wasting still more time. "I didn't think it was worth bothering about," Pease wrote.

On their second day, Pease couldn't help but notice Roosevelt starting to doubt his prowess as a lion hunter. Wanting to make sure Roosevelt got his animal, the local authorities had even come to Pease with the suggestion that he "place askaris on every hilltop to watch for lions." To this Pease responded that what he really wanted were lions on the hilltops and not a lookout squad to scare them off. He found both R. J. Cuninghame and the government official "rather fussy and troublesome about the coming of the great man," and he wanted everyone to simply relax and let him do what he knew how to do best—shoot lions. As Pease put it, he was always being "bothered by other people's ideas."

By their third day they had still not even seen a lion, but Pease was determined, and he told Roosevelt that his best chance was to "leave the men and noise" and come with him and a smaller party that included just him and his wife and daughter along with a couple of neighbors. Roosevelt concurred, and after first checking, then double-checking, to make sure that their rifles were in perfect working order, he and Kermit mounted their horses and prepared themselves mentally for the hunt. Pease, on the other hand, old pro that he was, nonchalantly helped his unarmed wife and daughter up onto their steeds. For Sir Pease, the hunt was an occasion no different from an afternoon picnic. A couple of lion dogs followed, and Pease set them out to beat their first donga—a gully full of dense vegetation snaking its way through the open plains. It was the best cover for miles around, perhaps hiding Roosevelt's coveted lion prize. They had seen the tracks of a big lion and lioness in a patch of sandy soil nearby, which made that possibility very promising. Sliding off their horses, they walked carefully along each side of the donga, hoping to flush out the animals. As they dismounted, the dogs smelled a lion, and they growled and snarled while the natives joined in by shouting and throwing stones into the grass. Then one of the natives yelled *Simba! Lion!* Roosevelt caught a glimpse of a tawny hide through the bush, and then a lion darted right in front of him. If it charged, its claws could be sinking into him or Kermit in an instant. Someone yelled, "Shoot!"

Roosevelt fired blindly into the tawny masses crashing through the brush. Kermit fired immediately after. Bursting out from the brush were two *Panthera leo*—but not the magnificent, roaring lions they were imagining, rather, cubs the size of dogs. Both were horribly wounded and had to be shot again to put them out of their misery. Pease was disappointed at their size, and Roosevelt tried to hide his humiliation.

Sir Pease certainly understood Roosevelt's predicament. As safari leader, Roosevelt needed to demonstrate that he was in charge. The failure to locate and shoot an adult lion felt personal to him, and as the party rode back to the ranch, Pease desperately scoured the landscape for signs of a bigger beast. Mile after mile, they saw nothing, but then Pease rushed off to a donga on the left, where he found tracks, but they were old, and there were no lions. Riding a little farther to a second spot favored by the animals, the group beat the bushes again, but for nothing. Exhausted and deflated from the day's disappointments, they decided to hit one last site, one that was very brushy. As they rode up, the response from the donga was immediate and definite— there was a loud grunting from a big lion and the crashing about of at least one other large cat. Eagerly jumping from his horse, Roosevelt prepared to face a charge, but, instead, the lions retreated, running away from him about thirty yards. Roosevelt followed with his gun. He later wrote, "Crack! The Winchester spoke; and as the soft-nosed bullet ploughed forward through his flank the lion swerved so that I missed him with the second shot; but my third bullet went through the spine and forward into his chest. Down he came, sixty yards off, his hind quarters dragging, his head up, his ears back, his jaws open and lips drawn up in a prodigious snarl, as he endeavored to turn to face us. His back was broken; but of this we could not at the moment be sure, as if it had merely been grazed, he might have recovered, and then, even though dying, his charge might have done mischief. So Kermit, Sir Alfred, and I fired, almost together, into his chest. His head sank, and he died."

But this was just one lion; the second had darted from the other side of the bush and was by this time galloping across the plains several hundred yards away. Roosevelt let rip an impossibly long volley of shots in its general direction, but the bullets all fell harmlessly to the ground. This prevented Pease from getting a good start after it, but, telling Kermit to join him and to do exactly as told, he promised to find the second lion and to hold it at bay for his father to shoot. The two men mounted their horses and chased after the animal, Theodore following. As they finally closed in a mile later, the lion turned to face them.

The elder Roosevelt tried shooting from the saddle, but his horse was too wild with excitement, and he kept missing. At this moment his horse tender, called Simba, ran up to his side. "Good, Simba, now we'll see this thing through," Roosevelt said. Exhausted, the lion now faced his opponents while trying to figure out whom to charge. He looked at one group of horses and then another, "his tail lashing to and fro, his head held low, and his lips dropped over his mouth." All the while, the lion's harsh growling "rolled thunderously over the plain," recalled Roosevelt. "I had never seen a lion so bombarded without charging," said Pease. "But every time he 'set' to charge, a shot from the other rifle, or a yell from me distracted him. Kermit fired some 20 shots." Seeing Roosevelt and Simba just standing there, the beast turned toward them, "his tail lashing quicker and quicker," Roosevelt recalled with alarm. Resting his elbow in the crook of Simba's shoulder, Theodore took aim and fired. "The bullet went in between the neck and shoulder, and the lion fell over to his side, one foreleg in the air. He recovered in a moment and stood up, evidently very sick, and once more faced me, growling hoarsely. I think he was on the eve of charging. I fired again at once, and this bullet broke his back just behind the shoulders; and with the next I killed him outright, after we had gathered round him."

Thus, Roosevelt got his lions, and as they carried them to camp, the porters danced and chanted in the moonlight, the two big cat carcasses swaying between the carrying poles on their shoulders. In one spectacular day of shooting, Roosevelt had killed four lions. In just a few days he would kill two more; by the end of the trip, he would have killed a total of nine, while Kermit would bag eight more.

Chapter 16

BWANA TUMBO—
MR. BIG BELLY

*R*oosevelt's lion hunting marked the official start of his adventure, the two bigger animals being the center of attention as his safari caught up to him at Pease's ranch. After staring down two large lions, he had earned the respect of his men. They called him *Bwana Makuba*, a Swahili honorific meant to convey that they thought him a great leader. The lions had set the tone, and his epic adventure—the actual, marching expedition—was set to begin.

The plan for the first leg of the expedition was to trace a broad arc through the ranchlands north of the railroad. Travel over the flat plains was easy, and it gave the 250-plus members of the expedition a chance to work out their daily routines on forgiving terrain. Depending on Roosevelt's hunting, camps were established for as little as one day or for more than a week. On days when the safari was on the move, the men broke camp early and divided their supplies into easily transported parcels of between fifty-five and sixty pounds. Their caravan was led by Roosevelt and an outsize American flag, its bearer sometimes joined by an African drummer or a man with a whistle. This gave the procession a cacophonous Fourth of July air, the long trains of porters supporting loads on their heads while beating hand drums and chanting a rhythm to keep the safari moving at pace.

At the end of each march, Roosevelt's tent was always pitched first. Right next door was Kermit's, and beside this was the dining tent, outfitted with a folding table and chairs. The cook's tent, skinning tent, supply tents, and long rows of the porters' tiny white pup tents all followed, and at night, these were all illuminated by dozens of little fires as the porters cooked their meals of rice and wild-game meat.

Marching northward, the expedition snaked its way through a bleak landscape of thorny scrub, where a large number of the Wakamba tribe had gathered. It had been a bad year for crops, and their chief was waiting to present Roosevelt with a fat sheep—a generous gift, considering that his tribe was on the brink of starvation. The chief was hoping to receive more than a sheep's worth of fresh game meat in return, and Roosevelt delivered, shooting a lone eland (a large cattle-like animal with spiral horns), which he shared with the Wakamba. As soon as he had done so, a second Wakamba man came running up with news of a rhinoceros nearby. From the top of a hillock, Roosevelt spotted the rhino standing out in the open. "The beast stood like an uncouth statue . . . a monster surviving over from the world's past." Creeping to within thirty yards of the animal, Roosevelt roused it, and the rhino immediately jumped to its feet with "the agility of a polo pony" and instantly began a charge. This was unexpected, but Roosevelt instinctively shot the rhino with his heavy double-barreled rifle, the rapidly advancing animal "ploughing up the ground" as it skidded to a halt, collapsing just thirteen paces away from him.

Skinning the rhino at dawn, Edmund Heller, who oversaw the preparation of all of Roosevelt's specimens, was closely watched by a dozen or so hungry Wakamba who had gathered during the night. As Heller recorded the encounter, they were "real savages who filed their teeth and delighted in raw flesh," and several were recruited to help with the carcass. Every one of them had a large knife, and they darted around the fallen animal, wildly hacking off chunks of meat. So chaotic was the scene that the *askari* soldiers had to drive the starving men back with whips. As the skinning proceeded, the blood about the carcass grew ankle deep, and the men waded through stomach contents as they cut away at the animal. After about an hour and a half of this mob labor, the rhino's skin was removed, and the Wakamba, grateful for a large meal in the face of the region's recent famine, rushed the carcass, picking the skeleton clean of flesh. "The intestines were also eaten by these people," Heller noted in his journal, seemingly amazed at the quick work they made of the enormous beast.

Heller and his team spent the next three days preparing the rhino skin for transport. Every time Roosevelt shot such a large animal, it meant that Heller was in for days of hard work as he raced against time to preserve the skin before it could rot. Since these animals were not easily moved, Heller had to constantly shift his camp—a handful of skinners and as many as forty porters—to wherever Roosevelt's dead animals had fallen. It was not only the inevitable decomposition that they raced against, but also the very real threat of scavengers—lions, hyenas, jackals, ravens, vultures, and even storks—tearing the animal to pieces.

Roosevelt took the preservation of each animal seriously. He insisted on saving the skull and, in many cases, the whole skeleton, of virtually every animal he shot. More than mere trophies, he knew that these were "absolutely necessary for the determination of the species" and that they would make valuable additions to the Smithsonian's collection. All these bones had to be "roughed out" in the field, meaning Heller and his team had to cut off as much of the muscle as possible before drying the skeleton for transportation. Later, back at the museum, technicians would clean off the last bits of dried flesh still adhering to bone. Since saving all the skins required that the porters carry tons of fine-grained salt for preservation, Roosevelt admitted that this was an expensive process. The salt's sheer weight added considerably to the cost of transport, but it was absolutely essential to the expedition's efforts to build the Smithsonian's African collection.

The salt method used was essentially one that had been perfected by Carl Akeley, the salt working by drawing moisture out of the hides and halting the decay that caused the hairs to slip out. Immediately after skinning, the hide needed to be scraped clean of any adhering tissue and fat to expose the under layer of skin where the roots of the hairs were embedded. This layer needed to be thoroughly rubbed with salt, and, stretching portions of the hide taut over a makeshift wooden table, Heller and his men spent hours scraping down each one. A layer of fine salt was poured on and rubbed into every square inch of the hide. This had to be done by hand, the salt also stinging every nick and cut on the work-roughened hands of the men. The skins were then rolled and packed into tightly sealed tins or barrels for transport to Nairobi, where they were stored in a warehouse before being shipped to the Smithsonian. The salt was only a temporary preservative, however, and once in the United States, these skins had to be tanned and turned into leather before they could be installed in the museum's collections or mounted for taxidermy displays. It was heavy, messy, tedious work, and Heller grew so tired of skinning and scraping rhinoceros that he jokingly complained of suffering from an acute case of "rhinoceritis."

As Heller's team worked, Roosevelt sat on a hilltop lunching under the shade of a huge fig tree. Reaching for his old army field glasses, he scanned the plains and spied three tall giraffes in the distance. Deliberate stalking them would have been too obvious, so Roosevelt called on his knowledge of native customs. The giraffes were accustomed to natives walking by in single file, so Roosevelt attempted to approach the animals by nonchalantly walking at a slight angle toward them. Taking care to not look at them directly, he slowly closed the distance before dropping to one knee and firing his first shot. *Smack!* He heard the bullet hit the animal's side, but the giraffe kept running. Roosevelt continued to fire until his rifle was empty. Jumping onto his horse and riding full-tilt, he fired more salvos into the wounded animals until he finally brought down two of the three giraffes.

Heller was just finishing the rhino hide when Roosevelt returned to camp with the news that he had just killed a cow and a bull giraffe and that Kermit was in hot pursuit and very likely to kill a third. Three giraffes in one afternoon, now spread out across some three miles of desolate terrain. As it was dusk, Heller and his team rushed to find the dead animals. In the confusion, Heller got separated from his men, but, seeing the flicker of their lanterns in the distance, he rode his horse directly toward them. Hearing his galloping getting closer in the night, the men bolted, thinking a rhinoceros was charging.

Such were some of the dangers for Edmund Heller and his skinners, camped out in the open amid smelly carcasses and dangerous animals. Several days later—and still scraping giraffe skins—they were awakened by lions roaring near camp. And this time it was no false alarm. With no fires burning, the lions came to within a few paces of their tents, attracted to the now-ripe smell of giraffe offal and drying bones.

This was the daily routine for Heller—skinning animals, roughing out skeletons, scraping and salting hides—and even before his team finished one batch, Roosevelt had moved on to his next hunting ground. This one was Juja Farm, owned by William Northrup McMillan, a wealthy American who had taken to the life of East Africa. Juja sat at the juncture of the Nairobi and Rewero rivers—a place where hippopotamus were known to congregate. Shooting a hippopotamus should have been a simple matter, but just as Roosevelt was getting into position on a river embankment overlooking the water, a burst of loud snorts and heavy trampling of feet sounded off to his side as an enormous black rhino crashed through the brush, twitching its tail and tossing its head as it charged Roosevelt, who instinctively raised his rifle yet again.

SALT AND GIRAFFE blood still clung to Edmund Heller as he made his way to Juja Farm. He had made a quick detour through Nairobi to drop off an oxcart load of big salted skins, and his horse was kicking up dust as he rode over the parched short-grass plains to this next expedition camp. He may have been dreaming of a refreshing bath and a restful night's sleep, but on arriving in camp, he met his biggest pile of carnage yet. Roosevelt had neatly dispatched the rhino that charged him, and, seemingly oblivious to Heller's workload, he also shot his hippopotamus. Two enormous animals, each weighing more than a ton, were waiting for Heller, and on top of all this was a leopard—killed by Kermit Roosevelt after it mauled one of their porters and charged him—two impala, a waterbuck, a warthog, and, mysteriously, a domestic house cat.

Roosevelt was clearly having a great time shooting, and it earned him a new nickname—*Bwana Tumbo*—the master with the big stomach. Newspapermen coined the term, which was as much a reflection of Roosevelt's waistline as it was his appetite for more mammal specimens.

Edmund Heller was experiencing his own great excitement. Examining the skulls of some of the mole-rats J. Alden Loring had collected—squat, burrowing rodents with short, stout legs and giant gnawing teeth—he could see that they were different from those of other known mole-rats of East Africa. They lacked a distinctive white fur patch on the top of their head. The absence of this trait made them seem more like a species from South Africa, but from measurements of skulls he had taken before leaving the Smithsonian, Heller knew that Loring's mole-rats were different from that species, too. The teeth were much bigger than anything previously described. The expedition had discovered its first new species, and in a feat of efficiency, Heller started writing up the scientific results even while the men were still in the field. Remarkably, the Smithsonian published Heller's description of the new species, complete with photographs of the mole-rat skull, on September 24, 1909—a mere 144 days from the time Loring trapped the specimen on the Kapiti Plains.

While Heller was busily preparing the rhino and hippo skins back at Juja Farm, Roosevelt galloped a dozen miles to Kamiti Ranch, where the landowner, Hugh H. Heatley, was protecting a herd of Cape buffalo in a large papyrus swamp. Only a favored few people were allowed to shoot from his herd, but Heatley invited Roosevelt to collect as many as he needed. Scouting around the first day, they saw seventy or eighty buffalo grazing in the open about a hundred yards from the edge of the swamp. It was too dark to shoot, but, heading out again early the next morning, Roosevelt and his party let fly a hail of ammunition to bring down three of the massive bulls.

As animals piled up, Roosevelt took a break from hunting, much to Heller's relief, to finish his articles for *Scribner's*, which were seriously overdue. It was a real chore for him to write while in the field, and he joked that it was his way of paying for his fun. Borrowing the formula that had worked so well for him when writing about his western adventures, Roosevelt mixed detailed descriptions of the landscape with natural-history anecdotes and the excitement of his hunts.

He also began to think about having a little more control over the news that was leaking out of camp. Initially, Roosevelt had allowed reporters to follow him only to Nairobi but no farther. He had even gone so far as to secure the backing of the colonial officials to oust any reporter breaking this rule or spreading wild rumors. But these strict rules only had the effect of keeping most of the reporters at home, where they were forced to anticipate the results of his hunt or even invent stories outright. Roosevelt's first lion was "shot several times over in the imagination" by these newsmen even before he actually shot it. All these fabrications infuriated the small contingent of loyal reporters assembled in Nairobi, for they not only lacked news of Roosevelt's daily activities but were forbidden from making anything up under threat of expulsion.

Roosevelt was smart to keep a tight grip on the press, but he also understood the need for a carefully controlled news outlet. He had befriended a reporter named Francis Warrington Dawson while on board the *Admiral,* and Dawson was among the few he thought he could trust. Dawson had rushed to Roosevelt's defense when some false stories were printed while the men were still on their way to Africa, and so Roosevelt asked him to serve as the safari's news conduit, with the following conditions: Dawson had to agree to never ask him for an interview, to report only exactly what Roosevelt told him, and to share the news with the other reporters, so as to head off any claims of favoritism. At first, Roosevelt kept Dawson informed by sending him letters in Nairobi, but when Roosevelt heard the tragic news that Dawson's wife had just died, he thought back to his own personal tragedy so many decades before and immediately invited Dawson to his camp. Although strongly advised against the move on the grounds that it would beget a flood of new requests and visits from reporters, Roosevelt ignored the advice. "Dawson is in trouble in a new country where he has no friends except Kermit and myself. His place is here with us. I'll take the consequences," he said.

Roosevelt had Dawson out to his camp for a lunch of wild pig, antelope, local vegetables, and buffalo-marrow sandwiches at Kamiti Ranch. Carrying his typewriter, Dawson accepted, noting that "except perhaps for the vegetables" the entire lunch was the result of

Roosevelt's shooting. Sipping lime-juice soda, Roosevelt filled Dawson in on the events of his past several weeks of hunting. He showed him the skulls of the three trophy buffalo he had just shot. All three were males, and he needed to round out the collection by going back out again for a cow the next morning.

Dawson was not permitted to join the hunters, but he watched events unfold from a distance. Roosevelt found the herd hunkered down in a dry watercourse amid some high grass and reeds, where it was impossible to get a good shot. To draw them out, Hugh Heatley, the landowner, volunteered to ride back and forth along the donga's edge on his white pony. It was a dangerous, if not foolhardy, move, but it worked, and with Roosevelt, Kermit, and Cuninghame standing at the ready, the whole buffalo herd rose up from the reed bed and came forward.

Opening fire all at once, they shot a cow but were surprised to see the herd then form a semicircle around them—a solid phalanx facing off against the hunters. Their heads were lowered to show their massive inward-curled horns, and, inching forward, they seemed ready to begin a thunderous charge. Although only a few weeks into his African adventure, Roosevelt had already faced menacing lions and rhino. Now he was about to get a taste of yet another species of dangerous game. The hunters stood their ground, remaining motionless. "Stand steady! Don't run!" Roosevelt called out, to which Cuninghame added, "And don't shoot!" They were on the brink of a stampede— one false move or one unexpected sound, and the herd would be on them like an avalanche.

Nobody blinked. Later, some of those present admitted to nearly losing their heads under the pressure, but Roosevelt stood strong. After a few tense moments, one of the buffalo made a break for cover, followed by another and another, until the whole herd was in retreat. As he had done so many times in his life, Roosevelt stared death in the eye and survived.

Although constantly thrusting himself into danger, Roosevelt was troubled by his son's daring recklessness. His decision to bring Kermit to Africa in the first place had everything to do with wanting to instill in his boys the virtues of courage, but he was rather alarmed at how daring his rather slim-cut son had proven himself in Africa.

In a letter home to Theodore III, Roosevelt had earlier expressed his concerns: "I am really proud of Kermit. It is hard to realize that the rather timid boy of four years ago has turned out a perfectly cool and daring fellow. Indeed he is a little too reckless and keeps my heart in my throat, for I worry about him all the time: he is not a good shot, not even as good as I am, and Heaven knows I am poor enough; but he is a bold rider, always cool and fearless, and eager to work all day long. He ran down and killed a Giraffe, alone, and a Hyena also, and the day before yesterday he stopped a charging Leopard within six yards of him, after it had mauled one of our porters."

And to his sister Corinne, Roosevelt confided: "Kermit is a great care and anxiety when we are in dangerous game country: since I have been out here twelve men have been killed or mauled by lions, and, naturally, when Kermit shows a reckless indifference to consequences when hunting them, I feel like beating him: but he is a dear boy and when once away from Lions and similar beasts he is a constant source of pleasure." Other members of the expedition were perhaps less enamored with the boy's recklessness, Sir Pease in particular noting in his diary that while Kermit was a nice boy, he was "a handful in the field."

As the safari eventually circled its way back to Nairobi, the first installment of specimens was at last ready to ship to the Smithsonian. The men had already collected hundreds of small mammals and birds and preserved nearly eighty-six large mammal skins and skulls—not bad for what was just the start of their expedition. Edgar Mearns took advantage of his time in Nairobi to meet with Acting Governor Jackson, who was an expert on East African birds and was able to confirm all his identifications, and Edmund Heller reported back to the Smithsonian that at the pace they were going, they would likely "fill every nook and cranny of the museum with large mammals." He also added that all three of the Smithsonian naturalists were "gleefully engaged in securing small animals and had shown no tendencies to become big-game hunters." In other words, nearly all the large mammal specimens had been shot by Roosevelt and his son.

Chapter 17

⊂ ⊃

DEEP IN PREHISTORIC THOUGHT

$\mathcal{E}$arly on the morning of June 5, 1909, Roosevelt awoke to drum thumps and the strange twangs of an African harp. Singing and dancing just outside his canvas-walled tent was his safari party, exuberant before heading out on a five-day journey across a waterless expanse to the south known locally as "the thirst." But beyond that ordeal lay a rich hunting ground called the Sotik, where Roosevelt hoped to experience a storybook hunter's paradise. Much as he had once ventured from his Dakota ranch to hunt in the Bighorns, Roosevelt's trek to the Sotik was meant to get him away from the more heavily hunted lands and into some "good game country."

To make the sixty-mile crossing with enough supplies, the porters loaded four enormous ox wagons to the gunwales with barrels of water. These wagons were of the Conestoga type made famous in the American West, but they were much bigger and constructed from such enormous timbers that they seemed more like wheeled ships. Drawn by yokes of up to sixteen humped oxen each, they rumbled ahead of the safari. The faint track they were to follow passed through brush and scrubby forest before opening up to a vast plain of withered grass and stunted thorn trees. It had been an especially dry year, and as the lines of the safari marched out, the landscape seemed all the more bleak for the clouds of choking dust kicked up under their feet. Nearly two hundred porters marched single file under the sun. The long whips of the oxcart men periodically "cracked like rifles," giving the march an uneasy sting, and, as if to remind all of the dangers of exhaustion, a detachment of three *askaris* brought up the rear to look after any laggards and to see that no weak or sick man was left behind. Everything and everyone was soon covered with a fine yellow grime, and the porters—who had been so exuberant before departing—had long since ceased their music in the blazing equatorial sun.

Although days were sweltering, nights in the desert were frigid, and during their brief rests Roosevelt simply lay down on the ground, using his saddle as a pillow and curling up under his great army over-coat, while underdressed porters shivered around him. Up before dawn, they were marching again, and as the red sun rose, the terrain became hilly, and, as if they were mirages, Roosevelt saw scenes that reminded him of his most pleasant days in the American West, the thorny acacia trees growing in the creek beds vaguely reminiscent of the cottonwoods outside his Elkhorn ranch. After five days of march-ing, the Smithsonian African Expedition reached its destination.

Camped beside the swift-flowing Southern Guaso Nyiro River, all the naturalists were together for the first time since stepping off the *Admiral*, and, sitting around the evening fire, Kermit Roosevelt might have pulled out his mandolin and plucked it in celebration of the reunion. It wasn't long before the men started swapping stories of their varied adventures in the wild. Heller recounted his elephant hunts with Carl Akeley, Loring told of trapping tiny mice and shrews in the Alaskan tundra, and Mearns went on about the teeming bird-life around camp. Roosevelt, perhaps tossing a little more fuel onto the fire, felt he would have been remiss if he did not tell the story of his harrowing close encounter with the grizzly in the Bighorns.

The campfire reminiscing was, sadly, short-lived. The naturalists again parted company the next day, Roosevelt moving on in search of big game. To get specimens of large mammals, he needed to rove. Loring and Mearns, however, stayed behind to conduct their survey. For Mearns, this meant getting out with his shotgun at first light so that he could hunt birds, keeping his eye out for species not yet rep-resented in their collection. Birds abounded beside the Guaso Nyiro, with the "gorgeously colored and diminutive sun birds" seeming to have a "special fondness for the gaudy flowers that grew near the river."

Loring set out long lines of mousetraps in wooded areas, in tall grass, and anywhere else he thought small mammals might wander. Pushing himself into thorny thickets, clambering along rocky stream-beds, and investigating burrows in the ground for the telltale signs of rodents, Loring left no likely spot unexplored. He could never predict what he might find the following morning. Traps set in tall grass might catch African climbing mice, which clamber through the stems with the aid of their long, twining tail; those traps set along the banks of swift-flowing streams might catch fishing rats, with their luxurious, waterproof fur. For Loring, setting a mousetrap was like asking a question—what strange new species of animal might I find here?

Dead animals rotted quickly in the hot equatorial climate, so for both Loring and Mearns, afternoons were devoted to skinning and stuffing specimens, which they pinned to boards for drying in the sun. On days when he had especially good success trapping mice, Loring had to rush to prepare all his specimens quickly. He needed to check his trapline again in the evening, to move some of the traps around to better spots, and to add fresh bait. Sometimes he even caught mice in the middle of the day, such as the beautifully striped zebra mouse. Wherever he went, Loring carried his shotgun, just in case he came across a squirrel or some especially coveted bird for Mearns.

The Sotik did not disappoint Roosevelt for big game: "My bag for the five days illustrates ordinary African shooting in this part of the continent, that is, fourteen animals, of ten different species: one lioness, one hyena, one wart-hog, two zebra, two eland, one wildebeest, two topi, two impala, one Robert's gazelle, one Thomson's gazelle." He expended a total of sixty-five bullets to get these animals, in part because of the excessive distances of his shots. As was Roosevelt's custom, his first few shots were often for "range-finding." Like a battleship at sea, Roosevelt carried enough shells to unleash a sustained barrage.

Kermit, whose tent doubled as a darkroom, had hurt his shoulder in a fall from his horse and had decided to set aside his rifle to concentrate on photography. Wildlife photography was becoming popular in East Africa, even rivaling hunting. But Kermit made no bones about his father shooting animals and, in fact, relied on him to provide cover for close-up shots of dangerous game. Setting out early one morning, the two men spotted an enormous black rhino. "Look at him," Kermit said, "standing there in the middle of the African plain, deep in prehistoric thought." Kermit took photographs while Roosevelt stood ready in case of a charge. Later, finding another big black rhino with a twenty-six-inch-long horn sleeping on the plains, Roosevelt wanted to test out some special sharp-pointed bullets from his little .30 Springfield to see if they could bring this animal down. Treading cautiously, he walked upwind and straight toward the animal. When he was a hundred yards off, the rhino rose and faced him, "huge and threatening, head up and tail erect." Roosevelt would get that rhino, but not before plowing a total of nine shots from the little Springfield into its vitals, all the while galloping after it for a total of four miles before finally killing it.

The relatively light caliber would have been perfectly fine for most North American big game—elk, moose, bear—but for thick-skinned African rhinoceros, it was wholly inadequate. Perhaps Roosevelt was thinking of the famed hunter Karamojo Bell, who felled over one thousand elephants in his career, most of them with bullets much smaller than Roosevelt's. Bell had learned the anatomy of the elephant skull so well that he could kill the creatures instantaneously with his carefully placed shots to the brain. He also used hard, nickel-plated bullets that penetrated bone better than the large lead slugs used by most other hunters in his time. As long as he was sure of the animal's anatomy and shot to the brain with accuracy, Bell could kill any number of these huge animals just as well as with a big-bore rifle. Roosevelt was likely trying something similar with his "sharp-pointed" bullets. When it came to marksmanship, however, Roosevelt was no Karamojo Bell.

Whenever he shot a male, Roosevelt always balanced that kill with some cows and calves for the museum exhibits. He found a cow rhino and her calf moments after felling the bull, and in his account for *Scribner's Magazine* he described their deaths: "Kneeling, I sent the bullet from the heavy Holland just in front of her right shoulder as she half faced me. It went through her vitals, lodging behind the opposite shoulder; and at once she began the curious death waltz which is often, though by no means always, the sign of immediate dissolution in a mortally wounded rhino. Kermit at once put a second bullet from his Winchester behind her shoulder; for it is never safe to take chances with a rhino; and we shot the calf, which when dying uttered a screaming whistle, almost like that of a small steam-engine."

Anti-hunting feelings were on the rise in America, and although he knew his actions were under scrutiny, Roosevelt was never one to apologize for his collecting, nor would he pander to sentimentality. Instead, his *Scribner's* accounts almost give the impression that he was trying to provoke a reaction from the anti-hunting factions, as he documented his kills—botched shots and all—in unashamed detail. Some readers were appalled. But as far as Roosevelt was concerned, violent death was just another part of living—even if some of his readers had lost touch with this harsh fact of life. Just after the Sotik leg of his safari, he delivered a one-two body punch of fierce African reality to the anti-hunting public at home:

> Civilized man now usually passes his life under conditions which eliminate the intensity of terror felt by his ancestors when death by violence was their normal end. . . . It is only in nightmares that the average dweller in civilized countries now undergoes the hideous horror which was the regular and frequent portion of his ages-vanished forefathers, and which is still an every-day incident in the lives of the most wild creatures. . . . In these wilds the game dreaded the lion and the other flesh-eating beasts rather than man. . . . The game is ever on alert against this greatest of foes, and every herd, almost every individual, is in imminent and deadly peril every few days or nights. . . . But no sooner is the danger over than the animals resume their feeding, or love making, or their fighting among themselves. . . . Death by violence, death by cold, death by starvation—these are the normal endings of the stately and beautiful creatures of the wilderness.

To Roosevelt, hunting—whether for sport or for museum collecting—was nothing more than predation, a natural part of life. Even humans could be prey, as the party learned. After Roosevelt was reunited with Loring and Mearns at the camp along the Southern Guaso Nyiro, he learned that Dr. Mearns had been kept especially busy tending to men wounded by lions. Even Loring came close to death when he was charged by a lion. He was skinning mice in front of his tent one afternoon, when a Maasai herd boy motioned for him to come and shoot a pair of lions feeding on a wildebeest near their drove of sheep and goats. Loring shot one of the lions as it charged him, the mortally wounded animal then hurtling past where he had stood as he leapt out of its way. Loring's shot had actually hit the lion straight through the heart, but the animal was still charging on its last pulse of blood. These daring reflexes earned Loring some welcome relief, for up until then he had been mocked as *Bwana Panya*: the "mouse master."

Mice were Loring's duty, and from the Sotik camp alone he had already trapped more than 170 small-mammal specimens representing at least 27 different species. He caught pouched mice, with enormous cheeks full of seeds; zebra mice, with beautiful longitudinal stripes; root rats with their big orange teeth for digging underground; dormice; hopping mice; groove-toothed mice; climbing mice; mice with spiny fur; hares; hedgehogs; and tiny shrews. In the eyes of the natives, his job was the most degrading position, and they couldn't understand how these small creatures could be of use to anyone. With big game everywhere, his preoccupation seemed a waste of time, and they presumed Loring was a coward—or, worse, that his position in the safari was some kind of punishment. The first gun bearer assigned to Loring had disappeared into the bush because he was so ashamed to be working for *Bwana Panya*. But after killing the charging lion, J. Alden Loring became known as the *Bwana Simba*, the "lion master."

Chapter 18

BENT ON MISCHIEF

*R*eunited with the scientists, the safari continued north, marching four days to the lush shores of Lake Naivasha and the watery world of the hippopotamus. Here they arranged to borrow a steamboat and a heavy wooden rowboat for Roosevelt's hippo hunt. Towing the rowboat behind, he and Kermit and the other men cruised up and down the papyrus-lined lakeshore, probing every lily-pad-choked lagoon along the way. Hippopotamus were easy enough to spot among the pink and purple lily flowers, but only their massive heads were visible above the water. Although hippo skulls can measure up to three feet long, their brains offer only a small target and are not easy to hit. Making hippos even more difficult to hunt was their tendency to submerge themselves and run along the bottom of the lake. They were only comfortable coming up on land at night, and Roosevelt found them "astonishingly quick in their movements for such shapeless-looking, short-legged things." But the whole safari knew not to be fooled by these comical-looking creatures. They were highly territorial, charging anyone who came too close and threatening to snap a man in half with their massive jaws.

The first few days of hunting the hippos proved difficult. Roosevelt caught only fleeting glimpses of the animals, until at last he surprised one standing onshore, wading along the edge of the papyrus. "We headed toward it, and thrust the boat in among the water-lilies." Why Roosevelt insisted again on using his light Springfield rifle against such large and dangerous game can only be imagined, but his first shot merely angered the enormous hippo, which then spun around and "with its huge jaws wide open came straight for the boat, floundering and splashing through the thick-growing water-lilies." As Roosevelt later pointed out, the cow's object may have been as benign as an escape to deeper water, but its wide-open jaws seemed to indicate that it was "bent on mischief." Roosevelt fired rapidly. Most of his shots missed, but after one went directly into its cavernous mouth, its huge jaws snapped shut "with the clash of a sprung bear trap." Roosevelt followed up with a shot to the brain, and down the animal went, sinking fast to the bottom. Several hours later, the inevitable decomposition produced enough gases to balloon the animal up to the surface, and the men towed it to shore for Heller.

Cutting up a partially decomposed and bloated hippopotamus would have been disgusting enough, but exacerbating the foulness of the task, the lake was infested with leeches. All the porters who had to go into the water to help haul the animal onshore came out covered in them, and Heller found an abundance of leeches living inside the hippopotamus's mouth.

On the same day that Roosevelt shot the hippo, Heller had also trapped a full-grown leopard, caught by a mere toe of its right hind foot. Heller had been using small steel leg-hold traps to catch carnivores, and while these were suitable for catching smaller cats and mongoose, Heller was amazed that such a light trap could also hold a leopard.

Leg-holds consist of two steel jaws held under the tension of springs that are released and snapped shut around the foot of an animal when it steps on a trigger pan in the center of the open jaws. Tricking an animal into placing its foot precisely on a tiny trigger mechanism requires a great deal of knowledge of both the habits of carnivores and the best methods of disguise. Naturally wary and with a keen sense of smell, carnivores are very adept at recognizing something amiss in their surroundings. Trappers will typically add some kind of bait or scent to the area to lure their prey, but for Heller, the smell of fresh meat wafting from the gut piles of Roosevelt's kills was enough to bring the jackals, hyenas, and all kinds of cats into the area. It then became a simple matter of carefully positioning his traps where these animals were most likely to step—along trails, on top of obvious vantage points where carnivores like to perch, and at natural choke points in the terrain. A good trapper might also lay twigs and branches on the ground in such a way as to guide an animal's footsteps precisely into the trap's jaws.

Heller set these traps by bedding them down in a small depression dug into the ground and then carefully covering them with some loose dirt sifted over the top. Since an animal caught by the foot could easily walk off with the trap, it had to be either staked down into the ground or wired to something heavy. Heller had wired the trap that snagged the leopard to a large fallen limb from a thorn tree, which served as "drag," granting the animal a certain degree of movement without allowing it to go very far. Heller followed the trail of this drag into a thorny thicket and got within ten feet before he realized he'd snagged a leopard. Scaling a nearby thorn tree, he fired several shots down into the animal to kill it.

Of course, all this talk of shooting hippos and trapping leopards certainly got the attention of animal activists back in America, and, not surprisingly, it was Reverend William J. Long, of "nature faker" fame, who was among Roosevelt's most vehement detractors. Speaking to a *New York Times* reporter, Long lambasted Roosevelt over the reports of his frequent killings in Africa: "They prove what I said two years ago, quoting from his own books, that he is a game butcher pure and simple, and that his interest in animals lies chiefly in the direction of blood and brutality." Elaborating further, Long assailed Roosevelt's bad example:

> The worst feature in the whole bloody business is not the killing of a few hundred wild animals in Africa, but the brutalizing influence which these reports have upon thousands of American boys. Only last week I met half a dozen little fellows in the woods. The biggest boy had a gun and a squirrel's tail in his hat, and he called himself *Bwana Tumbo*. They were shooting everything in sight, killing birds at a time when every dead mother

meant a nestful of young birds slowly starving to death. How could I convince them that their work was inhuman? Is not the great American hero occupied at this time with the same detestable business?

Long continued his anti-Roosevelt crusade in a subsequent article for the *Toledo Blade*: "The only thing we will ever get out of this much-heralded trip will be some more hunting yarns . . . and some more skins and bones, of which we already have too many. . . . The whole thing is atrocious."

Cruising up and down the lakeshores of Naivasha and oblivious to anything Reverend Long might have been spouting back home, Roosevelt hoped to bag an especially large bull to complete the hippo group for the National Museum. The first hippo he had shot had been mistakenly identified as a male, but on closer examination he was embarrassed to see that it was actually a very old, barren female. Before long Roosevelt spotted a few hippos in a little bay, floating with their heads above water. Like a team of harpoon men from the early days of whaling, Roosevelt and his oarsmen quickly launched their smaller wooden "chase boat" to close in for the kill, but they accidentally positioned themselves over an entire school of submerged hippos, and as the animals fled in panic, they bumped the bottom of the rowboat. The men held on to the sides as the boat rocked uneasily back and forth and "the shallow, muddy water boiled, as the huge beasts, above and below the surface, scattered every which way. Their eyes starting, the two rowers began to back water out of the dangerous neighborhood, while I shot an animal whose head appeared to my left, as it made off with frantic haste; for I took it for granted that the hippo at which I had first fired . . . had escaped. This one disappeared as usual, and I had not the slightest idea whether or not I had killed it. I had small opportunity to ponder the subject, for twenty feet away the water bubbled and a huge head shot out facing me, the jaws wide open. There was no time to guess at its intentions, and I fired on the instant. Down went the head, and I felt the boat quiver as the hippo passed underneath. . . . A head burst up twenty yards off, with a lily pad plastered over one eye, giving the hippo an absurd resemblance to a discomfited prize fighter, and then disappeared with great agitation." In an hour, four dead hippos floated to the surface—the big bull and three cows.

The unexpected carnage—and, more important, the thought of what the press would do when they heard the news—disturbed Roosevelt. He felt he had been forced by circumstances to fire into the herd, never imagining that he would kill so many animals. "I don't know what to do about it. We shall have to let the papers know. And this is not a game-slaughtering expedition." In the end, though, the public was no more concerned about his slaughter of the hippos than they were about the far greater numbers of smaller mammals that all the naturalists were collecting. Loring and Mearns had caught hundreds at Lake Naivasha, and, looking over their haul, they determined that a number of them were probably new species. Indicative of just how poorly known the region was, the group even found a new species while waiting for a train at the Naivasha railway station, a fox of the genus *Otocyon*. Mearns wrote to the Smithsonian to request "quick action" with regard to the new fox, so that if it was a truly new species, they should describe it without delay.

Chapter 19

HUNTERS
AND NATURALISTS

By the time of the Smithsonian African Expedition, big-tusked elephants had been so heavily hunted in British East Africa that they were essentially extirpated from the open plains. The few big bulls remaining had retreated to the bamboo forests on the upper slopes of Mount Kenya. Here they found refuge in the thick vegetation, where they were all but impossible to hunt. It was only after heavy rains, when the elephants sometimes moved down out of the bamboo and into the lower forest zone, that it was possible to hunt them, and it was here that Roosevelt hoped to find one.

Trudging up the slopes of Mount Kenya in his hobnailed boots, Roosevelt churned the ground into slick mud underfoot, with each step his legs brushing against the sodden understory vegetation, soaking his khaki trousers through. He ducked under vines and climbed over fallen timber. Poisonous nettles stung his hands. Through it all, Roosevelt carried one precious volume from his pigskin library.

Roosevelt was dependent on his guides, and it was Cuninghame together with some native Ndorobo trackers who went ahead to look for fresh elephant sign. In the misty forests, the landscape was suddenly dark and quiet. "The sun was shut from sight by a thick screen of wet foliage," Roosevelt reported. The gathered men stood on a carpet of spongy moss, with twisted vines and interlacing trees all around them. It was an eerie habitat, the only trails being those left by elephants, but they hardly saw any animals. A troop of black-and-white colobus monkeys bounded away through the treetops, and then all returned to silence. The Ndorobo trackers were like ghosts, appearing and disappearing before Roosevelt's eyes in the thick foliage, sometimes even unexpectedly dropping down from the trees in front of him. They examined every pile of dung in minute detail. Whenever they came upon fresh spoor, they followed up cautiously, testing the wind with charred matches to detect the subtle drift of the air (an elephant's nose commands respect, and hours of careful stalking can be ruined by a sudden shift in wind). Their first day of elephant hunting was a bust, so they pitched their camp by the side of a little brook at the bottom of a sheltered ravine, where they silently dined on bread, mutton, and tea, their clothing drenched through to their skin.

Resuming their careful stalk at dawn, they came across the fresh trail of a small herd of elephants, perhaps ten or fifteen cows and calves with a couple of big bulls among them. The wind was right, and, creeping along cautiously, they advanced close enough to hear the animals' telltale deep, rumbling calls. Readying his rifle, Roosevelt took care to step only in the elephant's footprints, the weight of the beast having left no twigs unbroken for him to crack underfoot. For nearly half an hour they tiptoed forward, Roosevelt's veins tingling with excitement. At last the trail twisted to one side, and they spied, not more than thirty yards ahead, the massive gray head of an elephant "resting his tusks on the branches of a young tree." A flock of noisy hornbills suddenly clambered overhead, but the elephants paid them no heed. The men were all hunkered down in the thick, wet foliage, speaking in whispers. Minutes passed before they could determine that the elephant in front of them was a bull with heavy tusks. The hunting party caught only fleeting glimpses of the animal—the flap of an ear, the flicker of a tail, the flash of a tusk—and then Roosevelt saw an eye. Having carefully studied a sectioned elephant skull in the American Museum before his trip, he visualized his shot. The elephant turned its head, and, aiming carefully just to the side of the eye, Roosevelt fired.

His shot missed the brain completely. The elephant stood stunned; then, as it stumbled forward, Roosevelt fired a quick second shot. This time the bullet connected, drilling a hole right through the center of the top of the skull, and as Roosevelt lowered his rifle, he saw the "great lord of the forest come crashing to the ground."

But the hunters were hardly out of danger. The moment the animal fell, the thick bushes parted, and a second bull came crashing straight toward Roosevelt, vines snapping "like packethread" before his rush. "He was so close, he could have touched me with his trunk," Roosevelt recalled, and had he not instinctively leapt to the side, he could have been snared in a curl of its trunk and whipped into the ground. Taking cover behind a tree, Roosevelt thrust two fresh shells into the big Holland rifle while Cuninghame fired off his two barrels nearly at once. The bullets hit home, and the bull stopped short in his charge, wheeled around, and immediately disappeared into the brush, trumpeting shrilly in wounded retreat. Then all was silent.

A joyful scene of nervous excitement followed as adrenaline pumped through every man's veins. The first elephant lay dead before them, but the second, although hard hit, fled at great speed. Hearing all the shots, Heller and his men charged up the side of the mountain and found everyone "chattering like monkeys," bellowing with elation. "I felt proud indeed as I stood by the immense bulk of the slain monster and put my hand on the ivory," said Roosevelt, and then everyone began the work of skinning under Heller's supervision.

The preservation of an entire elephant skin for taxidermy presents special problems. The sheer size of the animal means that it cannot be rolled or manipulated and must be skinned exactly as it falls. The skin itself is also too massive to handle in one piece, which calls for it to be cut off in sections to be sewn back together later, the seams sealed up with wax so that the animal looks whole. Cows and small bull elephant skins are cut into three sections. The head is cut off first, removed close behind the ears, where the cut will be hidden. The skin from the torso is then removed in two pieces down the midline, the result being two mirror images of the left and right side of the animal. For very large bulls it might also be necessary to divide each of these in half again; thus, a really big bull is sectioned into five separate pieces of skin, the head and four quarters, each of the latter with one leg.

Working this way, Roosevelt's hunters were all "splashed with blood from head to foot." One of the trackers even squatted inside the carcass to better use his knife. Others rewarded themselves by cutting off strips of meat for later consumption, festooning the surrounding branches as if with red ribbons. At dark, they camped in a small open glade about one hundred yards from the dead elephant, and as fires were kindled, the men sat and sang while roasting strips of meat on long sticks over the fire. "The flickering light left them at one moment in black obscurity, and the next brought into bold relief their sinewy crouching figures, their dark faces, gleaming eyes, and flashing teeth." Sitting right there among them, flashing his own gleaming white teeth, was Theodore Roosevelt, toasting thin slices of elephant heart on a pronged stick.

ROOSEVELT LEFT MOUNT Kenya shortly after shooting his first elephant. It would take Edmund Heller and his team ten days to fully process that animal, and Roosevelt wanted to use that time to embark on a solo hunt—to prove to himself that he was more than a tourist and could lead a hunt without help from the other naturalists and hunters. Gathering together a team of porters, gun bearers, *saises*, and tent boys, he set off for the plains of the headwaters of the Northern Guaso Nyiro River.

In the dry, thorny environs of this river through the desert, Roosevelt hunted roan and oryx—beautiful antelope with bold facial markings and curving, saber-shaped, or long, straight rapier-shaped horns, respectively. Ever since writing *Hunting Trips of a Ranchman*, Roosevelt had been perfecting his narrative style, incorporating nuggets of natural history into his descriptions of stalking game. For all his graphic descriptions of misplaced shots and animals running off wounded, Roosevelt recorded equally lengthy passages on the normal daily lives of these same animals. He made careful notes on the sizes of herds, their apparent breeding seasons, and even their gaits. The giraffe, he reported, had a very peculiar gallop, both hind legs coming forward at nearly the same time and to the outside of the forelegs. He discussed the different-shaped horns of the gazelles he saw on the

Guaso Nyiro compared to those he remembered from the Sotik or the Kapiti Plains, at the same time mentioning how the gazelles to the north seemed to twitch their tails more jerkily.

Feeling confident in his knowledge of the native fauna, Roosevelt began seriously contemplating writing a big book on the natural history of African mammals—a comprehensive tome summarizing the life histories of all the species he was hunting. Being a careful observer and having a steel-trap memory, Roosevelt was building a treasure trove of African-mammal anecdotes in his mind. Hunting these animals sharpened his naturalist's skills. The chase was what motivated him to get out and observe these animals in the wild, and in that pursuit he had gained a deep understanding of their lives.

Roosevelt's focus on the big mammals was just one part of the Smithsonian African Expedition, of course. The other half was the Biological Survey work of J. Alden Loring and Dr. Edgar A. Mearns. Roosevelt and Edmund Heller may have worked apart from these naturalists, but this was because one team needed to rove widely for large mammals while the others had to tend traps to obtain their study animals. The work of the hunters and the work of the naturalists, however, were entirely complementary, each recording observations and collecting specimens to study in more detail back at the museum. Having already made collections from the Kapiti Plains, the Sotik, and Lake Naivasha, Mearns and Loring each killed and preserved far more specimens than did Roosevelt and Kermit combined. But, absent Roosevelt and his support of the expedition, Loring and Mearns would not have had the opportunity to conduct their surveys at all. Roosevelt's hunting was the driving force behind the expedition.

As Roosevelt set off for his solo hunt to the west of Mount Kenya, Loring and Mearns embarked on a comprehensive survey of the western slopes of the mountain. While Roosevelt needed but a few days to go up and shoot his elephant, the other two men were planning to stay on the mountain for a full month, periodically shifting their camps to survey different elevations on their way up and down.

Mearns was the one who suggested to Roosevelt that he and Loring be allowed to conduct such an ambitious survey. At just over 17,000 feet, Mount Kenya is high enough to have glaciers despite being situated on the equator. Starting from the base of the mountain, with each few thousand feet of elevation the habitats changed, the lowland plains giving way to forest and then bamboo and, finally, cloud-shrouded grasslands and tundra near the top. They could expect the animals to be different in each new landscape, but just what species they would find was unknown.

Like Clinton Hart Merriam plotting his "life zones" of specimens throughout North America, Loring and Mearns endeavored to map the mysteries of how the fauna changed as one went farther up the mountain. Mearns, who boasted an ability to walk thirty miles a day over level ground, had to work "like fighting snakes" in this high country, which was lofty enough for the men to experience altitude sickness. It was dangerous work for the porters in particular, who did not have the best gear or even adequate clothing and were unaccustomed to the frosty weather on the upper slopes—one of the very few places in equatorial Africa where one could expect to experience a snow squall.

In anticipation of the cold conditions, Mearns chose his porters from among the Kikuyu inhabiting the surrounding Aberdare Mountains. Although their home was not nearly as high as Mount Kenya, these men were not entirely unaccustomed to the cold. Past explorers had considered themselves lucky if only a few of their native helpers died from exposure on Mount Kenya. Dr. Mearns vowed not to lose a single man.

A total of 150 Kikuyu porters carried the scientific gear up to their first base camp at 12,100 feet—traps, plant presses, shotguns, ammunition, tents, cook kits, specimen-preparation supplies, as well as all the food and even the firewood the group would depend on to keep warm and cook their meals. Working above the tree line, the men found themselves in a strange landscape of giant flowering plants, some towering more than thirty feet over their heads. Most of the porters went back down the mountain the next morning—the local people knew better than to spend much time way up there—but keeping a core group of thirty-six hardy Kikuyu, Mearns and Loring laid out a plan for collecting specimens from the most unusual habitats on the mountain.

From their base camp they ventured up to 13,700 feet, where Loring and Heller camped alone. Hiking all the way up to "the eternal ice and snow," Loring climbed to within 700 feet of the summit, where he was temporarily blinded from the glare off the glaciers. Meanwhile, Mearns walked along a snowbank and "had some fine slides down the snowfields." He was looking for animal tracks, hoping to perhaps spot the tracks of a "snow leopard." He settled for a collection of alpine plants from around a glacial lake instead.

From there they moved down to 10,700 feet, amid the thick bamboo and yellowwood trees, then down to a camp at 8,500 feet, finally finishing their survey work on the open plateau at 6,500 feet. Writing home to his wife and daughter, Mearns explained how he had "worked off some flesh" but said that the reward of specimens was worth the effort. They found some unusual animals, such as the rock hyrax—short, squat, woodchuck-size animals that were, in fact, more closely related to elephants than to rodents. They lived amid the alpine ledges at the highest elevations of the mountain. In places where these animals had sunned themselves for generations spanning centuries, these rock ledges were polished smooth. To Roosevelt's delight, the men also caught a giant shrew on Mount Kenya, and, true to form, it was ferocious, lashing out at anything within reach.

At the end of their mission, Roosevelt sent Mearns a note expressing his "great satisfaction at their results and especially the fact that they had been able to ascend the mountain and done their work without losing any natives from exposure." Roosevelt understood the scientific value of these collections, which were similar to those he had been making since he was a boy. However, he also understood the American public. He knew that, beyond the walls of museums, precious few people cared about such work or felt it important. Roosevelt may have nurtured a passion for shrews since he was a boy, but he also knew that, in this regard, he was exceptional and that hardly anyone else viewed these animals as affectionately as he did. Only among his fellow museum naturalists could Roosevelt share his passion for all kinds of animals, not just the big ones. If Americans were ever to appreciate natural history in its totality—from big showy mammals and birds to tiny rats and shrews—he knew that their best chance was through his popular writings and the museum taxidermy exhibits that were the focus of his ardent hunting. Roosevelt was as much a museum naturalist as Heller, Loring, or Mearns, but he also understood the importance of conveying his passion to a much broader audience. Cursed with poor vision, but never a myopic scientist, Roosevelt the naturalist understood how to go about winning the hearts and minds of the American people through both his writings and taxidermy.

AS ROOSEVELT WAS setting forth on his solo hunt, Carl Akeley was stepping off a German steamship in Mombasa. He boarded the Uganda Railway and sat in the same bench atop the cowcatcher that Roosevelt had ridden on months prior. But whereas Roosevelt was encouraged by his glimpses of wildlife along the way, Akeley was heartbroken. After a nearly five-year absence from the continent, Akeley couldn't believe how dramatically East Africa had changed. Where were the great herds of hartebeest? Why so few impala bounding over bushes? Wildlife had become scarce and more difficult to approach. Hunters were pouring into East Africa—Roosevelt among them— and Akeley was alarmed to see that they had left such a dark mark on the landscape.

Akeley was not fond of blood sport. He was principally an artist—a taxidermist—now on a very specific mission to collect specimens for a museum exhibit. Like Roosevelt, he was after elephants. He had just finished a taxidermy exhibit of a pair of elephants he had shot on a previous expedition for the Field Museum, when he approached the American Museum of Natural History to ask if they might want something similar for their main hall. All the great natural-history museums in America were trying to fill empty halls, and elephants were the perfect size to occupy the high-ceilinged spaces. Akeley capitalized on this unique moment in the development of these museums, and, knowing that the great game herds were doomed, he wanted to preserve a whole group of them for the American Museum of Natural History—a collection that would serve as the centerpiece of a great African mammal hall. The directors of the American Museum agreed.

But as he chugged up the Mombasa line, Akeley worried that maybe he had returned to Africa too late. Elephants had been far more abundant when he first conceived his idea, and those that remained were so spooked by humans that they were nearly impossible to hunt. He was facing the same problem that had vexed some of these same museums in their quests for specimens of American bison decades before—their expeditions arrived too late, the depletion of animals leaving little margin for success. Akeley wanted very specific elephants for his group—a big bull, a few cows, smaller males, and at least one calf—and, understanding the importance of publicity, he had earlier come to a gentleman's agreement that Roosevelt should kill at least one of the elephants for the group. But, confronted with the barrenness of wild Africa, he was gripped with concern for its future.

More pressing, Akeley worried about how to find Roosevelt in the vastness of the continent. Arriving in Nairobi, he was handed a sealed envelope from Roosevelt with a letter saying that he was hoping to rendezvous with him somewhere on the Uasin Gishu plateau—a rather desolate expanse more than a hundred miles away, but Akeley was under the impression that he might already be too late. Gathering up supplies, two transport wagons, and a hundred or so porters, Akeley set off for the eastern edge of the plateau anyway. His only chance for intercepting Roosevelt was to spot the safari from higher ground, and, climbing to a lofty promenade, Akeley gazed across the vast open plains of the Uasin Gishu. Mount Elgon towered in the distance, a backdrop to the hundreds of square miles of grassland stretching out before him.

Roosevelt had also sent out a few runners to try to find Akeley—tribesmen carrying sketch maps and notes on his general whereabouts—and at least one of these messengers completed that mission. From Roosevelt's note—by then several days old—Akeley reckoned that Roosevelt was probably nearing the Nzoia River. Akeley had no idea if the man would still be there when he arrived, but he had little choice but to set forth and hope.

Advancing straight toward the Nzoia the next morning, Akeley attempted to head off the safari. Trekking under the midday sun, he spotted a dust cloud in the distance, and, peering through his army field glasses, he saw that the dust was being kicked up by a very large safari on the move—a safari so large that it could have only been Roosevelt's. But Roosevelt was not with the main safari. As chance had it, he was returning from a place where he and Kermit had just photographed some cow elephants, when he saw a white man approaching. It was Carl Akeley, beaming with satisfaction at having located his friend at last.

Warm greetings ensued, after which Roosevelt revisited their plan to secure elephants for the American Museum of Natural History. He suggested they return to the spot where he and Kermit had just seen and photographed some suitable elephants. Once there, Akeley was relieved to see that the animals were not the least bit alarmed by their advance, perhaps made more comfortable by the fact that two of these three men had been with them moments before. There were six cows and two well-developed calves "taking their midday siesta, and milling about under the trees." Peering out from behind the cover of a large anthill, Akeley pointed out the ones he wanted—the two cows with the smaller but slightly better-shaped tusks. The elephants were but sixty yards away, well within range, and Akeley assumed that Roosevelt would simply step out from behind the mound and shoot them from where he stood. Instead, Roosevelt advanced to within a dangerous thirty yards, Akeley and Kermit following silently. "I had an impulse to climb on Roosevelt's shoulder and whisper that I wanted him to shoot her [the cow], not take her alive," Akeley later recalled, but Roosevelt wanted to make sure he hit his elephant. Shouldering his double-barreled elephant gun—the one that sometimes gave him nosebleeds when he fired it—he "put the bullet from the right barrel of the Holland through her lungs, and fired the left barrel for the heart of the other."

All at once, "an unwounded cow began to advance with her great ears cocked at right angles to her head." Then someone called out, "Look out! They're coming for us."

In the frenzy of shooting that followed, Roosevelt found himself fending off a stampede. "I put a bullet into the forehead of the advancing cow, causing her to lurch heavily forward to her knees, and then we all fired . . . 'round they spun and rushed off. As they turned, I dropped the second cow I had wounded with a shot in the brain, and the cow that had started to charge also fell, though I needed two or three more shots to keep it down as it struggled to rise." Meanwhile, the cow Roosevelt had first shot began running off with the rest of the herd but fell dead within a hundred yards. With three big elephants down, Kermit then used his Winchester to shoot a tiny bull calf needed to complete the museum exhibit.

For Akeley it was a bittersweet success. While he was pleased to have Roosevelt involved in his hunt, the men had shot one more elephant than they could use—a heartbreaking loss. They then parted ways, the taxidermist heading to Mount Kenya in the hope of securing his own big bull elephant to serve as the centerpiece of his exhibit. Knowing what Akeley was capable of as a taxidermist, and envisioning the monumental taxidermy tribute he had planned for the halls of the American Museum of Natural History, Roosevelt felt the killings justified. For Roosevelt, it was not so much the individual lives of animals that mattered as the survival of the species. At the very least he wanted people to have the chance to see good specimens preserved forever in a museum. That was his brand of naturalism.

"I SPEAK OF Africa and golden joys." The first line of Roosevelt's own retelling of his epic safari made it clear that he saw it as the unfolding of a great drama, and one that might have very well led to his own death, for the quoted line is from Shakespeare, the *Henry IV* scene in which the death of the king was pronounced. Roosevelt had been in the field for nearly nine months, and as 1909 drew to a close, he prepared to embark on a most dangerous mission. Disbanding his foot safari on the shores of Lake Victoria, he requisitioned a flotilla of river craft—a "crazy little steam launch," two sailboats, and two rowboats—to take him hundreds of miles down the Nile River to a place on the west bank called the Lado Enclave. A semiarid landscape of eye-high elephant grass and scattered thorn trees, it was the last holdout of the rare northern white rhinoceros, and it was here that Roosevelt planned to shoot two complete family groups—one for the Smithsonian's National Museum, and one for Akeley's African mammal hall at the American Museum.

Nestled between what was then the Anglo-Egyptian Sudan and the Belgian Congo, the Lado Enclave was a 220-mile-long strip of land that was the personal shooting preserve of Belgium's King Leopold II. By international agreement, the king could hold the Lado as his own personal shooting preserve on the condition that, six months after his death, it would pass to British-controlled Sudan. King Leopold was already on his deathbed when Roosevelt went to East Africa, and the area reverted to lawlessness as elephant poachers and ragtag adventurers poured into the region with "the greedy abandon of a gold rush."

Getting to the Lado, however, required Roosevelt to pass through the hot zone of a sleeping-sickness epidemic—the shores and islands at the northern end of Lake Victoria. Hundreds of thousands of people had recently died of the disease, until the Uganda government wisely evacuated the survivors inland. Those who remained took their chances, and Roosevelt noted the emptiness of the land.

The white rhino lived there—a completely different species from the more common black rhino Roosevelt had been collecting. Color, though, actually has little to do with their differences. In fact, the two animals are so different that they are usually placed in separate genera. The white rhino—*white* being the English bastardization of the Afrikaans word *wyd* for "wide," in reference to this species's characteristically broad upper lip—is specialized for grazing. By comparison, the more truculent black rhino has a narrow and hooked upper lip specialized for munching on shrubs. Although both animals are gray and basically indistinguishable by color, they display plenty of other differences: the white rhino is generally bigger, has a distinctive hump on its neck, and boasts an especially elongated and massive head, which it carries only a few inches from the ground. Roosevelt also knew that of the two, the white rhino was closest in appearance to the prehistoric rhinos that once roamed across the continent of

Europe, and the idea of connecting himself to a hunting legacy that spanned millennia thrilled him.

For many decades since its description in 1817, the white rhino was known to be found only in that part of South Africa south of the Zambezi River, but in 1900 a new subspecies was discovered thousands of miles to the north, in the Lado Enclave. Such widely separated populations were unusual in the natural world, and it was assumed that the extant white rhinos were the remnants of what was once a more widespread and contiguous distribution. "It is almost as if our bison had never been known within historic times except in Texas and Ecuador," Roosevelt wrote of the disparity.

At the time of Roosevelt's expedition, as many as one million black rhino still existed in Africa, but the white rhino was already nearing extinction. The southern population had been hunted to the point that only a few individuals survived in just a single reserve, and even within the narrow ribbon of the Lado Enclave, these rhinos were found only in certain areas and were by no means abundant. On the one hand, Roosevelt's instincts as a conservationist told him to refrain from shooting any white rhino specimens "until a careful inquiry has been made as to its numbers and exact distribution." But on the other hand, as a pragmatic naturalist, he knew that the species was inevitably doomed and that it was important for him to collect specimens before it went extinct.

As he steamed down the Nile, Roosevelt was followed by a second expedition of sorts, led by a former member of the British East Africa Police. But Captain W. Robert Foran was not intent on arresting Roosevelt—whom he referred to by the code name "Rex"; rather, he was the head of an expedition of the Associated Press. Roosevelt let Foran's group follow at a respectable distance, by now wanting regular news to flow back to the United States. Foran had also been instrumental in securing a guide for Roosevelt on his jaunt into the virtually lawless Lado Enclave. The guide, Quentin Grogan, was among the most notorious of the elephant poachers in the Lado, and Roosevelt was chuffed to have someone of such ill-repute steering his party.

Grogan was still recovering from a boozy, late-night revel when he first met Roosevelt. The poacher thought Kermit was dull, and he deplored the lack of alcohol in the Roosevelts' camp. Among some other hangers-on eager to meet Roosevelt was another character—John Boyes, a seaman who, after being shipwrecked on the African coast in 1896, "went native" and was so highly regarded as an elephant hunter there that he was christened the legendary King of the Kikuyu. Grogan, Boyes, and a couple of other unnamed elephant hunters had gathered in the hope of meeting Roosevelt, who characterized them all as "a hard bit set." These men who faced death at every turn, "from fever, from assaults of warlike native tribes, from their conflicts with their giant quarry," were so like many of the tough cowpunchers he had encountered in the American West—rough and fiercely independent men—that Roosevelt loved them.

Downriver they went, past walls of impenetrable papyrus, until they came upon a low, sandy bay that is to this day marked on maps as "Rhino Camp." Their tents pitched on the banks of the White Nile, about two degrees above the equator, Roosevelt was in "the heart of the African wilderness." Hippos wandered dangerously close at night, while lions roared and elephants trumpeted nearby. Having spent the past several months in the cool Kenyan highlands, Roosevelt found the heat and swarming insects intense, and he was forced to wear a mosquito head net and gauntlets at all times. The group slept under mosquito nets "usually with nothing on, on account of the heat" and burned mosquito repellent throughout the night.

Although their camp was situated just beyond the danger zone for sleeping sickness, Roosevelt was still bracing himself to come down with some sort of fever or another. "All the other members of the party have been down with fever or dysentery; one gun bearer has died of fever, four porters of dysentery and two have been mauled by beasts; and in a village on our line of march, near which we camped and hunted, eight natives died of sleeping sickness during our stay," he wrote. The stakes were certainly high in Rhino Camp, but Roosevelt would not have taken the risk if the mission was not important—the white rhino was the only species of heavy game left for the expedition to collect, and, of all the species, it was the one the Smithsonian would likely never have an opportunity to collect again.

In the end, Roosevelt shot five northern white rhinoceros, with Kermit taking an additional four. As game, these rhinos were unimpressive to hunt. Most were shot as they rose from slumber. But with a touch of poignancy, the hunts were punctuated with bouts of wildfire-fighting, injecting some drama into one of Roosevelt's last accounts from the field. Flames licked sixty feet high as the men lit backfires to protect their camp, the evening sky turning red above the burning grass and papyrus. Awakening to a scene that resembled the aftermath of an apocalypse, the men tracked rhino through miles of white ash, the elephant grass having burned to the ground in the night.

Whether the species lived on or died out, Roosevelt was emphatic that people needed to see the white rhinoceros. If they couldn't experience the animals in Africa, at least they should have the chance to see them in a museum. As a young hunter Roosevelt had set forth to hunt a trophy American buffalo "while there were still buffalo left to shoot." Now, as a mature naturalist, Roosevelt decided to collect some white rhino specimens while there were still some white rhinos left to collect—then and only then would he put away his rifle and bring his great African adventure to an end.

LIKE OLD FRIENDS, black-and-white chat thrushes greeted Roosevelt as he drifted down the Nile on his long journey home. It had been decades since he had first heard them, but he could still remember their call, a scolding *tsk-tsk-tsk* as they fluttered in the riverside brush. Spur-winged plovers still busied themselves in the mudflats along shore, emitting their loud and shrill *yak! yak!* Pied kingfisher still hovered over the water, looking to dive down on prey, and Roosevelt was thrilled to hear the *hoo-hoo* of the hoopoe again. When first visiting Africa as a boy, he had merely mimicked the duties of a faunal naturalist by shooting pigeons and buntings for his childhood museum; now, nearing the end of his life, he had collected some exceptionally valuable specimens for the National Museum of Natural History.

Thinking back on his life before the Smithsonian African Expedition, Roosevelt described his passion for natural history as "very real" but also acknowledged that his ambitions as a naturalist had never been fully realized. He derided his earliest efforts as a naturalist, considering his notes "copious but valueless," and he characterized his earlier contributions to science as being of "minimal worth," even though his boyhood notebooks showed his precociousness as a naturalist. Roosevelt held himself to the highest standards, and for much of his life he was disappointed with what he deemed a failure to really assert his own brand of naturalism—one that was adamant about getting out to do the hard and sometimes bloody work he deemed so necessary. But, coming to the end of the Smithsonian African Expedition, he finally felt he had stepped up to his own high standards and contributed something of value to the store of human knowledge.

Down the Nile to Edith, awaiting him in Khartoum, through Egypt and the cities of Europe, across the vast Atlantic Ocean and into New York Harbor, Roosevelt made his way back home. To the crowds gathering in Lower Manhattan, the muffled cannon blasts emanating from faraway Fort Wadsworth on Staten Island were the first indication that their beloved ex-president was near. Tens of thousands of people had gathered along the west shore of Manhattan to greet him, and they reached the height of excitement as a second twenty-one-gun salute announced his arrival on their shores. Standing on the deck of a regalia-festooned ship was Theodore Roosevelt, grinning and doffing his top hat as he set foot on his native land. The naturalist had come home.

⤐

THE END OF THE GAME

Nat•u•ral•ist /-list/ *n* **(1587) 1:** one that advocates or practices naturalism **2:** a student of natural history; *esp.*: a field biologist.

—*Merriam-Webster's Collegiate Dictionary,*
Eleventh Edition

*W*ho was Theodore Roosevelt the naturalist? Was he merely a big-game hunter justifying his hunts under the guise of museum collecting, or was he truly a man in pursuit of something higher in the name of science? To even ask such a question says something of our changed perception of naturalists today. Roosevelt was unquestionably considered a naturalist in his lifetime and was even profiled alongside Charles Darwin and John James Audubon in *Impressions of Great Naturalists,* a book written by the director of the American Museum of Natural History only a few years after Roosevelt returned from his Smithsonian African Expedition. Yet Roosevelt's brand of naturalism seems so alien to us today that we can legitimately question his bona fides. How many naturalists shoot animals and make museum specimens today? Whoever hears of a museum expedition going off to a remote, foreign place to trap and describe new species?

Further clouding our view is the rather bumpy course of Roosevelt's naturalist career. Perhaps because his enthusiasms pulled him in so many different directions, perhaps, also, for lack of mentors, Roosevelt bumbled along as a naturalist, ardently stuffing bird skins one year, racing off to kill bison the next, and then temporarily abandoning his pursuit of naturalism altogether. He certainly struggled to find himself as a naturalist, but the one thing that remained constant was his lifelong passion for adventurous, outdoor naturalism. Throughout his life, Roosevelt was in love with the idea of being a museum naturalist—the intrepid kind who went off on dangerous expeditions and shot exotic animals for natural-history museums— and it took him a lifetime finally to become one. The whole course of his life as a naturalist up until then—from his boyhood passion for collecting specimens to his western hunts and his emergence as a hunter-naturalist—led to the Smithsonian African Expedition, tying together all the disparate strains of his identity as a naturalist

From the day he discovered the dead seal on Broadway as a boy, Roosevelt had nurtured his desire to study nature through specimens. True, he had an ear for beautiful birdsong, and he trained himself to record the nuances of animal behavior in lyric prose, but in the end Roosevelt always preferred a specimen—something to hold in his hands—to bring natural history to vivid life.

And ever since dragging around his father's huge volume of David Livingstone's *Missionary Travels and Researches in South Africa* as a boy, Roosevelt saw Africa as the ultimate destination for outdoor adventure. Hunting dangerous game in Africa certainly accorded Roosevelt the status of an adventurer, but as he had learned through the course of his life, simply being a good hunter was not enough. He knew he needed to link his hunting closely to natural history.

In forming the Smithsonian African Expedition, Roosevelt didn't merely synthesize his own interests; he also brought together a tremendous team of hunters, naturalists, and scientists, and that union became a model for future exploration parties. On a Roosevelt expedition, hunters were expected to record and publish their observations the way naturalists did. Likewise, on a Roosevelt expedition, naturalists were expected to get out and hunt their own specimens. Roosevelt also insisted that the person who actually collected a specimen should have a hand in writing up any results for publication, much the way Edmund Heller did, describing new species even while the Smithsonian African Expedition was still in the field.

Returning to America, Roosevelt quickly settled into his newfound identity as a museum naturalist, publishing two great works as a result of his expedition. The first was a compilation of his *Scribner's Magazine* dispatches from the field: *African Game Trails: An Account of the African Wanderings of an American Hunter-Naturalist*. Some readers were aghast at his unabashed descriptions of death, and yet the book was a runaway best seller when it was first printed and was named 1910's "Book of the Year" by the *New York Herald*.

Less well known was his *Life Histories of African Game Animals*, a two-volume book he coauthored with Edmund Heller. It was a gem of a field study decades ahead of its time in providing detailed natural-history accounts of all the larger mammals encountered on the expedition. Although Roosevelt plainly knew that the book was not likely to be profitable, it brought together in one publication the most important results of his expedition. Dozens of scientific papers had already been published describing the results of the group's zoological surveys in East Africa, most of which were rather formulaic descriptions of new species and subspecies that were published in the Smithsonian's obscure "Miscellaneous Collections" series, where they were all but lost to anyone other than professional mammalogists. Roosevelt had always railed against Clinton Hart Merriam for publishing so many of these esoteric leaflets, but with his own new books he hoped to reach all of America—to bring naturalism to the general population. Together, *African Game Trails* and *Life Histories of African Game Animals* embody the two pillars upholding Roosevelt the naturalist—someone who loved both the science and the adventure of being a good naturalist.

Through the influence of George Bird Grinnell and the Boone and Crockett Club, Roosevelt developed a hunting ethic that combined the thrill of the chase with a need to give something back in return. Roosevelt opened the door for hunters to be more like scientists. Absent a strong conservation ethic, hunters would have been forever the enemies of wildlife, but Theodore Roosevelt made it possible for them to rejoin the ranks of naturalists. He resurrected the idea of being a naturalist in the vein of John James Audubon or Spencer Fullerton Baird—the kind who went out and hunted animal specimens for science, who told the stories of the animals they hunted.

Natural-history museums were central to Roosevelt's development as a naturalist, and his life was very much interwoven with the rise of the museums we know today. In Roosevelt's boyhood and youth, America's nascent natural-history museums—the Smithsonian and the American Museum of Natural History—were still in their curiosity stage. Like the youthful Roosevelt starting his boyhood museum with the seal he found on Broadway, the proprietors of America's first museums were still discovering their own brand of naturalism. All started out by simply displaying the wonders of nature. However, as collections grew, important and fascinating patterns emerged. Whether it was Roosevelt obsessively shooting and stuffing every bird he could find, or Baird sending his legions of collectors out west, naturalists shipping their specimens to the budding institutions were making real contributions.

Sending expeditions into the field with increasing regularity, museums were inundated with hundreds of thousands of specimens— everything from insects and birds to enormous mammals. And such a massive influx of new specimens meant that scientists no longer had to go out into the field to conduct their research. They could sort through thousands of incoming skins and skulls and churn out endless descriptions of new species. Clinton Hart Merriam was just one of these scientists, and he turned field biology into a machine for getting specimens into his hands. From Washington, D.C., Merriam drafted many new species descriptions. But absent from this assembly-line science was the classical faunal naturalist Roosevelt so loved.

AS A NATURALIST, Theodore Roosevelt is most often remembered for protecting millions of acres of wilderness, but he was equally committed to preserving something else—the memory of the natural world as it was before the onslaught of civilization. To him, being a responsible naturalist was also about recording the things that would inevitably pass, and he collected specimens and wrote about the life histories of animals when he knew it might be the last opportunity to study them extant. Just as the bison in the American West had faded, Roosevelt knew that the big game of East Africa would one day exist only in vastly diminished numbers. He had missed his chance to record much of the natural history of wild bison, but he was intent on collecting and recording everything possible while on his African expedition. Roosevelt shot and wrote about white rhinos as if they might someday be found only as fossils.

Interestingly, it was the elite European big-game-hunting fraternity that most loudly condemned Roosevelt's scientific collecting. He had personally killed 296 animals, and his son Kermit killed 216 more, but that was not even a tenth of what they might have killed had they been so inclined. Far more animals were killed by the scientists who accompanied them, but those men escaped criticism because they were mostly collecting rats, bats, and shrews, which very few people cared about at the time. Roosevelt cared deeply about all these tiny mammals, too, and he could identify many of them to the species with a quick look at their skulls. As far as Roosevelt was concerned, his work was no different from what the other scientists were doing—his animals just happened to be bigger. Roosevelt's kill rate amounts to about one large animal for each day he spent in Africa, a rate that he felt was scientifically and ethically justified.

Referring to his *African Game Trails* and *Life Histories of African Game Animals*, Roosevelt felt his most significant contributions were in simply "seeing, and recording, and interpreting facts" he felt were obvious but to which observers had been blind or had misinterpreted. By bringing disparate perspectives to the study of the natural world, Roosevelt was able to spot things that others missed. Reflecting back on his African expedition many years later, Roosevelt was proud of his work:

> In Africa, however, we really did some good work in natural history. Many of my observations were set forth in my book *African Game Trails*; and I have always felt that the book which Edmund Heller and I jointly wrote, the *Life Histories of African Game Animals*, was a serious and worthwhile contribution to science. Here again, this contribution, so far as I was concerned, consisted chiefly in seeing, and recording, and interpreting facts which were really obvious, but to which observers hitherto had been blind, or which they had misinterpreted partly because sportsmen seemed incapable of seeing anything except a trophy,

partly because stay-at-home systematists never saw anything at all except skins and skulls which enabled them to give Latin names to new "species" or "subspecies," partly because collectors had collected birds in precisely the spirit in which other collectors assembled postage stamps.

Roosevelt maintained that his style of being a naturalist was best—he got out into nature, made firsthand observations of animals' behavior while actively hunting them, collected his own specimens for scientific study, and did not get bogged down in the detailed work of the armchair naturalists who never left their offices.

But what do we think of this brand of naturalist today? Is there still a place for the hunter-naturalist? And should museums send expeditions to the last unexplored parts of the world? Much as in Roosevelt's time, the answers to these questions can be based on personal sentiments toward collecting animals as much as they can be based on the continuing need for scientific specimens.

Theodore Roosevelt's leadership of the Smithsonian African Expedition was one of the few instances in which museum-specimen collecting was in the spotlight of national attention, but naturalists of Roosevelt's ilk still exist. Our perceptions of naturalists have so changed over the years that this might seem surprising. Today, we are so conditioned not to disturb nature that the mere thought of actually collecting a specimen seems taboo. Part of the shift is valid—natural habitats have certainly diminished since Roosevelt's time—but it is equally true that we have so lost contact with the everyday struggles of the wilderness that we no longer accept death by the human hand as natural. We tend to see ourselves more as interlopers rather than valid members of the animal kingdom. By today's ethics, nature has become something to protect empathetically or observe from a distance and nothing more. Certainly there were those who reacted harshly to Roosevelt's killing of so many animals more than one hundred years ago, and this sentiment has only grown more prominent today.

This change of perception has affected the last remaining museum naturalists still eager to describe the great diversity of species on Earth. Despite all we *do* know, the natural world remains incompletely explored, and even looking at just one group—mammals—we still don't have a complete list of species. At last count there were over five thousand different kinds, but museum scientists are still discovering new ones at a rate of several dozen each year. There is now a new urgency to explore the zoological world, not only because habitats are disappearing at an alarming rate, but also because public sentiment about collecting specimens and conducting this kind of research is changing just as fast. Roosevelt saw the inevitable decline of the museum naturalists even as he ushered in their golden years. Like the white rhino, museum naturalists are now in the throes of what seems an inevitable decline—the era of the intrepid museum naturalist may very well be coming to an end.

As more time goes by, and as our views on what constitutes a true naturalist change, it is important to have some insight into the world of the museum naturalists of Roosevelt's time. To really understand Roosevelt the naturalist, we need to locate him in the naturalists' world that he knew—a world that wholeheartedly embraced guns, hunting, and taxidermy as equally important to the naturalist's craft.

Much of Theodore Roosevelt's greatness is, in fact, rooted in his being so thoroughly shaped by this kind of direct, and often bloody, involvement with nature. He loved the visceral knowledge that came from his wild adventures with animals. Steadfastly focused on both the tragic and the beautiful sides of the cycle of life, Roosevelt the naturalist has taught us to see and experience nature as it really is, whether we like it that way or not—both the giving and the taking of life.

Acknowledgments

Ib Bellew first suggested I write a book about Theodore Roosevelt, and with the encouragement of Patricia Wynne, I agreed. My good friend Bill Schutt introduced me to the agent who made this book a reality—Elaine Markson of the Elaine Markson Agency. Elaine got me off and running, but thanks are also due to Gary Johnson, who managed my contract when Elaine no longer could.

My editor at Crown—Kevin Doughten—together with Claire Potter, expertly guided me through to the completion of this book. More than simply walking me through the edits for just this one book, Kevin's multipage memos on everything he thought was going on with my book were like personalized guides to effective nonfiction writing. If I have any misgiving, it is that, upon publication of this book, those helpful lessons necessarily come to an end. Likewise, Claire filled multiple back-and-forth edits with hundreds of specific insights on how to best word difficult passages while identifying sections where I needed to add more context. Of equal importance, she helped me see the places where too much detail simply needed to be cut. A good wordsmith is a great asset, and Claire is certainly one.

I am grateful for the library and all the staff at the American Museum of Natural History, and in particular Barbara Mathe, Tom Baione, and Gregory Raml. Likewise, at the Smithsonian Institution Archives I thank Tad Bennicoff and Heidi Stover. Leslie Overstreet at the Smithsonian's Cullman Natural History Library shared with me a few choice treasures from the collection that were most welcome. At Harvard's Houghton Library, I thank Heather Cole.

To my many colleagues in the mammal collections at both the American Museum of Natural History and the Smithsonian Institution's National Museum of Natural History, I thank them all for their encouragement. I cannot name everyone, but those who most come to mind include, at the AMNH: John Wahlert, Neil Duncan, Eileen Westwig, Rob Voss, Nancy Simmons, Guy Musser, Patricia Wynne, and, of course, Bill Schutt, who was always eager to listen. At the NMNH: Esther Langan, Nicole Edmison, Stephanie Canington, Megan Krol, Marissa Altmann, Jenna Drake, John Ososky, Charley Potter, Kristofer Helgen, Brian Schmidt, and so many others. In the very last months before I submitted my manuscript, Simon Roosevelt provided a much-needed dose of encouragement, listening intently to all my thoughts and enthusiasms for Theodore Roosevelt, hunting, and museum collecting and expeditions. This book happened to go into the final production stages just as I was scheduled to join a two-month-long museum expedition to—of all places—Mount Kenya, as part of an effort by the Smithsonian Institution to revisit and resample the same places on that mountain that were surveyed by Edgar Mearns and J. Alden Loring more than a century ago. The expedition—which was something entirely independent of my writing—precluded me from having as active a role in the final production stages of this book as I would have liked, and once again I need to thank Claire Potter for seeing it through to production without me, and also Bill Schutt for stepping up and agreeing to address any end-game issues while I was collecting mammal specimens on Mount Kenya—thanks again, Bill; I owe you one.

Finally, and most important of all, I need to thank my family—my wife, Sakiko, and our three children, Sakura, Asahi, and Midori. This book was written over many hundreds of weekends, late nights, and holidays spanning more than ten years, and up until this moment, Midori in particular has never known me *not* to be working on this book, as I started before she was born. For Sakura and Asahi, who saw me delve ever deeper into this project over the years, I hope to make up for the lost time. My absence—both mentally and physically—to my whole family during these times was a real strain, and they must know that I am grateful for their patience. My parents, Stuart and Judith Lunde, provided a place for me to work when I really needed some peace and quiet to write or, more often, welcomed the rest of my family up to visit while I stayed home to write. I have dedicated this book to my wife, Sakiko, but of our three children, I can only ask that they remember how persistence and hard work pays off—a book written and now handsomely standing on my library shelf.

Sources and Notes

Part I: The Museum Naturalist

7 **"The country is the place for children"** Roosevelt, *Theodore Roosevelt: An Autobiography*, 337.

Chapter 1: The Seal on Broadway

9 **This was "Ladies' Mile"** Aaron, *Ladies' Mile*, 650; Burrows and Wallace, *Gotham: A History of New York City to 1898*, 945–46; Homberger, *The Historical Atlas of New York City*, 102–03.

9 **It was the dull mass** Roosevelt, *Theodore Roosevelt: An Autobiography*, 14.

10 **It was probably a harbor seal** This species (*Phoca vitulina*) still inhabits the waters of outlying New York City today.

10 **"the first day"** Roosevelt, *Theodore Roosevelt: An Autobiography*, 14.

10 **From his redbrick mansion** McCullough, *Mornings on Horseback*, 20; Roosevelt, *Theodore Roosevelt: An Autobiography*, 6.

11 **Tall, bearded, and with fierce** My characterization of the senior Theodore Roosevelt is drawn largely from E. Morris, *The Rise of Theodore Roosevelt*, 5; McCullough, *Mornings on Horseback*, 22–23; Robinson, *My Brother, Theodore Roosevelt*, 2–5; and Roosevelt, *Theodore Roosevelt: An Autobiography*, 7–11.

11   **To his own family** Roosevelt, *Theodore Roosevelt: An Autobiography*, 7.

11   **"the best man"** Ibid.

11   **"the only man of whom"** Ibid., 8.

11   **"muscular Christian"** Putney, *Muscular Christianity: Manhood and Sports in Protestant America, 1880–1920*.

11   **In sharp contrast** My characterization of Martha is drawn largely from McCullough, *Mornings on Horseback*, 40–46, 66; Dalton, *Theodore Roosevelt, A Strenuous Life*, 21; and Putnam, *Theodore Roosevelt: The Formative Years, 1858–1886*, 52.

12   **"purest woman he ever saw"** A. E. Roosevelt, *Hunting Big Game in the Eighties: The Letters of Elliott Roosevelt*, 46. Elliott was relaying to his mother the kind words of a fellow rider who admitted to having often admired Mrs. Roosevelt while he "sat in the cars" of the Long Island Railroad.

12   **delicate china doll** McCullough, *Mornings on Horseback*, 45; E. Morris, *The Rise of Theodore Roosevelt*, 21.

12   **No amount of money** Descriptions of Theodore's illnesses are drawn largely from E. Morris, *The Rise of Theodore Roosevelt*, 11; Roosevelt, *Theodore Roosevelt: An Autobiography*, 13.

12   **never entirely certain that he would survive** Dalton, *Theodore Roosevelt: A Strenuous Life*, 35; E. Morris, *The Rise of Theodore Roosevelt*, 11.

12   **doctors mistakenly attributed to a narrow chest** Hagedorn, *The Boys' Life of Theodore Roosevelt*, 21; E. Morris, *The Rise of Theodore Roosevelt*, 4; McCullough, *Mornings on Horseback*, 36.

12   **"gloomy respectability"** Roosevelt, *Theodore Roosevelt: An Autobiography*, 5.

12   **Sitting on his favorite velvet stool** E. Morris, *The Rise of Theodore Roosevelt*, 16.

12   **standing with one leg propped against the wall** E. Morris, *The Rise of Theodore Roosevelt*, 32; Morison, *The Letters of Theodore Roosevelt*, vol. 1, 12.

12   **One of his favorites was** E. Morris, *The Rise of Theodore Roosevelt*, 15.

13   **"I have ridden wildly"** Reid, *The Hunters' Feast; or, Conversations Around the Camp-Fire*, author's preface.

14   **"boy men"** Reid, *The Boy Hunters; or Adventures in Search of a White Buffalo*, 25, of my undated edition (chapter 4).

15   **This method literally stinks** The very best museum bone cleaners develop a certain palate for rotting flesh, and, like a wine connoisseur detecting certain hints of oak and cherry in a vintage, a good osteological preparator can smell when a maceration vat is decaying just right.

16   **"At the commencement"** The original *Record of the Roosevelt Museum* is held in the Theodore Roosevelt collection at Harvard University. I examined a copy held by the library of the American Museum of Natural History.

16   **"In your letter you write to me"** Morison, *The Letters of Theodore Roosevelt*, vol. 1, 3.

16   **"tiger-cat"** Ibid., 4.

16   **"I have one request"** Cutright, *Theodore Roosevelt: The Making of a Conservationist*, 10.

17   **When he acquired a live snapping turtle** E. Morris, *The Rise of Theodore Roosevelt*, 19.

17   **"the higher authorities"** Roosevelt, *Theodore Roosevelt: An Autobiography*, 14.

18   **"loss to science"** E. Morris, *The Rise of Theodore Roosevelt*, 19.

Chapter 2: Collections Make Museums

19   **cabinets of wonders and curiosities** Dennett, *Weird and Wonderful: The Dime Museum in America*, 1.

19   **One of the earliest naturalist enthusiasts** Mauriès, *Cabinets of Curiosities*, 18–19.

20   **One of the most famous** Mauriès, *Cabinets of Curiosities*, 202–03.

20   **After visiting one in Germany** Roosevelt, *Theodore Roosevelt's Diaries of Boyhood and Youth*, 79.

20   **Even Benjamin Franklin** Orosz, *Curators and Culture: The Museum Movement in America, 1740–1870*, 15.

20   **Soft-spoken and warm, Peale** Much of my characterization of Peale comes from Sellers, *Mr. Peale's Museum: Charles Willson Peale and the First Popular Museum of Natural Science and Art*, 1980.

21   **"diffuse a knowledge of the wonderful"** Ibid., 18.

21   **To populate his museum** Ibid., 23–25.

21   **One paper even suggested** Faber, "The Development of Taxidermy and the History of Ornithology," 552.

21   **Jean-Baptiste Bécoeur invented arsenical soap** Ibid., 559.

22   **Even as a child, Roosevelt** N. Miller, *Theodore Roosevelt: A Life*, 48.

22   **Eventually, Peale's sons took over** Dennett, *Weird and Wonderful: The Dime Museum in America*, 14.

23   **Situated in Lower Manhattan** Ibid., 23–38.

23   **After obtaining a taxidermy mount** Kohlstedt, "Entrepreneurs and Intellectuals: Natural History in Early American Museums," 32.

25   **Spencer Fullerton Baird** My characterization of Baird comes from two sources: Dall, *Spencer Fullerton Baird: A Biography; Including Selections from His Correspondence with Audubon, Agassiz, Dana, and Others*; and Rivinus and Youssef, *Spencer Baird of the Smithsonian*.

25   **Hunting means different things** Kellert, "Attitudes and Characteristics of Hunters and Anti-hunters," 412–23.

26   **"I well remember when a lad of eight"** Rivinus and Youssef, *Spencer Baird of the Smithsonian*, 1.

26   **Baird kept his bird collection** The wooden secretary that Baird's grandmother gave him is still housed in the Smithsonian Institution "castle" just outside the office of the Secretary of the Smithsonian. (Author's behind-the-scenes tour of the Smithsonian castle, summer 2015.)

26   **then called *Muscicipa pusilla*** Baird's new species is today classified
        as *Empidonax minimus* and *M. pusilla* is today's widow flycatcher
        (*E. trailli*).

27   **"but a boy"** Deane, "Unpublished Letters of John James Audubon
        and Spencer F. Baird: I," 199.

27   **"This letter is already too long"** Ibid.

27   **"Although you speak of yourself"** Ibid., 200.

27   **"Assisted as we hope and trust to be"** Dall, *Spencer Fullerton
        Baird: A Biography; Including Selections from his Correspondence
        with Audubon, Agassiz, Dana, and Others*, 48.

28   **"very unlike my preconceived idea of him"** Ibid., 55.

29   **"to found at Washington"** Ewing, *The Lost World of James
        Smithson: Science, Revolution, and the Birth of the Smithsonian*, 317.

30   **"My object is to make the Smithsonian Museum"** Herber,
        *Correspondence Between Spencer Fullerton Baird and Louis Agassiz—
        Two Pioneer American Naturalists*, 13.

Chapter 3: The Mind but Not the Body

31   **As the most formal** Roosevelt, *Theodore Roosevelt: An
        Autobiography*, 5–6.

31   **April 8, 1869** *The First Annual Report of the American Museum of
        Natural History*, 1870, 11. Also, Gable, "Theodore Roosevelt and
        the American Museum of Natural History," unpaginated.

31   **Unlike the other men** My characterization of Bickmore
        is drawn from Hellman, *Bankers, Bones and Beetles*, 10–
        11; Preston, *Dinosaurs in the Attic*, 13–18; and Bickmore's
        unpublished autobiography in the Rare Book Room of the library
        of the American Museum of Natural History. See Kennedy,
        "Philanthropy and Science in New York City," and Osborn, *The
        American Museum of Natural History*, for details on the founding
        and early history of the AMNH.

33   **Wealthy men began thinking** Kennedy, "Philanthropy and
        Science in New York City," 1.

35   **a snarling lion** This specimen is the first entry in the first of what
        is now more than thirty ledger books of specimens in the mammal

collection of the AMNH. Although no longer on exhibit (at the time of this writing the specimen was housed in a warehouse in Sunset Park, Brooklyn), a photograph of "AMNH 1" was published on page 14 of *The American Museum Journal*, vol. 14, no. 1 (1914), 3–15.

35   **"the cost of mounting this collection"** Blodgett, "Report on Purchases Made in Europe for the American Museum of Natural History," 22.

35   **Wishing to contribute** *Third and Fourth Annual Reports of the American Museum of Natural History*. The whereabouts of the various bats, mice, and squirrels mentioned in the museum's annual report for 1872 are not known. The specimens are not currently in the museum, and there is no record of them in the Department of Mammalogy catalogues.

35   **Theodore visited regularly** Cutright, *Theodore Roosevelt: The Making of a Conservationist*, 32. Roosevelt later recalled that he had "worked in the museum," and he specifically recalled "skinning some rather reddish white-footed mice." He also remembered "looking over a large number of South American mice in the museum . . . and appealing to Dr. Bickmore to know how I could get at the relationship of the South American with the northern mice of the same family."

35   **"armchair naturalist"** That Roosevelt enjoyed spending time in museums is evidenced by his making a point to visit natural-history museums in other cities around this time of his life. In Philadelphia, he wrote his father: "I think I will stay until Saturday as I am having a splendid time. I go to the Academy of Natural Sciences of Philadelphia every spare moment and am allowed to have the run of all the 38,000 books in the library. They have got quite a number of specimens, also" (quoted in Cutright, *Theodore Roosevelt: The Making of a Conservationist*, 32).

36   **He found that caffeine** McCullough, *Mornings on Horseback*, 94; E. Morris, *The Rise of Theodore Roosevelt*, 25.

36   **Nicotine was also** E. Morris, *The Rise of Theodore Roosevelt*, 25.

36   **In the span of just a few months** Putnam, *Theodore Roosevelt: The Formative Years, 1858–1886*, 71.

36 **"Of course I came here"** Roosevelt, *Letters from Theodore Roosevelt to Anna Roosevelt Cowles, 1870–1918*, 1.

36 **Theodore was always happy** Putnam, *Theodore Roosevelt: The Formative Years, 1858–1886*, 71.

36 **Always the naturalist** Robinson, *My Brother, Theodore Roosevelt*, 52.

36 **"clamoring country people"** Ibid.

36 **just as sickly as ever** Putnam, *Theodore Roosevelt: The Formative Years, 1858–1886*, 73; E. Morris, *The Rise of Theodore Roosevelt*, 32, footnote.

37 **"You have the mind"** Robinson, *My Brother, Theodore Roosevelt*, 50; Putnam, *Theodore Roosevelt: The Formative Years, 1858–1886*, 72; E. Morris, *The Rise of Theodore Roosevelt*, 32.

37 **"You must *make* your body"** Robinson, *My Brother, Theodore Roosevelt*, 50.

37 **Seated on a big settee** Putnam, *Theodore Roosevelt: The Formative Years, 1858–1886*, 72.

38 **The workouts were pure toil** Robinson, *My Brother, Theodore Roosevelt*, 50; E. Morris, *The Rise of Theodore Roosevelt*, 32–33.

38 **The Adirondacks** My overview of the geography and history of the Adirondacks is drawn from a number of sources, the most important of which include Donaldson, *A History of the Adirondacks* (1921); Jenkins and Keal, *The Adirondack Atlas: A Geographic Portrait of the Adirondack Park* (2004); McMartin, *Hides, Hemlocks, and Adirondack History: How the Tanning Industry Influenced the Growth of the Region* (1992); McMartin, *The Great Forest of the Adirondacks* (1994); Schneider, *The Adirondacks: A History of America's First Wilderness* (1998); Terrie, *Wildlife and Wilderness: A History of Adirondack Mammals* (1993); Terrie, *Forever Wild: A Cultural History of Wilderness in the Adirondacks* (1994); Terrie, *Contested Terrain: A New History of Nature and People in the Adirondacks* (1997).

39 **They searched the ruins of Fort George** Roosevelt, *Theodore Roosevelt's Diaries of Boyhood and Youth*, 241.

39   **Dangling their feet** Ibid., 245; E. Morris, *The Rise of Theodore Roosevelt*, 33.

39   **Paul Smith's was the leading** Schneider, *The Adirondacks: A History of America's First Wilderness*, 184.

40   **"went to a sort of half swamp"** Roosevelt, *Theodore Roosevelt's Diaries of Boyhood and Youth*, 245.

41   **One of the Roosevelt guides** Ibid., 248.

41   **an encounter with a mountain lion** Mountain lions (*Puma concolor*) were thought to have been extirpated from the Adirondacks and, indeed, much of the eastern United States, by about 1890. Only a few small populations persisted in Florida, with all the remaining populations occurring west of the Mississippi. For much of the first half of the twentieth century, there were only occasional reports of the species holding out in the Adirondacks; but by about 1980, things began to change, with many more sightings reported (see Jenkins and Keal, *The Adirondack Atlas*, 51). Whether or not these represented resident populations or occasional wanderers from the west was never certain. That mountain lions can roam widely was recently confirmed when DNA samples were used to track the wanderings of a single individual from the Black Hills of South Dakota, through Minnesota and Wisconsin and over to Lake George in the Adirondacks and down to Milford, Connecticut, where the animal was killed by a car (*New York State Conservationist*, vol. 67, no. 2 [2012], 8–11).

41   **When finally it was too dark** Roosevelt, *Theodore Roosevelt's Diaries of Boyhood and Youth*, 250.

Chapter 4: Full-Bore Birder

44   **Ornithology was considered a more masculine** Cooper and Smith, "Gender Patterns in Bird-Related Recreation in the USA and UK," 2010.

45   **Ornithology as a practice** Faber, "The Development of Taxidermy and the History of Ornithology," 550–66; Faber, *Discovering Birds: The Emergence of Ornithology as a Scientific Discipline, 1760–1850*, 1–191.

46   **"It will always give me much pleasure"** Dall, *Spencer Fullerton Baird: A Biography; Including Selections from His Correspondence with Audubon, Agassiz, Dana, and Others,* 307.

46   **Taxidermy shops** Cutright, *Theodore Roosevelt, the Naturalist,* 7; Cutright, *Theodore Roosevelt: The Making of a Conservationist,* 31–32.

46   **"As I entered the room"** Shufeldt, "Scientific Taxidermy for Museums," 377.

48   **"clumsy and often absent-minded"** Roosevelt, *Theodore Roosevelt: An Autobiography,* 18.

48   **"open it with a brick"** Ibid.

49   **"ran against or stumbled over"** Ibid., 17.

49   **Roosevelt had no idea how beautiful** Roosevelt, *Theodore Roosevelt: An Autobiography,* 18; Putnam, *Theodore Roosevelt: The Formative Years, 1858–1886,* 80.

49   **Theodore was crushed** E. Morris, *The Rise of Theodore Roosevelt,* 21; Putnam, *Theodore Roosevelt: The Formative Years, 1858–1886,* 80.

50   **"another terrible trip"** Putnam, *Theodore Roosevelt: The Formative Years, 1858–1886,* 80.

50   **"Roosevelt Museum"** Hagedorn, *The Boys' Life of Theodore Roosevelt,* 43. Standard museum practice is to treat the original label (known as the "field tag") as part of the specimen. Although Roosevelt's childhood specimens were later donated to other museums (notably the National Museum of Natural History and the American Museum of Natural History), most still bear Roosevelt's original "Roosevelt Museum" labels, the red ink now faded and appearing more pink.

Chapter 5: Egypt, Land of My Dreams

51   **The air must have been heavy** My characterization of what Roosevelt might have experienced on boarding the *Russia* is drawn from "The Ocean Steamer," *Harper's New Monthly Magazine,* vol. 41, no. 242 (August 1870), 185–198.

51   **After watching the low hills** Roosevelt, *Theodore Roosevelt's Diaries of Boyhood and Youth*, 263.

52   **He observed kittiwakes** Ibid.

52   **When a snow bunting alighted** Ibid.

52   **Roaming the streets of the English city** Ibid., 264.

52   **"Paris, November 14th 1872. Thursday"** Ibid., 270–71.

53   **"I suppose that all growing boys"** Roosevelt, *Theodore Roosevelt: An Autobiography*, 20. Roosevelt's grubbiness nearly led to his poisoning on one occasion when a well-meaning maid extracted from his taxidermy kit an old toothbrush used for applying arsenic to his bird skins—she left it with the rest of his wash kit for his personal use. Ibid., 20.

54   **"How I gazed on it!"** Roosevelt, *Theodore Roosevelt's Diaries of Boyhood and Youth*, 276.

54   **"The green water was alive"** Putnam, *Theodore Roosevelt: The Formative Years, 1858–1886*, 85.

54   **"When I undress tonight"** Ibid.

54   **"Numerous birds of various species"** Roosevelt, *Theodore Roosevelt's Diaries of Boyhood and Youth*, 280.

55   **Theodore seized the bird** Ibid., 278–79.

55   **He had become so fixated on collecting birds** Robinson, *My Brother, Theodore Roosevelt*, 56.

55   **Even his younger brother** Hagedorn, *The Boys' Life of Theodore Roosevelt*, 45.

55   **Surveying the vast Sahara** Putnam, *Theodore Roosevelt: The Formative Years, 1858–1886*, 86–87.

56   **"the nicest, cosiest"** Ibid., 87.

56   **"blew a chat to pieces"** Roosevelt, *Theodore Roosevelt's Diaries of Boyhood and Youth*, 290. Roosevelt was most certainly admitting an early failure. A good bird collector strives to kill a bird while inflicting the least amount of damage possible.

56   **"proportionately delighted"** Ibid.

57   **"ruthlessly lope"** Robinson, *My Brother, Theodore Roosevelt*, 57.

57   **Few dared ride** Ibid.

57   **The procedure used to prepare a bird study skin** See the following link to the Beaty Museum website, which includes a number of links highlighting procedures used to prepare bird study skins: http://beatymuseum.ubc.ca/research/birds.

58   **"between one and two hundred"** Putnam, *Theodore Roosevelt: The Formative Years, 1858–1886*, 92.

59   *"Bill long, without bristles"* Cutright, *Theodore Roosevelt: The Making of a Conservationist*, 62.

60   **bony wrists and ankles** Roosevelt, *Theodore Roosevelt: An Autobiography*, 20.

60   **"à la mop"** McCullough, *Mornings on Horseback*, 121.

60   **best to stand upwind of him** E. Morris, *The Rise of Theodore Roosevelt*, 36.

60   **"sharp, ungreased squeak"** Ibid.

60   **The family of six** McCullough, *Mornings on Horseback*, 127.

60   **Their new home** E. Morris, *The Rise of Theodore Roosevelt*, 48.

61   **"trustees meeting"** Ibid.

61   **"Record of the Roosevelt Museum"** Cutright, *Theodore Roosevelt: The Making of a Conservationist*, 71.

61   **Nevertheless, Theodore was undeterred** Putnam, *Theodore Roosevelt: The Formative Years, 1858–1886*, 126; Cutright, *Theodore Roosevelt: The Making of a Conservationist*, 73.

61   **unusually strong in history** E. Morris, *The Rise of Theodore Roosevelt*, 47.

62   **christened their new summer home** Putnam, *Theodore Roosevelt: The Formative Years, 1858–1886*, 117.

62   **"pursuing this plan"** Giraud, *The Birds of Long Island*, iv.

62   **"interesting facts would be acquired"** Ibid.

63   **"now and then one is seen."** Cutright, *Theodore Roosevelt: The Making of a Conservationist*, 78.

63   **"guttural joch joch"** Ibid., 81.

63   **"rather jingling trill"** Ibid., 82.

63   **"rollicking, bubbling notes"** Ibid.

63   **"sweet and plaintive song"** Ibid.

63   **"exasperatingly monotonous notes"** Ibid.

63   **"such horrible noises"** Ibid.

63   **"exasperating 'pay, pay'"** Ibid.

63   **"a very bright, short song"** Ibid.

63   **"*tseet-see-tseetsee*"** Ibid.

63   **"somewhat like *tchea, tchea, tchea, tchea, tchea*"** Ibid.

64   **"Its song is loud and cheerful"** Ibid.

64   **"Its delightful song"** Cutright, *Theodore Roosevelt: The Making of a Conservationist*, 82–83.

64   **Theodore Roosevelt was a self-made ornithologist** When asked how he came to love nature so much, Roosevelt replied that he could "no more explain why I like 'natural history' than why I like California canned peaches; nor why I do not care for that enormous brand of natural history which deals with invertebrates any more than why I do not care for brandied peaches" (Roosevelt, "My Life as a Naturalist," 321; also Cutright, *Theodore Roosevelt, the Naturalist,* 9).

Chapter 6: Alone at Harvard

65   **a single but sunny room** Cutright, *Theodore Roosevelt: The Making of a Conservationist*; 97; E. Morris, *The Rise of Theodore Roosevelt*, 60.

65   **It was furnished** Morison, *The Letters of Theodore Roosevelt*, 16; Cutright, *Theodore Roosevelt: The Making of a Conservationist*, 97; E. Morris, *The Rise of Theodore Roosevelt*, 60.

65   **A fire was burning** Morison, *The Letters of Theodore Roosevelt*, vol. 1, 16; Putnam, *Theodore Roosevelt: The Formative Years*, 128.

65   **Eventually, the walls** Cutright, *Theodore Roosevelt, the Naturalist*, 10.

65   **"Take care of your morals first"** Morison, *The Letters of Theodore Roosevelt*, vol. 1, 33; Putnam, *Theodore Roosevelt: The Formative Years, 1858–1886*, 141.

66   **Aside from the unspoken culture** Putnam, *Theodore Roosevelt: The Formative Years, 1858–1886*, 130–31; McCullough, *Mornings on Horseback*, 202.

66   **There was a lazy saunter** Putnam, *Theodore Roosevelt: The Formative Years, 1858–1886*, 131; E. Morris, *The Rise of Theodore Roosevelt*, 57.

66   **he actually *ran* to his lectures** E. Morris, *The Rise of Theodore Roosevelt*, 58.

66   **In his high-pitched** McCullough, *Mornings on Horseback*, 207–08; Cutright, *Theodore Roosevelt: The Making of a Conservationist*, 105.

66   **Henry Davis Minot** Cutright, *Theodore Roosevelt, the Naturalist*, 13; Cutright, *Theodore Roosevelt: The Making of a Conservationist*, 98; Putnam, *Theodore Roosevelt: The Formative Years, 1858–1886*, 134; Dalton, *Theodore Roosevelt: A Strenuous Life*, 64; McCullough, *Mornings on Horseback*, 215.

66   **In an attempt to adopt an air of sophistication** Morris, *The Rise of Theodore Roosevelt*, 88; McCullough, *Mornings on Horseback*, 203.

67   **"By the way"** Morison, *The Letters of Theodore Roosevelt*, vol. 1, 26; Cutright, *Theodore Roosevelt, the Naturalist*, 15.

67   **Roosevelt was planning a collecting trip** Cutright, *Theodore Roosevelt, the Naturalist*, 15; Cutright, *Theodore Roosevelt: The Making of a Conservationist*, 100; Putnam, *Theodore Roosevelt: The Formative Years, 1858–1886*, 144.

67   **His buddy Hal** Minot, *The Land and Game Birds of New England*, 1877.

68   ***"Anorthura troglodytes"*** Cutright, *Theodore Roosevelt: The Making of a Conservationist*, 91.

68   **"Perhaps the sweetest music"** Cutright, *Theodore Roosevelt, the Naturalist*, 16–17; Cutright, *Theodore Roosevelt: The Making of a Conservationist*, 101.

69   **"By far the best of these"** Cutright, *Theodore Roosevelt, the Naturalist*, 18.

70   **"Along with my college preparatory studies"** Roosevelt, *Theodore Roosevelt: An Autobiography*, 21.

70   **"scientific man"** Cutright, *Theodore Roosevelt, the Naturalist*, 2; Roosevelt, *Theodore Roosevelt: An Autobiography*, 18, 23, 24.

71   **"sparrow wars"** Cutright, *Theodore Roosevelt, the Naturalist*, 22–25.

71   **English sparrow's extermination** Many years later, while he was president of the United States, Roosevelt's attitude toward the English sparrow remained just as strong. From the White House he wrote Clinton Hart Merriam to ask, "Is there any kind of air gun which you would recommend which I could use for killing English sparrows around my Long Island place? I would like to do as little damage as possible to our other birds, and so I suppose the less noise I make the better." See Morison, *The Letters of Theodore Roosevelt*, vol. 6, 971.

71   **"a good rowing up"** Morison, *The Letters of Theodore Roosevelt*, vol. 1, 31.

72   **"My own sweet sister"** Putnam, *Theodore Roosevelt: The Formative Years, 1858–1886*, 150.

73   **"Old Hal Minot has left college"** Kohn, *A Most Glorious Ride: The Diaries of Theodore Roosevelt, 1877–1886*, 29.

73   **"really intensively desired to do scientific work"** Roosevelt, *Theodore Roosevelt: An Autobiography*, 24.

73   **"grinding like a Trojan"** Kohn, *A Most Glorious Ride: The Diaries of Theodore Roosevelt, 1877–1886*, 31.

73   **"Every nook and corner"** Ibid., 34.

73   **Theodore got the idea** Putnam, *Theodore Roosevelt: The Formative Years, 1858–1886*, 153.

74   **"Guffle-ing"** Hagedorn, *The Boys' Life of Theodore Roosevelt*, 59.

75   **"loved her as soon as he saw"** Donald, *Lion in the White House: A Life of Theodore Roosevelt*, 47.

75   **Seeking a picture** Brands, *T.R.: The Last Romantic*, 95.

77   **"endure fatigue and hardship"** N. Miller, *Theodore Roosevelt: A Life*, 94.

77   **"beautiful condition"** Vietze, *Becoming Teddy Roosevelt: How a Maine Guide Inspired America's 26th President*, 26.

77   **"as tough as a pine knot"** N. Miller, *Theodore Roosevelt: A Life*, 94.

77   **Theodore Roosevelt graduated magna cum laude** See Wilhelm, *Theodore Roosevelt as an Undergraduate*, 23–24. Citing the same source, Edmund Morris, *The Rise of Theodore Roosevelt*, 108, puts the total class at 177, but this appears to be one of Morris's few errors of fact—one that has been carried on through a number of subsequent works.

77   **Harvard had been good for him** Roosevelt, *Theodore Roosevelt: An Autobiography*, 24.

78   **"With Alice to love me"** Private diaries, June 29, 1880, as transcribed by Putnam, *Theodore Roosevelt: The Formative Years, 1858–1886*, 196.

78   **"perfectly blue"** N. Miller, *Theodore Roosevelt: A Life*, 94.

78   **"I write to you to announce"** Morison, *The Letters of Theodore Roosevelt*, vol. 1, 43.

78   **"utterly ignored the possibilities"** Roosevelt, *Theodore Roosevelt: An Autobiography*, 24.

78   **"There was a total failure"** Ibid., 25.

Part II: All Hunters Should Be Nature Lovers

81   **"It is to be hoped that"** Roosevelt, *Outdoor Pastimes of an American Hunter*, 339–40.

Chapter 7: Roosevelt Rebels

83   **But, seeing a physician** Hagedorn, *The Boys' Life of Theodore Roosevelt*, 63.

83   **"Doctor, I am going"** Ibid., 64.

84   **"wanted to very much"** A. E. Roosevelt, *Hunting Big Game in the Eighties: The Letters of Elliott Roosevelt, Sportsman*, 26.

84   **Theodore envied his brother's adventurous life** Ibid., 12.

84   **Theodore and Elliott organized everything** Putnam, *Theodore Roosevelt: The Formative Years, 1858–1886,* 202.

85   **Now, seeing the region for the first time** Ibid., 87. "To look out on the desert gives one somewhat the same feeling as to look over the ocean or over one of the North American prairies."

86   **"a huge bull, encircled"** Allen, "History of the American Bison, *Bison Americanus,*" 471.

87   **Like a naturalist recording** Putnam, *Theodore Roosevelt: The Formative Years, 1858–1886,* 203.

88   **"all the parties were fitted"** Baird, *Reports of Explorations and Surveys, to Ascertain the Most Practicable and Economical Route for a Railroad from the Mississippi River to the Pacific Ocean,* xiii.

89   **a must-have reference that young Theodore owned** Roosevelt referred to Baird's book in a letter he wrote to Elliott Coues dated April 21, 1882. Roosevelt referred to the work, which was officially published in 1857, by the print date of 1858, but that it was Baird's volume 8 is clear from the content of the letter. The letter is deposited in the Joseph F. Cullman III Library of Natural History at the Smithsonian's National Museum of Natural History.

89   **"cropped heads"** Morison, *The Letters of Theodore Roosevelt,* vol. 1, 46.

89   **"The trip was great fun"** Brands, *T.R.: The Last Romantic,* 108.

90   *Win* **was the word** E. Morris, *The Rise of Theodore Roosevelt,* 102.

90   **The summer house** It would be late 1882 before Theodore and Alice finally bought their own home at 55 West 45th Street; Brinkley, *The Wilderness Warrior,* 147.

91   **Most of the specimens** Cutright, "Theodore Roosevelt Disposes of His Boyhood Bird Specimens," 1–8.

92   **still restless and impatient** Putnam, *Theodore Roosevelt: The Formative Years, 1858–1886,* 219.

92   **"a caged lynx"** E. Morris, *The Rise of Theodore Roosevelt,* 812.

92   **socially unjust and even repellant** Roosevelt, *Theodore Roosevelt: An Autobiography,* 54.

92   **Law was a fine occupation, but** Ibid., 54–55.

92   **Barnlike in construction** Ibid., 56.

92   **"had to break into the organization with a jimmy"** Ibid.

93   **Hedging his bets** Brands, *T.R.: The Last Romantic*, 143.

93   **"dreadful misfortune"** Roosevelt, *Theodore Roosevelt: An Autobiography*, 55.

93   **While Theodore grappled** A. E. Roosevelt, *Hunting Big Game in the Eighties: The Letters of Elliott Roosevelt*, 69.

94   **As it became fashionable** Reiger, *American Sportsmen and the Origins of Conservation*, 45–46.

94   **An opportunity for Roosevelt to profit** E. Morris, *The Rise of Theodore Roosevelt*, 182.

95   **Perhaps Theodore would like to be one of the first** Ibid., 183.

96   **"while there were still buffalo"** DiSilvestro, *Theodore Roosevelt in the Badlands: A Young Politician's Quest for Recovery in the American West*, 28.

Chapter 8: Hell with the Fires Out

97   **American buffalo** Roosevelt often used "buffalo" for the species whose scientific name is *Bison bison*. "Buffalo" is the common name more appropriately used for either the Asian water buffalo (*Bubalis bubalis*) or the African buffalo (*Syncerus caffer*). "Bison" makes the distinction clear.

98   **"fond of politics"** Putnam, *Theodore Roosevelt: The Formative Years, 1858–1886*, 309.

99   **There was no platform** Hagedorn, *Roosevelt in the Bad Lands*, 3.

99   **dragging his baggage** Ibid., 4.

99   **"the bull pen"** Ibid.

100   **one with funny glasses** Ibid., 13

100   **ride in the back of the wagon** Ibid., 16.

100   **A stocky man with bespectacled blue eyes** Ibid., 19.

101   **Roosevelt spent this first night talking** Lang, *Ranching with Roosevelt*, 107.

101   **Everyone was tired from the long ride** Hagedorn, *Roosevelt in the Bad Lands*, 23; Lang, *Ranching with Roosevelt*, 112.

101   **"plumb good sort"** Hagedorn, *Roosevelt in the Bad Lands*, 28.

101   **Clumsy Roosevelt blundered into a cactus** Ibid., 31.

102   **"Don't mind me"** Ibid., 33.

103   **"If I didn't trust you men"** Ibid., 42–43. But see also note 135 in DiSilvestro, *Theodore Roosevelt in the Badlands*, 281.

103   **"The wind was just right"** DiSilvestro, *Theodore Roosevelt in the Badlands*, 56.

103   **"I never saw anyone so enthused"** Hagedorn, *Roosevelt in the Bad Lands*, 45.

104   **"the most extraordinary man"** Ibid., 46.

104   **"the American people's own official museum"** Bechtel, *Mr. Hornaday's War: How a Peculiar Victorian Zookeeper Waged a Lonely Crusade for Wildlife That Changed the World*, 4.

105   **"There are no buffalo anymore"** Ibid., 25.

105   **"ghastly monuments of slaughter"** Ibid., 28.

105   *Hurrah!* N. Miller, *Theodore Roosevelt: A Life*, 151. Roosevelt had taken the raw salted hide and cape to a local taxidermist (Barsness, *Heads, Hides and Horns: The Complete Buffalo Book*, 131–32).

105   **Three days later** N. Miller, *Theodore Roosevelt: A Life*, 576.

105   **"very cautiously"** Ibid., 152.

105   *The Beef Bonanza* Putnam, *Theodore Roosevelt: The Formative Years, 1858–1886*, 334.

106   **"But, my own darling"** N. Miller, *Theodore Roosevelt: A Life*, 152.

107   **Roosevelt learned of the birth** Morison, *The Letters of Theodore Roosevelt*, vol. 1, 65.

107   **Democrats and Republicans alike** Ibid., 228.

107   **A great fog** Ibid., 229.

108   **"There is a curse on this house"** Ibid., 230.

108   **"The light has gone out of my life"** Ibid.

108 **a man who refused to talk** N. Miller, *Theodore Roosevelt: A Life*, 157.

108 **But, as at least one biographer** Brands, *T.R.: The Last Romantic*, 163–65.

109 **"For joy or for sorrow"** Ibid., 172.

Chapter 9: Change in the West

110 **Born in Brooklyn** Reiger, *The Passing of the Great West: Selected Papers of George Bird Grinnell*, 6.

111 **"I had been brought up"** Ibid., 29.

112 **"a beautiful, white-haired old lady"** Ibid., 22.

112 **"perpetually in trouble"** Punke, *Last Stand: George Bird Grinnell, the Battle to Save the Buffalo, and the Birth of the New West*, 8.

114 **"was really wild and woolly"** Ibid., 1.

114 **one with an arrow sticking** Jaffe, *The Gilded Dinosaur: The Fossil War Between E.D. Cope and O.C. Marsh and the Rise of American Science*, 28.

116 **"two or three hours in the evening"** Reiger, *The Passing of the Great West: Selected Papers of George Bird Grinnell*, 58.

117 **"100 deer or more"** Ibid., 91.

117 **a kind of outdoor museum** Ibid., 109.

118 **"Their days are numbered"** Ibid., 61.

119 **"Arrived at my cattle ranch"** Brands, *T.R.: The Last Romantic*, 172.

119 **"He does not know what he does or says"** E. Morris, *The Rise of Theodore Roosevelt*, 231.

119 **"hell with the fires out"** Attributed to Brigadier General Alfred Sully. See Brooks and Mattison, *Theodore Roosevelt and the Dakota Badlands*, 4–5.

119 **Thousands of financial institutions collapsed** Smalley, *History of the Northern Pacific Railroad*, 199.

119 **He had only lost 25** Putnam, *Theodore Roosevelt: The Formative Years, 1858–1886*, 452.

120   **a buckskin suit** Lang, *Ranching with Roosevelt*, 151.

120   **"lopes and pauses"** Ibid., 153.

121   **"basted the life out of"** Ibid., 154.

121   **Arriving at Old Lady Maddox's** Ibid., 157.

121   **the fringed-buckskin hunting garb** Putnam, *Theodore Roosevelt: The Formative Years, 1858–1886*, 453–54; Lang, *Ranching with Roosevelt*, 151–60; Hagedorn, *Roosevelt in the Bad Lands*, 95–97.

121   **"the most picturesque"** DiSilvestro, *Theodore Roosevelt in the Badlands*, 92.

122   **"I got him!"** Ibid., 93.

122   **"inexpressibly touching"** E. Morris, *The Rise of Theodore Roosevelt*, 261.

122   **"sweet, sad songs"** Ibid., 263.

123   **"One day I would canter"** Brands, *T.R.: The Last Romantic*, 173.

123   **"Nowhere, not even at sea"** E. Morris, *The Rise of Theodore Roosevelt*, 263.

123   **"She was beautiful in face and form"** N. Miller, *Theodore Roosevelt: A Life*, 158.

Chapter 10: Winchester Naturalist

125   **At his Chimney Butte Ranch** Roosevelt, *Letters from Theodore Roosevelt to Anna Roosevelt Cowles*, 62; Morison, *The Letters of Theodore Roosevelt*, vol. 1, 123. Chimney Butte Ranch was also called the Maltese Cross Ranch. The former name refers to the location; the latter is in reference to the shape of his cattle brand.

125   **to any cowboy passing by** Lang, *Ranching with Roosevelt*, 80; Hagedorn, *Roosevelt in the Bad Lands*, 148. Roosevelt's Maltese Cross Ranch was situated right in front of the main thoroughfare south. Loquacious cowpunchers were constantly stopping in to talk.

125   **antlers interlocked** Hagedorn, *Roosevelt in the Bad Lands*, 149.

125   **"Theirs had been a duel"** DiSilvestro, *Theodore Roosevelt in the Badlands*, 112.

125　**That the eponymous elk** Roosevelt would later shoot a pair of vagrant elk wandering into the area. See "Still-Hunting Elk" in Roosevelt's *Hunting Trips of a Ranchman*, in the Modern Library edition: "I killed an elk near my ranch; probably the last of his race that will ever be found in our neighborhood" (p. 286).

126　**The Bighorns** My descriptions of Roosevelt's hunt in the Bighorns are drawn largely from Putnam, *Theodore Roosevelt: The Formative Years, 1858–1886*, 472–89, and Roosevelt's own retelling of these hunts in *Hunting Trips of a Ranchman*.

126　**"No one who has not tried"** Roosevelt, *Hunting Trips of a Ranchman*, 269.

127　**"plenty of handkerchiefs"** Kohn, *A Most Glorious Ride: The Diaries of Theodore Roosevelt, 1877–1886*, 230.

127　**Swift-flowing brooks** Roosevelt, *Hunting Trips of a Ranchman*, 269.

127　**"inner life"** Ibid., 282.

127　**"Each animal"** Ibid., 282–83.

127　**"The true still-hunter"** Ibid., 283.

128　**"I saw Merrifield"** Morison, *The Letters of Theodore Roosevelt*, vol. 1, 82.

130　**From there he worked so furiously** Ibid., 89.

130　**Lavishly bound** E. Morris, *The Rise of Theodore Roosevelt*, 291.

130　**"Mr. Roosevelt is not well-known"** Reiger, *American Sportsmen and the Origins of Conservation*, 147.

130　**"Where Mr. Roosevelt details"** Ibid.

131　**As Grinnell later recalled** Hagedorn, *The Works of Theodore Roosevelt*, vol. 1, xiii–xviii.

133　**"not been nice"** S. J. Morris, *Edith Kermit Roosevelt: Portrait of a First Lady*, 59.

133　**"I have always considered"** Brands, *T.R.: The Last Romantic*, 195.

134　**Edith and Theodore settled** My description of Theodore and Edith's settling into Sagamore in May 1887 is drawn from S. J.

Morris, *Edith Kermit Roosevelt: Portrait of a First Lady*, 109; Dalton, *Theodore Roosevelt: A Strenuous Life*, 116; Hagedon, *The Roosevelt Family of Sagamore Hill*, 15.

135   **"gun room"** Roosevelt, *Letters from Theodore Roosevelt to Anna Roosevelt Cowles, 1870–1918*, 93; S. J. Morris, *Edith Kermit Roosevelt: Portrait of a First Lady*, 110.

135   **"drearily on by fits and starts"** Dalton, *Theodore Roosevelt: A Strenuous Life*, 116.

135   **"vigorously"** Ibid.

Chapter 11: Real Men and Mousers

138   **"We regretted"** Hagedorn, *The Works of Theodore Roosevelt*, vol. 1., xviii.

139   **Gathering a small number** Grinnell, *Hunting at High Altitudes*, 500.

139   **"archetype of the American hunter"** Jeffers, *Roosevelt the Explorer*, 62.

139   **"perhaps the best shot"** Ibid.

139   **"the hardier and manlier"** Roosevelt, "The Boone and Crockett Club," 267.

139   **"a head or two of game"** Grinnell, *Hunting at High Altitudes*, 437.

140   **Someone even chopped out** Ibid., 447.

140   **"This occurrence"** Grinnell, "A Premium on Crime."

141   **"Congress has put a premium"** Grinnell, "Save the Park Buffalo."

141   **John F. Lacey** Senator Lacey from Iowa is remembered more for the Lacey Act of 1900, which outlawed interstate commerce in wildlife and established authority for enforcement, effectively ending an era of indiscriminate commercial market-hunting. The Lacey Act is still a cornerstone of U.S. wildlife law.

141   **"At least Congress"** Grinnell, "A Step Forward."

141   **"The bill for the protection"** Grinnell, "Protection for the Park."

142   **"I wanted to make it"** DiSilvestro, *Theodore Roosevelt in the Badlands*, 249.

142   **Pitifully little** Osgood, *Biographical Memoir of Clinton Hart Merriam, 1855–1942*, 9.

143   **As Merriam proudly noted** Merriam, *Report on the Mammals and Birds of the Expedition*, 661.

144   **"I was fortunate"** Ibid., 667.

145   **"It is in no sense"** Merriam, *The Mammals of the Adirondack Region: Northeastern New York*, vol. 1, preface.

145   **the Cyclone trap** A. L. Gardner, back matter in *Journal of Mammalogy*, vol. 78, no. 1 (February 1997).

146   **"I do not believe"** Kohler, *All Creatures: Naturalists, Collectors, and Biodiversity, 1850–1950*, 188.

147   **U.S. Biological Survey** Originally called the Office of Economic Ornithology in the Division of Entomology of the U.S. Department of Agriculture, the office was soon renamed the Division of Economic Ornithology and Mammalogy. In time Merriam started calling his office the "Biological Survey"—a moniker that President Theodore Roosevelt later made official. The office survives today as the Biological Survey Unit of the United States Geological Survey and is still closely tied to the National Museum of Natural History at the Smithsonian Institution.

148   **"cold frying-pan bread"** Roosevelt, *"Hunting Trips of a Ranchman: Sketches of Sport on the Northern Cattle Plains"* and *"The Wilderness Hunter: An Account of the Big Game of the United States and Its Chase with Horse, Hound, and Rifle,"* 458.

148   **"suddenly a small animal"** Ibid.

148   **"That was the end of the shrew"** Ibid., 459. Brinkley, *The Wilderness Warrior*, 210, gives a rather different account, describing Roosevelt as first inspecting the shrew alive and then sending it to Baird in Washington, D.C., "where it became part of the Smithsonian's natural history collection." This runs counter to Roosevelt's own description of the event, and no shrew from that time and place can be found in the mammal collections at the Smithsonian's National Museum of Natural History.

148 **"In proportion to its size"** Cutright, *Theodore Roosevelt, the Naturalist*, 36.

149 **"The little snake"** Ibid.

150 **"I know these scientists"** Morison, *The Letters of Theodore Roosevelt*, vol. 1, 663.

151 **According to** Merriam, "Preliminary Synopsis of American Bears," 65–83.

151 **None of Merriam's** See ibid., and Merriam, "Review of the Grizzly and Big Brown Bears of North America (Genus *Ursus*) with Description of a New Genus, *Vetularctos*." All of the species names he proposes in these are currently classified as synonyms under *Ursus arctos*, the brown bear. See Wozencraft, "Order Carnivora."

151 **Shortly after presenting his astonishing** Merriam, "Suggestions for a New Method of Discriminating Between Species and Subspecies."

152 **"It is not the business of the naturalist"** Merriam, "Review of the Grizzly and Big Brown Bears of North America (Genus *Ursus*) with Description of a New Genus, *Vetularctos*," 9.

153 **"I believe that with fuller"** Morison, *The Letters of Theodore Roosevelt*, vol. 1, 612. Morison used French quotation marks to indicate editorial interpretations of illegible words. In this instance—Roosevelt's letter to Osborn dated May 18, 1897—Morison interpreted the word "lumpers" to be "Campers." That "lumpers" is correct is not only clear from the context of the letter ("lumpers" being taxonomist jargon), but is also shown in Roosevelt's subsequent exact use of the same wording from his letter to Osborn in a published Letter to the Editor of *Science*. See vol. 5, no. 127 (1897), 879–80.

Chapter 12: A Tiffany Knife to the Heart

156 **These were more than just hunting narratives** Reiger, *American Sportsmen and the Origins of Conservation*, 180.

156 **As one historian has pointed out** Ibid., 181–82.

156   **"most orthodox"** R. L. Wilson, *Theodore Roosevelt: Hunter-Conservationist*, 119.

157   **"rather be anything"** Morison, *The Letters of Theodore Roosevelt.* vol. 2, 1157.

159   **"This kind of hunting"** Roosevelt, *Outdoor Pastimes of an American Hunter*, 33.

160   **"She was a powerful female"** Ibid., 40–41.

160   **"I almost broke the heart"** Morison, *The Letters of Theodore Roosevelt*, vol. 1, 674–75.

160   **Roosevelt understood** If only he could shoot enough specimens, Roosevelt was sure he could prove Merriam wrong: Roosevelt killed fourteen cougar on his Colorado hunt, and in his narrative account he provides a table summarizing the wide range of size and color data for what was essentially one interbreeding population of the species collected over the span of one month from mid-January 1901. Most of the specimens were females of either a "blue" or a "red" hue, and these ranged in size from just under five feet in length to seven feet long. Males were of either the red or the blue type and ranged between 7.5 and 8 feet long. See Roosevelt, *Outdoor Pastimes of an American Hunter*, 30–31.

161   **"Astonishingly little"** Ibid., 16.

161   **"No beast has been the subject"** Ibid., 16–17.

161   **It was mid-September** My description of the events leading up to Roosevelt's rise to the presidency are distilled from the prologue of E. Morris's *Theodore Rex*.

162   **His ascension coincided with America's** See Morison, *The Letters of Theodore Roosevelt*, vol. 3, xv.

162   **"unhappily prominent"** Ibid.

163   **"Very few people are aware"** Cutright, *Theodore Roosevelt, the Naturalist*, 92.

163   **"One evening at my house"** Ibid.

164   **"I wonder how I ever got on"** Bishop, *Theodore Roosevelt and His Time*, vol. 2, 113.

164   **"Not only shall I enjoy the book"** Cutright, *Theodore Roosevelt: The Making of a Conservationist,* 240.

164   **"You have the most extraordinary power"** Ibid., 241.

164   **"not only because it was entirely"** Selous, *African Nature Notes and Reminiscences,* dedication page.

165   **"Oh, Heavens!"** Cutright, *Theodore Roosevelt: The Making of a Conservationist,* 242.

166   **Early in his first term** Descriptions of and quotes from Roosevelt's Mississippi black-bear hunt are drawn from E. Morris, *Theodore Rex,* 172–74; and Brinkley, *The Wilderness Warrior: Theodore Roosevelt and the Crusade for America,* 434–40.

Chapter 13: Who's a Nature Faker?

168   **In the spring of 1903** My description of Roosevelt's western tour with John Burroughs is drawn largely from Cutright, *Theodore Roosevelt, the Naturalist,* 104–17; Burroughs, *Camping and Tramping with Roosevelt*; and Barrus, *The Life and Letters of John Burroughs,* vol. 2, 59–74.

169   **"Some of our newspapers"** Burroughs, *Camping and Tramping with Roosevelt,* 6.

170   **"He craved once more"** Ibid., 29.

170   **He leapt from the sled** Ibid., 66.

170   **Even from the presidential residence** This section is drawn largely from Cutright, *Theodore Roosevelt, the Naturalist,* 148–50; also, Roosevelt, *Outdoor Pastimes of an American Hunter,* 360.

170   **red-headed woodpecker** Roosevelt, *Outdoor Pastimes of an American Hunter,* 318. Roosevelt lamented that this species was less common compared to forty years earlier, when Burroughs described them as being one of the most abundant of all the birds in the region.

170   **"creaking gurgling"** See Cutright, *Theodore Roosevelt, the Naturalist,* 149.

170   **"little bits of fellow"** Roosevelt, *Outdoor Pastimes of an American Hunter,* 320.

171   **"Gentlemen, do you know what has happened"** Brinkley, *The Wilderness Warrior: Theodore Roosevelt and the Crusade for America*, 1.

171   **"The birds have come back"** Roosevelt, *Letters to Kermit from Theodore Roosevelt, 1902–1908*, 96–97. The cardinal outside his window is also mentioned in Roosevelt, *Outdoor Pastimes of an American Hunter*, 319.

171   **Even with the best binoculars** Cutright, *Theodore Roosevelt, the Naturalist*, 150.

171   **There were myrtle warblers** Roosevelt, *Outdoor Pastimes of an American Hunter*, 360.

171   **Roosevelt grew frustrated** Cutright, *Theodore Roosevelt, the Naturalist*, 150.

171   **"Very early for a fox-sparrow"** Robinson, *My Brother, Theodore Roosevelt*, 232.

171   **He specifically targeted the plume hunters** This section is drawn largely from Cutright, *Theodore Roosevelt: The Making of a Conservationist*, 222–24.

172   **Roosevelt declared Pelican Island** Ibid., 223; Chapman, *Autobiography of a Bird-Lover*, 182.

173   **"on an animal with a head"** Cutright, *Theodore Roosevelt, the Naturalist*, 94.

173   **"both the head and the tail"** Ibid.

173   **"whole lot of goody-goody books"** Lutts, *The Nature Fakers: Wildlife, Science, and Sentiment*, 36.

174   **"I have never read such nonsense"** Cutright, *Theodore Roosevelt, the Naturalist*, 131.

174   **"I don't believe for a minute"** Lutts, *The Nature Fakers: Wildlife, Science, and Sentiment*, 106.

174   **"dove shot at by an elephant gun"** Cutright, *Theodore Roosevelt, the Naturalist*, 135.

175   **"whooping through the woods"** Lutts, *The Nature Fakers: Wildlife, Science, and Sentiment*, 112.

175   **"didn't know the heart of a wild thing"** Cutright, *Theodore Roosevelt, the Naturalist*, 135.

175   **"Every time Mr. Roosevelt gets near the heart"** Ibid.

175   **"If it is charged"** Ibid., 136.

175   **"skin Long alive"** Lutts, *The Nature Fakers: Wildlife, Science, and Sentiment*, 68.

175   **"The Reverend Dr. Long is possessed of that rare gift"** Ibid., 138.

176   **"We abhor deliberate and reckless untruth"** Ibid.

Part III: Roosevelt's New Naturalism

177   **"Most big-game hunters never learn anything"** Roosevelt, "My Life as a Naturalist," 329.

Chapter 14: I Am Going to Africa

179   **To anyone who asked** Official presidential term limits did not yet exist, so Roosevelt could have hoped to stay in power for as many terms as he could be reelected.

179   **At forty-six** Roosevelt made frequent mention of his rheumatism as something that might keep him from hunting. Wagenknecht, *The Seven Worlds of Theodore Roosevelt*, 28–29; Millais, *Life of Frederick Courteney Selous*, 281.

179   **"I am fond of politics"** Putnam, *Theodore Roosevelt: The Formative Years, 1858–1886*, vol. 1, 309.

180   **"all kinds of people crowd"** Roosevelt, *Letters to Kermit from Theodore Roosevelt, 1902–1908*, 20.

180   **From British conservationist Edward North Buxton's** For a list of some of Roosevelt's favorite African game and hunting books see the bibliography in Roosevelt and Heller, *Life-Histories of African Game Animals*, vol. 2, 759–74.

180   **He even read African hunting stories** K. Roosevelt, *The Happy Hunting-Grounds*, 5–6.

180   **"the greatest of the world's great"** Roosevelt, *African Game Trails*, ix.

180 **"We had bear meat"** Roosevelt, *Letters to Kermit from Theodore Roosevelt, 1902–1908*, 227.

181 **Any time Selous came to visit** See Introduction in Selous, *African Nature Notes and Reminiscences*.

181 **"I mean to be like Livingstone"** Bull, *Safari: A Chronicle of Adventure*, 94.

181 **Leaving England for South Africa** Selous's life is here largely recounted from Millais, *Life of Frederick Courteney Selous*; and Bull, *Safari: A Chronicle of Adventure*, 93–121.

181 **"You are only a boy"** Bull, *Safari: A Chronicle of Adventure*, 98.

181 **"Who could wish a better life"** Millais, *Life of Frederick Courteney Selous*, 375.

182 **"I have found it more and more difficult"** Ibid., 225.

182 **greatest ambitions** Cutright, *Theodore Roosevelt, the Naturalist*, 186.

183 **Roosevelt had previously admired** Bodry-Sanders, *Carl Akeley: Africa's Collector, Africa's Savior*, 41.

183 **Roosevelt later visited** Akeley, *In Brightest Africa*, 158.

183 **"store bought"** Bodry-Sanders, *Carl Akeley: Africa's Collector, Africa's Savior*, 106.

183 **Akeley had just returned** My account of Akeley's White House dinner is taken from his own account of the event in Akeley, *In Brightest Africa*, 158–59.

183 **One of Akeley's most vivid** Ibid., 97–103.

183 **But the story that most** Ibid., 79, 158–59.

184 **"As soon as I am through"** Ibid., 159.

184 **"How would it do for me"** Cutright, *Theodore Roosevelt, the Naturalist*, 186.

184 **This breathless note** See footnote in Morison, *The Letters of Theodore Roosevelt*, vol. 6, 978. See also the following entries in Morison, *The Letters of Theodore Roosevelt*, vol. 6: 4645, 4723, 4825, 4854, 5111, 4885, 5112.

184   **"You blessed fellow"** Roosevelt, *Letters to Kermit from Theodore Roosevelt, 1902–1908,* 240.

184   **Like his father** Ibid., 221.

184   **Roosevelt took it all with humor** Cutright, *Theodore Roosevelt, the Naturalist,* 196–97.

184   **"do its duty"** O'Toole, *When Trumpets Call,* 15.

185   **Theodore's old friend** J. L. Gardner, *Departing Glory,* 111.

185   **An article in the Philadelphia *Ledger*** Morison, *The Letters of Theodore Roosevelt,* vol. 6, 1236.

185   **Roosevelt found it all very amusing** J. L. Gardner, *Departing Glory,* 111.

185   **More than disease** Abbott, *The Letters of Archie Butt,* 203.

185   **"wanton outrage"** Thompson, *Theodore Roosevelt Abroad,* 16.

185   **For years he had been writing** Roosevelt, *Letters to Kermit from Theodore Roosevelt, 1902–1908,* 202–03.

186   **"just in time to see"** Millais, *Life of Frederick Courteney Selous,* 231.

186   **"dignified and appropriate"** Thompson, *Theodore Roosevelt Abroad,* 12.

186   **"lions, mosquitoes and the tsetse fly"** Morison, *The Letters of Theodore Roosevelt,* vol. 7, 2.

186   **Two British hunters** Cutright, *Theodore Roosevelt, the Naturalist,* 187.

186   **Selous felt very strongly** See letter to Alfred Pease transcribed in Millais, *Life of Frederick Courteney Selous,* 269–72.

186   **"trust to the native"** Ibid., 269.

186   **Roosevelt was puzzled** Thompson, *Theodore Roosevelt Abroad,* 10.

186   **Following Buxton's advice** See E. Morris, *Colonel Roosevelt,* 584–86, for an overview of all of these smaller two-month hunting excursions.

186   **"good game country"** Thompson, *Theodore Roosevelt Abroad,* 10.

187   **"upon the habits of the game"** Ibid.

187 **"mere holiday after big game"** Hagedorn, *The Boys' Life of Theodore Roosevelt,* 292.

187 **Tjäder Expedition** Allen, "Mammals from British East Africa, Collected by the Tjäder Expedition of 1906," 1909.

187 **Founded in 1846** The Smithsonian Institution did not include a museum—at least not officially—until Spencer Baird argued for the creation of the United States National Museum (USNM) in 1879. It was a combined art, history, and natural-history museum at first. Not until 1960 did the museum become an exclusively natural-history museum under a new name: the National Museum of Natural History (NMNH).

188 **"As you know"** Morison, *The Letters of Theodore Roosevelt,* vol. 6, 1093.

188 **Always a tough negotiator** Ibid., 1093–94.

189 **He also agreed to set up** Thompson, *Theodore Roosevelt Abroad,* 11.

189 **An elated Roosevelt** Millais, *Life of Frederick Courteney Selous,* 267.

189 **"last chance for something"** Thompson, *Theodore Roosevelt Abroad,* 13.

189 **"devote full attention"** Ibid., 15.

189 **Having studied the accounts** Millais, *Life of Frederick Courteney Selous,* 270.

190 **He made a list** Thompson, *Theodore Roosevelt Abroad,* 14.

190 **Roosevelt did use the power** Ibid.

190 **"I shall leave Mombasa"** Millais, *Life of Frederick Courteney Selous,* 268.

190 **"crush out the old school"** Morison, *The Letters of Theodore Roosevelt,* vol. 3, 72.

190 **"little scientific men"** Ibid., 708.

191 **the "best field naturalist"** Mearns and Mearns, *The Bird Collectors,* 223.

191   **Given this robust résumé** Hume, *Ornithologists of the United States Army Medical Corps: Thirty-six Biographies,* 310.

191   **At thirty-four, Heller** H. W. Grinnell, "Edmund Heller: 1875–1939," 209–18.

192   **"He is well aware"** O'Toole, *When Trumpets Call,* 36.

192   **As Roosevelt's venture grew** Millais, *Life of Frederick Courteney Selous,* 270.

192   **Cracking open a can** Morison, *The Letters of Theodore Roosevelt,* vol. 2, 855. Colonel Roosevelt so cared for the men serving under him while at war in Cuba that he bought them canned beans and tomatoes out of his own pocket: "My men are in tatters and their shoes are like those of tramps. . . . The few delicacies—if beans and tomatoes can be called such—which they have had I have had to purchase myself."

192   **His only luxury** Cutright, *Theodore Roosevelt, the Naturalist,* 191.

192   **"I do not believe"** Ibid., 191–92.

192   **Test-firing** K. Roosevelt, *The Happy Hunting-Grounds,* xi.

193   **"exceedingly proud"** R. L. Wilson, *Theodore Roosevelt: Hunter-Conservationist,* 179.

193   **"I should like in case of an emergency"** Morison, *The Letters of Theodore Roosevelt,* vol. 6, 1223.

193   **But by far the most magnificent** See R. L. Wilson, *Theodore Roosevelt: Hunter-Conservationist,* 174–77, for details on the Roosevelt armament, including specifics on the royal-grade elephant gun and a full-page color photo.

193   **It came with a list** Roosevelt, *African Game Trails,* 28–29.

193   **"In recognition"** Ibid., 28.

193   **Clothing was something** Cutright, *Theodore Roosevelt, the Naturalist,* 192.

194   **Even the lantern** The newly patented "Stonebridge folding lantern" was a marvel of Yankee ingenuity in having lightweight crystalline mica "glass" and back reflector that allowed the beam to be directed somewhat like a flashlight. One of these

lanterns appears to be hanging from the center post in the photo of Roosevelt's tent on page 170 of Bull, *Safari: A Chronicle of Adventure*. Also seen in the image are some of the paint cans that were used for storing smaller skeletons scattered about, and there is a bird-drying box with Roosevelt's name on it and with a bird skin already drying. Overall, Roosevelt's tent looks very much like a specimen collector's tent.

194   **He packed nine pairs** Cutright, *Theodore Roosevelt, the Naturalist*, 192–93.

194   **"not even into the jungles of Africa"** J. L. Gardner, *Departing Glory*, 112. See also Robinson, *My Brother, Theodore Roosevelt*, 251–53.

194   **"pigskin library"** Roosevelt included a full list of the contents of his field library in Appendix F of his *African Game Trails*.

194   **"reading in some little mosquito cage"** Thompson, *Theodore Roosevelt Abroad*, 17.

195   **Having lived for more than fifty years** Bishop, *Theodore Roosevelt and His Time: Shown in His Own Letters*, vol. 2, 122.

195   **"It is no child's play"** Morison, *The Letters of Theodore Roosevelt*, vol. 6, 1060.

195   **Roosevelt warned Kermit** Ibid.

195   **"rifle sense"** K. Roosevelt, *The Long Trail*, 31.

195   **Finally, on the morning of March 23** Descriptions of Roosevelt's departure are taken from O'Toole, *When Trumpets Call*, 13–17.

196   **"Three cheers!"** Millais, *Life of Frederick Courteney Selous*, 268.

196   **"drying in my room at the moment"** Morison, *The Letters of Theodore Roosevelt*, vol. 7, 7.

196   **"nicely prepared"** Edgar Mearns to Mrs. Mearns, April 21, 1909, RU 7083, Box 1, Mearns Papers, Smithsonian Institution Archives.

196   **"That's a wonderful sight"** J. L. Gardner, *Departing Glory*, 117.

Chapter 15: A Railroad Through the Pleistocene

197   **As swiftly as he might have shouldered** O'Toole, *When Trumpets Call*, 42.

198   **That first night** Mearns Papers, Smithsonian Institution Archives.

198   **Excluded from this prime seating** Thompson, *Theodore Roosevelt Abroad*, 33.

198   **Here and there Roosevelt caught glimpses** Roosevelt, *African Game Trails*, 16.

198   **The only indication** Ibid., 16–18.

198   **On awakening in his coach** Ibid., 19.

199   **Roosevelt's comparison** Humans trace their origins to Africa, and one theory holds that having lived side by side with mankind for millennia, the wild animals of Africa kept pace with the incremental advances in human hunting techniques, thus persisting. Elsewhere, such as in Pleistocene Europe, many of these same animals succumbed to the predations of newly arriving humans, the theory holding that they were naïve and vulnerable to humans' hunting techniques.

199   **"vast zoological garden"** Thompson, *Theodore Roosevelt Abroad*, 33.

199   **"naturalist's wonderland"** Roosevelt, *African Game Trails*, 13.

199   **Roosevelt believed wildlife conservation** Ibid., 13–15.

199   **"mushy sentimentality"** Ibid., 14.

199   **"well-meaning persons"** Ibid.

199   **"There should be certain sanctuaries"** Ibid.

199   **"merely aesthetic reasons"** Roosevelt, *Outdoor Pastimes of an American Hunter*, 272–73.

200   **There were no fewer than 265** Tweed Roosevelt, "Theodore Roosevelt's African Safari," 422.

200   **As befit a Newland, Tarlton & Co. safari** Trzebinski, *The Kenya Pioneers*, 139.

201 **"pine and birch and frosty weather"** Roosevelt, *African Game Trails*, 24.

201 **"like spectacles"** Ibid., 37.

201 **"like barnacles on an old boat"** Ibid.

201 **"Nature is merciless indeed"** Ibid.

202 **"Few laymen"** Ibid., 21.

202 **"owing to the enormous masses"** J. G. Pease, *A Wealth of Happiness and Many Bitter Trials*, 281.

202 **Making matters worse** Ibid.

203 **Not knowing the names** Roosevelt, *African Game Trails*, 41. ·

203 **"a little red-billed finch"** Ibid.

203 **"pretty, alert little things"** Ibid., 32

203 **"among the most beautiful"** Ibid.

203 **"mole rats with velvety fur"** Ibid., 42.

203 **"heavy woodchucks"** Ibid.

203 **"wee rhinoceros"** Ibid.

203 **"It had been hanging from a mimosa twig"** Ibid.

203 **"absolutely out of condition"** Thompson, *Theodore Roosevelt Abroad*, 15.

206 **"men who, having in earlier days"** Fitter and Scott, *The Penitent Butchers: The Fauna Preservation Society, 1903–1978*, 8–9.

206 **To Roosevelt, these were merely** Roosevelt, *African Game Trails*, 72–74.

207 **"If I can only get my lion"** Dawson, *Opportunity and Theodore Roosevelt*, 57.

207 **One man was yanked** Roosevelt, *African Game Trails*, 78.

208 **"Roosevelt had mapped out"** J. G. Pease, *A Wealth of Happiness and Many Bitter Trials*, 282.

208 **"It can be done alone"** A. E. Pease, *The Book of the Lion*, 239.

209 **"Away went Kermit after a Hyena"** J. G. Pease, *A Wealth of Happiness and Many Bitter Trials*, 282.

209   "so we went back and took it" Ibid.

209   "I didn't think it was worth bothering" Ibid.

209   "place askaris on every hilltop" Ibid., 280.

209   "rather fussy and troublesome" Ibid.

209   "bothered by other people's ideas" Ibid., 282.

209   "leave the men and noise" Ibid.

210   Then one of the natives yelled *Simba!* Roosevelt, *African Game Trails*, 83.

210   Pease was disappointed J. G. Pease, *A Wealth of Happiness and Many Bitter Trials*, 283.

210   "Crack! The Winchester spoke" Roosevelt, *African Game Trails*, 85.

211   This prevented J. G. Pease, *A Wealth of Happiness and Many Bitter Trials*, 283.

211   "Good, Simba" Roosevelt, *African Game Trails*, 86.

211   "I had never seen" J. G. Pease, *A Wealth of Happiness and Many Bitter Trials*, 283.

211   The bullet went in Roosevelt, *African Game Trails*, 87.

Chapter 16: Bwana Tumbo—Mr. Big Belly

214   "The beast stood" Roosevelt, *African Game Trails*, 105.

214   "the agility of a polo pony" Ibid., 106.

214   "ploughing up the ground" Ibid.

214   "real savages" Ibid., 118.

214   So chaotic was the scene Heller Papers, Smithsonian Institution Archives.

215   "The intestines were also eaten" Ibid.

215   "absolutely necessary" Roosevelt and Heller, *Life-Histories of African Game Animals,* 746.

215   Roosevelt admitted Ibid., 747.

215   The salt method Ibid.

216   "rhinoceritis" Mearns Papers, Smithsonian Institution Archives.

218   **Newspapermen coined the term** E. Morris, *Colonel Roosevelt*, 589.

218   **Remarkably, the Smithsonian published** Heller, "A New Rodent of the Genus *Georychus*," 1909.

218   **paying for his fun** K. Roosevelt, *The Happy Hunting-Grounds*, 23.

219   **"shot several times over"** Dawson, *Opportunity and Theodore Roosevelt*, 68.

219   **"Dawson is in trouble"** Ibid., 62.

219   **"except perhaps for the vegetables"** Ibid., 76.

220   **"Stand steady! Don't run!"** Roosevelt, *African Game Trails*, 167–68.

221   **"I am really proud of Kermit"** Morison, *The Letters of Theodore Roosevelt*, vol. 7, 10.

221   **"Kermit is a great care and anxiety"** Ibid., vol. 7, 26.

221   **"a handful in the field"** O'Toole, *When Trumpets Call*, 50.

221   **"fill every nook and cranny"** Ibid., 52.

Chapter 17: Deep in Prehistoric Thought

222   **"good game country"** Thompson, *Theodore Roosevelt Abroad*, 10.

223   **"cracked like rifles"** Roosevelt, *African Game Trails*, 180.

223   **using his saddle as a pillow** Ibid., 181.

223   **It wasn't long before** Ibid., 186–89.

224   **"gorgeously colored"** Ibid., 189.

224   **"My bag for the five days"** Ibid., 203.

224   **"range-finding"** Ibid.

225   **"Look at him"** Ibid., 206.

225   **"huge and threatening"** Ibid., 212.

225   **"Kneeling, I sent the bullet"** Ibid., 217.

226   **"small steam-engine"** Ibid.

226 **"Civilized man"** Ibid., 239.

227 **Even humans could be prey** Ibid., p 245.

227 **Even Loring came close to death** Ibid., 226.

227 *Bwana Simba,* **the "lion master"** Loring, *African Adventure Stories,* 58.

Chapter 18: Bent on Mischief

228 **"astonishingly quick"** Roosevelt, *African Game Trails,* 252.

228 **"We headed toward it"** Ibid., 258.

229 **"with its huge jaws"** Ibid.

229 **"bent on mischief"** Ibid.

229 **"with the clash of a sprung bear trap"** Ibid.

229 **Heller had been using** The leopard was caught with a #2 double long spring trap, which would be used for an animal the size of a fox in the United States. Roosevelt, *African Game Trails,* 261; Heller Papers, Smithsonian Institution Archives.

230 **"They prove what I said"** "Long Attacks Roosevelt," *New York Times,* May 27, 1909.

230 **"The worst feature"** Thompson, *Theodore Roosevelt Abroad,* 50.

231 **"The only thing"** Long, "Roosevelt a Butcher, Declares Dr. Long," *Toledo Blade,* June 10, 1909.

231 **"the shallow, muddy water boiled"** Roosevelt, *African Game Trails,* 266.

232 **"I don't know what to do"** Dawson, *Opportunity and Theodore Roosevelt,* 108–09.

Chapter 19: Hunters and Naturalists

233 **Trudging up the slopes of Mount Kenya** Roosevelt, *African Game Trails,* 294–95.

233 **"The sun was shut"** Ibid., 294.

234   **The Ndorobo trackers** Ibid., 297.

234   **"resting his tusks"** Ibid., 298.

235   **"great lord of the forest"** Ibid.

235   **"like packethread"** Ibid.

235   **"chattering like monkeys"** Ibid.

235   **"I felt proud indeed"** Ibid.

235   **The preservation of an entire elephant** Roosevelt and Heller, *Life-Histories of African Game Animals,* vol. 2, 755.

236   **"splashed with blood"** Roosevelt, *African Game Trails,* 300.

236   **"The flickering light"** Ibid.

237   **As Roosevelt set off for his solo hunt** My account of Mearns and Loring's survey of Mount Kenya is drawn from Mearns's letters written at that time (Mearns Papers, Smithsonian Institution Archives).

243   **"I speak of Africa"** Roosevelt, *African Game Trails*, ix.

243   **"crazy little steam launch"** Ibid., 459.

244   **"the greedy abandon of a gold rush"** Bull, *Safari: Chronicle of Adventure,* 151.

244   **The white rhino** The idea that "white" had its origins in the Afrikaans *wyd* was first suggested to me by Helmut Sommer, Senior Technician in the Department of Mammalogy at the American Museum of Natural History.

244   **Roosevelt also knew that of the two** Roosevelt, *African Game Trails*, 2.

245   **"It is almost as if our bison"** Ibid., 464.

245   **"until a careful inquiry"** Ibid.

246   **"a hard bit set"** Ibid., 457.

246   **"the heart of the African wilderness"** Ibid., 474.

246   **"usually with nothing on"** Morison, *The Letters of Theodore Roosevelt,* vol. 7, 46.

246   **"All the other members"** Ibid., 47.

247   **"very real"** Roosevelt, "My Life as a Naturalist: With a Presentation of Various First-hand Data on the Life Histories and Habits of the Big Game Animals of Africa," 321.

248   **"copious but valueless"** Ibid., 325.

Epilogue: The End of the Game

253   **Interestingly, it was the elite European** See various letters in Lyell, *African Adventures: Letters from Famous Big-Game Hunters.*

253   **"In Africa, however, we really did some good work"** Roosevelt, "My Life as a Naturalist: With a Presentation of Various First-hand Data on the Life Histories and Habits of the Big Game Animals of Africa," 329.

Bibliography

Aaron, Amanda. "Ladies' Mile." In *The Encyclopedia of New York City*, edited by Kenneth T. Jackson, p. 650. New Haven: Yale University Press, 1995.

Abbott, Lawrence F. *The Letters of Archie Butt: Personal Aide to President Roosevelt*. Garden City, New York: Doubleday, Page, 1924.

Akeley, C. R. "Elephant Hunting in Equatorial Africa." *The American Museum Journal*, vol. 12, no. 2 (1912), pp. 43–62.

Akeley, Carl E. *In Brightest Africa*. Memorial Edition. Garden City, New York: Doubleday, Page, 1923.

Akeley, Mary L. Jobe. *Carl Akeley's Africa: The Account of the Akeley-Eastman-Pomeroy African Hall Expedition of the American Museum of Natural History*. New York: Dodd, Mead, 1930.

Alderson, William T. (Editor). *Mermaids, Mummies, and Mastodons: The Emergence of the American Museum*. Washington, D.C.: American Association of Museums, 1992.

Alexander, Edward P. "Mermaids, Mummies, and Mastodons: An Exhibition on the Evolution of Early American Museums." In *Mermaids, Mummies, and Mastodons: The Emergence of the American Museum*, edited by William T. Alderson, pp. 17–21. Washington, D.C.: American Association of Museums, 1992.

Alexander, Edward P. *Museum Masters: Their Museums and Their Influence.* Nashville: American Association for State and Local History, 1983.

Allen, Joel Asaph. "History of the American Bison, *Bison Americanus.*" Extracted from *The Ninth Annual Report of the [U.S. Geological] Survey, for the Year 1875.* Washington, D.C.: Government Printing Office, 1877.

Allen, Joel Asaph. "Mammals from British East Africa, Collected by the Tjäder Expedition of 1906." *Bulletin of the American Museum of Natural History,* vol. 26 (1909), pp. 147–75.

Amos, James E. *Theodore Roosevelt: Hero to His Valet.* New York: John Day, 1927.

Anthony, Harold E. "The Capture and Preservation of Small Mammals for Study." Guide Leaflet No. 61. New York: American Museum of Natural History, 1925.

Asma, Stephen T. *Stuffed Animals and Pickled Heads: The Culture and Evolution of Natural History Museums.* Oxford: Oxford University Press, 2001.

Baird, Spencer F. *Reports of Explorations and Surveys, to Ascertain the Most Practicable and Economical Route for a Railroad from the Mississippi River to the Pacific Ocean. Made Under the Direction of the Secretary of War, in 1853–4, According to Acts of Congress of March 3, 1853, May 31, 1854, and August 5, 1854,* vol. 8. Washington, D.C.: Beverley Tucker, Printer, 1857.

Baldwin, William C. *African Hunting from Natal to the Zambesi: Includes Lake Ngami, the Kalahari Desert, &c. from 1852–1860.* London: Richard Bently, 1863.

Barber, Lynn. *The Heyday of Natural History, 1820–1870.* Garden City, New York: Doubleday, 1980.

Barnum, Phineas T. *The Life of P. T. Barnum, Written by Himself.* Reprinted with Introduction by Terrence Whalen. Urbana: University of Illinois Press, 2000. Originally published 1855 by J. S. Redfield (New York).

Barrus, Clara. *The Life and Letters of John Burroughs.* 2 vols. Boston: Houghton Mifflin, 1925.

Barsness, Larry. *Heads, Hides and Horns: The Compleat Buffalo Book.* Fort Worth: Texas Christian University Press, 1985.

Beard, Peter H. *The End of the Game.* 4th ed. San Francisco: Chronicle Books, 1988.

Bechtel, Stefan. *Mr. Hornaday's War: How a Peculiar Victorian Zookeeper Waged a Lonely Crusade for Wildlife That Changed the World.* Boston: Beacon Press, 2012.

Bickmore, Albert S. "An Autobiography with a Historical Sketch of the Founding and Early Development of the American Museum of Natural History." Unpublished manuscript, Rare Book Room, American Museum of Natural History.

Bishop, Joseph Bucklin. *Theodore Roosevelt and His Time: Shown in His Own Letters.* 2 vols. New York: Charles Scribner's Sons, 1920.

Black, Gilbert J. (Editor). *Theodore Roosevelt, 1858–1919.* Dobbs Ferry, New York: Oceana, 1969.

Blodgett, W. T. "Report on Purchases Made in Europe for the American Museum of Natural History." In *The First Annual Report of the American Museum of Natural History,* 1870.

Bodry-Sanders, Penelope. *Carl Akeley: Africa's Collector, Africa's Savior.* New York: Paragon House, 1991.

Boyes, John. *The Company of Adventurers.* Reprinted with a Foreword by Mike Resnick. Alexander, North Carolina: Alexander Books, 2001. Originally published 1928 by East Africa Ltd. (London).

Brands, H. W. *T.R.: The Last Romantic.* New York: Basic Books, 1997.

Brands, H. W. (Editor). *The Selected Letters of Theodore Roosevelt.* New York: Cooper Square Press, 2001.

Brinkley, Douglas. *The Wilderness Warrior: Theodore Roosevelt and the Crusade for America.* New York: HarperCollins, 2009.

Brooks, Chester L., and Ray H. Mattison. *Theodore Roosevelt and the Dakota Badlands*. Washington, D.C.: National Park Service, 1958.

Bull, Bartle. *Safari: A Chronicle of Adventure*. New York: Viking, 1988.

Burroughs, John. *Camping and Tramping with Roosevelt*. Boston: Houghton Mifflin, 1907.

Burrows, Edwin G., and Mike Wallace. *Gotham: A History of New York City to 1898*. New York: Oxford University Press, 1999.

Butt, Archie. *Taft and Roosevelt: The Intimate Letters of Archie Butt, Military Aide*. 2 vols. Garden City, New York: Doubleday, Doran, 1930.

Buxton, E. N. *Two African Trips*. London: Edward Stanford, 1902.

Cartmill, Matt. *A View to Death in the Morning: Hunting and Nature Through History*. Cambridge: Harvard University Press, 1993.

Chapman, Frank M. *Autobiography of a Bird-Lover*. New York: D. Appleton-Century, 1933.

Charnwood, Godfrey Rathbone Benson, Baron. *Theodore Roosevelt, by Lord Charnwood*. Boston: Atlantic Monthly Press, 1923.

Chessman, G. Wallace. *Governor Theodore Roosevelt: The Albany Apprenticeship, 1898–1900*. Cambridge: Harvard University Press, 1965.

Churchill, Winston. *My African Journey*. New York: Norton, 1990. Originally published 1908 by Hodder and Stoughton (London).

Clark, James L. *Good Hunting: Fifty Years of Collection and Preparing Habitat Groups for the American Museum*. Norman: University of Oklahoma Press, 1966.

Clark, James L. *Trails of the Hunted*. Boston: Little, Brown, 1928.

Cooper, C. B., and J. A. Smith. "Gender Patterns in Bird-Related Recreation in the USA and UK." *Ecology and Society*, vol. 15, no. 4 (2010), http://www.ecologyandsociety.org/vol15/iss4/art4/.

Cordery, Stacy A. *Alice: Alice Roosevelt Longworth, from White House Princess to Washington Power Broker*. New York: Penguin, 2007.

Cutright, Paul Russell. *Theodore Roosevelt: The Making of a Conservationist*. Urbana: University of Illinois Press, 1985.

Cutright, Paul Russell. "Theodore Roosevelt Disposes of His Boyhood Bird Specimens." *Journal of the Theodore Roosevelt Association*, vol. 9, no. 4 (Fall 1983), pp. 1–8.

Cutright, Paul Russell. *Theodore Roosevelt, the Naturalist*. New York: Harper & Brothers, 1956.

Dall, William Healey. *Spencer Fullerton Baird: A Biography; Including Selections from His Correspondence with Audubon, Agassiz, Dana, and Others*. Philadelphia: J. B. Lippincott, 1925.

Dalton, Kathleen. *Theodore Roosevelt: A Strenuous Life*. New York: Alfred A. Knopf, 2002.

Dary, David A. *The Buffalo Book: Saga of an American Symbol*. Chicago: Swallow Press, 1974.

Daubenmire, Rexford F. "Merriam's Life Zones of North America." *The Quarterly Review of Biology*, vol. 13, no. 3 (Sept. 1938), pp. 327–32.

Davis, Oscar King. *Released for Publication: Some Inside Political History of Theodore Roosevelt and His Times, 1898–1918*. Boston: Houghton Mifflin, 1925.

Dawson, Warrington. *Opportunity and Theodore Roosevelt*. Privately published in 1923 by Warrington Dawson.

Deane, Ruthven. "Unpublished Letters of John James Audubon and Spencer F. Baird: I." *The Auk*, vol. 23 (1906), pp. 194–209.

Deane, Ruthven. "Unpublished Letters of John James Audubon and Spencer F. Baird: II." *The Auk*, vol. 23 (1906), pp. 318–34.

Deane, Ruthven. "Unpublished Letters of John James Audubon and Spencer F. Baird: III." *The Auk*, vol. 24 (1907), pp. 53–70.

Dennett, Andrea Stulman. *Weird and Wonderful: The Dime Museum in America*. New York: New York University Press, 1997.

DiSilvestro, Roger L. *Theodore Roosevelt in the Badlands: A Young Politician's Quest for Recovery in the American West*. New York: Walker, 2011.

Donald, Aida D. *Lion in the White House: A Life of Theodore Roosevelt.* New York: Basic Books, 2007.

Donaldson, A. L. *A History of the Adirondacks.* New York: Century, 1921.

Doughty, Robin W. *Feather Fashions and Bird Preservation: A Study in Nature Protection.* Berkeley: University of California Press, 1975.

Ellsworth, Lincoln. *The Last Wild Buffalo Hunt.* New York: Privately printed in 1916.

Ewing, Heather. *The Lost World of James Smithson: Science, Revolution, and the Birth of the Smithsonian.* New York: Bloomsbury, 2007.

Faber, Paul Lawrence. "The Development of Taxidermy and the History of Ornithology." *Isis,* vol. 68, no. 244 (1977), pp. 550–66.

Faber, Paul Lawrence. *Discovering Birds: The Emergence of Ornithology as a Scientific Discipline, 1760–1850.* Baltimore: Johns Hopkins University Press, 1997.

Faber, Paul Lawrence. *Finding Order in Nature: The Naturalist Tradition from Linnaeus to E. O. Wilson.* Baltimore: Johns Hopkins University Press, 2000.

Fitter, Richard, and Sir Peter Scott. *The Penitent Butchers: The Fauna Preservation Society, 1903–1978.* Fauna Preservation Society, 1978.

Foran, W. Robert. *A Cuckoo in Kenya: The Reminiscences of a Pioneer Police Officer in British East Africa.* London: Hutchinson & Co., 1936.

Foran, W. Robert. *The Elephant Hunters of the Lado.* Unpublished manuscript copyrighted by W. R. Foran and subsequently published. Long Beach, California: Safari Press, 2007.

Foran, W. Robert *Kill or Be Killed: The Rambling Reminiscences of an Amateur Hunter.* Peter Capstick Adventure Library, edited by Peter Capstick. New York: St. Martin's Press, 1988. Originally published 1933 by Hutchinson & Co. (London).

Fortey, Richard. *Dry Storeroom No. 1: The Secret Life of the Natural History Museum.* New York: Alfred A. Knopf, 2008.

Gable, John A. "Theodore Roosevelt and the American Museum of Natural History." *Theodore Roosevelt Association Journal*, vol. 8, no. 3 (1982).

Gardner, A. L. Back matter in *Journal of Mammalogy*, vol. 78, no. 1 (February 1997).

Gardner, Joseph L. *Departing Glory: Theodore Roosevelt as Ex-President.* New York: Charles Scribner's Sons, 1973.

Garretson, Martin S. *The American Bison: The Story of Its Extermination as a Wild Species and Its Restoration Under Federal Protection.* New York: New York Zoological Society, 1938.

Giraud Jr., J. P. *The Birds of Long Island.* New York: Wiley and Putnam, 1844.

Graham Jr., Frank. *The Adirondack Park: A Political History.* New York: Alfred A. Knopf, 1978.

Grinnell, George Bird. "A Premium on Crime." *Forest and Stream,* vol. 42, no. 12, March 24, 1894.

Grinnell, George Bird. "Protection for the Park." *Forest and Stream,* vol. 42, no. 19, May 12, 1894.

Grinnell, George Bird. "Save the Park Buffalo." *Forest and Stream,* vol. 42, no. 15, April 14, 1894.

Grinnell, George Bird. "A Step Forward." *Forest and Stream,* vol. 42, no. 16, April 21, 1894.

Grinnell, George Bird (Editor). *Hunting at High Altitudes.* New York: Harper & Brothers, 1913.

Grinnell, Hilda Wood. "Edmund Heller: 1875–1939." *Journal of Mammalogy*, vol. 28, no. 3 (1947), pp. 209–18.

Groneman, Carol, and David M. Reimers. "Immigration." In *The Encyclopedia of New York City*, edited by Kenneth T. Jackson, pp. 181–87. New Haven: Yale University Press, 1995.

Hagedorn, Hermann. *The Boys' Life of Theodore Roosevelt.* New York: Harper & Brothers, 1918.

Hagedorn, Hermann. *The Roosevelt Family of Sagamore Hill.* New York: Macmillan, 1954.

Hagedorn, Hermann. *Roosevelt in the Bad Lands.* Boston: Houghton Mifflin, 1921.

Hagedorn, Hermann (Editor). *The Works of Theodore Roosevelt.* Memorial Edition. Vol. 1 of 24. With an Introduction by George Bird Grinnell. New York: Charles Scribner's Sons, 1923.

Hagedorn, Hermann, and Gary G. Roth. *Sagamore Hill: An Historical Guide.* Oyster Bay, New York: Theodore Roosevelt Association, 1977.

Hayden, F. V. (Editor). *Sixth Annual Report of the United States Geological Survey of the Territories Embracing Portions of Montana, Idaho, Wyoming, and Utah; Being a Report of Progress of the Explorations for the Year 1872.* Washington, D.C.: Government Printing Office, 1873.

Hays, Samuel P. *Conservation and the Gospel of Efficiency: The Progressive Conservation Movement, 1890–1920.* Reprinted with a new Preface by the author, New York: Atheneum, 1969. Originally publsihed 1959 by Harvard University Press.

Heller, Edmund. "A New Rodent of the Genus *Georychus.*" *Smithsonian Miscellaneous Collections,* vol. 52, no. 1879 (1909).

Heller, Edmund. "The White Rhinoceros." *Smithsonian Miscellaneous Collections,* vol. 63 (1913), pp. 1–77.

Hellman, Geoffrey. *Bankers, Bones and Beetles: The First Century of the American Museum of Natural History.* Garden City, New York: Natural History Press, 1968.

Herber, Elmer Charles (Editor). *Correspondence Between Spencer Fullerton Baird and Louis Agassiz—Two Pioneer American Naturalists.* Washington, D.C.: Smithsonian Institution, 1963.

Herman, Daniel Justin. *Hunting and the American Imagination.* Washington, D.C.: Smithsonian Institution Press, 2001.

Hollister, N. "East African Mammals in the United States National Museum: Insectivora, Chiroptera, and Carnivora." *Bulletin of the United States National Museum,* no. 99, pt. 1 (1918), pp. 1–194. Plates 1–55.

Hollister, N. "East African Mammals in the United States National Museum: Rodentia, Lagomorpha, and Tublidentata." *Bulletin of the United States National Museum*, no. 99, pt. 2 (1919), pp. 1–184. Plates 1–44.

Homberger, Eric. *The Historical Atlas of New York City: A Visual Celebration of Nearly 400 Years of New York City's History*. New York: Henry Holt, 1994.

Hume, E. E. *Ornithologists of the United States Army Medical Corps: Thirty-six Biographies*. Baltimore: Johns Hopkins Press, 1942.

Irmscher, C. *Louis Agassiz: Creator of American Science*. Boston: Houghton Mifflin Harcourt, 2013.

Jackson, K. T. (Editor). *The Encyclopedia of New York City*. New Haven: Yale University Press, 1995.

Jaffe, M. *The Gilded Dinosaur: The Fossil War Between E. D. Cope and O. C. Marsh and the Rise of American Science*. New York: Crown, 2000.

Jeffers, P. H. *Roosevelt the Explorer: T.R.'s Amazing Adventures as a Naturalist, Conservationist, and Explorer*. New York: Taylor Trade Publishing, 2002.

Jenkins, Jerry, with Andy Keal. *The Adirondack Atlas: A Geographic Portrait of the Adirondack Park*. Syracuse: Syracuse University Press, 2004.

Johnston, Jeremy. "Preserving the Beasts of Waste and Desolation: Theodore Roosevelt and Predator Control in Yellowstone." *Yellowstone Science* (Spring 2002), pp. 14–21.

Kellert, S. "Attitudes and Characteristics of Hunters and Anti-hunters." *Transactions of the 43rd North American Wildlife and Natural Resources Conference* (1978), pp. 412–23.

Kennedy, J. M. "Philanthropy and Science in New York City: The American Museum of Natural History, 1868–1968." Ph.D. dissertation. New Haven: Yale University, 1968.

Kirk, Jay. *Kingdom Under Glass: A Tale of Obsession, Adventure, and One Man's Quest to Preserve the World's Great Animals*. New York: Henry Holt, 2010.

Kline, Benjamin. *First Along the River: A Brief History of the U.S. Environmental Movement.* San Francisco: Acada Books, 1997.

Kohler, Robert E. *All Creatures: Naturalists, Collectors, and Biodiversity, 1850–1950.* Princeton: Princeton University Press, 2006.

Kohler, Robert E. *Landscapes and Labscapes: Exploring the Lab-Field Border in Biology.* Chicago: University of Chicago Press, 2002.

Kohlstedt, Sally Gregory. "Entrepreneurs and Intellectuals: Natural History in Early American Museums." In *Mermaids, Mummies, and Mastodons: The Emergence of the American Museum,* edited by William T. Alderson, pp. 22–39. Washington, D.C.: American Association of Museums, 1992.

Kohlstedt, Sally Gregory (Editor). *The Origins of Natural Science in America: The Essays of George Brown Goode.* With an Introduction by Sally Gregory Kohlstedt. Washington, D.C.: Smithsonian Institution Press, 1991.

Kohn, Edward P. (Editor). *A Most Glorious Ride: The Diaries of Theodore Roosevelt, 1877–1886.* New York: Excelsior Editions, 2015.

Lang, Lincoln A. *Ranching with Roosevelt.* Philadelphia: J. B. Lippincott, 1926.

Lay, William O. *J. Alden Loring: A Naturalist Afield.* Owego, New York: Tioga County Historical Society, 1999.

Livingstone, David. *Missionary Travels and Researches in South Africa.* New York: Harper & Brothers, 1858.

Lodge, Henry Cabot. *Selections from the Correspondence of Theodore Roosevelt and Henry Cabot Lodge, 1884–1918.* 2 vols. New York: Charles Scribner's Sons, 1925.

Loring, J. Alden. *African Adventure Stories.* New York: Charles Scribner's Sons, 1914.

Louv, Richard. *Last Child in the Woods: Saving Our Children from Nature-Deficit Disorder.* Updated and expanded. Chapel Hill, North Carolina: Algonquin, 2008.

Louv, Richard. *The Nature Principle: Human Restoration and the End of Nature-Deficit Disorder.* Chapel Hill, North Carolina: Algonquin, 2011.

Lucas, F. A. "The Preparation of Rough Skeletons." Science Guide No. 59. New York: American Museum of Natural History, 1950.

Lutts, Ralph H. *The Nature Fakers: Wildlife, Science, and Sentiment.* Charlottesville: University Press of Virginia, 1990.

Lyell, Denis D. *African Adventures: Letters from Famous Big-Game Hunters.* Peter Capstick Adventure Library, edited by Peter Capstick. New York: St. Martin's Press, 1988. Originally published 1935.

Mauriès, P. *Cabinets of Curiosities.* London: Thames and Hudson, 2002.

McCullough, David. *Mornings on Horseback.* New York: Simon & Schuster, 2001.

McMartin, Barbara. *The Great Forest of the Adirondacks.* Utica, New York: North Country Books, 1994.

McMartin, Barbara. *Hides, Hemlocks, and Adirondack History: How the Tanning Industry Influenced the Growth of the Region.* Utica, New York: North Country Books, 1992.

Mearns, Barbara, and Richard Mearns. *The Bird Collectors.* San Diego: Academic Press, 1998.

Merriam, Clinton H. *The Mammals of the Adirondack Region: Northeastern New York.* 2 vols. New York: Transactions of the Linnaean Society, 1882–1884.

Merriam, Clinton H. "Preliminary Synopsis of American Bears." *Proceedings of the Biological Society of Washington,* vol. 10 (1896), pp. 65–83.

Merriam, Clinton H. "Report on the Mammals and Birds of the Expedition." In *Sixth Annual Report of the United States Geological Survey of the Territories Embracing Portions of Montana, Idaho, Wyoming, and Utah; Being a Report of Progress of the Explorations for the Year 1872,* edited by F. V. Hayden, pp. 551–715. Washington, D.C.: Government Printing Office, 1873.

Merriam, Clinton H. "Review of the Grizzly and Big Brown Bears of North America (Genus *Ursus*) with Description of a New Genus, *Vetularctos.*" *North American Fauna,* no. 41 (1918).

Merriam, Clinton H. "Suggestions for a New Method of Discriminating Between Species and Subspecies." *Science*, vol. 5, no. 124 (1897), pp. 753–58.

Metzler, Sally. *Theatres of Nature: Dioramas at the Field Museum.* Chicago: Field Museum, 2007.

Millais, J. G. *Life of Frederick Courteney Selous, D.S.O., Capt. 25th Royal Fusiliers.* London: Longmans, Green, 1919.

Millard, Candice. *The River of Doubt: Theodore Roosevelt's Darkest Journey.* New York: Doubleday, 2005.

Miller, C. *Gifford Pinchot and the Making of Modern Environmentalism.* Washington, D.C.: Island Press, 2001.

Miller, G. S. "Directions for Preparing Specimens of Mammals." Part N of *Bulletin of the United States National Museum*, no. 39 (1914).

Miller, Nathan. *Theodore Roosevelt: A Life.* New York: William Morrow, 1992.

Minot, Henry D. *The Land and Game Birds of New England.* Boston: Estes & Lauriat, 1877.

Morison, Elting E. (Editor). *The Letters of Theodore Roosevelt.* 8 vols. Cambridge: Harvard University Press, 1951–1954.

Morris, Edmund. *Colonel Roosevelt.* New York: Random House, 2010.

Morris, Edmund. *The Rise of Theodore Roosevelt.* New York: Random House, 1979.

Morris, Edmund. *Theodore Rex.* New York: Random House, 2001.

Morris, Sylvia Jukes. *Edith Kermit Roosevelt: Portrait of a First Lady.* New York: Coward, McCann and Geoghegan, 1980.

Nash, Roderick. *Wilderness and the American Mind.* 3rd ed. New Haven: Yale University Press, 1982.

Naylor, Natalie A., Douglas Brinkley, and John Allen Gable (Editors). *Theodore Roosevelt: Many-Sided American.* Interlaken, New York: Heart of the Lakes Publishing, 1992.

Ornig, J. R. *My Last Chance to Be a Boy: Theodore Roosevelt's South American Expedition of 1913–1914.* Baton Rouge: Louisiana State University Press, 1994.

Orosz, Joel, J. *Curators and Culture: The Museum Movement in America, 1740–1870.* Tuscaloosa: University of Alabama Press, 1990.

Ortega y Gasset, J. *Meditations on Hunting.* Translated by Howard B. Wescott. Introduction by Paul Shepard. New York: Charles Scribner's Sons, 1985. Originally written in Lisbon in 1942, as a prologue to *Venite años de caza mayor* by Edward, Count Yebes.

Osborn, Henry Fairfield. *The American Museum of Natural History: Its Origin, Its History, the Growth of Its Departments to December 31, 1909.* 2nd ed. New York: Irving Press, 1911.

Osborn, Henry Fairfield. *Impressions of Great Naturalists: Reminiscences of Darwin, Huxley, Balfour, Cope and Others.* New York: Charles Scribner's Sons, 1924.

Osgood, Wilfred H. *Biographical Memoir of Clinton Hart Merriam, 1855–1942.* National Academy of Sciences Biographical Memoirs, vol. 24, 1944. Washington, D.C.: National Academy of Sciences, 1947.

O'Toole, Patricia. *When Trumpets Call: Theodore Roosevelt After the White House.* New York: Simon & Schuster, 2005.

Pakenham, Valerie. *Out in the Noonday Sun: Edwardians in the Tropics.* New York: Random House, 1985.

Patterson, John H. *The Man-Eaters of Tsavo.* Peter Capstick Adventure Library, edited by Peter Capstick. New York: St. Martin's Press, 1986. Originally published 1907 by Macmillan (London).

Pease, Alfred E. *The Book of the Lion.* New York: Charles Scribner's Sons, 1914.

Pease, Joseph Gurney. *A Wealth of Happiness and Many Bitter Trials: The Journals of Sir Alfred Edward Pease, a Restless Man.* York, England: William Sessions Ltd., 1992.

Poliquin, Rachel. *The Breathless Zoo: Taxidermy and the Cultures of Longing.* University Park: Pennsylvania State University Press, 2012.

Pomeroy, Daniel E. "Akeley's Dream Comes True: The Akeley Hall of African Mammals—a Monument to the World's Greatest Wonderland of Wild Life." In *The Complete Book of African Hall*. New York: American Museum of Natural History, 1936.

Powell, Jim. *Bully Boy: The Truth About Theodore Roosevelt's Legacy*. New York: Crown Forum, 2006.

Preston, Douglas. *Dinosaurs in the Attic: An Excursion into the American Museum of Natural History*. New York: St. Martin's Press, 1986.

Pringle, Henry F. *Theodore Roosevelt: A Biography*. New York: Harcourt, Brace, 1931.

Punke, Michael. *Last Stand: George Bird Grinnell, the Battle to Save the Buffalo, and the Birth of the New West*. Washington, D.C.: Smithsonian Books, 2007.

Putnam, Carleton. *Theodore Roosevelt: The Formative Years, 1858–1886*. Vol. 1. New York: Charles Scribner's Sons, 1958.

Putney, Clifford. *Muscular Christianity: Manhood and Sports in Protestant America, 1880–1920*. Cambridge: Harvard University Press, 2001.

Quinn, S. C. *Windows on Nature: The Great Habitat Dioramas of the American Museum of Natural History*. New York: Abrams Books, 2006.

Rattenbury, R. C. *Hunting the American West: The Pursuit of Big Game for Life, Profit, and Sport, 1800–1900*. Missoula, Montana: Boone and Crockett Club, 2008.

Reid, Thomas Mayne. *The Boy Hunters; or Adventures in Search of a White Buffalo*. Chicago: M. A. Donahue & Co. Undated reprinting. Originally publsihed 1855.

Reid, Thomas Mayne. *The Hunters' Feast; or, Conversations Around the Camp-Fire*. New York: Robert M. Dewitt. Undated. Originally published 1856.

Reiger, John F. *American Sportsmen and the Origins of Conservation*. 3rd ed. Corvallis: Oregon State University Press, 2001.

Reiger, John F. (Editor). *The Passing of the Great West: Selected Papers of George Bird Grinnell*. New York: Winchester Press, 1972.

Renehan Jr., Edward J. *The Lion's Pride: Theodore Roosevelt and His Family in Peace and War.* Oxford: Oxford University Press, 1998.

Ripley, S. Dillon. *The Sacred Grove: Essays on Museums.* New York: Simon & Schuster, 1969.

Rivinus, E. F., and E. M. Youssef. *Spencer Baird of the Smithsonian.* Washington, D.C.: Smithsonian Institution Press, 1992.

Robinson, Corinne Roosevelt. *My Brother, Theodore Roosevelt.* New York: Charles Scribner's Sons, 1922.

Roosevelt, Anna E. *Hunting Big Game in the Eighties: The Letters of Elliott Roosevelt, Sportsman.* Edited by his daughter, Anna Eleanor Roosevelt. New York: Charles Scribner's Sons, 1933.

Roosevelt, Kermit. *The Happy Hunting-Grounds.* With an Introduction by Jennifer Ham. New York: Barnes and Noble, 2004. Originally published 1920.

Roosevelt, Kermit. *A Sentimental Safari.* New York: Alfred A. Knopf, 1963.

Roosevelt, Robert B. *Game Fish of the Northern States of America and British Provinces.* Abercombie and Fitch Library. New York: Arno Press, 1967. Originally published 1862 by Carleton (New York).

Roosevelt, Robert B. *Superior Fishing, or, the Striped Bass, Trout, and Black Bass of the Northern States.* With a new Introduction by Ernest Schwiebert. St. Paul: Minnesota Historical Society Press, 1985. Originally published 1865 by Carleton (New York).

Roosevelt, Theodore. *African Game Trails: An Account of the African Wanderings of an American Hunter-Naturalist.* Peter Capstick Adventure Library, edited by Peter Capstick. New York: St. Martin's Press, 1988. Originally published 1910 by Charles Scribner's Sons (New York).

Roosevelt, Theodore. *A Book-Lover's Holidays in the Open.* New York: Charles Scribner's Sons, 1916.

Roosevelt, Theodore. "The Boone and Crockett Club." *Harper's Weekly,* vol. 37, no. 1891, March 10, 1893, p. 267.

Roosevelt, Theodore. *"Hunting Trips of a Ranchman: Sketches of Sport on the Northern Cattle Plains" and "The Wilderness Hunter: An Account of the Big Game of the United States and Its Chase with Horse, Hound, and Rifle.*" Introduction by Stephen E. Ambrose. New York: Modern Library, 1998. *Hunting Trips* was originally published in 1885; *The Wilderness Hunter,* in 1889.

Roosevelt, Theodore. *Letters from Theodore Roosevelt to Anna Roosevelt Cowles, 1870–1918.* New York: Charles Scribner's Sons, 1924.

Roosevelt, Theodore. *The Letters of Theodore Roosevelt.* Edited by Elting Morison, John Morton Blum, and Alfred Chandler. 8 vols. Cambridge: Harvard University Press, 1951–1954.

Roosevelt, Theodore. *Letters to Kermit from Theodore Roosevelt, 1902–1908.* Edited with an Introduction and Prefaces by Will Irwin. New York: Charles Scribner's Sons, 1946.

Roosevelt, Theodore. Letter to the editor. In *"Discussion and Correspondence: The Discrimination of Species and Subspecies." Science,* vol. 5, no. 127 (1897), pp. 879–80.

Roosevelt, Theodore. "My Life as a Naturalist: With a Presentation of Various First-hand Data on the Life Histories and Habits of the Big Game Animals of Africa." *The American Museum Journal,* vol. 18 (1918), pp. 321–50.

Roosevelt, Theodore. *Outdoor Pastimes of an American Hunter.* Classics of American Sport series. With a Foreword by Paul Schullery. Harrisburg, Pennsylvania: Stackpole Books, 1990. Originally published 1892 by *Forest and Stream.*

Roosevelt, Theodore. "Revealing and Concealing Coloration in Birds and Mammals." *Bulletin of the American Museum of Natural History,* vol. 30 (1911), pp. 119–231.

Roosevelt, Theodore. *Theodore Roosevelt: An Autobiography.* New York: Charles Scribner's Sons, 1920. Originally published 1913 by Macmillan (New York).

Roosevelt, Theodore. *Theodore Roosevelt's Diaries of Boyhood and Youth.* New York: Charles Scribner's Sons, 1928.

Roosevelt, Theodore. *Theodore Roosevelt's Letters to His Children.* Edited by Joseph Bucklin Bishop. New York: Charles Scribner's Sons, 1919.

Roosevelt, Theodore. *Through the Brazilian Wilderness*. Reprinted with a new Introduction by H. W. Brands. New York: Cooper Square Press, 2000. Originally published by Charles Scribner's Sons (New York).

Roosevelt, Theodore, and Edmund Heller. *Life-Histories of African Game Animals*. 2 vols. New York: Charles Scribner's Sons, 1914.

Roosevelt, Theodore, and Henry D. Minot. "The Summer Birds of the Adirondacks in Franklin County, N.Y.," pp. 1–4. Privately published and distributed, 1877.

Roosevelt, Theodore, Theodore S. Van Dyke, Daniel G. Elliot, and Andrew J. Stone. *The Deer Family*. Illustrated by Carl Rungius and others. New York: Macmillan, 1902.

Roosevelt, Tweed. "Theodore Roosevelt's African Safari." In *Theodore Roosevelt: Many-sided American*, edited by Natalie A. Naylor, Douglas Brinkley, and John Allen Gable, pp. 413–32. Interlaken, New York: Heart of the Lakes Publishing, 1992.

Rothfels, Nigel. "Preserving History: Collecting and Displaying in Carl Akeley's *In Brightest Africa*." In *Animals on Display: The Creaturely in Museums, Zoos, and Natural History*, edited by Liv Emma Thorson, Karen A. Rader, and Adam Dodd, pp. 58–73. University Park: Pennsylvania State University Press, 2013.

Rotundo, Anthony A. *American Manhood: Transformations in Masculinity from the Revolution to the Modern Era*. New York: Basic Books, 1993.

Schillings, C. G. *In Wildest Africa*. Translated by Frederic Whyte. New York: Harper & Brothers, 1907.

Schneider, Paul. *The Adirondacks: A History of America's First Wilderness*. New York: Owl Books, Henry Holt, 1998.

Schullery, P. (Editor). *American Bears: Selections from the Writings of Theodore Roosevelt*. Boulder, Colorado: Roberts Rinehart, 1977.

Sellers, Charles Coleman. *Mr. Peale's Museum: Charles Willson Peale and the First Popular Museum of Natural Science and Art*. New York: Norton, 1980.

Selous, Frederick Courteney. *African Nature Notes and Reminiscences*. Foreword by President Theodore Roosevelt. Library of African

Adventure, edited by Mike Resnick. New York: St. Martin's Press, 1993. Originally published 1908 by Macmillan (London).

Selous, Frederick Courteney. *A Hunter's Wanderings in Africa: Being a Narrative of Nine Years Spent Amongst the Game of the Far Interior of South Africa*. Library of African Adventure, edited by Mike Resnick. New York: St. Martin's Press, 2001. Originally published 1881.

Sewall, William W. *Bill Sewall's Story of T.R.* New York: Harper & Brothers, 1919.

Shufeldt, R. W. "Scientific Taxidermy for Museums (Based on a Study of the United States Government Collections)." *Smithsonian Institution. United States National Museum*. Washington, D.C.: Government Printing Office, 1894.

Smalley, Eugene V. *History of the Northern Pacific Railroad*. New York: G. P. Putnam's Sons, 1883.

Smith, Alfred Charles. *Attractions of the Nile and Its Banks: A Journal of Travels in Egypt and Nubia Showing Their Attractions to the Archéologist, the Naturalist, and General Tourist*. London: J. Murray, 1868.

Smith, Victor Grant. *The Champion Buffalo Hunter: The Frontier Memoirs of Yellowstone Vic Smith*. Edited by Jeanette Rodgers. Helena, Montana: Twodot, 1997.

Spiro, Jonathan Peter. *Defending the Master Race: Conservation, Eugenics, and the Legacy of Madison Grant*. Burlington: University of Vermont Press, 2009.

Terrie, P. G. *Contested Terrain: A New History of Nature and People in the Adirondacks*. Syracuse: Syracuse University Press, 1997.

Terrie, P. G. *Forever Wild: A Cultural History of Wilderness in the Adirondacks*. Syracuse: Syracuse University Press, 1994.

Terrie, P. G. *Wildlife and Wilderness: A History of Adirondack Mammals*. New York: Purple Mountain Press, 1993.

Thayer, William Roscoe. *Theodore Roosevelt: An Intimate Biography*. New York: Houghton Mifflin, 1919.

Thompson, J. Lee. *Theodore Roosevelt Abroad: Nature, Empire, and the Journey of an American President*. New York: Palgrave Macmillan, 2010.

Thorson, Liv Emma, Karen A. Rader, and Adam Dodd. *Animals on Display: The Creaturely in Museums, Zoos, and Natural History.* University Park: Pennsylvania State University Press, 2013.

Trefethen, James B. *An American Crusade for Wildlife.* New York: Winchester Press and the Boone and Crockett Club, 1975.

Trzebinski, Errol. *The Kenya Pioneers.* New York: Norton, 1986.

Van Dyke, Theodore S. *The Still-Hunter.* With Illustrations by Carl Rungius and the author and a new Foreword by Robert Wegner. Originally published: New York: Macmillan, 1904. Classics of American Sport Edition. Mechanicsburg, Pennsylvania: Stackpole Books, 2004.

Vietze, Andrew. *Becoming Teddy Roosevelt: How a Maine Guide Inspired America's 26th President.* Camden, Maine: Down East, 2010.

Wagenknecht, Edward. *The Seven Worlds of Theodore Roosevelt.* New York: Longmans, Green, 1958.

Wallace, Joseph. *A Gathering of Wonders: Behind the Scenes at the American Museum of Natural History.* New York: St. Martin's Press, 2000.

Walters, Michael. *A Concise History of Ornithology.* New Haven: Yale University Press, 2003.

Washburn, W. E. "Joseph Henry's Conception of the Purpose of the Smithsonian Institution." In *A Cabinet of Curiosities: Five Episodes in the Evolution of American Museums.* With an Introduction by Walter Muir Whitehill, pp. 106–66. Charlottesville: University Press of Virginia, 1967.

Weidensaul, Scott. *Of a Feather: A Brief History of American Birding.* Orlando, Florida: Harvest Books, 2007.

White, G. Edward. *The Eastern Establishment and the Western Experience: The West of Frederic Remington, Theodore Roosevelt, and Owen Wister.* New Haven: Yale University Press, 1968.

Wilhelm, Donald. *Theodore Roosevelt as an Undergraduate.* Boston: Luce, 1910.

Wilson, D. E., and D. M. Reeder (Editors). *Mammal Species of the World: A Taxonomic and Geographic Reference*, 3rd ed. 2 vols. Baltimore: Johns Hopkins University Press, 2005.

Wilson, R. L. *Theodore Roosevelt: Hunter-Conservationist*. Missoula, Montana: Boone and Crockett Club, 2009.

Wilson, R. L. *Theodore Roosevelt: Outdoorsman*. New York: Winchester Press, 1971.

Wister, Owen. *Roosevelt: The Story of a Friendship, 1880–1919*. New York: Macmillan, 1930.

Wozencraft, C. W. "Order Carnivora." In *Mammal Species of the World: A Taxonomic and Geographic Reference*, 3rd ed., edited by D. E. Wilson and D. M. Reeder, pp. 532–628. 2 vols. Baltimore: Johns Hopkins University Press, 2005.

Photography Credits

Pages ii, 7, 81, and 177: Library of Congress.

Photograph insert page 1: 520.11-004, Houghton Library, Harvard University (top left); 560.11-020, Houghton Library, Harvard University (top right); Image 337999, American Museum of Natural History Library (bottom); **insert page 2:** 520.12-17, Houghton Library, Harvard University (top left); 570.R67a-001, Houghton Library, Harvard University (top right); 570.R67ed-003, Houghton Library, Harvard University (bottom left); 570.P69a-11, Houghton Library, Harvard University (bottom right); **insert page 3:** Smithsonian Institution Archives, Image 76-4354 (top); Smithsonian Institution Archives, Image MAH-46853 (middle left); Library of Congress (right and bottom left); **insert page 4:** 560.51-1903-031, Houghton Library, Harvard University (top); Image 31715, American Museum of Natural History Library (middle); Smithsonian Institution Archives, Image 82-3231 (bottom); **insert page 5:** Library of Congress (top left); 560.61-053, Houghton Library, Harvard University (right); Reproduced from *African Game Trails*, 1908, by Theodore Roosevelt (bottom left); **insert page 6:** 560.61-148, Houghton Library, Harvard University (top); Smithsonian Institution Archives, Image 95-253. (bottom); **insert page 7:** Smithsonian Institution Archives, Image NHB-24881 (top); American Museum of Natural History Library, Image 330591 (bottom); **insert page 8:** American Museum of Natural History Library, Image 319065 (top left); Megan Krol (bottom right).

Index

Note: Page numbers after 261 refer to notes.

A

Adam, animals named by, 19
Adirondack Mountains:
  Lake Tear of the Clouds in, 161
  Theodore's bird list of, 69–70
  Theodore's trips to, 38–42, 67, 68–69, 74
  tourists in, 84
Africa:
  Akeley's expeditions to, 183, 186, 191, 223, 240–43
  animals sought in, 190, 198
  anticolonial sentiment in, 184
  arrangements for trip to, 189–96
  big-game mammals in, 164, 206–10, 214–18, 225–26, 228–32, 233–36, 240–43, 244–47, 252–53
  birds in, 55, 203, 223–24, 247
  boyhood trip to Egypt, 53–60
  hazards of trip to, 194–95, 201, 208
  human origins in, 294
  Lado Enclave, 243–47
  naturalists for trip to, 190–91, 237
  news controlled about, 218–19, 245
  Nile excursion for Smithsonian in, 243, 245, 246, 247
  outfitting Smithsonian trip to, 192–94, 200, 202
  railroads in, 180, 186, 198, 207, 240
  safaris to, 199–206, 240–42
  sleeping sickness in, 244, 246
  small-mammal collecting in, 204–5, 218, 223, 224, 227, 237, 239, 253
  Smithsonian support of trip to, 187–88, 197, 205, 221, 223, 244, 246, 247, 250, 251, 254–55
  Sotik hunting ground, 222, 224–27
  species diversity in, 198–99
  specimen collecting for Smithsonian in, 204–6, 207, 214–18, 220–21, 224–25, 227, 237, 238–39, 247, 253
  tent boys in, 201
  Theodore's arrival for Smithsonian expedition in, 197–99
  Theodore's Smithsonian expedition to, 199–212, 213–21, 222–27, 228–32, 233–48, 250, 252–53
  Theodore's homecoming from, 248
  Theodore's interest in, 180–81, 182–89, 250
  Theodore's notes for publications on, 186, 202, 204, 205–6, 218, 225–26, 236–37, 240, 243, 250–51
  Tjäder Expedition to, 187
  traveling in, 222–24, 238–39
  wildfire-fighting in, 247
African Game Trails (T. Roosevelt), 250–51, 253
African Hunting from Natal to the Zambezi (Baldwin), 181
African Nature Notes and Reminiscences (Selous), 164

Agassiz, Louis, 31–33, 61, 64, 113
Agriculture Department, U.S., 147
Akeley, Carl, 163, 182–84
    African expeditions of, 183, 186, 191,
        223, 240–43
    and American Museum, 244
    and salt method, 215
    as taxidermist, 182–83, 205, 240, 243
    and Theodore's African trip, 183–84,
        186, 241–43
Alaska, Harriman Expedition to, 158–
    59, 182
Alexander Philipp Maximilian of Wied-
    Neuwied, Prince, 35
Ali (tent boy), 201
Allen, Joel A., 71, 176
American Big-Game Hunting (T.
    Roosevelt), 156
American Midwest, hunting trip to,
    83–87, 89, 98
American Museum of Natural History,
    252
    buildings of, 35
    founding of, 2, 24, 31, 34–35
    holdings of, 35, 142, 189
    museum naturalists' contributions to,
        4, 34–35
    and new species, 153
    and Theodore's African trip, 205, 240,
        243, 244
    Theodore's museum specimens
        donated to, 91
American Museum of P. T. Barnum,
    23–24
American School of Mammalogy, 145
American Sportsman's Library, 173
American West:
    decimation of game in, 206
    exploration of, 115
    fauna of, 115, 116, 118
    fossils in, 113, 115, 118, 121
    hunting in, 95–96, 98–104, 126–29,
        170, 186
    Native American tribes in, 114
    opening of, 94, 113, 132
    preservation of, 138–41
    specimens collected in, 113
    stories of, 125–26
    Theodore's writings about, 129–30
    as Wild West, 114
antelope hunting:
    pronghorn (American West), 120,
        121–22, 136
Army Arsenal Building, 35

arsenical soap, 21–22
Atlantic Monthly, 174
Attractions of the Nile and Its Banks
    (Smith), 54–55
Audubon, John James, 142, 145
    and Baird, 27–28, 45
    and Bell's taxidermy, 46
    estate of, 110–12
    influence of, 45, 70, 111–12, 249, 251
    Viviparous Quadrupeds of North
        America (with Bachman), 27–28
Audubon, John Woodhouse, 112
Audubon, Lucy "Grandma," 112, 132
Audubon Park, New York, 110, 116
Audubon Society, 132

B

Bachman, John, 142, 145
    Viviparous Quadrupeds of North
        America (with Audubon), 27–28
bacterial maceration, 15
Badlands Cowboy, 119
Baird, Spencer Fullerton, 25–30, 45–46
    and Audubon, 27–28, 45
    and Bell's taxidermy, 46–47
    bird collection of, 26, 27, 264
    and bison specimens for exhibit,
        104–5
    as hunter-naturalist, 25–26, 28, 31
    influence of, 25, 45, 46, 49, 70, 85,
        113, 251
    and Merriam, 143
    and new species, 26–27
    and railroad surveys, 87, 88–89, 147,
        252
    and Smithsonian, 29–30, 45–46
    and U.S. Exploring Expedition,
        28–29
Baird's rabbit, 144
Baldwin, William Charles, African
    Hunting from Natal to the Zambezi,
    181
Barnum, P. T., 23–24, 35
bears:
    decimation of, 206
    hunting, 128–29, 136, 141, 142, 146,
        166–67, 180, 207
    as iconic species, 126
    of Kodiak Island, 158
    species of, 151
Beaty Museum, California, 271
Bécoeur, Jean-Baptiste, 21–22
bee-eater, green, 59

Beef Bonanza, The (Brisbin), 105
Bell, John, 28, 46–47, 48, 50, 59, 116
Bell, Karamojo, 225
Bickmore, Albert S., 31, 32–34, 49, 50,
    61, 64
    Travels in the East Indian Archipelago,
    33
Bighorn Mountains, Wyoming, 126–29
Bill (tent boy), 201
biodiversity, 3, 254–55, 284
Biological Society of Washington,
    151–52
Biological Survey, U.S., 69, 147, 175,
    191, 283
birds:
    in Africa, 55, 203, 223–24, 247
    extinction of, 63
    feathers in hats, 107, 171–72
    migration of, 63
    ornithology, 28, 44–46, 62, 69–70,
        144, 164
    scientific collections of, 86–87, 196,
        254
    shooting for sport, 86–87, 89, 111
    skinning, 57–58, 271
    songs of, 63–64, 68–69, 122–23, 124,
        170, 247, 250
    study skins of, 27
    at White House, 170–71
    writings about, 164
bird sanctuaries, 6
Birds of Long Island, The (Giraud), 62
Birds of the Eastern United States
    (Chapman), 164
bison/buffalo:
    decimation of, 96, 98, 104–5, 118, 129,
        136, 138, 206, 241, 252
    fossil record of, 120
    hunting, 84–86, 96, 97–105, 106, 114,
        116–17, 180
    meanings of terms, 277
    protection of, 140
    robes, 107
    trophy head, 135
Blackfeet Indians, 131
Boone, Daniel, 121, 139
Boone and Crockett Club, 139–41
    ethic of, 139–40, 141, 166–67, 199,
        251
    founding of, 139, 147, 187
    and land protection, 140
    membership requirements of, 139
    as model for other groups, 206
    and Theodore's African trip, 186

Theodore's association with, 138–39,
    141, 143, 166, 199, 206, 251
    and Yellowstone National Park,
    140–41, 168
Boyes, John, 246
Boy Hunters, The (Reid), 14, 38, 46, 111,
    129
Brisbin, James S., *The Beef Bonanza,*
    105
Bulletin of the Nuttall Ornithological
    Society, 69
Burroughs, John, 158, 163, 169–70, 174
Buxton, Edward North, 186, 193, 206
    Two Africa Trips, 180

C

cabinets of natural curiosities, 19–20, 24
Cambridge, Massachusetts, Theodore
    in, 65–66
Camps and Cruises of an Ornithologist
    (Chapman), 164
Cape buffalo, hunting in Africa, 218,
    220
caping, 104
caribou hunting, 141, 142, 148
Carow, Edith Kermit, 132–36
    wedding of, *see* Roosevelt, Edith
    Carow
Central Pacific Railroad, 88
Central Park Menagerie, New York, 35
Chapman, Frank, 163, 172
    Birds of the Eastern United States, 164
    Camps and Cruises of an Ornithologist,
    164
Cheyenne tribe, 131
Chimney Butte Ranch, 125
Churchill, Winston, *My African Journey,*
    180, 190
Civil Service Commission, 155
Clark, James L., 205
Cleveland, Grover, 141
Collier, Holt, 166
Colorado, hunting trip to, 159–61, 285
Columbia Law School, Theodore's
    studies in, 90, 91–92
Congress, U.S.:
    and Smithsonian, 188, 189
    and U.S. Biological Survey, 147
    and wilderness protection, 140–41
conservation, 5, 6, 44, 106, 118–19,
    131–32, 156, 199, 206
Coues, Elliott, 276
cougars, killing, 285

Crater Lake, Oregon, 162
Crockett, Davy, 121, 139
Cuba, and Spanish-American War,
    156–57
Cuninghame, R. J., 197, 202, 209, 220,
    233, 235
Custer, George Armstrong, 117, 131
Cyclone trap, 145

D

Dakota Badlands:
    hunting in, 95, 98–104, 120–24
    Theodore's cattle ranch investment
        in, 102–3, 105–6, 119–20, 134, 135,
        136
Darwin, Charles, 249
    and evolution, 115
    On the Origin of Species, 113
Dawson, Francis Warrington, 219–20
Deer Family, The (T. Roosevelt), 172–73
deer hunting, 136
dime museums, 23
dinosaurs, 115

E

Egypt:
    bird market in, 55
    Roosevelt family travel to, 50, 53–59,
        85
    specimens collected in, 58
elephants:
    decimation of, 233, 241
    hunting in Africa, 233–36, 240–43
    ivory hunters, 181
elk:
    decimation of, 130, 136, 206
    hunting, 127–28, 129, 146
    as iconic species, 126
    protection of, 140
    taxidermy of, 235, 240–41
Elkhorn (ranch), 125
Everybody's Magazine, 174
    "Nature Fakers," 176
    "Real Naturalists on Nature Faking,"
        175–76
    "Roosevelt on the Nature Fakirs,"
        174
evolution, 113, 115
"Ex Ex squadron," 28–29
extinction, 116
    and fossil remains, 115, 118
    looming possibility of, 96, 98, 104–5,

106, 136–37, 148, 150, 240, 243,
    245, 247, 252–53
market hunting leading to, 63

F

"Fejee Mermaid," 23–24
Ferris, Joe, 99–104
Ferris, Sylvane, 99–100, 103, 119–20
Field Museum of Natural History,
    Chicago, 4, 183, 189, 205, 240
fish and fisheries, destruction of, 43–44
flycatchers, tyrant, 26–27
Foran, W. Robert, 245
Forest and Stream, 118, 130, 131, 132,
    138, 140, 141, 156
Fort McKavett, Texas, 84
Fort McPherson, 114
fossil remains, 21, 113, 115, 118, 120,
    121, 199
Franklin, Benjamin, 20
frass, 21
Free Trade Club, 95
frontier spirit, 45

G

game animals, legislation to protect, 6
Game Birds of the Coasts and Lakes, The
    (R. Roosevelt), 43
giant ground sloths, fossils of, 120
Giraud, J. P. Jr., *The Birds of Long
    Island,* 62
Goff, John B., 159
gold, discovery of, 131
Gorringe, Henry Honychurch, 95, 98
Gouverneur Morris (T. Roosevelt), 135
G. P. Putnam's Sons, 125
Grant, Ulysses S., 35
Green-Wood Cemetery, family burials
    in, 109
Grinnell, George Bird, 110–18, 130–32,
    153
    in the American West, 110, 113–18,
        131
    and Boone and Crockett Club, 139,
        140–41, 147, 187, 251
    conservation efforts of, 131–32,
        140–41
    on extermination of species, 136–37
    as *Forest and Stream* editor, 118, 130,
        131, 132, 138, 156
    and Harriman Alaska Expedition,
        158

on national park protection, 140,
141
as professional naturalist, 115, 131
Theodore's collaboration with, 132,
138, 156, 163
and Theodore's writings, 130, 156
Grinnell, Tom, 111
Grogan, Quentin, 245–46
Gros Ventres Indians, 131

H

Harriman, Edward, 158
Harriman Alaska Expedition, 158–59,
182
Harrison, Benjamin, 155
Harvard College:
Agassiz at, 31–32
entrance exam for, 61
Museum of Comparative Zoology, 32,
61, 113
Porcellian Club, 75
Theodore's time at, 64, 65–67, 70–72,
76, 77–78, 135
Hay, John, 157
Hayden Geological Survey, 143–44
Heatley, Hugh H., 218, 220
Hellene, Signor, 22
Heller, Edmund:
and large-mammal collecting, 204,
229–30, 237
Life Histories of African Game Animals
(with T. Roosevelt), 251
and new species, 218, 250
skinning big-game specimens, 214–17,
218, 235, 236
and Theodore's African trip, 191–92,
214–17, 221, 229–30, 235
Henry, Joseph, 29, 45
hippopotamus, hunting in Africa, 228–
29, 230–32
Holophusicon, 20
Hornaday, William Temple, 104–5, 163,
175
hunter-naturalists:
Baird's army of, 45–46
changing perceptions of, 5–6, 249
field experiences of, 13–14, 142–43,
146–47
and museum collections, 24–25
respect for and knowledge of nature,
127, 138, 169–70
and Theodore's African trip, 187
writings of, 156, 161

hunters:
commercial, 87, 97, 106, 131, 172
hypermasculinity promoted by, 94,
139, 142, 207
and the military, 94
moral code for, 138, 141, 156, 166–67
nature, *see* hunter-naturalists
restrictions on, 44, 137, 138–39
hunting:
anti-hunting feelings in U.S., 226,
230–32, 253, 254
for "final trophy," 106
for food, 25
as moral good, 94
popularity of, 106–7
as predation, 227
in prehistoric times, 294
profitability of, 107, 131
for sport/challenge, 25, 86–87, 89,
94–96, 106–7, 111, 127–29, 156,
165, 187, 251
and trapping, 229–30
types of, 25–26
Hunting in Many Lands (T. Roosevelt),
156
Hunting Trips of a Ranchman (T.
Roosevelt), 129–32, 141–42, 175,
236

I

Impressions of Great Naturalists, 249
Independence Hall, Philadelphia, 22
ivory hunters, 181

J

Jackson, Sir Frederick John, 197, 221
Juja Farm, Kenya, 183, 217, 218

K

Kodiak Island, bears of, 158

L

Lacey, John F., 141, 282
Lacey Act (1894), 141, 282
Lake George, New York, 39
*Land and Game Birds of New England,
The* (Minot), 66
Lang, Gregor, 99–104, 120
Lang, Lincoln, 101, 120–21
Lebo (teamster and cook), 126, 127

Lee, Alice Hathaway:
    courtship of Theodore and, 76, 78–79,
        83, 89
    meeting of Theodore and, 75
    wedding of, 90–91, 133
    see also Roosevelt, Alice Lee
Leeholm, Oyster Bay, 90, 134
legislation, roles of, 6
Leopold II, king of Belgium, 244
Lever, Sir Ashton, 20
Lewis and Clark Expedition, 151
Life Histories of African Game Animals
        (T. Roosevelt and Heller), 251, 253
life zones, 153–54, 238
lions:
    fossils of, 120
    hunting in Africa, 206–12, 213
Livingstone, David, 41, 186, 208
    *Missionary Travels and Researches in
        South Africa,* 12–13, 33, 38, 250
Lodge, Henry Cabot, 135
Long, Rev. William J., 173–76, 230–31
Longfellow, Henry Wadsworth, 74
Loring, J. Alden:
    and Biological Survey, 191
    charged by lion, 227
    and new species, 232
    and small-mammal collecting, 204–5,
        218, 223, 224, 227, 237
    and Theodore's African trip, 191,
        204–5, 218, 224, 227, 232
Ludlow, William, 117, 131
Lunde, Darrin, early years of, 4–5

M

Maddox, Old Lady, 120, 121
Maine, 157
mammalogy, 142–43, 144–50
    study of small mammals, 145–46,
        147–50, 154, 253
Mammals of the Adirondack Region
        (Merriam), 144–45, 148, 150, 165
mammoths, fossils of, 120
Man-Eaters of Tsavo, The (Patterson),
        180, 207
Marsh, Othniel Charles, 113–16
Marsh Expedition, 113–16
masculinity, 11, 94, 139, 142, 207
McKinley, William, 157, 158
    assassination of, 161–62
McMillan, William Northrup, 217
meadowlark, song of, 122
Mearns, Edgar A., 163

and new species, 232
and small-mammal collecting, 204–5
and Theodore's African trip, 191, 198,
        221, 227, 232
Merriam, Clinton Hart, 143–48, 163,
        251
    and American School of Mammalogy,
        145
    and Baird, 143
    and Biological Survey, 69, 147, 175,
        191, 283
    and Harriman Expedition, 158–59
    and Hayden Geological Survey,
        143–44
    on life zones, 153–54, 238
    Mammals of the Adirondack Region,
        144–45, 148, 150, 165
    on new species, 144, 145, 150–51,
        164–65, 182, 252
    and species lumpers vs. splitters,
        152–54, 160
Merriam, Clinton Levi, 143
Merrifield, Bill, 99–100, 103, 119–20,
        126–29
Minot, Henry Davis, 78
    and Adirondacks trip, 67, 68, 69
    at Harvard, 66–67, 70, 72–73
    *The Land and Game Birds of New
        England,* 66
*Missionary Travels and Researches in
        South Africa* (Livingstone), 12–13,
        33, 38, 250
Mohannis, Chief Sagamore, 135
mole-rats, 218
Montana Territory, bison hunting in,
        104–5
Morton Hall, New York City, 92
Mose (Adirondack guide), 41
mountain lions:
    hunting, 159–61
    species of, 160–61
Mount Katahdin, Maine, 76–77
Mount Kenya, 237–38, 243
Mount Marcy, New York, 161
mourning-dove, song of, 123
mousetraps, 145, 147
muscular Christianity, 11, 17, 37
museum hoaxes, 23–24
museum naturalists, 2–3
    adventure sought by, 4, 70
    contributions to science, 24
    instinct to collect, 19
    as nature hunters, 26
    research papers written by, 67

scientific study by, 4
  writings of, 163–64
Museum of Comparative Zoology, 32,
  61, 113
Museum Wormianum, 19–20
My African Journey (Churchill), 180,
  190

N

National Museum of Natural History,
  Smithsonian, 4, 25, 29–30, 45–46,
  291
national parks, 6, 162
  see also specific parks
National Wildlife Refuges, 162, 172
Native Americans, 114, 116–17, 131
natural history:
  exploration, 115
  scientific study of, 113
natural-history museums:
  accessibility of, 33
  back rooms of, 1
  cabinets as sources of, 19–20, 24
  collections as essence of, 24
  collectors commissioned by, 2, 45
  dime museums, 23
  European, 33
  exhibits of, 22, 23–24, 252
  expeditions funded by, 187–89
  functions of, 21, 24, 251–52
  historical record maintained in, 3, 6
  Holophusicon, 20
  Peale's collection, 21, 22, 24
  in the Smithsonian, 25, 29–30
  specimens in, *see* specimens
  Theodore's collection, 16–18, 50, 61,
    64, 91
  wealthy donors to, 33–34
  Wormianum, 19–20
naturalist:
  changing image of, 255
  defined, 249
Natural Theology (Paley), 17
"Nature Fakers" (T. Roosevelt), 176
nature study:
  European style of, 32
  field guides, 45
  popularity of, 173
  as Victorian moral good, 17, 44
Naval War of 1812 (T. Roosevelt), 93,
  95, 125
Newland, Tarlton & Co., 192, 200
New York City:

founding a museum in, 33, 34
"Ladies' Mile" in, 9, 172
Roosevelt home in, 31, 60, 61–62, 108,
  135
Theodore as police commissioner of,
  155–56
New York Fisheries Commission, 44
New York State Legislature, Theodore's
  election to, 93, 106, 131
Nile River, 243, 245, 246, 247, 248
Northern Pacific Railroad, 88, 95, 99,
  140
North Maine Woods, Theodore's travel
  to, 73–74, 75–77
Notes on Some of the Birds of Oyster Bay
  (T. Roosevelt), 70
Nuttall Ornithological Society, 69, 70,
  71, 144

O

On the Origin of Species (Darwin), 113
ornithology, 28, 44–46, 62, 69–70, 144,
  164
Osborn, Henry Fairfield, 153
owls, saw-whet, 170
Oyster Bay, New York:
  Roosevelt homes in, 61–62, 69, 90, 96,
    105, 117, 134–35
  Theodore's pamphlet on birds of, 70
  Theodore's zoology notes on, 64

P

Pacific Railroad Surveys (1853–1855),
  87–89
Paley, William, *Natural Theology,* 17
Panama Canal, 162
passenger pigeon, 63
Patterson, John Henry, *The Man-Eaters
  of Tsavo,* 180, 207
Paul Smith's lodge, 39, 73–74
Pawnee tribe, 116–17, 131
Peabody, George, 113
Peabody Museum of Natural History,
  Yale, 113, 115, 116, 117
Peale, Charles Willson, 20–21, 22
Peale, Titian, 29
Peale family, 20–23, 24
Pease, Sir Alfred, 202, 203, 207, 208–11,
  221
peccary hunting, 141, 142
Pelican Island, Florida, 172
Philippines, insurrection in, 162

Plains Indians, 131
Pleistocene era, 198, 294
preservation, 5, 165–66, 199, 206, 252
pterodactyl, 115

R

railroads:
  and bison hunting, 97, 98
  Pacific Railroad Surveys, 87–89
  transcontinental, 88, 95, 99, 114, 140
  Uganda Railway, 180, 186, 198, 207,
    240
  westward-moving, 87–89, 95, 126
  and wildlife industry, 107, 132
Ranch Life and the Hunting-Trail (T.
    Roosevelt), 142
Reid, Capt. Thomas Mayne, 13–14, 112,
    151
  The Boy Hunters, 14, 38, 46, 111, 129
"Remarks on the Zoology of Oyster Bay,
    L.I" (T. Roosevelt), 64
Republican Party:
  internal divisions in, 93
  and McKinley-Roosevelt election,
    157–58
  Theodore's initial interest in, 92–93
  21st District Republican Association,
    92–93
rhinoceros:
  black, 217, 225, 244
  hunting in Africa, 214–17, 225–26,
    244–47
  white, 244–47, 253, 255, 299
Rice, Cecil Spring, 185
Roosevelt, Alice (daughter), 107, 108,
    129, 134, 155
Roosevelt, Alice Lee (first wife):
  early years of, *see* Lee, Alice
    Hathaway
  illness and death of, 107–9, 119, 122,
    133
  pregnancy of, 98, 107
  Theodore's devotion to, 91, 106,
    109
  Theodore's tribute to, 123–24
  wedding of, 90–91, 93, 133
Roosevelt, Anna "Bamie" (sister), 11,
    60, 107, 133
  and father's death, 72
  and Theodore's specimens, 36
  and young Alice, 108, 129
Roosevelt, Corinne "Conie" (sister), 11,
    55, 107, 171, 194, 196

Roosevelt, Cornelius (grandfather), 10
Roosevelt, Edith Carow (second wife):
  and African trip, 184–85, 186, 195,
    248
  children of, 135–36, 155
  early years of, *see* Carow, Edith
    Kermit
  pregnancy of, 135
  wedding of, 134, 155
Roosevelt, Elliott (brother), 11, 41, 55,
    107
  and father's death, 72
  hunting trip to Midwest, 83–84, 89,
    98
  personal traits of, 84
  world travels of, 94
Roosevelt, Emlen (cousin), 60–61, 73
Roosevelt, Kermit (son), 171
  and African trip, 184, 185–86, 194–
    95, 213, 220–21, 246
  as big-game hunter, 187, 204, 209–12,
    216, 217, 226, 243, 247, 253
  guns and hunting, 193
  mandolin of, 194, 223
  photography of, 224–25
  travel to Africa, 198, 202
Roosevelt, Martha Bulloch "Mittie"
    (mother), 10, 11–12, 15, 37, 54, 92
  children of, 11
  illness and death of, 107–8, 109, 119,
    122
Roosevelt, Quentin (son), 195
Roosevelt, Robert Barnwell, 43–44, 48,
    131
  *The Game Birds of the Coasts and
    Lakes,* 43
Roosevelt, Theodore:
  Adirondack trips of, 38–42, 67,
    68–69, 74
  adventure sought by, 2, 5, 14, 38, 46,
    93, 106, 131, 156–57, 179–80, 189,
    249–50
  African Game Trails, 250–51, 253
  African trip of, *see* Africa
  aging, 179
  and Alice, *see* Lee, Alice Hathaway;
    Roosevelt, Alice
  American Big-Game Hunting, 156
  as assistant secretary of navy (ASN),
    156, 157
  autobiography of, 14
  as big-game hunter, 5, *81,* 214–15,
    225–26, 230–32, 237, 242–43, 245,
    249, 253

birds as interest of, 43, 44–45, 46, 48, 51–52, 55, 59, 62–64, 67
and Boone and Crockett Club, 139–41, 143, 166, 168, 186, 187, 199, 206, 251
buckskin suit of, 120, 121, 122, 125, 127
building his strength, 37–38, 61, 76, 83
as *Bwana Makuba,* 213
as *Bwana Tumbo,* 217–18
cattle ranch investment of, 102–3, 105–6, 119–20, 134, 135, 136
childhood of, 12–18, 22
competitiveness of, 89, 90
as conservationist, 5, 6, 44, 156, 162, 168, 199, 245
The Deer Family, 172–73
early years of, 4
and Edith, *see* Carow, Edith Kermit; Roosevelt, Edith
Egyptian travel of, 50, 53–59, 85
energy of, 74, 76, 77, 92, 101, 249
European travel of, 49–50
family of, 155
Gouverneur Morris, 135
as governor of New York, 157, 171–72, 183
guns and hunting, 4–5, 48–49, 56–57, 95, 141, 175, *177,* 192–93
and Harvard, 61, 64, 65–67, 70–72, 75, 76, 77–78, 135
health of, 12, 14, 18, 36–38, 42, 49, 61, 74, 83, 84, 106, 135, 179
and his father's death, 72, 73, 74–75, 76, 93, 108–9, 122
as hunter-naturalist, 5–6, 25, 57–59, 87, 91, 132, 142–43, 146, 165, 168–69, 186–87, 188, 239–40, 245, 247–48, 249–55
Hunting in Many Lands, 156
Hunting Trips of a Ranchman, 129–32, 141–42, 175, 236
hunting trips to the West, 98–104, 105–6, 120–24, 126–29, 166–67
hunting trip to Midwest, 83–84, 87, 89, 98
income of, 155, 186
journals kept by, 41, 44, 52–53, 58–59, 62–63, 64, 67–69, 76, 119, 127, 142, 203, 248
law studies of, 90, 91–92
Life Histories of African Game Animals (with Heller), 251, 253

and McKinley assassination, 161–62
media attention to, 166–67, 169, 180, 185, 190
as museum naturalist, 1–2, 7, 17, 19, 22, 36, 49, 50, 62, 64, 76, 162–63, 187, 250
museum of, 16–18, 50, 61, 64, 91, 117, 135, 162, 247
on nature fakers, 174–75, 176
Naval War of 1812, 93, 95, 125
as New York City police commissioner, 155–56
in North Maine Woods, 73–74, 75–77
Notes on Some of the Birds of Oyster Bay, 70
personal traits of, 66–67, 70, 99
personal view of naturalism, 176, 272
and politics, 92–94, 106, 107, 108, 131, 155–56, 157–58, 168, 179–80
as preservationist, 5, 40, 165, 168, 199, 206
as president, 162–63, 166–67, 168–76, 180, 185, 189
public speeches by, 95
Ranch Life and the Hunting-Trail, 142
reinventing himself, 77, 78–79, 93
"Remarks on the Zoology of Oyster Bay, L.I.," 64
role models and mentors of, 25, 28, 43, 47–48, 59, 62, 70
as romantic dreamer, 120, 182
and seal carcass, 9–10, 14–16, 252
self-identity of, 163
and small-animal specimens, 147–50
social circle of, 75, 76, 92–93
and Spanish-American War, 157
and species lumpers vs. splitters, 152–54, 160, 284
as specimen collector, 1–2, 4–5, 19, 35, 40, 48, 60, 64
The Summer Birds of the Adirondacks, 69–70
and taxidermy, 46–47, 49, 59, 116, 240
as teenager, 43, 44, 48, 53, 62, 65
Trail and Camp-fire, 156
as vice president, 157–58, 161
vision problems of, 49, 204, 240
as visitor to American Natural History Museum, 35
The Wilderness Hunter, 142, 175
and Yellowstone, 138, 168–70
Roosevelt, Theodore III (son), birth of, 136

Roosevelt, Theodore Sr. (father), 10–11,
    40, 65, 78, 133
    Egyptian travel of, 56, 60
    and his son's health, 36–38, 42, 49,
        83
    illness and death of, 71–72
    and muscular Christianity, 11, 17, 37
    and natural-history museum, 24, 31,
        34–35
    and politics, 93
Roosevelt, West (cousin), 39, 41, 60–61,
    73, 136
Roosevelt & Son, 11
Roosevelt family, 10–12, 36, 66
    Adirondack trip of, 39–41
    Egyptian travel of, 50, 53–59, 85
    homes of, 31, 60, 61–62, 108, 135
Roosevelt Museum of Natural History,
    The, 162–63
    accumulating specimens for, 16–17,
        20
    dissolved, 91
    field tags from, 269
    precursors of, 20
    Record of, 16–18, 61
    in Roosevelt home, 16, 17–18
"Rough Riders," 157

S

Sagamore Hill, Oyster Bay, 135
Saltonstall, Dick, 75
Science, 151
Scott, Sir Walter, 74
Scribner's Magazine, 186, 202, 204, 205,
    218, 225, 250–51
seal, carcass of, 9–10, 14–16, 252
Selous, Frederick Courteney, 163,
    181–82
    African Nature Notes and
        Reminiscences, 164
    and Theodore's African trip, 184, 186,
        189, 192, 195–96, 198, 202
Sewall, William, 73–74, 75–76, 77
Shakespeare, William, Henry IV, 243
Sheridan, Philip, 114
Sherman, William Tecumseh, 94, 114
shrews, study of, 148–49, 239, 253
Simba (horse tender), 211
Sioux warriors, 114
Smith, Rev. Alfred Charles, Attractions
    of the Nile and Its Banks, 54–55
Smith, Paul, 39, 73–74
Smithson, James, 29

Smithsonian Institution, Washington
    DC, 251–52
    expeditions supported by, 187–89
    founding of, 29, 291
    holdings of, 45–46, 142, 187–88,
        189
    "Miscellaneous Collections," 251
    National Museum of Natural History,
        4, 25, 29–30, 45–46, 291
    railroad naturalists of, 88–89
    and Theodore's African trip, 187–88,
        197, 205, 221, 223, 244, 246, 247,
        250, 251, 254–55
    Theodore's museum collection sent
        to, 91
    and U.S. Biological Survey, 69
Society for the Preservation of the Wild
    Fauna of the Empire, 206
Sommer, Helmut, 299
Southern Pacific Railroad, 88
Spanish-American War, 156–57
sparrows:
    English, 70–71, 274
    songs of, 63
    white-throated, 63, 68
"sparrow wars," 71
species:
    distribution of, 154
    diversity of, 3, 254–55, 284
    extinction of, see extinction
    invasive, 71
    loss of, 172
    lumping vs. splitting of, 152–54, 160,
        284
    new, 26–27, 70, 145, 150–51, 164–65,
        182, 218, 232, 252, 254, 255
    proliferation of, 150–51
    survival of, 243
    variability within, 160–61
specimens:
    anatomical complexities of, 32
    bacterial maceration of, 15
    caping, 104
    collected before extinction, 63
    collected for exhibition, 104–5, 142,
        183, 200, 202, 205, 225, 240, 247,
        252
    collected for scientific study, 1–2, 6,
        24, 27–28, 29, 32, 45, 48, 87, 88–89,
        91, 115–16, 145–47, 205, 215, 251,
        252, 254
    collected in Africa, 204–6, 207,
        214–18, 220–21, 224–25, 227, 232,
        235–36, 237, 238–39, 253

as data points, 145
field collections of, 45, 49, 146–48
living, 137, 142
paper tag IDs of, 3, 91, 146, 269
prepared for exhibition, 48
preservation of, 21–22, 32, 215–17
shooting, stuffing, preserving, 1–2,
    28, 47–48, 58, 62, 215
skinning, 47, 57–58, 235–36, 271
taxonomic order of, 2–3, 19, 153–54
Theodore's private collection of, 16–
    18, 20; *see also* Roosevelt Museum
    of Natural History
as trophies, 106, 128, 205, 207, 215
value for posterity, 3, 6, 137
SS *Russia,* 51
Stonebridge folding lantern, 292–93
Strand Magazine, 190
Summer Birds of the Adirondacks, The
    (T. Roosevelt), 69–70

T

Tarlton, Leslie, 197
taxidermy, 5, 46–48, 49, 59, 182–83,
    205, 240, 243
taxonomic order, 2–3, 19
    lumpers vs. splitters of, 152–54, 160,
        284
thrush, hermit, 68–69, 123
Tjäder Expedition, 187
Trail and Camp-fire (T. Roosevelt),
    156
Tranquility, Oyster Bay, 62
trapping, 229–30
Travels in the East Indian Archipelago
    (Bickmore), 33
21st District Republican Association,
    92–93
Two Africa Trips (Buxton), 180

U

Uganda Railway, 180, 186, 198, 207,
    240
Union Pacific Railroad, 114
United States Army, 45, 88, 94
United States Exploring Expedition "Ex
    Ex squadron," 28–29
United States National Museum
    (USNM), 291
urbanization, 6
U.S. Biological Survey, 69, 147, 175, 191,
    223, 237–40, 283

V

Vanderbilt, Cornelius, 110
Verreaux, Édouard, 34–35
*Viviparous Quadrupeds of North America,
    The* (Audubon and Bachman),
    27–28

W

Wakamba tribe, 214
Walcott, Charles Doolitle, 188–89,
    191
Washington, George, 20, 179
water-shrew, 148
White House:
    bear hunt dinner in, 180–81
    birds in area of, 170–71
Whittier, John Greenleaf, 74
wilderness:
    encroachment into, 137
    protection of, 6, 40, 140–41, 165–66,
        252
    railroad incursions into, 87–89
    romanticization of, 45
Wilderness Hunter, The (T. Roosevelt),
    142, 175
wild game:
    in Africa, *see* Africa
    decimation of, 118, 131–32, 136, 206
    poachers of, 118
    protection of, 118–19, 132, 168, 206
    reserves of, 199
    in restaurants, 107
    see also specific animals
wildlife:
    anthropomorphic stories of, 173–76
    life zones of, 153–54, 238
    vulnerability of, 156
wildlife conservation, 199
wildlife refuges, 6, 141, 162, 172
Wood, Leonard, 157
woodpeckers, red-headed, 286
Wood's Gymnasium, New York, 37
Worm, Ole, 19
Wormianum, 19–20
wren, winter, 68

Y

Yellowstone National Park:
    bison slaughtered in, 138
    exploration of, 117–18, 131
    Hayden Geological Survey, 143–44

Yellowstone National Park *(continued):*
    protection of, 140–41, 168, 169
    Theodore's trip to, 168–70
Yellowstone Park Improvement
        Company, 140
Yellowstone Protection Act (1894), 141

Z

zoological exploration, 2–4, 28–29

About the Author

DARRIN LUNDE is a Supervisory Museum Specialist in the Division of Mammals at the Smithsonian's National Museum of Natural History, in Washington, D.C. Previously he was Collections Manager for the Department of Mammalogy at the American Museum of Natural History, in New York City. As a museum naturalist, he has conducted fieldwork throughout the world and has named more than a dozen new species of mammals. He lives in Maryland.